GULLIVERIANA: II

*The Travels of Mr. John Gulliver,
Son to Capt. Lemuel Gulliver* (1731)

by

PIERRE FRANÇOIS GUYOT DESFONTAINES

Modern Gulliver's Travels: Lilliput (1796)

by

LEMUEL GULLIVER, JUN. (pseud.)

FACSIMILE REPRODUCTIONS

EDITED WITH AN INTRODUCTION

BY

JEANNE K. WELCHER

AND

GEORGE E. BUSH, JR.

Three Volumes in One.

GAINESVILLE, FLORIDA
SCHOLARS' FACSIMILES & REPRINTS
1971

SCHOLARS' FACSIMILES & REPRINTS

1605 N.W. 14TH AVENUE

GAINESVILLE, FLORIDA 32601 U.S.A.

HARRY R. WARFEL, GENERAL EDITOR

Grateful appreciation is expressed to the following libraries for permission to reprint the works in this book:

YALE UNIVERSITY LIBRARY: *The Travels of Mr. John Gulliver* (1731).

BRITISH MUSEUM: *Modern Gulliver's Travels: Lilliput* (1796).

LC CATALOG CARD NUMBER: 72-162479

ISBN 0-8201-1098-1

MANUFACTURED IN THE U.S.A.

GULLIVERIANA: II

W. Hogarth inv.   Ger. Vandergucht sculp

Gulliver presented to the Queen of Babilary.

From *The Travels of Mr. John Gulliver*, Vol. I

INTRODUCTION

Of the more than sixty eighteenth-century works which were inspired by *Gulliver's Travels,* about one third remain close to the original in matter or manner. In recognizable fashion they employ one or more of Jonathan Swift's essential elements: a travel framework, interspersed with descriptions and adventures; fantastic objects and events, particularly those chosen to provide fresh perspectives on familiar experiences; descriptions, more or less ironic, of ideal states; unusual characters and imaginary locations; and satire in the handling of people and institutions. Only seven of these works imitate by actual borrowing: that is, they use the original Gulliverian lands and tell more about some of the original characters.

Into this last group fall the two works reprinted here, *The Travels of Mr. John Gulliver, Son to Capt. Lemuel Gulliver* by Desfontaines and the anonymous *Modern Gulliver's Travels, Lilliput: Being a New Journey to that Celebrated Island by Lemuel Gulliver, Jun.* Both are direct imitations, reproducing the original in many unmistakable respects. At the same time, both innovate and do it similarly. As their titles and authorial pseudonyms indicate, both employ the rather pat idea of having an offspring of Gulliver as the narrator and returning traveller.

Obvious as the idea is, it was not used often. The only other notable example in the eighteenth century was the series of anonymous articles, "Debates in the Senate of Magna Lilliput," which ran in *Gentleman's Magazine* between 1738 and 1746 (H. Teerink, *Bibliog-*

v

raphy of Jonathan Swift, ed. Arthur Scouten, 1963, item no. 1247). To get around a new law forbidding Parliamentary debates to be printed, a grandson of Gulliver intermittently reported the substance of important speeches, using Gulliverian substitutes for actual names and pretending he was giving news from Lilliput. The idea was perhaps Samuel Johnson's; at least he was the outstanding contributor (see C. Lennart Carlson, *The First Magazine: A History of the Gentleman's Magazine,* 1938, pp. 95-104). Although they gain satiric perspective from the Lilliputian parallel and illustrate the continuing prominence of the *Gulliver,* the interest of the sixteen essays lies far more in their political connection than their Swiftian. By contrast, the interest of *The Travels of Mr. John Gulliver* and *Modern Gulliver's Travels* is distinctly their many Gulliverian features.

Among these the new narrators are of primary importance, producing as they do two very different viewpoints. In the Desfontaines the narrator is the son John whom Swift mentions in the account of Lilliput, born of Lemuel and Mary before Gulliver, Sr., starts on his travels (1696). According to Desfontaines, John completed his own travels and wrote his account by 1720, although the work did not appear for ten years. The son in the *Modern Gulliver* has no prototype in *Gulliver's Travels,* being the offspring of a Blefescudian, begotten when Gulliver was in Blefescu, which would mean sometime between 1703 and 1705 according to the dates in *Gulliver's Travels.* Lemuel, Jr., is thus only a little younger than Desfontaines' John; yet he lives to write this autobiography in 1796. Almost a century separates the elder Gulliver's first voyage and the close of the younger Lemuel's account, although the two men are but a generation apart.

Differing in temperaments, styles, and values, the authors of these two continuations use *Gulliver's Travels* for their own distinct purposes. Each emphasizes different features of the original and implies a very different estimate of it. What this shows of the author's own talents is mildly interesting. Far more important, examining two such contrasting continuations of the *Gulliver* reveals from a new angle the range and vitality of the original.

A̶b̶b̶é̶ *The Travels of Mr. John Gulliver*
by PIERRE-FRANÇOIS GUYOT DESFONTAINES (1731)

A humorless, thin-skinned, flagrantly immoral moralizer, Pierre-François Desfontaines would not seem a likely person to translate and imitate *Gulliver's Travels*. He was not entirely expert in English. He was critical of fantasy and allegory, his own taste running to long-winded platitudes. Yet in the event he was indisputably successful.

More a rewriting than a translation, his *Les Voyages de Gulliver* was immensely popular (Teerink, no. 385). It sold at a phenomenal rate, running into as many editions as did the original. The reviews of the day praised indiscriminately both those parts that were faithful to the original and the passages by Desfontaines which had no Swiftian counterpart. None of the critics commented on the degree of alteration, not even Swift. Having received a servile letter from Desfontaines admitting but justifying "une traduction peu fidèle," Swift wrote a scathing reply which confines itself to ridiculing Desfontaines' inaccurate, hedging preface to the first edition (*The Correspondence of Jonathan Swift*, ed. Harold Williams, 1963, Vol. III, Desfontaines' letter of 4 Juillet [o.s. 23 June] 1727 and Swift's undated reply, pp. 217 and 225; Sybil Goulding gives a full account of Desfontaines and Swift in *Swift en France*, 1924, pp. 58 ff.).

One cannot deny Desfontaines' promptness in recognizing what he could do with the *Gulliver's Travels*. It was not three months after its publication that he started his translation, which he completed and published in April 1727. As for his continuation, while not the first, it was one of the earliest. *Le Nouveau Gulliver*, as Desfontaines entitled his continuation, appeared in 1730. English, Dutch, German, and Italian translations followed in the very next year.

The English version, *The Travels of John Gulliver*, was made by John Lockman, a practiced translator who gained some little acclaim later for doing various works by Voltaire. While the French and German texts were reprinted several times, there was but one English edition, the text reprinted here (Teerink, no. 1238). Where an earlier English continuation, *Travels into Several Remote Nations*, Vol. III, 1727 (Teerink, no. 1219 etc.), had pretended to be an additional part of the original *Gulliver's Travels*, written by the same author, Desfontaines was content with a lesser fiction: he claimed, on the title page, that the French edition was "Traduit d'un Manuscrit Anglois," and he followed this with his initials. This pretense was dropped in the English translation, as was any identification of the author.

The Travels of John Gulliver has evoked more critical comment than most Gulliveriana, the concentration being on the way the work differs from and falls short of the Swift. The most sympathetic attitude among modern critics is the suggestion, not pursued, that the work may more profitably be considered on its own terms than always in comparison with *Gulliver's Travels* (William A. Eddy, *Gulliver's Travels: A Critical Study*, 1923 & 1963, p. 198). Since modern critics see Desfontaines' spirit as singularly at odds with Swift's and emphasize the contrast between the original and the imitation, it is somewhat surprising that no one has really considered precisely what in Swift's work attracted Desfontaines. If his motives were simply mercenary and moralizing,

many another work might profitably have occupied him
too. Yet he did no other imitations and his only other
translation was of Virgil's works. Furthermore, in spite
of what the critics imply and Desfontaines himself says
—"the only conformity is in the title" (p. 2)—the Gulliverian borrowings in his work are substantial.

The whole design is not just an imaginary journey,
but a strongly Gulliverian one, telling the adventures of
a single hero in several very different lands, each ob-
served with care and wonder and reported with a re-
markable number of the elder Gulliver's enthusiasms and
prejudices. From the start, young Gulliver undertakes
his travels voluntarily, although his destinations are al-
tered by nature and people. Very early in the tale he
is separated from his companions, but in each new lo-
cale he quickly ingratiates himself with the natives,
learns the language, studies and records their ways, an-
tagonizes someone or aligns himself with a local feud,
and engages in battle or just moves on. Like his father's,
his aim after each adventure is to return to Europe.

The way in which Desfontaines varies his invented
countries is like Swift's. Some of the lands are ideal,
some embody undesirable qualities, and some are fantastic in one or another feature designed to illustrate a
principle. Specifically Swiftian ideas characterize three
of the lands: one is a series of different islands (in Tierra
del Fuego), each with its own extreme peculiarities as
in Part III of the *Gulliver*; two deal with length of human life as in the Struldbrug episode. Even the original features of *The Travels of John Gulliver* owe something to Swift. John's first adventure is in Babilary
where women hold men's offices and vice versa. The
reversal provides the same tacit irony as is found in Lilliput and Brobdingnag. Similarly Desfontaines creates a
new image—the crump-backed people (Vol. II, Chap. I)
—to explore the relative nature of beauty, again a topic
which Swift had treated in Parts I and II of *Gulliver*.

While generally Desfontaines' style lacks the vigor, acidity, and economy of Swift's, occasional passages bear resemblances. Perhaps the most striking is the comparison of European and Letalispon manners and politics (Vol. II, Chap. X), which echoes discussions in Lilliput (Chap. VI), Brobdingnag (Chap. VI), and Houyhnhnmland (Chaps. V-VII).

What is unusual about *The Travels of John Gulliver* is that it does so frequently echo the Swift, though in an alien voice. Partly that voice is keyed to other literary sources: moral tales, romances, and nonsatiric imaginary journeys. Such works account for many of the non-Swiftian topics and attitudes, such as the interest in women and romantic love. Whatever interest the work may have in itself and in the context of eighteenth-century moral tales, the primary effect for the student of Gulliveriana is seeing *Gulliver's Travels* in a distorting mirror, discovering there what features remain identifiable, and learning from this something more about the very essence of Swift's work.

Modern Gulliver's Travels, Lilliput:
Being A New Journey to That Celebrated Island
by Lemuel Gulliver, Jun., (1796)

Modern Gulliver's Travels is a work of exuberance if not of art, a jumble of somewhat Swiftian techniques and ideas, used with varying degrees of success. Just who the author was remains uncertain; Philip Gove cites two possibilities: H. Whitmore and Mrs. Elizabeth Graham (*The Imaginary Voyage in Prose Fiction*, 1941, p. 394). Internal evidence shows a writer well-acquainted with the ways of eighteenth-century hack journalism and with a strong feeling about the political situation of the day. He tends to parody when he imitates, overdoing effects as would presumably be suitable for the mass public. Yet he has an uncommonly sharp apprehension of what Swift was doing in the *Gulliver* and has something of his moral earnestness. The work comes across as part pot-boiler and part sincere political comment.

In form *Modern Gulliver's Travels* is a hodge-podge. Like the Swift it is basically an imaginary journey, with an intermixture of travel and utopian literature, autobiography, debate, and sermon. Satire is, as with Swift, the controlling tone. Not content with these, the author added other genres and topics, chosen with neither harmony nor propriety. All these elements he simply interspersed, rather than assimilating them into a homogeneous result as Swift had done. Written at a time when the romance form frequently served as a catch-all frame for descriptions, poems, and other set pieces, the *Modern Gulliver* is—even by contemporary standards—astonishing eclectic.

The story of Lemuel Jr.'s birth and parentage is a sentimental romance. Scenes from this background interrupt the account of his adult life like the episodes of a serialized novel in a magazine. Parts of the story are in the form of lyrics and verse epistles. This is all highly romantic but, whether deliberately or not, the tone is that of Sterne or Diderot rather than of the straight sentimental tale. Furthermore, the fact that one or both of young Lemuel's presumed parents were members of a religious order associates the story with the many scandalous accounts of convent life popular in the seventeenth and eighteenth centuries. Here, too, the treatment borders on burlesque in the number and variety of alleged vices, the blasé attitude of the narrator, and the many contradictory discoveries he makes.

Within this double framework of imaginary journey and sentimental-scandal tale appear many set pieces. In prose are samples of character writing, a Gothic tale, a will, and "Confessions à la Rousseau" (p. 196). In poetry, besides the sentimental verses, are odes, laments, brief satires, other lyrics, and a very ambitious "moral satiric poem" of nearly six hundred lines, complete with annotations (pp. 145-73).

To this already diverse combination is added the most intriguing element of this book, the very obvious indications that it is to be read as a roman à clef, attacking members of the royal family and prominent political figures. This is conveyed primarily through an invented language which the author supplies in unusual abundance. He makes the first examples transparently clear to show that it is a cipher. To embark for Lilliput, young Lemuel goes to a coastal town of Blefescu, "Balono" (p. 7), clearly Boulogne. He crosses a narrow body of water and arrives at "Doph'r" (p. 13), Dover faintly disguised.

More common than these homonym-like constructions are various kinds of anagrams. Some are simply reverse spelling: the title "Noble Renommoc" (p. 26), commoner spelled backward. Some are perfect anagrams ("Blefescudianized" as the text labels the process, p. 67): "Chtmhaa" (p. 23) for Chatham, "Calxhosfer" (p. 51) for Charles Fox, and a title for Gulliver Jr., "Norab Glulplew," meaning Baron Plug-Well, describing a surgical feat he performs for the king. Some are anagrammatic scrambles with letters added or omitted, for euphony or mystery. The context makes unmistakable that "The Sublime Pekrub" (p. 37) is Burke. At "Elsac Sinwrod" (Windsor Castle) Gulliver is presented to "Log-Ereg," King George III. One of the main characters in the new Lilliput is "Vilpi-Tico" (p. 26), presumably William Pitt, beclouded by substitution, omission, and addition, with perhaps a further play on the word politics.

Other ciphering principles are used also, including an occasional example of a formation based on foreign words. For instance, the family name of young Lemuel's mother, Belciglia, is an Italian understatement of her beauty. Because of this cryptographic variety and the obscurity of some references, the terms are not equally decipherable. In the text reproduced here, interlinear annotations in an unknown hand identify with varying degrees of clarity some two dozen of the scrambled names. Many remain unglossed, but even what is supplied here shows the richness of the author's allusion to the contemporary political scene, as well as the fascination of the anagram game.

The invented languages of imaginary journeys have been but slightly explored by scholars, with attention limited to the more sophisticated examples—those based on foreign languages or ideal concepts of language. The *Modern Gulliver* invites more study than it has received. Edward Seeber, one of the few to cite it, notes the extraordinary number of madeup words, but his analysis consists of one enigmatic remark, "some of them [the words] suggest English influence (Pekrub, Oro-Bluff), but the majority do not (Juknig, Norab Glulplew)" ("Ideal languages in the French and English Imaginary Voyages," *PMLA*, 60, 1945, 593).

Another respect in which *Modern Gulliver's Travels* imitates the Swift with some significance is its use of obscene material. William Eddy described the *Modern Gulliver* as "a lengthy account of Gulliver's amorous intrigue with a Lilliputian lady, stated in the preface to be an integral part of the original, omitted by Lemuel through delicacy. Readers will remember that there is a hint of scandal in the work of Swift itself, a hint which was expanded in the imitation to unnecessary length of indecency." Eddy compares the somewhat similar content of Garrick's *Lilliput* and concludes, "It must be admitted that both are amusing; but the humor of Garrick is suited to the drawing room, while the other—well it could be read in a smoking car, by the members of the

Society for the Suppression of Indecent Literature" (p. 199).

One may smile at Eddy's phrasing (even while being befuddled by his description, which does not accurately describe either Gulliver's alleged amours), but his reaction is not a rare one. A study of Gulliveriana shows that many eighteenth-century readers were so forcibly struck by Swift's explicit references to parts and functions of the body which polite literature generally chose to ignore or to handle in a discreetly comic manner that for them the essence of his style was its obscenity.

Modern Gulliver's Travels makes no such error. It occasionally introduces taboo elements gratuitously or uses sniggering circumlocutions, unlike Swift's explicit, almost clinical vocabulary (the phallic "crocodile" of Chap. X is a Scribblerian ribaldry, found in *Three Hours After Marriage* and not characteristically Swiftian). But, in spite of Eddy's emphasis, obscenity plays no disportionate part in the work. What is even more distinctive, the author of *Modern Gulliver's Travels* grasped Swift's intentions and apparently strove to achieve the same effects, attacking like Swift the evils of gossip, false ideas of modesty and morality, and the ridiculous extremes of scientific experimentation. The indelicate terms and scenes relate to plot and character. They mainly derive in substance from Swift. And they contribute positively to the satiric aim. In these respects the work differs markedly from the bulk of imitations featuring pseudo-Swiftian obscenity.

The objects of satire in *Modern Gulliver's Travels* are like Swift's in that the author focusses vigorously on paramount abuses. Besides attacking individuals, he satirizes the theater, balls, hunting, gambling, money-lending, financial fraudulence, and bribery. All of these, however, are subordinate to his major concern, the French Revolution. Both its occasion and its conduct pose, to his mind, a monumental threat. In the light of this, he attacks ludicrous forms of taxation, corruption in the law courts, religious institutions, and the war. He vividly parodies the levity of the English as they spend themselves in childish plots and counterplots. He sees, deplores, and wishes the reader similarly to see their self-absorption and their dangerous indifference. The ideas are not novel—they come from the political writers and satirists of the past decade. But the sharpness of the ridicule is his own, and the employment of the Swiftian vehicle is eminently appropriate if not a total success.

The copy of Desfontaines' *The Travels of Mr. John Gulliver* used for this facsimile edition is in the Beinecke Rare Book and Manuscript Library of Yale University. *Modern Gulliver's Travels* is reprinted from a copy in the British Museum. We wish to thank both of these libraries for giving permission to use these copies for reproduction. We are grateful also to the American Philosophical Society and the Research Committees of C. W. Post College and Saint Francis College for grants which helped finance this work.

JEANNE K. WELCHER

C. W. Post College
Greenvale, New York

GEORGE E. BUSH, JR.

Saint Francis College
Brooklyn, New York

October 8, 1970

THE
TRAVELS
OF
Mr. *John Gulliver,*
Son to Capt. *Lemuel Gulliver.*

Tranſlated from the *FRENCH,*
By *J. Lockman.*

VOL. I.

LONDON:
Printed for SAM. HARDING, at the
Bible and *Anchor,* on the Pavement
in St. *Martin's-Lane.* MDCCXXXI.

TO THE

RIGHT HONOURABLE

THE

COUNTESS

OF

HAROLD.

Madam,

HOSE who de-
vote themſelves to
the Muſes, are ſo
little encourag'd
by the Great, that
I cannot but eſteem your
Ladyſhip's goodneſs, in indulging

Dedication.

dulging the ambition I had of inſcribing this tranſlation to you, as a peculiar happineſs, and an omen of its ſucceſs.

Your known diſinclination to applauſe, eſpecially that of a publick nature, tho' every action of your life deſerves it, lays me under a double obligation to your Ladyſhip.

That your Ladyſhip ſhould be eminent for the practice of all the milder virtues, is no wonder, when we conſider the illuſtrious family from which you are ſprung. Your noble

Dedication.

noble anceſtors, at the ſame time that they were the ornament of the *Britiſh* court, were conſpicuous for all thoſe qualities which render human nature amiable. And here your Ladyſhip's excellent Father the Earl of *THANET*, ſhines with diſtinguiſh'd luſtre, who, of all men, ſeems to have had the deepeſt ſenſe of thoſe admirable words of *Pythagoras*; that, " If we can in any " thing reſemble the Gods, " 'tis in doing good, and " ſpeaking the truth.

The

Dedication.

The tranſition from this great character to that of your Ladyſhip, would be natural; but your commands to the contrary, force me, tho' with the greateſt reluctance, to be ſilent. I am with the higheſt reſpect,

Madam,

Your Ladyſhip's

moſt devoted

humble Servant,

John Lockman.

(i)

THE

Tranſlator's Preface.

I ſhall not attempt a character of the following work, nor enter into the genius and moral of it; the author, under the feign'd name of the editor, having done it at large.

Nor ſhall I, tho' poſſibly it may be expected, pretend to draw a contraſt between the inimitable Travels of captain Lemuel Gulliver and thoſe of his ſon: ſuch a task, as it would be very difficult, and of too delicate a nature, at leaſt for me; ſo it might perhaps give ſome perſons, for whoſe judgment I have the greateſt deſerrence, a mean opinion of my taſte. All I ſhall obſerve on this head, is, that the invention, the ſpirit and humour in the following travels, made the tranſlation of them a delightful exerciſe.

As the adventures of our young traveller, have been receiv'd very favourably by the French, I hope his countrymen will ſhew them the ſame indulgence. This I wou'd

not

not doubt of, were I at liberty to point out the author, whose works have made him deservedly famous in the republic of letters; but as he has thought proper to conceal his name on this occasion, 'twould, methinks, be equally rude to publish it, as to force off a lady's mask.

With regard to my Version, I've endeavour'd to give it in as easy a dress, as the time I had for it wou'd allow ; to infuse a little of that spirit, which is the life of translations; and to file away those roughnesses which make them flat and languid, and so very unlike their originals. Nor have I, I hope, been wanting in fidelity, except in two or three places of no consequence to the beauty of the work, in which our author happen'd to mistake, occasion'd by his being unacquainted with some of our customs.

Notwithstanding the writings of the French are so much sought after by us, yet 'tis well known, that in general, they are look'd upon as light, wordy, as 'tis term'd, and consequently uninform'd with the manly sense of our English writers. How far this may be true, I shall not take upon me to determine

termine directly; but if I may be allow'd to speak my thoughts, my humble opinion is, that 'tis chiefly owing to the bad Versions which have been made from that tongue, especially of the great Writers in it; and well may they be found wordy, since their words only are translated. Was an artless sculptor to imitate a beautiful antique busto, or a sign-painter to copy a Raphael *or a* Titian; *'tis certain that the grace, the spirit and fire of the originals would be entirely lost in their performances.*

Tho' I've presum'd to give my opinion so freely on this head, I yet wou'd not have it imagin'd I mean it as a compliment to my own talents. And, indeed, as this is the farthest from my thoughts, so were my capacity in this province ever so great, I yet shou'd think I had very little to boast of.

I cannot but take notice of the contempt in which Romances *in general are had, (and consequently the writers of them,) tho' the moral be ever so excellent, by multitudes of persons, merely because they are fictitious. That the greatest part of our* Romances *are very trifling, I readily grant; but*

but tho' I wou'd not presume to lessen the dignity of history; its vast usefulness, or the merits of a good historian, I yet believe that a greater genius is requir'd for the former. The historian has materials to work upon, whereas the other is oblig'd to spin them out of his own fancy, and to strike out a new creation, as it were, of his own.

But to return to my translation. As several arts are transiently treated of, and some burlesq'd in the course of this work, it consequently made my task the harder; however, I flatter myself I've translated those passages with tolerable propriety. What I have chiefly to crave the reader's indulgence for, is with regard to the sea terms, in which, tho' I took the utmost care, I possibly may sometimes not have hit upon the true dialect.

If this piece meets with some success, I intend to prepare for the press, a translation of an excellent work entitled Critical Reflections on Poetry and Painting, by l'Abbé du Bos, Secretary of the French Academy at Paris, who has done me the honour to offer me his assistance, in order to make the English Edition as complete as possible.

THE

THE

French Editor's

PREFACE.

*T*HE *Travels of Capt.* Lemuel Gulliver *have met with such success,
that 'tis with the utmost diffidence we
publish the following*; *and as the public are so justly prejudic'd against the continuation of all celebrated pieces, we dare
not flatter ourselves so far as to think,
this will pass uncensur'd. The general
opinion is, that a writer who continues a
a work, is a kind of copist, that treads ser-
vilely in his author's steps*; *that he does
no more than glean after him*; *and having no talent at invention, the most he
can do, is merely to enlarge and adjust his
own ideas by those of the original writer.
The public always suspects, that he has
no other view, than, under the auspices
of another work, to raise the reputation*

a   *of*

of his own ; *not knowing (unhappily for him) that the more they have ap-plauded a piece, the less inclination they have to approve another in the same taste.*

This being suppos'd, it may be pro-per to observe here, that notwith-standing the following work is entitled the New Gulliver, *it yet is in no man-ner a sequel of that publish'd under the name of Capt.* Lemuel Gulliver. *There is neither the same traveller, the same kind of incidents, nor is the cast of the allegory like that of the former ; in a word, the only conformity is in the title. The former was the father, ours is the son, and the reader will soon perceive, we might justly have given another name to our hero ; and that the only reason why we prefer'd this to any other, was from a supposition, that as the public have made the philosophical, and bold ideas of Capt.* Lemuel Gulliver *familiar to them ; they would be less surpriz'd at those of* John Gulliver *his son, when they saw them united together in some measure, under a like title : for tho' the fictions are very*
                                            different,

different, there yet is a kind of analogy between them.

In Capt. Lemuel's *travels, we are entertain'd with dwarfs and giants of an unaccountable fize; a race of immortal men; an aerial ifland, and a republic of rational horfes. In thofe of the fon, the reader will be connvey'd into one country where the fair fex have the fuperiority; a fecond whofe men foon grow old, and enjoy but a very fhort life; a third whofe inhabitants, tho' fuperlatively deform'd and ugly, do neverthelefs appear handfome in the eyes of their countrymen; laftly, another, whofe natives are indulg'd a long life, and the advantage of returning to the bloom of youth, when they have attain'd to half their years. 'Tis by the fingularity of thefe fuppofitions, that the two works in queftion may refemble in general; but the fuppofitions differ widely in themfelves, and the morals which refult from each, have no manner of affinity. The fon's adventures are entirely different from thofe of the father, and altogether independant on them; and are no otherwife a fequel of Capt.* Lemuel's, *than,*

(pardon

(4)

(pardon the comparison) *the* Adventures
of Telemachus *are a continuation of the*
Odyſſey. *'Tis well known, that thoſe
two poems (if both may be allow'd that
name) are entirely independant ; are neither in the ſame caſt, nor have the ſame
object : and 'twas merely from the faint ſi-
militude of a few features, and a very
ſlight conformity, that the* Archbiſhop of
Cambray's Telemachus, *was ſaid to be
a ſequel of* Homer's Odyſſey.

*As fiction of every kind is contemptible,
unleſs it be of uſe to mankind, and has
truth couch'd under it ; we flatter ourſelves
that the reader will eaſily diſcover the moral which is ſhadow'd under the images
we here preſent him with ; not to mention
thoſe we have interſpers'd up and down
the dialogues, wherever there was an opportunity for ſo doing. The firſt fiction,
for inſtance, will ſhew, that the maxim
with regard to* Baſhfulneſs, *which has taken deep root among us, and receives a
ſanction from the depravity of the age, is
a very pernicious one. We imagine, that
this virtue is reſtrain'd wholly to the fair
ſex ; and upon that pretence, men fancy
that*

that the lofs of it, or the perfuading women to banifh it from their minds, is no
reflection on their honour. In reading of
a place where the very reverfe happens;
a country where the female inhabitants
enjoying a fuperiority over the other fex,
act the fame part as the men do among
us, and imitate their depravity; we cannot but think their conduct very ftrange
and unaccountable, and muft neceffarily dif-
approve it. Neverthelefs, when once women are fuppos'd fuperior to the other fex,
we are not to wonder much at this difor-
der; whence 'tis plain, that men wou'd
not be fo corrupt on this article, did they not
abufe their fuperiority. But muft then
the predominant fex be, in one fenfe, the
weakeft; and take advantage of their
power, to attack inceffantly, with a preme-
ditated contempt, thofe whom they will triumph over? This moral of theirs is univerfally known; nothing was wanting,
but to draw it forth into action, in like
manner as we have done feveral others,
which the reader will meet with in the
body of the work.

The

*The country whose inhabitants, tho'
they soon grow old and die early, do nevertheless in some measure live longer than
we ; will of itself suggest so many reflections, that it were needless to acquaint the
reader with the moral of this allegory,
which alludes to the vain and idle use we
make of life.*

The particulars of Gulliver's dwelling
among savage nations; and his discourse
with the people, are not so surprizing
as the preceeding adventures, and include
a self-evident, paradoxical philosophy.
Here all regularly-constituted nations, are
censur'd by a virtuous savage, who being
guided by no other light than that of nature ; pronounces, that what we call civil
society, politeness, and decorum, is no other
than a vicious commerce, and the creature
of a corrupted fancy, which prejudice only
makes us esteem.

The grotesque shape of the people, subject to the emperor Doſlogroboskow, and
the agreeable idea they form to themselves
of one another's persons, denote, that beauty
and deformity, a good and ill grace, are
mere arbitrary qualities.

Lastly,

Laftly, The Letalifpons, *a people, who return to the bloom of youth at a certain age, and enjoy a long life, will fhew how ridiculoufly the greateft part of mankind act, in valuing life fo much, and taking fo little thought to prolong it; and fpending it in fuch a manner, as tho' they did not think it worth their care. As to the fingular notions which this people have form'd to themfelves, with regard to animals, and their laws of health, let thofe who will make their advantage of them. Thefe opinions, tho' they poffibly may have fome foundation, will hardly ever be put in practice.*

It were needlefs to mention the different iflands, which are here fuppos'd to be in Terra del Fuego. *We thought proper to make a* Dutchman *defcribe them, left, thofe whimfical ideas, which have no manner of probability, and are merely allegorical, would, had our traveller related them, have made him talk out of character; and ruin'd his veracity with the public, in cafe he himfelf had told thofe particulars.*

Dr. Ferruginer's *letter, inferted at the end of the fecond volume, will*

be

be of service in giving an air of probability to the several astonishing particulars that are related in these travels, and told, as so many matters of fact. The great erudition of that gentleman, who peruses all books antient and modern, purposely to extract from them such particulars, as may seriously support the grotesque ideas which compose this work, may possibly form a pretty agreeable contrast. After all, these learned quotations are of use to young Gulliver, or to the person who speaks in his name; for whenever we attempt to shadow truth under images, we ought to have probability chiefly in view.

Here D . . . S . . . . . t's genius has been very much admir'd, who in his travels of Capt. Lemuel Gulliver, imposes in such a manner, upon the imagination, that he almost gives an air of verisimility, to things manifestly impossible; and by a series of incidents delicately describ'd and connected, seduces agreeably the judgment. As the fictions in the following work are less singular and bold, they consequently cost the author less pains, in his endeavours to elude the understanding.

We

We only wish, that this little work, may be indulg'd part of the favourable reception which the translation of that of D... S ..... t, *met with in* France. *I am sensible that the public have been very much divided in opinion, with regard to the merits of that work; which some look'd upon, as one of the best that has been publish'd these many years; while others consider'd it merely as a rhapsody of trifling and insipid fictions. The reason of this latter judgment, is, that those people consider'd only the naked circumstances, abstracted from the wit and allegory, which nevertheless is very obvious in almost every page. They complain'd there were no intrigues, no situations, or circumstances of things to effect the imagination; These would have had a regular romance, instead of which, they were entertain'd with nothing but a series of allegorical travels, unenliven'd with so much as one single love adventure. Some regard has been had to their taste in the present work; but at the same time, care has been taken to do this sparingly, for fear of deviating*

ting

ting too much from the work, from which our hint was first borrow'd.

These are the reflections I thought proper to prefix to this work, agreeable to the intentions both of the author and translator. The latter, who was pleas'd to entrust me with the publication of his work, has, by certain expressions which dropt from him, given me some reason to believe it was written by himself; however, this is a circumstance I dare not positively assert.

THE

(i)

THE
CONTENTS.

CHAP. I.

THE author's education. His natural inclination to travel. His application tohis studies. His diftafte of the fchool philofophy; is divided whether he fhall devote himfelf to letters or bufinefs. Embarks for China.

CHAP. II.

A ftorm arifes; the veffel is drove into the eaftern ocean, and afterwards taken by pirates of the Ifland of Babilary. The author is carried into the queen's feraglio.

CHAP.

C H A P. III.

The author soon learns the Babilarian *tongue, by a new and uncommon method. His conversation with the director of the seraglio, who informs him that the posts and employments of the state are fill'd by women. The origin of this custom.*

C H A P. IV.

Sequel of the discourse between the author and the director of the seraglio. Manners of the women and men of the island of Babilary. *Description of the seraglio, and of those who were confin'd in it with the author; their employments, jealousies, &c.*

C H A P. V.

The queen visits the seraglio. The author is presented to her; has the good fortune to please her. He is nominated and declared the queen's husband for the

C H A P.

C H A P. VIII.

C H A P. IX.

C H A P. X.

ing to knock out his brains, and eat him. In what manner he is deliver'd. **p. 134.**

C H A P. XI.

Whilst part of the crew is on shore, those who staid on board the vessel, weigh anchor. The author, with several Portugueze, *is oblig'd to continue a long time in the island of* Mahoonam. *They make an alliance with a nation of savages.* **p. 151.**

C H A P. XII.

The author falls in love with a pretty female savage. His conversation with her and her father, who censures the manners of the Europeans. **p. 163.**

C H A P. XIII.

Battle between the Kistrimaux *and* Taouaous. *The latter, being assisted by the* Portugueze, *are victorious.*
The

The author makes a speech, to diffuade the favages from putting the prifoners to death. A peace is concluded between the two nations. p. 195.

THE

THE
TRAVELS
OF
John Gulliver, &c.

CHAP. I.

*The author's education.   His natural in-
clination to travel.   His application to
his studies.   His diftaste of the fchool
philofophy ; is divided whether he fhall
devote himfelf to letters or bufinefs.
Embarks for* China.

 have obferv'd, that children generally have the
fame inclinations with
their fathers, unlefs e-
ducation happens to
change their natural
bent. I know, however, that they
fome-

sometimes take after their mothers only; whence it follows, for instance, that the son of a poet is found to be a prudent, sagacious man; the son of a philosopher, a coxcomb or a devotee; and the son of a traveller, unactive and sedentary.

As to my self, I can say that I take very much after my father, not only with regard to the exterior qualities, but also those of my mind; whence, I presume to flatter my self, that I am the genuine son of the celebrated Capt. *Lemuel Gulliver*, and of Mrs. *Mary Burton* his wife, a woman whose conduct was ever irreproachable. As I had been brought up in my father's house, where the discourse generally turn'd upon his travels, and the wonderful discoveries he had made, in the various oceans he had run over; I had an insuperable inclination from my infancy, to go to sea. 'Twas to no purpose, that descriptions were sometimes made to me of storms and other casualties, and the dreadful dangers to which my father had been expos'd:

curiosity

curiofity prevail'd over fear; and I was
willing to fuffer as many hardfhips as
my father had done, provided I might
fee as many wonders.

He found me thus difpos'd at his
return from his third voyage, which
was that of *Laputa*; when overjoy'd
to find fo great a conformity between
his inclinations and my own, he promis'd to carry me along with him, the
next time he went to fea. 'Tis probable he did not intend to fet out immediately; for I being but fourteen
years of age, was too young to follow him at that time. And indeed he
was not as good as his word; for
fhortly after, embarking at *Portfmouth*
the 2d of *Auguft* 1710, he took leave
of no body but my mother, and left
me inconfolable for his hafty and unexpected departure.

Never child in the world wifh'd
more earneftly to be a man than I
did; however, this was not merely
that I might be fecur'd from the accidents to which childhood is liable;
or for the fake of injoying my liberty,

and

and of acting as I thought proper; but only that I might be enabled to bear the hardships which are so frequently met with at sea; and be big enough to be taken on board a ship. I went to school against my inclination, when I us'd to argue thus with my self; Why should I apply my self to languages, that will never do me the least service? Will the *Indians*, the *Chineze*, the *Americans*, value me the more for understanding Greek and Latin? Why am I not rather taught the *Asiatic*, the *African*, or *American* languages, since these undoubtedly wou'd be of infinitely greater advantage to me? However, notwithstanding these reflections, which sometimes made me hate my studies, I nevertheless made a very good progress in them.

That which gave me the greatest disgust, was the study of philosophy as taught in our universities. The famous professor under whom I learnt, us'd to tell his pupils with a grave face and tone, that the logic of the schools

fchools was abfolutely ufeful in all
fciences ; that it directed the mind in
its feveral operations, and gave it a
juftnefs which could not be obtain'd
by any other means. He even made
us frequently difpute on this very fubject ; but then he himfelf argued fo
wretchedly on all occafions, and the
feveral operations of his dull, heavy
foul were fo ill directed; that I may
juftly affirm, he himfelf was for ever
arguing againft the ridiculous opinion
he pretended to maintain.

Metaphyficks, methoughts feem'd
more adapted to contract and blunt the
faculties of the mind, than to give it
a juft turn of thinking; and I abhorr'd
its chimerical fubtilties. Morality,
whofe views are to rectify the heart,
was made dubious and problematical,
and caft into abftrufe and knotty queftions. As to phyficks, fo little is
learnt in the fchools, that the fruit which
refults from them, does not compenfate the time they engrofs. In my opinion, the fyftems of Sir *Ifaac Newton,*
Des Cartes, and fome other modern phi-

B 3   lofophers,

lofophers, is the beft courfe of philofophy a man can go through; thefe not
employing a barbarous feries of fcho-
laftic diftinctions to impofe upon the
mind. And indeed, I can affirm I am
wholly obliged to thofe Books for the
little philofophy I know; and that I have
very much enlarg'd my knowledge in
that branch of fcience, ever fince I
forgot all I had learnt at college.

During my Studies, I applied my
felf very clofely to geography; and
by that means, tho' I cou'd not travel
in perfon, I yet had the pleafure of
rambling up and down the world in
imagination. I was extremely delighted with all relations of foreign countries; I us'd to ask travellers a thoufand queftions, and convers'd frequently
with failors; and the fight of a fhip
compleatly rigg'd, wou'd raife fudden
and involuntary tranfports in my foul,
like to thofe which *Achilles* felt, at the
fight of a fword or lance.

My mother finding herfelf burthen'd with feveral children, and no
great matter to maintain them with, bid
me

me ufe all my endeavours to get fome
fmall place in the treafury or exchequer.
She wou'd often tell me, of a great
number of wealthy commiffioners, and
others employ'd in the revenue, who
had once condefcended, to accept of the
meaneft and moft infignificant employments. However, notwithftanding all
the arguments fhe brought on thefe
occafions, fhe yet could never perfuade
me to embrace fo flippery a ftate of life,
which at the fame time is not very
reputable; where knavery is not always fuccefsful; and where a man runs
the hazard of fpending his days in the
infupportable dependance of a numberlefs multitude of mafters, more imperious than venerable; whofe ficklenefs,
frequently plunges their fubalterns into the misfortunes of the famifh'd
* *Erefichthon.*

Had it been poffible for me to lead a
fedentary life, methinks I fhould have
chofe the profeffion of a fcholar, pre-

B 4   ferable

* *See* Ovid's Metamorphofes, *Book XI.*

ferable to all others. You are born,
says an amiable man of learning one day
to me, with a moſt happy diſpoſition to
ſcience: nature has indulg'd you memory, underſtanding, genius; a fruitful
imagination, and taſte: you may, by the
uncommon aſſemblage of all theſe qualities, and a proper exerciſe of your
talents, do the higheſt ſervice to the
literary world, and be an honour both
to your family and country. You are
very ſenſible, that perſons who make
a figure in the ſciences, are here had in
the higheſt eſteem. *England* becomes
more and more the glorious ſeat of ſcience, and of all that is curious in the
whole compaſs of knowledge. Among
us, a learned philoſopher, a judicious
and knowing hiſtorian, a delicate writer of fine ſenſe, is never ſuffer'd to
pine away in miſery; preferments, to
which the learned and witty have the
moſt juſt claim, are beſtow'd on them
only. Literary merit is here always
call'd forth from obſcurity, and rewarded in a ſuitable manner. Embrace,
my dear child, a calm and honourable

able way of life, in which, without amaffing fo much wealth as many of our commiffioners, you will acquire a fum, as by falling infinitely fhort of the wealth abovemention'd, will be more worthy a man of honour upon that very account.

Thus was I alternately prompted to apply my felf to bufinefs or letters. But how wide is the difference between thofe two conditions of life! the man of bufinefs is enflam'd with a defire of heaping up wealth; the Scholar bends his thoughts wholly to the enriching his mind; the one raifes his fortune, the other gains nothing but a name; the one enriches himfelf with the fpoils of the living, the latter with thofe of the dead; the former has learning and learned men in equal contempt, the latter defpifes rich men more than he does riches; the former enjoys life, the latter exifts after death.

In 1714, being then eighteen years of age; of a tall ftature, and a ftrong, robuft complexion, I pack'd up my things, and without once taking leave

of

of my mother, or any of my relations, having got a fmall fum of money which fome good friends had lent me, and a few books, I went to *Woolwich*, where I had heard that an under-writer was wanted for a veffel that was juft ready to fet fail for *China*.

Tho' I had neither experience or recommendation, I neverthelefs flatter'd my felf with the hopes of getting this place; and in that view, I went and offer'd my fervice to Capt. *Harrington*, who was to command the fhip. My poft was not very advantageous or honourable; however, as it gave me an opportunity of going to fea, there was nothing in the world I fo earneftly defir'd. Befides, I knew that feveral of our moft celebrated Tars, as well as a great number of our wealthieft traders, had firft fet out in an infinitely meaner capacity.

I told the captain, that I was a pennylefs young fellow, whofe only refuge was a little education, and a great deal of honour; that having gone thro' a courfe of ftudies with tolerable
fuccefs,

fuccefs, I knew fomething; that I had
a ftrong inclination to go to fea; and
concluded with faying, that I thought
my felf qualified for the place, and
therefore begg'd him to let me have it.
The captain taking very little notice of
what I told him concerning my ftudies,
only ask'd me whether I underftood
accompts. As my mother had made
me learn them very early, it was an
eafy matter for me to fatisfy him in
that particular. He continued to ask
me feveral queftions, to all which I
gracefully made the moft fatisfactory
replies; fo that feeming to approve of
my underftanding, my perfon and behaviour, he gave me the employment
I defir'd. I was overjoy'd at my fuccefs, particularly when we weigh'd
anchor, which was the 23d of *July*,
1714.

My firft endeavours were to infinuate
my felf into the favour of our captain
and the officers, and to gain the efteem
of the whole crew. Tho', one would
think that the women only fhould confider a man's perfon; 'tis yet certain,
that

that a handſome, well-built young
fellow, commonly pleaſes univerſally,
when the qualities of his mind corre-
ſpond with thoſe of his body; eſpecially if he be vertuous, and a perſon of
good ſenſe. I cannot ſay whether this
happy aſſemblage was found in me;
and whether my advantageous exterior, did not as much conduce to
gain me the eſteem of all, as my prudence, my polite behaviour, and my
eaſy, even, and complaiſant temper.
Captain *Harrington* diſcover'd the
eſteem and friendſhip he had for me
upon all occaſions. My cloſe application to buſineſs; the progreſs I made
in navigation; the judicious reflections I form'd on various ſubjects; my
prudent and circumſpect behaviour;
and the bravery I ſhew'd on all occaſions, made him frequently ſay, that I
ſhou'd one day be very rich, and perhaps attain the higheſt honours in the
navy. This applauſe inſpir'd me with
emulation, and rais'd a ſecret pride in
my mind, which I nevertheleſs conceal'd with the utmoſt caution; firmly
                                    perſuaded

perfuaded that nothing is more apt to
make us lofe the efteem the world may
have for us, than our feeming to fancy
we have obtain'd it. I was already
puff'd up with the ambitious thoughts of
a young *Oxonian*, who has taken his bat-
chelor's degree, and fancies he fees a
bifhop's chair preparing for him in
diftant profpect; happily for my felf,
I had neither vices or ignorance to difguife.

C H A P. II.

*A ftorm arifes; the veffel is drove into
the eaftern ocean, and afterwards taken
by pirates of the Ifland of* Babilary.
*The author is carried into the queen's
feraglio.*

I fhall not give an account of the different winds that blew during our
courfe; the fine or bad weather we
had; the various adventures we met
with; or the Iflands we were oblig'd
to put into, to take in water and provifions; fuch a detail wou'd be neither
inftructive

inftructive or amufing, and 'tis not my
defign to write any thing merely to
tire the reader.

We had already pafs'd the ftraits of
Sunda, and found our felves oppofite
to the gulph of *Conchinchina*, in the
month of *June* 1715, when we met
an englifh veffel commanded by Captain
Jefferies. We fent out our long-boat
to enquire how trade went at *Canton*, a
port of *China*, where moft *European*
fhips generally touch, in order to fell
their lading, and take in the commodities of thofe countries. He inform'd
us, that the port abovemention'd was
crouded with *European* veffels, fo that
the commodities they had brought
from *Europe*, fold for a very trifle;
and that thofe of *China*, efpecially the
raw filk of *Namkim*, fold very dear;
for which reafon he advis'd us to make
for the port of *Emoui* in the province of
Fokien.

We confider'd, that it wou'd be much
better for us to put into that port,
fince, purfuant to the inftructions of our
owners, we were to return by the fouth
fea.

fea. Accordingly we follow'd the fatal advice which Capt. *Jefferies* gave us, when leaving the ifland of *Macao* and the port of *Canton* to our ftarboard, we enter'd the fea of *China* about the middle of *July*. We knew that 'tis dangerous failing on that fea, in the months of *Auguft* and *September*; however we hop'd we fhould get into the road of *Emoui* the beginning of *Auguft*, and not be overtaken by a *Tifon*. Thefe *Tifons* are hurricanes, which generally begin eaftward, tho' they often veer round the compafs in lefs than four hours. The *Chineze* call them *Tufans*, whence they are call'd *Tifons* by the *Europeans*.

Auguft the 2d, we got within 30 leagues of *Emoui*, and were overjoy'd to find our felves fo near the port, when on a fudden we were overtaken by the terrible hurricanes abovemention'd. At the fame time a dreadful ftorm arofe, and the fea ran mountains high. Our main-maft was carried away, and moft of our fails were tore to pieces. For four and fourty
hours

hours together, we were furrounded with a pitchy darknefs; death with all its train of terrors was prefent to our imagination; and we found we had been drove a vaft many leagues, without knowing whither we were going. Our captain difcover'd the greateft intrepidity, experience, and prefence of mind on this occafion; and animated the whole crew by his example. As for my own part, I was indefatigable, which afterwards increas'd very much the love and efteem he had for me. At laft the ftorm abated infenfibly.

At day break, we computed we were got into the eaftern ocean, above the ifland of *Niphon*, the largeft of the iflands of *Japan*. We then thought proper to fteer fouth-weft, in order to reach *Emoui*. A week after we difcover'd an ifland, that appear'd of a great extent, which we miftook for the ifland of *Formofa*. We made for that ifland, the wind being favourable, when we faw a large veffel bearing down upon us, which feem'd

to

to be a pirate, and refolv'd to give us chafe, and board us if poffible. They crouded all their Sail, and being come within cannon fhot, pour'd in feveral broad fides upon us, fo that we were oblig'd to ftrike, after having fought an hour and half. The conquerors boarded us fabre in hand, and having bound us, they carried us into their own veffel, where the prifoners were divided into three claffes, *viz.* the old, the middle-ag'd, and young men. The latter were fubdivided into two claffes; one whereof was of fuch as were hand-fome and well-fhap'd, among which laft I had the honour of being included. Thefe barbarians, who while their fa-bres were drawn, wore a terrible af-pect, now appear'd polite and humane; they were all beardlefs; had long hair; and moft of them feem'd fhort of fta-ture, young, and exquifitely beautiful.

Some time after, the captain of the pirates came to the place where I and my companions lay, and having view'd us all, he came up to me, kifs'd my hand, and carried me into his cabbin,

C   where

where he carefs'd me in fuch a manner as furpriz'd me very much, for
I had no notion that this captain was
a woman.

I then faw a man come in to us, who
feem'd advanc'd in years. The majefty of his face was heightned by a
venerable beard. He was much taller
than the reft of the barbarians, and had
a more mafculine air. I was afterwards
inform'd that he was a royal commiffioner, whofe office was to fuperintend the
prizes. Affoon as the captain faw him,
he began to difguife his paffion, and
foon after left me alone with him.
Zindernein, for that was the comptroller's
name, having obferv'd that the captain
was very fweet upon me, gave me to
underftand it would be for my advantage to be prudent, and preferve my
honour with the ftricteft care. Immediately he order'd me to go into his cabbin, where a bed was prepar'd for me;
and he feem'd to watch me narrowly
till we arriv'd in the ifland.

This ifland, as I then found, was
call'd *Babilary,* a word fignifying in
the

the language of the country, the *glory of women.* We caft anchor in the port two days after, when we immediately faw a great number of the inhabitants advancing towards us, who congratulated their countrymen on the prize they had taken. All my companions having been expos'd to fale the next day, were bought at different prices, according to their age and perfonal qualities; and Capt. *Harrington* was fold cheaper than the reft, becaufe he was the oldeft of the crew; but as for my felf, I was not put up. Upon our landing, *Zindernein* took me with him in a kind of calafh drawn by four beafts very like ftags; and in lefs than two hours, we arrived at *Ramaja,* the capital of the ifland, where the court refided, about twelve leagues from the port we landed at. At our arrival, a numberlefs multitude of people crouded about us; and I heard them crying aloud on all fides, *Sa-bala-cooroocoocoo,* that is, as I afterwards underftood, *how handfome this foreigner is!*

We alighted at the gate of a palace,

C 2 which

which appear'd very magnificent, the entrance whereof was guarded by a confiderable number of young foldiers. *Zindernein* having introduc'd me, carried me through many apartments, where I was met by feveral young men very fplendidly dreft. They all view'd me, but without once opening their lips, being aw'd by the prefence of my conductor I was afterwards made to repofe my felf in an apartment, whither cloaths were immediately brought me by a dozen old women, whom I took for fo many men, and thefe made figns for me to undrefs my felf; I obey'd with all the decency poffible, and immediately was dreft in a white veft of the fineft flax, and a red filk gown.

Soon after I was conducted into a hall, where a noble banquet was prepar'd. I was order'd to place my felf at table in the moft honourable feat. *Zindernein* fat down next to me, and the reft of the feats were fill'd by thofe young perfons, who had crouded about me upon my arrival at the palace.

The

The reader will suppose, I was very much astonish'd at every thing I saw, and that I did not know what to judge of my condition. *Zindernein* cheer'd me with his caresses; and by the signs he made, gave me to understand I was to be happy. During the entertainment, several matters were discours'd upon that I did not understand, which consequently made the time move a little heavily: however, being prodigiously hungry, I eat very heartily, which seem'd to please *Zindernein*. I found, by the motion of the eyes of those who sat at table, that I was the topic of a great part of their conversation: sometimes they wou'd direct their glances to me, when I seem'd to be the subject of their dispute, whence I imagin'd, that they differ'd in opinion about me. At the conclusion of the feast, we were entertain'd with a consort of music both vocal and instrumental, which gave me but very little pleasure; for their music, to my ear, seem'd vastly languid, artless, insipid, unvaried, and grate-

ingly

ingly effeminate, in ſhort like that of the † *French.*

Being very much tir'd, I gave *Zindernein* to underſtand that I wanted a little reſt. He himſelf conducted me into an apartment magnificently furniſh'd, where two old women who waited my coming, undreſs'd me. I went to bed, and *Zindernein* taking his leave, promiſ'd to come and viſit me the next morning. I was left alone, and my chamber door was lock'd.

I then gave my ſelf up to the moſt melancholy reflections. I now, ſays I, am confin'd in a real priſon; I have loſt my liberty, and ſhall be forc'd to ſpend my days in this place, without the leaſt hopes of ever recovering it. But wherefore then is this magnificence, and all theſe gaudy ſcenes of delight? How auguſt is this priſon! What is to be my fate? Am

I

† *As our author is an* engliſhman, *we have made him ſpeak agreeable to the idea which his countrymen have of the* french *muſic.* - - - - - *This is the author's note.*

I not us'd in this fplendidly-kind manner, purely to prevent my dying with
grief and anxiety? I am undoubtedly kept alive, purpofely to be offer'd up
in facrifice, to the god who is worfhip-
ped by the inhabitants of the country.
But if this be fo, How was it poffible
for the young men that fat at table
with me, and who in all probability
are captives as well as my felf, to appear fo gay and unconcern'd? If I am
only to be a flave, does the treatment I
have hitherto met with wear the face
of captivity? None of thofe who are
in the fame circumftances with my
felf, have in any manner a fervile air.
Where am I, what am I, what fhall
I do? Alas! they poffibly defign to
force me to change my religion, but
I will fuffer ten thoufand deaths, fooner than confent to it.

These uneafy thoughts kept me from
fleeping for fome time; however I at
laft clos'd my eyes and fell into a found
fleep. The next day 'twas a pain to
me to wake; the longeft flumbers are
always too fleeting for the wretched.

C H A P. III.

The author soon learns the Babilarian *tongue, by a new and uncommon method. His converfation with the director of the feraglio, who informs him that the pofts and employments of the ftate are fill'd by women. The origin of this cuftom.*

Z*Indernein* came to me a little after I was got up, and finding me very uneafy, he was extremely kind, and gave me to underftand that I had no reafon to defpond. A moment after, a man came into the room, who taught the language of the country to foreigners by a moft furprizing method, without the affiftance of a regular Grammar. He was a painter in miniature, who drew wonderfully fine, and had collected in two large volumes, the reprefentations of all natural objects, which he himfelf had painted, and afterwards got engrav'd. His whole art lay in immediately prefenting

senting to a scholar, the pictures of
the most common and ordinary things:
whenever he shew'd him a print, he
told him the name by which it was
call'd in the *Balibarian* tongue, and
made him write it underneath, in the
character which was peculiar to him;
so that his draughts taken together,
made a kind of dictionary, that was
vastly useful to his pupils.

Among us, the only method of learning foreign languages, is by joining the
idea of a word, whose signification we
would remember, with the idea of
another word that is familiar to us; so
that we retain one found by the medium of another. Now all that comes
into the mind by the organ of sight,
imprints it self much stronger than
whatever enters it by the medium of
the other senses, as experience plainly
shews. Hence I conclude, that this gra-
matic-painter's method was excellent,
and that it ought to be us'd in our universities, for the instructing of our youth
in greek and latin. The only reason
why children learn to tattle so soon
from

from their nurfes, is becaufe they fee
and look attentively upon every thing
they hear fpoke. However, I am perfuaded that this new fyftem of gram-
mer will not meet with better reception, than the new methods which are
daily invented in *Europe* for fhortning
the way to fcience, which in reality,
add but very little to the number of
learned men.

I fpent a fortnight in learning all the
noun fubftantives of the *Babilarian*
tongue ; at the fame time I alfo learnt
the adjectives, becaufe there was no
print but reprefented the Thing with
a variety of attributes. Several of thefe
prints were illuminated, otherwife it
would have been impoffible for me to
learn the names of the feveral colours.

With regard to thofe verbs which
exprefs an action of the foul or body,
my mafter finding I had a very good
memory, and had already learnt the
nouns, gave me the fecond volume of
his collections, comprehending the
verbs; that is, pictures or reprefentations of the different actions and paffions.

ons. The nouns in that language are indeclinable, and the verbs are not conjugated, wherein it bears a great affinity to the english; which in that particular, boasts a greater perfection than most other languages, they being clogg'd with useless difficulties. Neither has it, any more than ours, nouns masculine or feminine to express inanimate Beings, which I always look'd upon as vastly absurd. To instance in an examplo or two, why is *ensis* in latin which signifies a sword, of the masculine gender; and *vagina*, that is a scabbard, of the feminine. Are the sword and scabbard of a different sex? I could add several other observations on this head, were such enquiries proper for a mariner.

Most of the prints which were to express the verbs, were pretty much complex'd? but then I never saw any thing so beautifully design'd in my life, particularly when they express'd any impulse of the soul, such as hatred, desire, fear, hope, esteem, respect, contempt, anger, submission; and the virtues,

virtues, fuch as chaftity, obedience, fidelity; or the vices, as knavery, avarice, pride, cruelty, &c.

As we exprefs thefe things by metaphorical terms, which are analogous to the motions and modifications of the body; 'tis plain that nothing is eafier than to defcribe all this to the eye in painting. Adverbs, which are of ufe in heightning or lefs'ning the force of verbs, and to exprefs a gradation in our ideas, were alfo painted; fo that at the fame time I was taught the verbs by the expreffions of the feveral actions defcrib'd in painting, I alfo learnt the adverbs by the reprefentation of the mode of thofe actions. As for inftance, the various degrees of love were exprefs'd in fo many different pictures, to which a common term or word corresponded; with the addition of another term to exprefs the feveral degrees of the paffion, and this was what form'd the adverb.

Zindernein ufed to vifit me every day, and was greatly pleas'd with the progrefs I made in the *Babilarian* language;
and

and indeed in about a month's time, I
was able to converfe with him. Sometimes I cou'd not hit upon the proper
expreffion; but then, as he underftood
what I meant, he would immediately
recall it to my memory. Befides,
the inhabitants fpeak very flow, fo
that a man has time to recollect the
word as he fpeaks: and as 'tis a foft
language, the pronounciation is very
eafy. With regard to the accent, I
learnt it by degrees. The reafon why
I got the *Babilarian* tongue fo foon,
was, becaufe I confin'd my felf clofe
to it for two months, and convers'd
with no body but my mafter and *Zin-*
dernein. By application we adorn and
embellifh the mind, and improve in
every kind of knowledge.

In my firft converfation with *Zinder-*
nein, I ask'd him why fo much civility
had been paid me? what were the motives of the kind ufage I met with?
what place that was in which I liv'd,
and what they intended to do with me?
He made no fcruple to fatisfy my curiofity, by telling me, that I was in the
queen's

queen's feraglio, in which there were about a dozen young foreigners, like my felf whom fhe lov'd ; and had educated, merely to adminifter to her pleafures. The men of this ifland, fays he, are not worthy of her majefty, who would think fhe fullied the majefty of her diadem, were fhe to ftoop fo low as to beftow her affection on a fubject ; and that it would even be dangerous, in a political view, were fhe to do them fo great an honour; becaufe the families of the ifland, out of which fhe might make choice of husbands, would poffibly take advantage of the grandeur to which it would raife them. What! fays I to him, am I then intended to be given in marriage to the queen? Yes, fays he, in cafe fhe approves of your perfon and underftanding. But all the young men here are your rivals. Surely, fays I, this is very unaccountable in a queen; is it poffible for the modefty of a woman to go fuch lengths, as to marry a dozen husbands?

She never has but one at a time, replied *Zindernein*; but then fhe is at liberty

ty to change him every year, in cafe fhe
thinks proper. On this occafion fhe
takes him, among the young men, fhe
loves beft out of the feraglio, in order
to raife him to that honour; and then
fhe fends back the husband fhe quits
into the fame feraglio, and marries
him again afterwards if fhe pleafes.
Her prefent husband has liv'd ten
months with her, fo that his time is
near expir'd, and 'tis thought he won't
be continued.

There is in this palace a young man
of great beauty and merit, who, 'tis
generally thought, will fucceed him.
Poffibly it may one day be your lot,
and you may be fo happy as to pleafe
her majefty. Who knows but fhe may
prefer you to that young man, who is
defign'd to fill her auguft arms?

Such an honour, fays I, would be
delightful, were it of long duration;
and were I to be a king upon marrying
her majefty. That can never be, fays
Zindernein, the law being exprefs to
the contrary. What! fays I, is there
a law in this ifland which excludes
                                    males

males from the throne, and fuffers none but women to afcend it? 'Tis not fo with us. 'Tis true indeed, that the fcepter is now in a * female hand, but that, was only by accident, and becaufe the majority of the people thought her next heir to the crown. After her deceafe, we fhall have a king, which is much more natural in every refpect; we thinking it mean to fubmit our felves to a woman. The male fex, is the fuperior, and 'tis their bufinefs to command. Thus, fays he, fhould it be in this ifland, and 'twas fo formerly; but the manners of the inhabitants are quite chang'd, and the reins are held by women. They fill up all pofts and employments both civil and military; our fea and land forces are compos'd of them only; in fhort, the men among us act the part of the women in your country.

What! fays I to him, are not you then who prefide here, and fuperintend

the

---

* *Queen* Anne *was fuppos'd to reign when the author writes.*

the prizes, a man? Are thofe who took us prifoners, women? Yes, fays he, your veſſel was taken by females. They are drefs'd like men, except that their gowns defcend but to the calf of the leg; whereas thofe of the men are much longer and wider. I am indeed a man, and the only one that has any thing to do in the adminiſtration, none but a man being allow'd to execute my office.

I then felt a kind of ſhame and confufion, when I found that I had been taken prifoner by women, tho' I was arm'd, and cou'd not forbear bluſhing. *Zindernein* perceiving it, told me, that ſuch women of the iſland as devoted themfelves to a military life, were very brave and well difciplin'd; were furious in battle, and that the men could hardly make head againſt them. Befides, fays he, they are very vigorous: as they are train'd up very young in all bodily exercifes, and learn to ride, and fence; as they often go a hunting, and drink ſtrong liquors, they become more ſtrong and robuſt than the male inhabitants of this country, whom decorum will not permit to

D   imitate

imitate the women in thofe particulars.
However, fays he, this was not always
the cuftom; and I'll acquaint you
with the rife of it, in cafe you have
any curiofity that way. I entreated
him to gratify it, when he began as
follows.

About feven thoufand two hundred
moons fince, *Ameneininus* was fovereign of this ifland. In his reign, men
began to have a prodigious value for
women, infomuch that the female reign
feem'd already come. The king, and
in imitation of the pattern he fet them,
all the men of the ifland, neglecting
their moft important affairs, apply'd
themfelves no more to the ftudy of the
laws or politicks; difdain'd glory; fled
from war; never adminiftred juftice;
defpis'd knowledge, and all the polite
arts; were ignorant of hiftory and philofophy; abhorr'd labour of every kind;
were regardlefs of honour, and dead to
emulation, and, in a word, were eternally fighing at the feet of an enchant-
ing fex. Now the women who are naturally ambitious, refolv'd to take advantage

vantage of this fcandalous effeminacy of the men, in order to fhake off the yoke, which the wifdom of antient times had laid on their fhoulders ; a yoke which the weaknefs of the prevailing fex had fince made too eafy. They fucceeded too well in this fatal attempt; and the charms of queen *Aigina*, being neglected by her royal confort, fhe began the black crime. Accordingly fhe ftep'd into the throne, and threw from it, a weak, indolent monarch, who was immers'd in pleafure, and the flave of a multitude of miftreffes.

The confpiracy which the women had form'd, broke out at the fame juncture: having gain'd a fuperiority over their husbands, they not only undertook to manage all domeftic affairs, which thefe had entirely abandon'd; but alfo thofe of the adminiftration of all publick affairs; of politicks, the revenues, war, and juftice which was now wholly difregarded. However, at firft they did not dare to ufurp openly the rights and privileges of the other fex, but contented themfelves

with

with managing every thing in their name. Had they then carried their machinations farther, the men might poffibly have rouz'd from their lethargy; or at leaft have difputed for abfolute power with the females, fince both nature and reafon have given them that prerogative. But the women, who are naturally artful and of a moft fubtil caft of mind, took a quite different courfe; they flatter'd their husbands, and feduc'd their lovers; fo that at laft, their charms having gain'd a very great afcendent, they began to prepare the fatal revolution.

The male world fubmitted infenfibly to the laws of the other fex. As thefe manag'd the adminiftration tolerably well, and did not fuffer the State to be in as much confufion as before, no one repin'd. In procefs of time 'twas imagin'd, that fince they held the reins fo fteadily, they certainly were born to empire. In the mean time, the men immers'd themfelves ftill more and more in floth; and their indolence increas'd in proportion as it was fomented

by

by inactivity. 'Twas then, as we are told, that a furprizing comet blaz'd in the sky, the tail whereof feem'd to be eclips'd; a circumftance which the female aftrologers did not fail to interpret in their own favour.

King *Ameneininus* dying, *Aiginu* put to death fuch of her husbands relations as might have difputed the crown with her, or have ruin'd her fchemes; and, 'tis fuppos'd, that her fon fell a facrifice to her horrid ambition. A few old men, who were grown uneafy, after weighing every thing ferioufly, attempted to revive the antient cuftoms, and reftore the male fpecies to their original rights and privileges; but thefe were banifh'd by an act of parliament, compos'd of the moft diftinguifh'd females of the ifland. Some other old men, who poffibly might have attempted to rebel, were fo intimidated at the example which was made of the former; that reflecting on their advanc'd age and inability to fight, they thought proper to lie ftill. The reft, after having trifled away life at the feet

of

of their miſtreſſes, were afraid to take up arms againſt them; and ended their days under a tyranny, to which they had voluntarily ſubmitted in their youth. As to the young men who were born in ſlavery, they never once thought of freeing themſelves.

While *Zindernein* was giving me this account, I reflected that the male part of the *Europeans*, conſidering their preſent way of life, might one day be ſubject to ſome ſuch revolution as that I have been ſpeaking of. Their igno-rance and effeminacy, have long pav'd the way to it, if the female world have but the art of making a proper ad-vantage of it.

Neverthelefs, continued *Zindernein*, the inhabitants of the northern part of this great iſland, which then was a kingdom apart and independant from ours; fearing leſt the infection ſhould reach them, and their wives ſhould form ſuch another conſpiracy, ſent emiſſaries ſecretly into our provinces. Theſe endeavour'd to ſpirit up the men to rebel, and to aboliſh the new empire.

Accordingly

Accordingly twenty thousand men having broke out into actual rebellion, they requir'd her majesty to summon a male-parliament, and elect a king; and in case of refusal, threatned to chuse one themselves. Their proposal was haughtily rejected by the queen, who threatned to make the rebels feel the effects of her power, in case they did not immediately lay down their arms. Immediately she rais'd a body of fifty thousand women, in order to reduce the rebels. The most scandalous circumstance is, that three thousand faint-hearted young fellows, suffer'd themselves to be incorporated among the female regiments. The army was commanded by the queen in person, who had under her twelve she-lieutenant-generals, twelve female-major-generals, thirty six she-brigadiers, and fourty eight colonels of that sex.

The two armies met in the plains of *Camaraca.* The males were arm'd with bows and arrows, and their cavalry was very well mounted. The queen, justly suppos'd that as her for-

ces

ces were undifciplin'd, nor had ever
feen a battle, they confequently would
fcarce be able to make head againft an
army of men, and therefore employ'd
a ftratagem highly worthy her genius.
She fet at the head of her army, which
was now drawn up in battle array,
four thoufand very beautiful young
women. Their hair fell in treffes on
their naked fhoulders; their fnowy
breafts were uncover'd, as alfo their
legs and their arms. Thefe were their
only weapons; and 'twas in this dangerous and formidable condition, they
appear'd before the oppofite army,
whofe fury died away at the fight: accordingly they threw down their arms,
and they who juft before were the moft
formidable enemies, now became the
tendereft lovers and moft cringing flaves.

Others relate this incident in a different manner, and fay, that the queen
having thought proper to treat with
the rebels, fent twenty exquifitely beautiful females into their camp, who immediately captivated the hearts of all
the confpirators; and that afterwards
fomenting

fomenting a spirit of discord among the leaders, the male army broke up. This has so much the greater air of probability, as women are well known to have a most admirable knack at setting men together by the ears.

Be this as it will, the women gain'd as much advantage by this pacific victory, as they could have promis'd themselves from the most bloody battle, tho' they had had the glory to cut the male army to pieces. From that period their authority has always increas'd. We, for our parts, are excluded all the posts and employments of state: 'tis they alone profess the sciences, and none but themselves are allow'd to cultivate them: nay, to so ridiculous a a pitch is this carried, that any man who should pretend to set up for a scholar, would be laugh'd at by every body, and be sent back to his distaff and needle. In fine, they only preside over the altars, and the mysteries of religion; and 'tis they offer solemn sacrifices to the Gods in our temples, and are at the head of all our religious ceremonies. As

As for my own part, fays he, who
have the misfortune to be of the male
fpecies; and who neverthelefs would
have reafon to thank nature for it,
were I born under another climate; I
fecretly deplore that fhameful fubverfion of the order which nature had
eftablifh'd; and will never fubfcribe in
my heart, to that falfe maxim, which
is taught by all our fhe-pedants, that
the female fpecies is the moft perfect
throughout the whole animal creation.
This, in my opinion, is a new and er-
roneous doctrine, that clafhes with antient tradition, and may be confuted
by unanfwerable arguments. 'Tis true
indeed, that females only are able to
bring forth their like; and that all
animated fubftances iffue immediately
from theirs. But then, is it poffible
for them to produce the effect of this
admirable power, which indeed is a
noble prerogative, without the affiftance
of the male fpecies? 'Tis to no purpofe
to fay, that the principle of fertility
is inherent in them; and that the action of the males only prepares and mo-
difies

difies it, like the dew of the fpring,
which defcending into the bowels of
the earth, unfolds the infant bud, and
calls forth the plants from it. I, for
my own part, affert that every thing is
perform'd by the males; that the pri-
mitive bud is inherent in them, and
that females are directly, with regard
to them, what the earth is with refpect
to an induftrious hand that cultivates it.
This was the opinion of the learned
part of our male anceftors, whofe books,
whence we might have borrow'd numberlefs arguments to confute their pretenfions, the women have burnt. Neverthelefs, no one dares in this age to
maintain this opinion publickly, upon
pain of paffing for a dangerous innova-
tor, and a factious perfon.

Such, dear *Gulliver*, is the country
you now inhabit. If you can extinguifh
that pride, which the excellence of
your fex infpires you with, and eradicate the juft prejudices of education, you
then will be happy. As you are very
handfome, all the women in general
will treat you with refpect; and flatter
and

and ogle you in such a manner, as
will sufficiently sooth your vanity.
For notwithstanding that the women
look upon our sex as inferiour to theirs,
they neverthelefs have the utmost regard for us: they treat us respectfully;
give us the precedency upon all occafions, and dare not let drop one difo-
bliging expreffion; and were a woman
to ufe us with the leaft uncivility, fhe
would be thought frantic, and quite
lofe her reputation. This is a precious
remainder of our antient cuftoms; a
natural right which female pride has not
been able to abolifh; and an antient title,
we ftill preferve againft them. However, they pretend that the fole reafon
why they treat us fo tenderly, is from
the confideration of our weaknefs,
which, fay they, claims the moft gentle ufage. Alas! this complacency is
now degenerated to an empty honour.
Women, when we love them, call us
their mafters, and yet we are for ever
their flaves.

CHAP.

C H A P. IV.

Sequel of the difcourfe between the author and the director of the feraglio. Manners of the women and men of the ifland of Babilary. *Defcription of the feraglio, and of thofe who were confin'd in it with the author; their employments, jealoufies,* &c.

I liftned attentively to this difcourfe, which furpriz'd me very much. While *Zindernein* was talking to me, I fometimes cou'd hardly forbear burfting out a laughing; but I check'd my felf as much as I cou'd, becaufe I obferv'd, that it always made him more ferious, and feem'd to throw him into fome confufion. When he had done fpeaking, I told him with an air of gayety and freedom, that fince the fair-fex had the fuperiority in that ifland, I would conform to cuftom; and endeavour to compenfate for the lofs of the rank which nature had given me, by the foft and eafy enjoyment of thofe

pleafures

pleafures which now offer'd themfelves.

In cafe, fays he, you have the honour to marry the queen, you then will
be remov'd out of this feraglio, and be
allow'd to range up and down her majefty's palace, where you'll be furrounded with a numberlefs multitude
of officers of both fexes. But be fure
you take care not to give a loofe to
criminal defires, or fall in love with
any woman. If you difcover the leaft
frailty, you'll be defpis'd by the whole
nation: it being an eftablifh'd maxim,
that modefty, which is here look'd upon
as an inconfiderable quality in the
female fex, is an effential virtue in ours.
A man who keeps miftreffes, and devotes
himfelf entirely to them, lofes his reputation, when his irregularities are
once made public, which it is fcarce
poffible to prevent, becaufe the women
of this country are furprizingly indif-
creet; and are often prompted by vanity, to blaze abroad the favours they
are indulg'd. The queen's confort is
particularly oblig'd to be vaftly upon
his

his guard, and to take care that his conduct be irreproachable. He muſt not only be chaſt, but muſt not even be ſuſpected of incontinency.

Are all the courtiers, ſays I, very modeſt? yes, ſays *Zindernein*; however many of them are not always what they affect to appear, and the greateſt part are ſuſpected to have miſtreſſes. 'Tis the glory of women to ſubdue the hearts of men, and that of men to defend them. They themſelves would be pardon'd in every thing, tho' they pretend to be leſs frail than men, whom at the ſame time, they won't excuſe in one ſingle particular. However, when a man careſſes one woman only, the public is ſo indulgent as to excuſe him: but in caſe he devotes himſelf to ſeveral, and that his ſhame is once ſpread abroad, his wife, who is dishonour'd after a moſt ridiculous manner, generally divorces him from her. Sometimes indeed, ſhe winks at her husband's intrigues, and is prudently ſilent. Beſides, 'tis not very eaſy to comprehend

hend on this occasion, what is wanting
to a man's honour.

Our women, says he, rail very much
at the other sex, who yet are not
much offended, provided they don't
fall upon their persons, or their parts,
whose reputation they value infinitely
more than they do their virtue. They
look upon the art of pleasing the women, as the noblest quality; and that
of engaging their respect the lowest.

I then ask'd him, in what manner
marriages were carried on in this island.
There is no circumstance, says he, in
the world, that is conducted and concluded with so much caution, and so little prudence as this. We have several
superannuated old fellows, who are
marriage-brokers, and employ themselves wholly in pairing the youths of
both sexes. Nothing is hardly ever
consider'd, but the outside of a young
fellow, his birth, his estate, and his
person; as for his temper, that is never
enquir'd into, till after the indissoluble
knot is tied. 'Tis true indeed, that the women have the convenience of repudia-
ting

ting their husbands, for which reason
they have no occasion to be so very scru-
pulous, with regard to a similitude of
inclinations: but as the male part are
denied this privilege, 'tis surprizing so
many of them should be negligent,
in an article of such great importance
to married people.

After I understood a little of the
Babilarian tongue, I was allow'd the
liberty to see all my companions of the
seraglio, and to amuse myself with
them. They generally went to bed
and rose late, and spent part of the day
in dressing, and going to music-houses
and theatres, whither the queen often
resorted with her whole court. There
was not the least friendship between
these young men, because they all as-
pir'd to the same honour, and each fancied he deserv'd it, preferable to the
rest of his rivals. They were for ever
blackning one another's reputation, and
were particularly zealous to depreciate
that man, who was look'd upon as the
greatest beauty; and was generally sup-

E   pos'd

pos'd would be pitch'd upon by the queen for her confort.

This happy rival was call'd *Sirilu.* One of them told me he had a moft infipid air, and that his eyes had too great a languifh: another affirm'd he was a ftupid creature: a third affur'd that the queen wou'd not like him, and wou'd hardly keep him a week. If at any time I applauded one of the Band, the reft wou'd fay he was an aukward fellow; that he had very dif-agreeable eyes, and was horridly ill-natur'd. In fhort, tho' they us'd one another very handfomely in outward fhew, they yet bore a mortal averfion to one another. As I was thought to be a very pretty young fellow, the reader may fuppofe, I too had my fhare of cenfure.

Their converfation was vaftly infipid, except when it turn'd upon fcandal. They would frequently difcourfe of their drefs, and the difpofition of their attire. Sometimes they wou'd argue, but then the topic which they ufually debated upon, was to enquire, whe-

ther

ther it were more graceful, to let the
hair defcend in ringlets upon the fhoulders, or to tie it up in a ribbon; whether an artificial red fpread upon the
cheeks, did not heighten their beauty;
and if the colour with which nature
paints the face, is not more faint than
thofe which art has invented; whether
a complexion that inclines to brown is
not more lovely in the eyes of women,
than a complexion that has too much of
the lilly and rofe in it. Each of them
pronounc'd upon thefe important particulars, as the looking-glafs directed.

A great number of the women of the
feraglio, waited upon thofe who were
confin'd in it; and were commanded
not to admit any other women into it,
upon pain of death, unlefs brought by
the queen, who us'd to vifit it fometimes. Thefe female-goalers of ours
were all frightfully ugly, and, as I
was afterwards inform'd, incapable of
the focial embrace. They all had
different employments in the feraglio;
and fhe who prefided over the reft,
was call'd the *Great Maramouk*. She
E 2   and

and all her subalterns, were subordinate to *Zindernein*, who was super-intendant-general of all her majesty's pleasures, and grand purveyor of her seraglio; an employment to which that of comptroler of the prizes taken at sea, was annex'd. When the reader considers the manners and customs of these females, he will be of opinion, that this employment was more suited to a man, than to one of their own sex.

CHAP. V.

The queen visits the seraglio. The author is presented to her; has the good fortune to please her. He is nominated and declared the queen's husband for the ensuing year. He leaves the seraglio and resides in the palace.

WHen *Zindernein* thought I understood the tongue so well, as to be able to discourse with the queen; and observ'd I had contracted a certain air, which all the men, who are desirous of insinuating themselves into
the

the favour of the ladies, ftudy to acquire; he bid me prepare to fee her
majefty, who, he faid, wou'd vifit the
feraglio on the morrow. He bid me
be fure not to be over forward in difcourfe when the queen was prefent;
to affume a plain, unaffectected air; to
foften my glances with the greateft
modefty and referve; to let every gef-
ture be ftudied; to put on at the fame
time a calm and ferene countenance;
and fometimes to ogle her majefty in
the moft lively, the moft tender, and
refpectful manner. I promis'd to obferve his inftructions, and began to
prepare my felf for the honour I was
to receive the next day.

That day I was drefs'd more fplendidly than ufual. I fhone in jewels,
and was cloath'd in a moft magnificent habit. I had been order'd to
bathe in fcented waters; and *Zindernein* gave me a wonderful liquor to
drink, that gives a clearnefs to the
skin, and makes it look agreeably
plump; and a moift and fparkling caft
to the eye. When my companions

E 3   beheld

beheld my beauty lighted up in this manner, they could not forbear difcovering their envy.

Sirilu was apprehenfive I fhould fufpend his glory and happinefs. Thro' a certain faint red, with which he always artfully conceal'd his natural, wan complexion, I cou'd perceive he grew pale as he look'd at me. The women of the feraglio, faid I was of a more advantageous ftature; that my leg was more finely fhap'd, and my hair more graceful; that the turn of my face was more agreable, my eyes larger, my mouth fmaller, and my features more delicate. However, *Sirilu* was finely fhap'd, and very handfome; but then he had a melancholy air, and a moft fenfelefs countenance.

Her majefty came to the feraglio in the evening, and *Zindernein* prefented me to her in private; telling her at the fame time, that I was the young foreigner he had frequently mention'd to her, who was on board the laft veffel that was taken. The queen was of a majeftic ftature; her gracious and noble

noble afpect, correfponded to her exalted dignity; fhe, like moft of the women of that country, had what we *Europeans* call a mafculine beauty, but which goes by another name in that ifland, becaufe all its male inhabitants have an effeminate air.

She made me fit down by her, and the firft queftion fhe ask'd me, was, what country I was born in. Having told her I was an *European*, and born in an ifland call'd *Great Britain*; fhe faid, matters fhould be fo ordered, that I wou'd no longer think of my country. I replied, I had already begun to forget its manners and cuftoms, and refolv'd to follow thofe intirely of the country into which providence had caft me. Our cuftoms, fays fhe, muft certainly appear very odd to you, fince you have been educated in quite oppofite maxims; however, you'll quickly find you have gain'd by the change. In your country, women are more happy than men, in ours 'tis the very reverfe. Your whole life is one continual round of pleafure, and

E 4   it

it is fpent in an agreeable viciffitude of amufements; your days are unruffled by cares or difquietudes of any kind. Your dependance is purely fpecious and imaginary, 'tis we in reality are dependant on you; our whole concern is to pleafe you; 'tis you gather all the fruit of our labours, and we live only to make you happy. Enjoy, fays fhe, therefore and relifh a happinefs, which you may depend upon as long as you live in this ifland; and confent to promote my felicity, which here-after may poffibly increafe your own. But, you blufh! how am I charm'd with your modefty! One would really think you were a native of this ifland, and yet you was born in *Great Britain*. You certainly muft have been king of that country; for a man who boafts fo many perfections, ought to command over the reft of his fellow-creatures. You have nothing of that immodefty I have obferv'd in foreigners; you feem to have liv'd feveral years among us, and yet you have been but three months in my kingdom.

Not-

Notwithſtanding I was prepar'd to talk as rationally as I poſſibly cou'd to the queen, I muſt confeſs my wit and ſenſe forſook me at this juncture ; the modeſty which had been ſo ſtrongly inculcated to me, together with my ſurprize, ſtruck me quite dumb. I am certain there's no woman of faſhion in *Europe*, but wou'd be in ſome confuſion, were a mighty monarch to addreſs her in the ſame manner. Being a man and an *European*, it was impoſſible for me to anſwer the overtures of an auguſt queen, whoſe majeſtic air fill'd me with awe; at the ſame time that her indecent diſcourſe ſhock'd the prejudices I had imbib'd : for her majeſty did not only ſay a thouſand obliging things which affected my modeſty, but was laviſh of the moſt tender, the moſt melting expreſſions ; but then, as I diſcover'd little gayety, I appear'd reſerv'd and judicious : I knew when to caſt my eyes to the ground ; when to raiſe, or turn them on one ſide ; when to ſmile, recline my head, or bluſh ; in ſhort, the queen

was

was extremely pleas'd both with my perſon and behaviour, tho' I had ſhewn but little wit. Poſſibly ſhe might agree in taſte with ſeveral men in *Europe*, who don't value whether a woman has any at all, provided ſhe is modeſt, beautiful, and has ſome little glimmerings of good ſenſe. She kiſs'd me with a moſt graceful air, and her kiſs ſeem'd more amorous than polite.

After her majeſty was gone, *Zindernein* ſaid ſhe was very well pleas'd with me, and told him, I had given her more ſatisfaction than any of the young men in the ſeraglio. If, ſays he, the queen keeps in the ſame mind, and your own behaviour does not check your good fortune, ſhe very probably will marry you firſt; and as ſhe's prodigiouſly ſmit with your perſon, you poſſibly may enjoy the honour of her bed for ſeveral years.

As the princeſs at her leaving the ſeraglio, was continually mentioning me to the Ladies and even Lords of the court; a report was ſoon ſpread, that ſhe was deeply in love with me.

From

From that minute I was abhorr'd, and my character tore to pieces by all my companions. *Sirilu* was inconfolable at the news; the melancholy which was natural to him, chang'd to the blackeft vapours: he loft his ftomach; fleep fled his eyes; he neglected his drefs, and took no further care of his beauty. He grew daily more pale and meager; the glory to which I was rais'd, having quite disfigur'd the love-linefs of his features. The reft, who were equally diftanc'd by my promoti-on, being fenfible that in the prefent affair, feniority in the feraglio was no title to acquire the honour which was defign'd me; cou'd not yet look upon the preference I was fhewn, as a pecu-liar prerogative; but were reduc'd to the fad confolation which patience ad-minifters in all the reverfes of fortune.

However, *Zindernein* having inform'd the queen, of the ftate of her feraglio fince her laft vifit, order'd him to tell all my companions not to defpond; that fhe wou'd think of their Intereft, and wou'd make them all happy in
their

their turns, but that they muſt wait; a way of expreſſion very familiar to grandeur.

However, as her majeſty was not willing the ſeraglio ſhou'd languiſh in a cruel uncertainty, ſhe thought proper to fix her choice. Hereupon I was nominated the queen's conſort, for the year 1716, with the uſual formalities. Publick rejoycings were made upon this account; and being remov'd out of the ſeraglio into her majeſty's palace, I receiv'd the compliments of the whole court, and the ſeveral corporations of the kingdom, upon that occaſion.

I ſpent, purſuant to cuſtom, a fortnight in the palace, before the marriage was to be ſolemniz'd. Sometimes I us'd to divert my ſelf in the calaſh attended with *Zindernein*, and certain lords and ladies of the court, whom I made choice of, when I viſited all the country houſes in the neighbourhood. I had a drawing-room, where the *Paratis*, or greateſt lords of the kingdom us'd to wait upon me, and had the privilege

vilege of fitting on a ſtool in my prefence. All royal honours were paid
me, tho' I was not yet king, becauſe
I was appointed to marry a queen; and
ſhould perhaps have given one to the
State, had heav'n acquieſc'd with the
wiſhes of the people.

C H A P. VI.

The learning of the women of Babilary.
Tribunals or courts compos'd of men.
Different religion of the ſexes. Man-
ner how women adminiſter juſtice, ma-
nage the revenues, and carry on Trade.
Different academies.

AS I at firſt gratified abundantly
my curioſity, I ſhall relate in
few words all the ſingularities I obſerv'd in the cuſtoms of the iſland of
Babilary. Being one day in the Play-
houſe with *Zindernein,* I ſaw ſeven ladies, who had a very witty aſpect,
ſeated on a diſtinguiſh'd bench. As
we were coming out, I aſk'd my conductor who thoſe ſeven perſons were;
he

he told me, they form'd a literary tribunal, whom the queen had lately e-
ftablifh'd to pafs fentence, in a fovereign manner, on all dramatic pieces.
Before, fays he, this tribunal was e-
rected, the public were pefter'd with a
numberlefs multitude of ftupid plays,
which a fett of infipid writers had the
affurance to prefent to them, under
the glorious aufpices of actors and
actreffes, without once confulting perfons of a refin'd and judicious tafte,
and well vers'd in the laws of the
Drama. But fince the time that all
dramatic poets, are, by a new ftatute,
oblig'd to obtain the approbation of
this learn'd and ingenious tribunal, before their plays are brought on the
ftage; there is not one damn'd, but all
are applauded according to their merit; and the public are no longer impos'd upon, during the firft reprefentations of a play.

Such a tribunal, fays I, is worthy
the wifdom of your adminiftration. But
wherefore is not fuch another eftablifh'd
for all books that are publifh'd? Her
majefty,

majefty, fays *Zindernein*, has taken care
of that alfo. Formerly, 'twas enough
that an author advanc'd nothing a-
gainft virtue or the State; but now care
is taken to prevent their depraving the
tafte or infecting the mind; fo that no
trifling, incoherent work, is now allow'd
to be printed. For this purpofe there
has been eftablifh'd a body of judicious
perfons, deep learn'd in the feveral
branches of literature, who are neither
fantaftic or captious; and thefe autho-
rize the publication of all works of wit.
Since this prudent inftitution, the public is no longer pefter'd with pieces abfolutely bad; and another very happy
circumftance, is, there are fewer new
books.

Moreover, learning is indulg'd a
great liberty, purpofely to advance the
progrefs of arts and fciences. Her majefty, in order to improve the genius and
underftanding of her fubjects, enriches
all thofe who write any valuable
pieces; by which means emulation increafes, arts flourifh, and excellent
works are produc'd. Letters were furprizingly

prizingly neglected in the preceeding
reign; and the laborious profeffion of
a writer, was look'd upon as the leaft
honourable. The queen, being robb'd
and plunder'd with impunity by the
Marajats, whofe employment was to
collect the revenues, thought of compen-
fating the lofs, by retrenching the feveral ftipends with which merit had always been rewarded. In all probability, virtue and politenefs would foon
have taken their flight with learning,
had not her prefent majefty wifely provided againft fo great an unhappi-
nefs.

I then ask'd *Zindernein,* whether the
books which met with the approbation
of the public, were very witty and ingenious. We, fays he, fet a greater
value on thofe works which inform the
judgment, than on fuch as are written
merely to the fancy. In general, we require genius and judgment in all works;
but then we † *had rather there fhould be*
no

† *According to the englifh proverb,* Rather than
all be wit, let there be none.

no wit at all, than too much. Some of
our moderns have introduc'd a certain
epigramatic, affected ſtile, which at
firſt dazled the imagination, but is now
very much exploded; ſo that in this
age, to hunt after wit, is the ſame as
hunting after impertinence. Nevertheleſs this flat, puerile ſtile, is ſtill admir'd by ſome, who, being at variance
with reaſon, have enter'd into a kind
of agreement among themſelves, to per-
petuate its precious feed. Our men
are more delighted with this ſtile than
the women; a ſure indication of their
fickleneſs, and at the ſame time of
the emptineſs of their underſtand-
ings.

'Tis ſurprizing, ſays I to *Zindernein*,
the women of your country ſhould
have devoted themſelves to learning;
and that a ſex, which in all parts of
the world, is lazy and ignorant, and
who look upon thinking as a very painful exerciſe, ſhould in your iſland be
ſo learned and laborious. Knowledge,
ſays he, is the child of ſelf-love, and
curioſity : are we then to wonder,

F   that

that women who are here indulg'd
every gratification, fhould thirft after
fcience, and make ftudy a ferious employment? The labour which learning
demands is light to them, becaufe they
are puff'd up by vanity, and prompted
by a reftlefs ambition. The only motive of their ftudy, is, that they may
obtain a prerogative to defpife all who
do not.

If women are ignorant in all other
countries, as you fay they are, the reafon
is, becaufe men, from the moft juft
and folid reafons, prohibit their application to fuch fciences as inflate the
mind. They judicioufly confider, that
women are too prone to vanity;
and that were they to devote themfelves ferioufly to ftudy, their innate curiofity would prompt them to
dive too far; that their delicacy and
penetration might occafion a thoufand
dangerous difputes; that their obftina-
cy would make their errors incurable;
that they would have an infatiable
thirft after knowledge; in a word,
that they would lofe fomething of that

fprightly

fprightly tafte which heav'n has indulg'd
them, for the capital and indifpen-
fable duty of their fex; all which
wou'd be of great prejudice to human
nature.

The confequence of this is found in
our country. Such women as cultivate
the *belles lettres* are inexpreffibly haughty;
moft of thefe lofe themfelves in abftracted fpeculations; they fometimes leave
good fenfe behind, purely for the fake
of wit and turn; they ftart queftions
that aftonifh the judgment; they write
huge folios on impoffibilities, and on the
properties of non-entity; and whenever they are miftaken, they never allow themfelves to be fo. In a word,
they not only defpife fuch of their fex,
as apply themfelves to bodily exercifes
only; but go fuch lengths, as to contemn
the male world, whom one would
think they confider merely as fo many
brute animals; and that their greateft
perfection is their poffeffing the inferior
part of the human foul. Whenever they
marry, 'tis, as it were, againft their inclinations, and merely in compliance with

the

the law, which prohibits their leading a fingle life. Nay, fo far have fome of them gone, as to advance that 'tis no crime to infringe this ftatute; in fhort, fome of them are fcepticks in every thing.

Undoubtedly, fays I, 'tis fince the revolution, that feveral of your women have been fo paffionately fond of learning. Alas! anfwer'd *Zindernein*, the revolution would perhaps have never happen'd, had we not been pefter'd with female-pedants, long before that fatal æra.

The learning of our women, who applied themfelves to ftudy, whilft the minds of the men, were overfpread with a thick mift of ignorance, is one of the chief caufes of our fallen ftate. The knowledge they had acquir'd, gave them a fatal fuperiority over us. As men, in general, would never have obtain'd a preeminence over all animals, were not their minds active and induftrious; by which they found out methods to tame the moft favage and ungovernable: in like manner, the
female

female mind acquiring a superiority over that of man, by the care the women took to cultivate, refine and enlarge it, eafily triumph'd over the male fpecies. Such was *Zinderncin*'s difcourfe, who gave me an ingenuous account of whatever he thought, concerning the manners and cuftoms of his country.

May all my countrymen, who fhall perufe this genuine account I give of my adventures, dread left the fame cataftrophe which has been fo fatal to the ifland of *Babilary*, fhould one day happen in *Great Britain*; and may they not rely too much on the fmall ftock of knowledge they boaft. But, on the other fide, may the women not flatter themfelves, they fhall fo foon arrive at the glorious pitch to which the *Babilarian* women have attain'd; the happy averfion they bear to every kind of application and ftudy, fecures to the male fpecies, for one century at leaft, the prefervation of their natural rights, and their lawful fuperiority over them. But ignorance now makes fo great a progrefs among the men in *Europe*, that I would

not

not dare affirm, whether, after having reduc'd a confiderable part of our neighbours under her empire, fhe may not attempt to crofs the fea; and add my countrymen to the number of her flaves. In this fatal extreme, fhould the *Englifh* ladies attempt to imitate the *Babilarian* women, lord have mercy upon us all!

I alfo enquir'd of *Zindernein*, whether his countrymen had not fome tribunal, where they exercis'd a kind of jurifdiction? Yes, fays he, they have tribunals, but of a moft ridiculous kind, which would have been abolifh'd long fince, had they not humbly intreated they might ftill fubfift, as a faint fhadow of the valuable ruins of their antient authority. There are therefore fix tribunals, all compos'd of fuperanuated, decripit men. The firft is to judge exactly of the degree of white and red, which each man, according to his age and complexion, may ufe, in order to pleafe the fair-fex in general; with the privilege of laying a Fine on all thofe who fhould be too lavifh

of

of this ridiculous varniſh, the offspring
of whim and folly. The ſecond court
is to judge of modes; to approve the
changes that are made in them, and to fix
the number of days a certain colour is
to reign, a ſilk of a peculiar taſte, or a
certain manner of dreſs. The third is
to ſettle the rank which men are to obſerve with regard to one another, and
their ſeveral preeminences, of which
they are ſurprizingly jealous. The
fourth, which is the moſt awful, takes
cognizance of their diſputes; the innocence or malignity of their raillery and
back-biting, and makes them either re-
tract or ſoften it, as the court ſhall ſee fitting. The fifth is to proſecute men advanc'd in years, who endeavour to paſs
for young fellows. They are not allow'd to retrench above ten years;
when they are convicted of making a
greater ſtretch, they are condemn'd to
wear a medal about their necks, which
deſcends a little below the girdle; the
year, the month, and day of the month,
being written in large characters.
Thoſe who out of malice, or by their

ſatyrical

fatyrical Difcourfes, add to the years
of other men, arc fentenc'd never to
paint their faces with red, and to appear with their naked faces the reft
of their lives. The fixth is to punifh
fuch as neglect the worfhip of the god
OSSOKIA.

What god is this, fays I to *Zindernein*, is he worfhipp'd only in your
ifland? He is the god of the men, as
OSSOK is the goddefs of women; an
imaginary goddefs and unknown on the
earth, till the women ufurp'd the
whole authority of this kingdom.

Formerly, worfhip was paid to *OS-
SOKIA* only, he not being known to
have a wife. But our females took it
into their heads to marry him to a goddefs, who, according to their modern
opinion, is vaftly fuperior to him; as
if their pretended goddefs cou'd have
triumph'd over the preeminence of a
god, as eafily as they have over ours.
Amazing blindnefs! frail and imperfect
man, has fuffer'd himfelf to be vanquifh'd by woman: but *OSSOKIA*,
who is perfect, and able to overturn
both

both heaven and earth, is too powerful
and intelligent to fubmit to a female
reign.

Such, fays I, is the corruption of the
human mind, which often forms to itfelf a fyftem of religion, agreable to
its intereft and prejudices. But fince
you have taken notice of your male
courts, give me fome account of your
female tribunals; and inform me in
what manner women adminifter juftice
in this country. With great judgment
and impartiality, replied *Zindernein*, if
we except that fome old women, who
have an infatiable thirft after *Simao*, or
gold, fometimes permit a quantity of it
to be thrown into their fcale; and that
the young judges feem fometimes to favour our juvenile, handfome councel-
lours, more than the old and ugly.
This abufe, fays I, muft not be afcri-
bed to the fex your judges are of. In
countries where your maxims don't
prevail, we meet with judges who
are no lefs fufpected of thofe petty
prevarications, which the dazling
fplendor of *Simao* and of beauty, fets

in

in a quite different light, and makes
them appear as venial in their eyes.
'Tis but too true, fays *Zindernein*, that
caufes will feldom be judg'd with
impartiality, fo long as they fhall
come under the cognizance of human
tribunals. Would to heav'n that *OS-
SOKIA* would himfelf determine all
difputes, which arife too often among
mortals! 'Tis in vain for fuch of our
women as have the adminiftration in
their hands, to affirm, that they are
upon earth the lively images of their
goddefs *OSSOK*: if this be true,
OSSOK, whom they tell us made
them fuch, has very little genius for
painting.

There are alfo, fays he, in this
ifland female courts, whofe office is to
maintain the public privileges, and
fuperintend the management of the revenues. Never was a reign more gentle, more prudent, and more impartial,
than that of our auguft queen, ever fince
fhe herfelf has prefided at the helm.
Affifted only by the counfels of her
nurfe, whofe zeal and difintereftednefs
are

are univerfally applauded, fhe employs all her endeavours to reftore trade to its former life and vigour, and to make her people happy. Her fub-jects hope her wifdom will confound the pride of a numberlefs multitude of *Marajats*, who have prefum'd to rival her in the magnificence of their palaces; and that at leaft her political equity, will clip their wings in fuch a manner, as to prevent their being quite fo rich as the princeffes of the blood. For we have feen *Marajats*, born from among the dregs of the people ; diffolute and dead to honour, amaffing immenfe riches by advancing money at an exor-bitant difcount, have eclips'd the mag-nificence of the moft illuftrious ladies ; appropriated to themfelves the moft ex-alted dignities and the fineft eftates; and had even the odious ambition to become the ftem of a pofterity of *Paratis*.

The only tax, fays he, that now fub-fifts in the ftate, is a general poll-tax, proportion'd to the fubftance of every individual, which produces a great fum of money, without draining the fub-ject.

ject. Under the preceeding reigns, twenty thousand *Marajats*, upon pretence of raising the subsidies of the crown, us'd to plunder the people, and did not bring one third part of it into the royal coffers. By a new and prudent regulation, those women who preside over the mysteries of *O S S O K* in every city, receive all her majesty's revenues. Hereby, a just and faithful payment of the lawful tributes, is become a kind of religious virtue; because those ministers of *O S S O K* take care to inculcate to the people from the pulpit, that unless they perform their duty in this particular, the goddess will punish them after death. Persons of the greatest quality and estate pay the largest sum; every one declares exactly what he is worth; and as women are always very vain, some pay more than they wou'd be tax'd, purely to seem richer than they really are. To heighten the public felicity, all foreign commodities are allow'd to be imported in our island, free. Trade is open, and in a flourishing condition. We never hear of any bankrupts;

bankrupts; the whole body of female merchants having rais'd a public fund, to endemnify all such she-traders as have sustain'd losses through misfortune, and to remedy the evils they could not foresee.

I listned very attentively to all he told me, but cou'd hardly believe that women had such just and prudent ideas, and that their administration sham'd that of men. I earnestly wish'd, not only that our english women might govern as prudently as those of the island of *Babilary*; but that the men would, at least, guide the helm with as much judgment, and follow as sagacious maxims. My opinion is, that the chief reason why women govern so well, is, that whenever they hold the reins, they suffer themselves to be guided by the other sex; whereas, when men govern, they blindly follow the desires and dictates of women. Possibly, in the island of *Babilary*, men govern in reality; as we find that women generally bear the sway in *Europe*. I acquainted
Zindernein

Social capitalism! (or capital socialism)

Zindernein with my thought, and he
feem'd to approve it.

I told him I intended to vifit the
great fquare of the city the next day.
Accordingly we went thither, and I
muft confefs I never faw fo noble an
area in the greateft cities of *Europe*.
'Tis in the fhape of an octogon, and
fix hundred yards over. The houfes
round it are built in a grand tafte, and
a moft beautiful fymmetry. In the
middle ftands the equeftrian ftatue of
queen *Rafalu*, who reign'd fifty years
ago, and built this magnificent fquare;
round which the ftatues of all fuch
women, as have diftinguifh'd themfelves, fince the revolution, by their
fingular merit, are plac'd. Thefe ftatues not only reprefent the moft illuftrious female generals, but learned fhe-ci-
vilians, famous mathematicians, illuftrious women, whether poetefses or orators
&c. On each fide of the octogon an
academy is built. The firft is for ma-
thematics; the fecond for phyfics; the
third for morality; the fourth for hiftory; the fifth for eloquence and
poetry;

poetry; the fixth for painting, fculp-
ture, and architecture; the feventh for
mufic; the eighth for mechanics in
general. All thefe academies are fill'd
with perfons of a diftinguifh'd merit.
Ladies of the firft quality are fometimes admitted into them, not fo much
in confideration of their exalted birth
and fortune, as for their perfonal worth
and knowledge. Every fhe-academi-
cian is oblig'd, before fhe is admitted
a member, to give a public proof of
her capacity.

C H A P. VII.

*Mejax, governefs of the principal port of
the ifland, falls in love with the author,
who alfo is captivated with her charms.
She carries him off; delivers at the
fame time all his companions out of
flavery, and flies away with them on
board a veffel, which fhe had got ready
for that purpofe.*

NOtwithftanding that I was often
in *Zindernein's* company, he neverthelefs us'd to leave me fometimes,
to

to give the neceffary orders in the feraglio. I was not alone in his abfence,
but had always a numerous levee of
both fexes. Sometimes too I us'd to
converfe in private with fome ladies of
high birth and dignity. She among
them who feem'd to be moft affiduous
in her addreffes to me, was the governefs of the port of *Pataka*, fituated
two leagues from the royal city; a
woman of noble birth, rich, young,
fprightly; a finifh'd beauty, and of a
moft amiable temper. I was fo inchanted with her, that I was no longer
fenfible to the glory of marrying the
queen; however, it was impoffible for
me to break my paffion to her, without
offending the rules of decorum; I
alfo knew how dangerous it would
be to footh fuch a flame, efpecially
when I found fhe was mutually ftruck;
but at the fame time I forefaw, that my
heart could not long refift the charms
of fo lovely a creature.

She one day came into my apartment when the company were gone,
and there remain'd only a few flaves
with

with me, who withdrew out of re-
fpeƈt the moment ſhe appear'd. *Mejax*, for that was her name, took this
opportunity to tell me with a languiſhing air, that 'twas a great unhappineſs
for her I was ſo beautiful ; that my
charms, which had awak'd the moſt
tender paſſion in her heart, made it abfolutely impoſſible for her ever to be happy, ſince they had inflam'd the queen.
Alas ! ſays ſhe, with a paſſionate tone
of voice, why did fate convey you into her majeſty's feraglio ! why did not
I prevent it ; why did not *Zindernein*
overlook your perfeƈtions ! or why did
I not bribe him when he firſt came a-
ſhore on our iſland, after he had taken your veſſel ! I then only might
have had the happineſs of knowing,
and poſſibly of pleafing you.

As I was highly pleas'd with this declaration, I did not think proper to
difguife my ſentiments, in imitation of
the mock ſeverity of our *European* ladies, who, on thefe delicate occaſions,
generally aſſume an angry air. Since,
ſays I, you make me ſo tender, ſo in-
       G   genuous,

genuous, and, as I believe, sincere a confeffion; I shan't scruple to own, that I
have the higheft fenfe of the value of
your love; that your merit has made
the ftrongeft impreffion on my heart;
and that in cafe her majefty had not
allotted me the glory of being her
confort, I should have thought it the
greateft happinefs to be yours only, and
to be at liberty to marry you; efpecially fince that fituation in life, tho' lefs
glorious, would perhaps have been
more permanent. But this is not a
time to entertain fuch thoughts. Stifle
thofe wishes as they interfere with my
glory, and efpecially fince they may
be of fatal confequence to you.

Alas! cruel creature, fays fhe, will you
then kill me? The queen is not yet
married to you, and 'tis in your power
to make me happy, without deftroying
your own felicity. Marry the queen,
if fate will have it fo, and fince 'tis
not in my power to oppofe your exalta-
tion; but then fuffer me, at leaft, to
breathe my paffion, and the tender refpect I bear you; and let me flatter my
felf

felf fo far, as to think you burn with a mutual flame.

Never did I fee fo much love in a woman, as *Mejax* difcover'd at that inftant. As I was paffionately fond of her, I fometimes wou'd refolve to follow the cuftom of my own country ; and act like a man of honour and an *European*. But then nature wou'd dictate to me that I was a man; and fometimes, the place, and the condition I was in, wou'd banifh the remembrance of it from my mind ; fo that the part I was to act of a man who was feminiz'd, as it were, perplex'd me very much; not knowing whether I fhould be bold or fearful, forward or referv'd. However, *Mejax* ftill talk'd in a moft languifhing and paffionate manner, and I continued to defend that virtue fhe was endeavouring to feduce. I beg our *Englifh* ladies to pardon the images and expreffions I employ, which tho' fo repugnant to our manners, are neverthelefs agreeable to thofe of *Babilary*, and the ambiguous fituation I was then in.

In

In the mean time, methoughts it would
be proper for me to take advantage of
Mejax's violent paſſion; not to gratify
both her's and my own, but, if poſſible,
to recover my liberty. *Mejax*, ſays I
to her, 'twill be impoſſible for me
ever to indulge your wiſhes, or ſuffer
you to languiſh for me. The inſtant
the queen does me the honour to take
me to her bed, if you once preſume to
mention your flame to me, you will
be baniſh'd my preſence for ever. Nevertheleſs, I won't diſguiſe myſelf ſo
far, as not to own that I love you
tenderly ; and that, notwithſtanding
the glory to which I ſhall be rais'd,
there is nothing I could more paſſionate-
ly wiſh than to be your husband. After all, this wou'd not be a fruitleſs
or chimerical wiſh, had you but courage enough to ſecond it, and make
choice of one of the expedients I ſhall
now venture to propoſe. The firſt is,
to divert the queen, if poſſible, from
the deſign ſhe has of marrying me. In
thus ſacrificing to you the exalted honour her majeſty prepares for me, I
ſhall

ſhall give you the ſtrongeſt proofs how
dear you are to me. But as you
may think this method impracticable;
and that the attempting to extinguiſh
her flame may be of dangerous conſequence, I had rather propoſe another
expedient. You are governeſs of the
port of *Pataka*, and have all that be-
longs to it at your diſpoſal: order a
veſſel to be immediately fitted out,
which we will go aboard on privately;
when being got out of the reach of
her majeſty's power, I'll gratify the
utmoſt of our mutual wiſhes, without
running the hazard of ruining you or
myſelf. I am ſenſible, that you will
thereby forfeit all the titles and eſtates
you poſſeſs in this iſland, and be for
ever depriv'd of them by this voluntary exile ; but if you have a real and
unreſerv'd paſſion for me, your generoſity will overlook thoſe conſidera-
tions.

Mejax, who had liſtned to me with
the deepeſt attention, ſeem'd quite loſt
in thought. After having been long
ſilent, ſhe broke into a ſigh, and an-

ſwer'd,

fwer'd, that I propos'd a very odd expedient; however that true love was a
ftranger to politics, intereft or dangers; that fince I was brave enough to
flight the honour of the queen's bed
for her fake, fhe, in return, ought to
facrifice her honours and poffeffions to
mine; that there was no danger to
which fhe would not expofe herfelf,
to prove the deep fenfe fhe had of my
love, that her refolution was fixt;
that as I was to marry the queen immediately, we had no time to lofe; and
that fhe'd ufe her utmoft endeavours to
carry me off on the morrow night, and
put me on board a fhip, which, happily for us, was going to weigh anchor
in the road of *Pataka*.

But this, fays I, is not all; you muft
free all our crew, who are flaves to
different inhabitants of this ifland.
They muft be taken on board with us,
and fhare in my good fortune. I'll indulge, fays fhe, the utmoft of your
wifhes, and will conduct you in triumph into your own country: thrice
happy to fpend the remainder of my
days

days with fo dear a man, tho' in the moft remote regions!

As I knew where Capt. *Harrington* liv'd, who had complimented me upon my promotion, I told *Mejax* the place. She promis'd to fend for him privately, and order him to be ready near *Pataka*, the next day, with as many of his fellow-captives as he could get together. She then took her leave, promifing to love me eternally, and be inviolably faithful; when immediately fhe went and prepar'd every thing for our departure.

I fpent the reft of the day in great anxiety, for fear left our plot fhould not fucceed; on which occafion, I form'd a thoufand imaginary tortures; for then I forefaw that my ruin and that of *Mejax* wou'd have been inevitable; and fhould have reproach'd myfelf with being the wretched caufe of her deftruction. In order that I might not betray myfelf involuntarily; and to conceal my confufion from the importunate glances of a prying court: I thought proper to feign an indifpofition,

G 4   and

and go to bed. In this perplexity,
I was in some measure, if I may be allowed the whimsical comparison, in the
condition of the author of a new tragedy, the first night of its representation.
Conceal'd in the most obscure part of
the box or gallery; actuated alternately
by hope and fear; the moment the curtain rises, he feels joy or sorrow, according to the various emotions of the
spectators, who are to pronounce his
fate. If they laugh, he desponds; if
they weep, he rejoices. He is tran-
sported with the hopes of its success;
while the dread of its being hiss'd off
the stage, freezes the blood in his veins:
thus is he fluctuating till the fifth act,
which pronounces his doom. Alas!
the part I dar'd to act was deep tragedy. The business was either to recover my liberty, and complete my
wishes and those of *Mejax*; or to see
us both deliver'd up, to the formidable vengeance of a despis'd, deluded
queen.

Whilst I was in this cruel condition,
her majesty, afflicted at my pretended
indisposition,

indifpofition, honour'd me with a vifit, attended by *Zindernein*. The husband fhe had enjoy'd a twelve month, had been juft before thank'd for his fervices, and was Conducted back into the feraglio; fo that fhe waited with extreme impatience, for the happy day appointed for the folemnization of our marriage. Finding me very much dejected, her majefty was afraid my illnefs would retard the completion of her defires. She fpoke to me in the moft affectionate terms; and I muft confefs, that in this inftant, the thoughts of my treachery forc'd a pang from my heart, which very much increas'd my anguifh and perplexity. But then, the defire of obtaining my liberty; the hope of feeing again my country and family; and the violent paffion I had for the charming *Mejax*, got the better of love and gratitude; fo that I ftrongly perfifted in the dangerous defign I had form'd of being run away with.

Her majefty intreated me to take the greateft care of my health, and not to defpond; and after having difcover'd

cover'd the moſt tender concern for my recovery, ſhe went away with a mournful and perplex'd air, and left *Zindernein* with me. As I had a great affection for him, the thoughts of being ſoon ſeparated from ſo good a friend, heightned my diſtreſs. I once reſolv'd to reveal my deſign to him, and perſuade him to follow me; however I did not dare to break it to him, leſt his ſevere and uncorruptible fidelity, ſhould prove an invincible obſtacle to my deſigns. I likewiſe was afraid leſt I ſhould thereby expoſe my miſtreſs to danger, to whom I was ſo much oblig'd, and lov'd with ſo great an exceſs of paſſion.

The queen's *Rebecaſſes*, or femalephyſicians, came then into my chamber, and after having felt my pulſe, which they found very high, they began a conſultation upon my pretended illneſs. Some fancied I had an impoſthume in my head; others ſaid I had a ſchirrus in the liver; and others again that I had taken a ſurfeit. One was for having me blooded in the foot; and
another

another wou'd have me take a kind
of emetic. Had I follow'd all their
prescriptions, I shou'd have swallow'd
down a thousand doses; and possibly
have met with the fate of so many *European* princes and great men, who have
frequently hast'ned their death, by an
overfond care of preserving their lives.
I assur'd all the *Rebecasses*, I was not
sick; and that my indisposition was so
slight, it would soon be cur'd without
their assistance.

I indeed, got up the next day, and
immediately had some discourse with
Mejax, who came to visit me in the
morning. She inform'd me, that all
things were prepar'd; that she had given the necessary orders; that *Harrington* had notice, and promis'd to be ready in the evening with the rest of the
English, in the road to *Pataka*. She
added, that in her opinion, our design
must succeed; that in the afternoon, I
should propose to take an airing in my
calash, towards *Pataka*; that *Zindernein* and she would do themselves the
honour to wait upon me. . . . .

What!

What! fays I interrupting her, is *Zindernein* in the plot? No, fays *Mejax* : but 'twont be decent for you to take an airing with me, unlefs there be a man in the company; and *Zindernein* is the moft proper perfon for our purpofe, as the court won't have the leaft fufpicion of him. When we fhall have got near the port, feveral of my women, who will follow on horfeback, fhall draw their fwords, at a certain fignal agreed upon between us; when *Harrington*, whom I have inftructed in what he is to do, fhall inftantly come up with his men completely arm'd. With this reinforcement, our women will foon difperfe the guards; when we will immediately make for the port; go on board the veffel that lies ready, and fend back *Zindernein*. The time and place for putting our defign in execution, are both mark'd out; and provided *Harrington* is but trufty, and behaves himfelf valiantly, our defign muft certainly fucceed. As *Harrington*, fays I, has given you his word and honour, you
may

may depend upon his affiftance, and that of his affociates; not to mention, that the fuccefs of this affair is of the higheft concern to them all.

I affected to be very jocund all the remaining part of the day, and receiv'd the compliments of the whole court, upon the recovery of my health. They did me the honour to affirm, that my indifpofition had heighten'd my beauty; and laugh'd heartily at the *Rebecaffes*, for intending to exhauft their whole art, in order to reftore me to my health. But whilft the whole court was rejoycing at my pretended recovery; and delighted themfelves with difcourfing on the fplendid preparations, which were ordain'd for the folemnization of our auguft nuptials; the news of an unexpected accident damp'd their joy, and threw them into the deepeft affliction; for fear left this misfortune fhould be of fatal confequence to her majefty. The beautiful and unfortunate *Sirilu*, who had flatter'd himfelf with the hopes of marrying the queen firft; fearing left his charms fhould
fade,

fade, by his being fufpended a year; afham'd to find himfelf loft to all his expectations; and fancying, poffibly, that fince her majefty was fo fond of me, fhe perhaps would keep me feveral years, had abandon'd himfelf to the deepeft defpair; and in the tranfports of his anguifh, heighten'd by his natural melancholy, had ftabb'd himfelf in the night; fo that the next morning he was found breathlefs,and weltring in his own blood. 'Twas fear'd, that the queen,who feem'd to love him tenderly; and who, before fhe knew me, intended to efpoufe him that year, would be extremely afflicted for his untimely end, fince fhe had brought him to it; and being of a foft and compaffionate caft, wou'd abandon herfelf too much to melancholy. However, her majefty was lefs afflicted at the news of this accident, than an *Englifh* lady is commonly for the lofs of her favourite lapdog. The queen's indifference upon this occafion, was a glorious teftimony of the great afcendant I had over her. *Mejax* being come to me in the evening according

according to appointment, I propos'd
to *Zindernein* our taking an airing towards *Pataka*. A little after, we got
into the calaſh, attended by a guard of
about twenty ſhe-ſoldiers. Theſe were
joyn'd in the way by about fifty women on horſeback, who ſeem'd deſirous of partaking in our diverſion, and
of having the honour to eſcort us.
Mejax and myſelf were both very un-
eaſy at it; ſo that *Zindernein* did not
know what conſtruction to put upon
our deep ſilence. He ſaw us throw
our eyes continually on all ſides ; and
obſerv'd in our looks that kind of
fear and confuſion, which is inſepa-
rable from all bold and hazardous at-
tempts.

Being got in ſight of the port, near a
little wood, a large company of men
came out of it and advanc'd towards
us. The guards ſeem'd ſurpriz'd to ſee
ſo great a company of men, without ſo
much as one woman among them, and
cou'd not forbear laughing. But how
great was their ſurprize ! when *Mejax*
giving the ſignal, they ſaw all thoſe
men

men whom they defpis'd, draw their
fabres from under their gowns, and
advance forward with a warlike and
menacing air. The guards wou'd
have fallen upon them; but the reft
of the women on horfeback, who
were in the plot, taking out their
piftols, check'd their defign, and
immediately put them to flight.

Zindernein was feiz'd with the deepeft tranfports of grief, and attempted
to kill himfelf; but *Mejax* told him,
fhe was refolv'd to carry me off, and
marry me in a foreign country. She
advis'd him to accompany us in our
flight; befides, fays fhe, as the queen
entrufted this beautiful youth to your
care, fhe'll never pardon you for fuffering him to efcape; fhe'll fancy you
was one of my accomplices, at leaft,
that you're bafe and negligent. The
moft gentle punifhment that will be
inflicted on you, will be the lofs of
your employment and her favour. To
make the ftronger impreffion upon his
mind, I faid, that fuppofing her majefty would pardon him, and he fhould
be

be able to juftify his conduct to her, he yet ought to abhor living in a country, where the men were fo fcandaloufly govern'd by the other fex. Have not I myfelf, fays I to him, heard you figh for this fhameful fubverfion of the laws of nature? Come along with us, and I'll carry you into *England*, where you'll meet with all the honours due to your merit. I have, fays *Mejax*, interrupting me, fent a casket of jewels on board; fo that, in what part foever of the world fortune may throw us, we fhall be perpetually happy, becaufe we fhall be rich. I'll divide my wealth with you; and *Gulliver*, who loves, and is belov'd by you, will complete your felicity.

Zindernein, after a moment's reflection, faid he was refolv'd to go along with us; that indeed it would be very dangerous for him to continue in the ifland; that as he had no children, he was not bound to it by any tyes; and therefore was determin'd to fhare our fate.

H   Being

Being all arriv'd at the port, we alighted from our horses. Our countrymen
got thither almost as soon as we did,
and all the women having dismounted,
they got into a boat, and row'd towards the vessel which lay at anchor.
They afterwards put all our *Englishmen*
on board. The she-sailors and the rest
of the female crew were for resisting,
but it prov'd to no purpose : *Mejax* no
sooner appear'd, but they all threw
down their arms, when the she-troop-
ers and our sailors seiz'd upon the ship,
on which *Mejax*, *Zindernein*, and I
went aboard. Immediately after we
weighed anchor, and steer'd eastward.
It was agreed that *Mejax* should command the ship during the whole course,
and that *Harrington* should be her second captain. Our sailors were commanded to work the ship, under the
conduct of our pilot, who was an able
and experienc'd man ; and the *Babilarian* women had orders to defend us in
case of an attack.

C H A P.

C H A P. VIII.

The queen of Babilary *fends two veffels
iu purfuit of* Mejax ; *a bloody engagement enfues.* Victorious Mejax *is
wounded and dies.* They caft anchor before an ifland. Danger the author is
in.*

THE wind was not very favourable, fo that the next day after
our departure, we had not got above
fix leagues from the port, when we
perceiv'd two fhips in purfuit of us.
We crouded all our fail, and being
refolved to go whither the wind would
carry us, we fteer'd fouthward, the
wind being north. However, the two
veffels ftill kept after us, and as they
were lighter than ours, they came
nearer to us infenfibly. We concluded
they would come up with us before
night, and prepar'd to fight them. Accordingly, about four in the evening
they were come within cannon-fhot;
and we then found, as we had ima-

gin'd,

gin'd, that they were two *Babilarian* veffels mann'd (if I may be excus'd the great impropriety) with women, according to the cuftom of that country.

When the two fhips were come up with us, they put out the long-boat to acquaint us with her majefty's orders, and commanded us to return into the port; threatning in cafe we refus'd, to fall upon us immediately. We declar'd we wou'd not obey; and were refolv'd to defend ourfelves in cafe of an attack. In the mean time we were all come upon deck: *Mejax* with her drawn fabre, at the head of all her women; *Harrington* and I, at the head of fuch of the male part of the crew, as were not fet to the guns, or employ'd in working the fhip. After feveral broad-fides, the two veffels grappled ours, and were for boarding us. The battle was dreadful and bloody; *Mejax* behav'd with inexpreffible bravery, as did all the women who fought with her. As the attack was chiefly carried on on that fide, we all, both men and women, reinforc'd her; and I fought
like

like a defperado at *Mejax*'s fide, who
feem'd to be in more concern for my
life than fhe was for her own. At laft,
we repuls'd the enemy, who defpairing
to conquer us, and fearing we fhould
board them, and take their veffels,
thought proper to fheer off.

However, we loft but four men and
ten women, who died in the bed of
honour; and had not above twenty
wounded of both fexes. But what
pangs did I feel, when I faw *Mejax* cover'd with her own blood! fhe had
fought to the laft gafp, and the heat of
the engagement had prevented her taking notice of three wounds fhe had
receiv'd, the moft dangerous of which
was in her breafts; the fword having
enter'd at her right, and run quite
through to her left breaft. Our furgeon
prob'd the wounds, and affur'd us they
were mortal; and *Mejax* herfelf was fenfible fhe had but a very fhort time to live.
I did not ftir from her in this extremity, and obferving I wept bitterly, fhe
did all that lay in her power to comfort me.

H 3   Cou'd

Cou'd I, fays fhe to me, have poffibly afpir'd to a more glorious death?
'Tis true indeed, that I die in open rebellion againft my fovereign; but then
is it a crime in a fubject, to difpute
with her queen, the dominion of a
heart? I have defended my conqueft;
love has feconded my bravery; I am
come off victorious: heaven will not
allow me to reap the fruit of my victory.
Live, adorable *Gulliver*: I die, alas!
in the dread of living for ever in
your heart. It grieves me to the foul,
when I think of the cutting pangs my
death will make you feel. Do all that
lies in your power, I befeech you, to
forget me; and hereafter devote yourfelf to every thing that may contribute,
to blot from your mind the fad remembrance of the tender *Mejax*. What
will it avail me to be in your thoughts
when I am no more? Your fighs and
tears will not be able to recal me to
life, nor be of any other ufe but to
difturb your own.

At the fame time that fhe was thus
taking an everlafting adieu, with the true
fpirit

fpirit of a heroine, fhe gave me all
her jewels, but advifed me to fell them
the firft opportunity, for fear left the
fight of them, fhould awake in my
mind, the mournful idea of the woman
who had lov'd me fo paffionately. She
then commanded her women to follow
me whitherfoever I fhould go, and
charg'd them to defend me valiantly on
all occafions. A little after, fhe
breath'd her laft, to the great grief of
all the women her followers, and the
whole *Englifh* crew, who ow'd their
freedom to her generofity; and whofe
valour had preferv'd them from falling into flavery a fecond time.

I was deeply afflicted at her death,
and found it impoffible for me to arm
myfelf with that philofophical infenfi-
bility, fhe had fo much recommended
in her dying moments. In her, I loft a
generous benefactrefs and an accom-
plifh'd lover. Capt. *Harrington* and
Zindernein did their utmoft to footh my
grief, which forc'd a flood of tears
from my eyes for three days fucceffively. While I was thus prey'd upon by

afflicticn,

affliction, I was oblig'd to take a little
fuftenance in order to fupport nature;
I wifh'd to go to *Mejax*, and life was
become odious to me. All the women
on board admir'd my tendernefs, and
efteem'd me much more upon that account.

In the mean time we ftill fteer'd
fouthward, as the wind drove us, and
endeavour'd to difcover fome ifland
to take in water, becaufe our fhip had
been equipp'd very precipitately; and
our fudden flight had not allowed us
time, to take a quantity fufficient for
our voyage. About a week after we
difcover'd a very fmall ifland, and taking it for one of the *Moluccas*, we
refolv'd to caft anchor before it. We
enter'd a fmall bay, in the weftern
part of the ifland, when part of our
men and women, I being in the company, got into the long-boat, and
went on fhore.

We went about half a league up the
country, in fearch of a fpring, and being got near a wood which ftood at a
little diftance from a mountain, we feperated

perated a little. *Harrington* went one way with ten or twelve *Englifh*, and myfelf another, with about the fame number of women, and not one man but myfelf. Thefe *Babilarian* women, who had a great affection for me, wou'd not fuffer me to go with the *Englifh*, imagining I fhould be fafer with them. We were all well arm'd, and in a condition to defend ourfelves, in cafe the inhabitants had attacked us. However, we march'd with great circumfpection, and endeavour'd to ftand upon our guard.

Scarce had my little company gone a quarter of a league along the wood fide, but we were perceiv'd by about a hundred favages, who fat on the top of the mountain. Immediately they came down very haftily, and fcour'd about on all fides. As they were fuperiour in number, and would have been too hard a match for us, we thought proper to haften back to the fhore; but, they intercepted us. We then faw a company of men, moft of them fix foot high,

high, naked, beardlefs, and their skins
quite red.

Having furrounded us, they threatned
to knock our brains out, in cafe we refus'd to furrender; and indeed, they
had already wounded two of our *Babilarian* women with their arrows.
Immediately they fell upon us, difarm'd us, and began to ftrip us. As I
was at the head of the company, they
difarm'd and ftript me firft. But how
great was their aftonifhment, when
they found that the reft were women,
and moft of them young and handfome!
They feem'd to be overjoy'd at this
difcovery; and laughing, immediately
fell a dancing.

In the mean time I was ty'd to a tree
with willow twigs, when I faw a moft
fhocking fcene. Thefe rude, barbarous favages, like the fabulous fatyrs
of antiquity, threw themfelves fud-
denly on the women, and fatiated in
fo furious a manner their ungovernable
luft, that moft of the unhappy creatures unable to bear up under it, fainted away in their arms. As they were
wholly

wholly employ'd in gratifying their
brutality, and took no notice of me, I
infenfibly unloos'd the willow bands,
when flipping into the wood unperceiv'd, I ran as faft as my legs would
carry me towards the fhore, where, to
my great joy, I perceiv'd our long-
boat, coafting along the ifland.

As foon as our People faw me, they
made towards the land, when jumping
into the long-boat, I told them the
danger I had been in, and the fad fate
the *Babilarian* women my companions
had met with. We thought fit to continue fome time in the bay, and coaft
along the fhore, in hopes that our female companions might be as fortunate
as myfelf, and efcape from the barbarians. But we waited to no purpofe,
and therefore return'd on board.

When the *Babilarian* women who
had ftaid on board, were told what
had happen'd to their companions, they
were immediately for revenging them,
and for that purpofe defir'd our captain
to put them afhore in order to attack
the inhabitants. A council was held,
and

and as we had no opportunity of taking in water in this ifland, it was refolv'd we fhould run all hazards. Accordingly an hundred and thirty of us went on fhore, ninety of whom were men and the reft women, all arm'd with fabres, muskets and bayonets.

We advanc'd in good order towards the place where the favages had come upon us by furprize, and found only two *Babilarian* women dead of their wounds. We then march'd towards the mountain, and being got on the top of it, difcover'd feveral huts. We naturally fuppos'd that this was the haunt of the favages, but not hearing the leaft noife, we drew near to it foftly, when we perceiv'd feveral of the inhabitants afleep. We advanc'd ftill farther, and faw at a diftance our *Babilarian* women bound together and lying near a hut. We march'd towards them, when inftantly feveral favages who were not afleep, fet up a dreadful roar, which wak'd all their companions.

Immediately we fell upon them, and having fhot the firft, the reft took

to

to their heels. But our *Babilarian* women furrounding the dwelling, prevented their flight, and cut a great many of them to pieces. The female-pri-
foners, who were then fet at liberty by
our *Englifhmen*, drefling themfelves, and
fnatching up their arms, which lay
in a neighbouring hut, they joyn'd us,
and compleated the defeat of the barbarians. Being tranfported with fury,
they would have referv'd thofe who
had feem'd moft eager in tormenting
them, for a cruel punifhment. They
bound ten of thefe, and carried them
to the fhore, where, in fpight of
all we could do, they burnt them
alive.

After this expedition, we advanc'd
into the wood along the fide of the
mountain, where we found a fpring.
Here we quench'd our thirft, and
fent for hogfheads in order to fill
them with water. Whilft part of
our crew were doing this, the reft
hunted in the wood, and kill'd a
great quantity of game, which being
carried

carried on board, ferv'd to folemnize our victory.

We did not think proper to continue longer in this ifland, for fear left a frefh company of favages fhould fall upon, and opprefs us with numbers. Accordingly we all return'd on fhipboard, after having fent thither our butts which we had fill'd with water, and immediately weigh'd anchor.

C H A P. IX.

The author is fhipwreck'd and efcapes in a canoo. He goes on fhore on the ifland of Tilibet, *where he is made a flave. Defcription of the manner of its inhabitants. The fhort term of years they are allow'd to live, and the ufe they make of life.*

"Short lives tribe

CApt. *Harrington's* defign, to whom I had given part of the jewels *Mejax* had bequeath'd me at her death, was to return to *England*; highly fatisfy'd with the prefent I made

made him, which was of much greater value than if he had brought a cargo of goods. As we had no commodities on board our veſſel, 'twou'd have been ridiculous in us to have made for any other place; and therefore I join'd with him in opinion, that we ſhou'd ſail for *Europe*, which we accordingly did. After ſix weeks ſail, during which we had a pretty favourable wind, we were overtaken by a violent ſtorm, in about twelve degrees of northern latitude, and an hundred and four of longitude. The raging winds, after having tore all our ſails to pieces, carried off our mizen maſt, and alſo our bolt-ſprit. As the boiſterous waves overwhelm'd the veſſel, pumping was of little ſervice; when running upon the rocks, it was bruis'd, and immediately ſprung a leak in ſeveral places, ſo that 'twas manifeſt we muſt inevitably ſuffer ſhipwreck.

However, the rocks we ſplit upon, ſhew'd we were not far diſtant from ſome land, which yet we could not ſee becauſe of the pitchy darkneſs.

In

In this extremity, we thought proper to leave the ſhip and run a-ground. We put out the long-boat, and immediately the whole crew of both ſexes got on board of her. I alſo was going to jump in, when unfortunately I took it into my head to look after my casket of jewels, which was in a cheſt that ſtood in the captain's cabin. Accordingly I ran to the cheſt, open'd it, and immediately took out the casket, but that very inſtant the veſſel was ſinking. I gave myſelf over for loſt, and began to run with all ſpeed towards the long-boat, but thoſe who were in her, were in ſuch trouble and confuſion, that not recollecting I was left behind, they cut the cable which held the long-boat to the ſhip; and immediately the impetuoſity of the waves drove them ſo far, that 'twas impoſſible for them to give me the leaſt aſſiſtance.

In this extreme, I had no time to debate, upon which I jump'd into one of the canoos, and inſtantly cut the cable that faſtned it to the ſhip, which immediately founder'd. 'Twas to no purpoſe

purpose for me to attempt to row to
the long-boat; the sea ran so high, and
'twas so dark, that I soon lost sight of
it.

I row'd a long time together, without knowing whether I drew nearer,
or further off from land; and all my
endeavours now were to struggle with
the waves, and preserve myself from
shipwreck. However, the sky clear'd
up by degrees; the wind fell, and the
sea grew pretty calm. I saw land, and
the sight of it sooth'd the agonies of
my soul. I took heart, and row'd with
all my strength in order to reach the
shore; flattering myself with the hopes
of meeting my companions there; but
alas! I never once set eyes on any of
them since, Capt. *Harrington* excepted,
as I shall relate hereafter. They were
swallow'd up by the waves; and I shall
ever deplore the remembrance of my
dear companions, especially *Zindernein*
and the brave *Babilarian* women.

After rowing five hours, I at last
reach'd the coast, and landed before
sun-set. As I was quite spent, I gather'd

I

ther'd fome fruits, which I happily
found at a little diftance from the fhore.
I went up to a rifing ground, whence
I faw a country very well cultivated,
and a few villages. I then concluded
that the inhabitants liv'd under a regular
form of government, which was fome
confolation to me. I wou'd have gone
towards thofe villages, but night came
upon me in the way; and now, not
knowing where to go, I ftopt and
climb'd up a tree, in order to fhelter
myfelf from wild beafts and fpend the
night. The reader will fuppofe I had
very little fleep, and that I revolv'd a
thoufand thoughts in my mind, all which
I would now relate, did I not know
that the reflections of the wretched
and unhappy, are always ungrateful.

The next morning, at day-break, I
was wak'd by the barking of dogs,
who were got about the tree where I
had hid myfelf; and at the fame time I
perceiv'd a handfome young man, with
a quiver of arrows over his fhoulders,
advancing towards the place where I
lay. He was come pretty near it, and
was

was going to let fly an arrow at me,
when I fet up a dreadful cry. The
young man, who poſſibly took me, as
he faw me through the leaves, for fome
great bird ; hearing a human voice, immediately ſtoop'd his bow, and drew
near to the tree. Finding the hunter
was humane, I came down from the
tree, threw myſelf at his feet, and
made a thouſand fupplicating geſtures,
in order to teſtify my reſpect and fub-
miſſion, and how much I ſtood in need
of his fuccour.

He look'd at me fome time, and by
feveral kind figns, gave me to underſtand he would take me under his protection, and that no evil ſhould befall
me. He then bid me follow him, and
pointing to a houfe, which appear'd
large and regularly built, he carried
me to it. Being come in, I faw a woman whom I fuppos'd to be his wife,
and feveral children and fervants,
who were all very kind, and offer'd
me victuals. The lady of the houfe,
feeing a casket of jewels under my arm,
defir'd to fee it. I prefented it to

her,

her, and thought myself indifpenfably
oblig'd to make her a prefent of it.
She open'd the casket, and viewing what
was in it, return'd it me, and wou'd
not touch one of the diamonds. Obferving I offer'd it to her in a very cour-
teous manner, and prefs'd her to accept of fome of the moft valuable jewels; fhe fmil'd with a kind of fcorn,
and gave me to underftand, that thofe
trifles were not worthy of being either
offer'd or accepted. I was afterwards
inform'd, that the inhabitants of this
country, had no manner of efteem for
diamonds, as being of no fervice to
the neceffities or pleafures of life: furprizing blindnefs! not to be fenfible of
the worth of thofe fhining ftones,
which having the admirable faculty of
reflecting light more ftrongly than all
other natural bodies, are therefore
juftly had in fo high efteem; and fo
much fought after in *Europe*, that the
ladies frequently prefer them, to what
they ought to value more than any
other thing in the world.

Having

Having given my patrons to understand that I was a foreigner; that I was come from a very remote country, and had been shipwreck'd on their coast, they seem'd to pity me; and endeavour'd to comfort me by giving me to understand that they'd be very kind to me, provided I serv'd them with affection and fidelity. A few days after, I had a dress given me, like that of the other slaves of the family; and was order'd to superintend the baths of *Jalassu*, for so was the mistress of the family call'd. I was under great terror when this employment was given me; and imagin'd, that since I was invested with a post of such considerable trust, I was to be serv'd in the same manner as the *Turkish* slaves, to whom this province is allotted. However, my fears were very ill grounded; for the men of this country, as I was afterwards inform'd, unprey'd upon by jealousy, are so firmly perfuaded of the chastity of their wives, that they don't use any expedients to secure themselves of it. As husbands repose

I 3   fo

fo generous a confidence in their wives,
thefe are inviolably true to their bed;
and never abufe a liberty, that
would make thofe criminal pleafures
infipid to them, in which the fufpicion of a jealous husband only, gives
a relifh to the enjoyment.

I had fcarce been a month in the
houfe, when all the flaves were wak'd
at midnight, becaufe *Jalaffu* was in
labour. We all enter'd her apartment,
in order to affift her if it were neceffary.
She had a good time, and was deliver'd
of a fon. But how great was my furprize, when I faw the babe fhe had
brought into the world but an hour before, feated on a chair, opening its
eyes, looking with curiofity round
about, and pronouncing fome words
that none underftood! Inftead of crying, as all our children do when they
come into the world, he laugh'd, fung,
and difcover'd the pleafure he felt, to
find himfelf iffued from his mother,
like a prifoner who is newly fet at liberty. He feem'd overjoy'd to fee
himfelf rifen from a ftate of non-exi-
ftance,

france, and to find himſelf numbred among the living.

Immediately he roſe up, and ran to his mother who gave him ſuck. Some hours after, a taylor was ſent for to take meaſure of him, and make him a ſuit, which was order'd to be diſpatch'd out of hand, becauſe the child almoſt grew up under the eye; for which rea-ſon they were oblig'd to make him a new ſuit every month. I admir'd that nature ſhould be ſo favourable to man-kind in thoſe countries, and indulge them the enjoyment of life the inſtant they are born.

The ſame day a maſter of languages was ſent for, to teach the new-born in-fant to ſpeak. The preceptor only found-ed a ſubſtantive or other part of ſpeech; this the child repeated, and immedi-ately treaſur'd it for ever in his me-mory. And indeed, in a fortnight's time, he talk'd as plain as the reſt of the children of the family. I took this opportunity to learn the language alſo. But how happy ſoever my me-mory may be, I muſt confeſs I employ'd

I 4   much

much more time in learning all thofe words. However, in three months, I knew enough to make myfelf underftood, and to comprehend whatever was faid to me.

Scarce was I able to exprefs my thoughts, when I ask'd one of the oldeft of my fellow-flaves, who had the greateft favour fhewn him by our mafter; if all the children of the houfe, refembled the laft our miftrefs was deliver'd off? Whether they all learnt the language at that age, with as much cafe as he did; and whether in three months, their minds were as ftrong and capacious? What's that you fay, fays he? This child knows nothing but his own tongue, whereas he ought by this time to have learnt a little mufic and dancing. I am certain, he'll hardly know his exercifes by that time he's two years old. He is little of his age, and hardly four foot in ftature. Children, fays I, fhoot up in a very fhort time in your country! Why don't they in yours, fays he? No, no, fays I, very far from it.

Why

Why now how old d'ye think I am?
Five, fays he, for you feem to be about
the fame age as I am. You are
mightily out, fays I, I am twenty.
Heavens, fays he, twenty! impoffible
fure. That is the longeft period of
our lives; at leaft, no man ever liv'd
to above four and twenty, and yet you
feem as young and robuft as I am.
Having affur'd him, that what I told
him of my age was fact; and that in
my country men liv'd to fourfcore,
and fometimes an hundred years of
age, he ftarted up, and ran to *Furofolo*,
for that was our mafter's name, to relate all I had told him.

Upon this, all the family began to
ftare at me, as if they had never feen
me before. They cou'd not believe
what I told them, and ask'd me a thoufand queftions, to afcertain themfelves
of the truth of it. An able mathematician, who was in the houfe, and
taught the mathematicks to the two
youngeft children, ask'd me flily, whether I remembred to have feen an
eclipfe of the fun in my country. As

I

I knew perfectly that I had seen six,
and had not forgot the year, the
month, the day, or hour when they
happen'd; becaufe, I had lov'd, from
my infancy, to enquire about every
thing which related to the heavens;
I gave him an exact account of all I
cou'd recollect. Immediately he turn'd
to his aftronomical books, and found
that the eclipfes happen'd at the very
time I mention'd. Thus, we are told,
the *Chineze* pretend to prove the antiquity of their empire, and the veracity
of their hiftory; by fhewing, that their
antient books mention feveral eclipfes,
agreable to the laws of the motion of
of the planets; and by proving that the
writers of thofe books muft neceffarily
have feen them, becaufe thefe volumes
exifted at a time when their anceftors
where wholly ignorant of aftronomy;
and incapable of making exactly retro-
gade calculations with refpect to the
combination, anteriorly poffible, of celeftial motions.

The mathematician, ftruck with my
anfwers, told the family I certainly
was

was as old as I affirm'd myfelf to be,
and that there was not the leaft room
to doubt of it. In what manner, fays
my mafter to me, have you fpent fo
long a courfe of years? During the
firft fix or feven years of my life, fays
I, I had not the leaft ufe of my reafon
or liberty. At three years of age I
founded words very imperfectly; at
four I began to talk a little; then I
was taught to read, and afterwards to
write, when I was fent to fchool,
where I ftudied feven years.

What did you ftudy, during fo
long a time, fays *Furofolo?* The *Greek*
and *Latin* tongues, fays I. I prefume,
fays he, they are the languages of
fome nations bordering upon your
own. No, fays I, they are dead languages. Why then, fays he, were you
made to learn them? Wou'd you not
have fpent your time to much better
purpofe, in ftudying things that might
have been of advantage to your family
and country, or capable of rendering
life more agreable? I anfwer'd, that feveral men among us, devoted three
parts

parts in four of their lives to the ſtudy
of thoſe tongues; that they alſo learnt
ſeveral other dead languages, ſuch as
the *Hebrew*, the *Samaritan* and *Chaldee*;
that indeed thoſe linguiſts did not
make the greateſt figure among our *Literati* ; but that we had thoſe in much
higher eſteem, who had the courage
to ſpend their whole lives in treaſuring
up in their memories, the æras and circumſtances of all incidents; and enquir'd into all the tranſactions which
had happen'd in the world before they
exiſted, from the creation to the preſent age.

How idly, ſays *Furoſolo*, do you employ the long life that is indulg'd you!
I find, that tho' you live four times as
long as we do, you yet don't live
longer, in reality, ſince three fourths of
your life are abſolutely loſt. Can any
thing be more ridiculous, than to employ ſo many years in learning the art
to expreſs the ſame thing by a variety
of terms? your conduct on this occaſion, is like that of a workman, who,
inſtead of learning his trade, and improving

proving himſelf in it, ſhould waſt a long courſe of years in getting by heart, the different names by which his tools were antiently call'd. With regard to your intenſe application to hiſtory, why are you ſo ſollicitous to know all that has occurr'd ſince the beginning of the world? Are not the preſent incidents ſufficient to employ or amuſe us? What have we to do with things that happen'd before we were born? Time paſt is fled and gone; and therefore can any thing be ſo trifling as to enquire into it? Time paſt exiſts no more than the future; and in my opinion, 'tis equally ridiculous to ſearch into either of them.

Such was *Furofolo*'s paradoxical philoſophy, agreable to the odd notions which the inhabitants of that iſland, call'd in their language *Tilibet*, have imbib'd. As theſe live but a ſpan, they employ it to very great advantage. Their whole aim is enjoyment, without once troubling themſelves with knowledge; nor do they, like us, devote a conſiderable part of life, in making

king superfluous provisions for a journey, which is always ended, before
we have got together a store sufficient
for our purpose.

What other employments do your
countrymen follow, says *Furofolo?*
Some, says I, apply themselves to trade,
others embrace a military life; others
again. . . . . . . What, says he, have
you so little regard to the long life you
are indulg'd, as to venture losing it in
battle? We, tho' our lives are so short,
do nevertheless look upon war as a real
madness; not but that we fight sometimes, when divisions happen to break
out among us. But cou'd we flatter
ourselves with the hopes of living so
long as you do, I am certain, not one
of my countrymen wou'd be so stupid,
as to hazard the losing so precious
so lasting a jewel. I find that long life
is a burthen to you, and that you sometimes endeavour to while and trifle
part of it away, and at others, to rid
yourselves of it at once.

This is but too true, says I: in our
opinion, the greatest misfortune that
can

can poſſibly befall us, is to be reduc'd
to think that we exiſt; a reflection,
which, in ſome meaſure, deſtroys us.
Hence it is, that we ſtrike into a thouſand different employments, in order
to baniſh that dreadful idea, which is
no other than that *tædium* or languor,
defin'd by our philoſophers, *the attend-
ing to the ſucceſſive parts of our duration.*
I cou'd ſcarce make *Furofolo* underſtand
the meaning of *tædium*; becauſe as theſe
people are always eaſy, they have no
word in their language to expreſs that
ſickneſs of the ſoul, nor the leaſt idea
of it. They are not, like a multitude
of our *Europeans*, melancholy thro' complexion, and ſad from caprice. The
joy and ſatisfaction of their ſouls,
ſparkles on their ever-vacant and ſerene
countenances; and they ſeem to practice in a literal ſenſe, the precept of
Horace, * *Dona præſentis rape lætus horæ.*
Wholly employ'd on the preſent,
they forget the paſt, and deſpiſe the
future ;

* *And ſnatch the bleſſings of the preſent hour*

future; and their hearts are equally free from frivolous fears and chimerical hopes. Life appears to them too short, to be spent in feeding ones self with boundless desires; and to waste the present moment, in thinking on what's to come. They are happy to day, and don't trouble themselves about being so to morrow.

During my stay in the island of *Tilibet*, I enquir'd very carefully into the manners of its inhabitants, and the genius of their government. That part of the island in which I liv'd, was rul'd by a monarch, who was then in the flower of his youth, being four years old. His first minister was sixteen; who, tho' so far advanc'd in years, was very hearty and vigorous both in body and mind. He directed the prince, and govern'd the kingdom, with the most consummate wisdom. The common people, as well as the Great, applauded his happy administration, and wish'd it might last forever. This great man, entirely devoted to the administration, and the interest of the people, inseperable infeperable from thofe of the fovereign; was modeft, polite, affable, and difinterefted; qualities which endear'd him very much to the king, who being a great lover of truth and juftice, cou'd not but follow exactly all the counfels of fo moderate and judicious a minifter. By his great affiduity, truth prevail'd at court, and juftice in the tribunals. There are alfo two other kingdoms in our ifland, each of which is govern'd by a particular prince. By the wifdom of this minifter, the three monarchs live in perfect harmony; and he himfelf is always chofen arbiter, whenever any difpute arifes among them.

Such arts and fciences as are ufeful to mankind, and all that contributes to the perfection of human nature, are, as indeed they ought to be, duly efteem'd by the inhabitants of this ifland; and all perfons who diftinguifh themfelves by the fuperiority of their talents, are always protected by the minifter, who obferv'd, that the inftant they ceas'd to be patroniz'd, learning

K   and

and arts, for want of emulation, and
motives for being cultivated, were
wholly forgot; and that the human
mind was over-run with ignorance and
ftupidity. And indeed, the king is
moft affiduous in fupporting fuch of his
fubjects, as are diftinguifh'd by a fuperiority of genius.

One particular circumftance in the
court of this prince, which cannot be
parallel'd in thofe of *Europe*, is, that
lefs regard is had to extraction, than
to innate greatnefs of mind; and that
virtue and merit only reflect a luftre on
the poffeffor. Perfons are rais'd to employments in the State, not by powerful cabals, or fimulated virtues, but
for rectitude of foul and capacity.
The prince's court confifts wholly of
perfons of a fuperior merit; and it
may be juftly affirm'd, that he fees the
beft company in his kingdom.

The *Tilibetans* are wholly ignorant
of navigation, becaufe they think life
too fhort and too precious, to be fpent
in troublefome voyages, and be expofed to the dangers of the Sea. The
reader

reader will eafily guefs the reafon, why the inhabitants of thefe iflands fleep as little as poffible, and much lefs than we do. *Furofolo* obferving me to fleep feven hours together, faid to me one day: you drowze away the third part of your life, fo that 'tis not fo long as I thought it was. As for us, whofe life is fhorter, we fpend every moment of it to advantage; and as fleep is a kind of death, we fly from it to the utmoft of our power, and ufe ourfelves not to fleep above an hour in the four and twenty.

I then told him, that among us the women, and fometimes the men, often flept ten or twelve hours together; or at leaft lay half the day in bed, purpofely to contract it as much as lay in their power: that we look'd upon the art of whiling away the time as a great happinefs; infomuch that we gave the name of paftime, to our moft darling pleafures: that a long and a forrowful day, were with us fynonimous terms; and that he was look'd upon as the

K 2 happieft

happieſt man, who had liv'd long, and thought his life very ſhort.

Furofolo, ſurpriz'd at what I told him, ask'd me at what age we began to enjoy our liberty and concern ourſelves with worldly affairs? Whether we were not afflicted with languiſhing diſeaſes, and corroding cares? Whether if in old age, and when we were threeſcore, we enjoy'd a perfect health, and were ſtill agreeable to ſociety.

I anſwer'd, that we did not begin to be free, and concern ourſelves with affairs, till about twenty: that we were frequently oppreſs'd with grief and ſickneſs, eſpecially, if we gave too great a looſe to our paſſions: that in the latter part of our courſe, we were obnoxious to a thouſand ſiniſter accidents; that we grew peeviſh and troubleſome; and that young people generally ſhunn'd the company of thoſe in years.

We have nothing of this among us, ſays he. We are free, and generally enter upon buſineſs at four years of age.

age. Our bodies are not fubject to infirmities of any kind; except, when we are in a very advanc'd age, that is about feventeen or eighteen, in which feafon, we neverthelefs preferve all the gayety of youth. So that, computing the time you fleep; that which you lofe before you come upon the ftage of the world; that which forrow and difeafe render infupportable; and the mournful courfe of years of which your old age is compos'd: I believe it will be found in the whole, that we live longer than thofe who among you, are indulg'd the longeft life.

K 3   C H A P.

CHAP. X.

The author escapes from the island of
Tilibet, and goes on board a Portugueze *vessel which puts into an island.*
He is taken by favages, who are
going to knock out his brains, and
eat him. In what manner he is
deliver'd.

NOtwithstanding *Furofolo*, his wife,
and the rest of the family were
very kind to me, I neverthelefs began to be weary of the island, which
I had now liv'd a twelve-month in, and
of the mean condition to which I was
reduc'd; fo that I was continually re-
volving day and night how to efcape
from it. I regretted the island of *Babilary*, and with grief compar'd my
prefent fhameful captivity, to the exalted rank I had abandon'd.

One day as I was walking alone on the
fea fhore, from which *Furofolo*'s houfe was
not far diftant, I perceiv'd a long-boat
lying at anchor, and ten or twelve men
well

well arm'd, who were juſt landed, and
ſeem'd looking about for a ſpring.
The ſight of men in *European* habits
gave me the higheſt joy; but then I
was afraid leſt they ſhould take me for
ſome ſpy, ſent out by the inhabitants,
and would therefore perhaps murther
me. For this reaſon I hid myſelf in a
little wood that was juſt by, in order
to obſerve their motions unperceiv'd.
In the mean time, they came ſo near
to the place where I lay, that I could
hear them ſpeak *Portugueze*. Upon
this, I came out of the place where I
was conceal'd; ſaluted them in a civil
manner, and addreſs'd them in that
language which I had learnt of a *Portugueze*, who was on board our veſſel
when we left *England*.

The *Portugueze*, taking me at firſt
for one of their countrymen, embrac'd
me; and after giving me the greateſt
teſtimonies of friendſhip, ask'd me
what I did in that iſland, which they
ſuppos'd had never been viſited by
any *European.* I told them, I had
been thrown on that coaſt by a ſtorm,

K 4   which

which had funk the veffel I came in;
and had been for a twelve-month a
flave in that ifland; that I befought
them to fet me at liberty; that as
they feem'd to be looking for a fpring,
in order to take in frefh water, I wou'd
fhew them one; and that whilft they
fhould be filling their hogfheads, I
wou'd go to the houfe where I liv'd,
which was not above a league's diftance from thence; in order to bring
away the little I had been able to
fave from fhipwreck.

They promis'd in the moft obliging
terms, not to go on board till my return. Then, after fhewing them the
fpring, I ran home to fetch my jewels.
Being got thither, *Furofolo*, with
whom I had entrufted them, was unluckily gone abroad. This was a fad
difappointment; but fearing left he
fhould not return home fome time, I
refolv'd to abandon my treafure.
However, my mafter return'd a little after, when I immediately defir'd
him to give me my cafket. What,
fays he to me, art thou going to do
with

with thofe glittering ftones? Haft thou
met with any perfon, who is filly
enough to purchafe them? I anfwer'd
with an air of confufion, that I had
met with an opportunity to difpofe of
them in fuch a manner as might afterwards be of fome advantage to me.
So much the better, fays he; I am
glad any benefit accrues to thee from
fuch trifles.

I took my casket, and immediately
leaving the houfe, without once bidding farewel to any one in it, I went a
bye way to the place where the *Portugueze* promis'd to wait for me. I
affifted them in filling their hogfheads,
and ftepping into the long-boat, went
on board their veffel, which lay at
anchor about half a league from the
fhore.

The captain receiv'd me with great
affability and politenefs, and tho' I
told him I was an *Englifhman*, he neverthelefs treated me as kindly as if I
had been his countryman. Having related to him the feveral adventures I
had met with, fince my leaving *England,*

land, which was three years; he congratulated me on my good fortune, in being deliver'd from so many dangers; and said, that I ought not to repine at my being shipwreck'd, or the slavery to which I had been reduc'd, since I had sav'd so rich a treasure. Thanks to my jewels, I was respected not only by the captain, but by the rest of the officers and the whole crew, who look'd upon me as a man, that wou'd soon make a splendid figure in his own country. Another advantage I drew from my jewels, was, that they stampt a kind of credit on whatever I told them, concerning my adventures in the island of *Babilary*; for otherwise, I possibly should have been thought a great liar, or at least a fellow that had a rare knack at invention.

The vessel was returning from *Macao,* an island subject to the *Chineze* empire, at the mouth of the gulf of *Quang-cheu,* where the *Portugueze,* who have a fort there, carry on an advantageous trade; which, however, is not so considerable, ever since the
Dutch

Dutch drove them out of the greateſt part of *India.* Our ſhip had a rich cargo on board; and was ſtor'd with proviſions ſufficient for the voyage it was to make to *Braſil,* before it return'd back to *Liſbon.*

We had now gone about three months of our courſe, and were got into the ſea of *Paraguai,* about the 35th degree of ſouthern latitude, when the ſhip leak'd in two places. We endeavour'd to ſtop the leaks with tow, and imagin'd we had done it effectually; but the next day, we found above four foot water in the hold. Then all hands were ſet to the pump, which we ply'd for five hours together, and ſtopt the leaks better than we had done before. Neverthelefs, as we were afraid of their opening again, and found that freſh ones broke out daily, we reſolv'd to put into an iſland, which we diſcover'd with the teleſcope, tho' we could not find it in the chart, in order to refit our veſſel.

The next day, having a very favourable gale, we got very near it, when
putting

putting out the long-boat, we entred a road, and about four in the morning, found ourſelves at the mouth of a river. Having caſt anchor, five and twenty of us got into the long-boat, of whom I was one, and went about two leagues up the river. We landed, and immediately ſaw a very large plain, winding round a hill, which having aſcended, we perceiv'd a long range of huts at the foot of it. We then ſtood upon our guard, for fear leſt the inhabitants ſhould come upon us by ſurprize; and being arm'd with muskets, bayonets, piſtols and ſabres, we were well prepar'd againſt an attack.

Soon after, we perceiv'd a great number of ſavages with clubs in their hands, come out of the huts, and a little wood that lay round them. Theſe no ſooner ſaw us, but they advanc'd towards us with a menacing air, howling dreadfully at the ſame time. We then drew up in a line, and prepar'd to receive them; and being come within musket-ſhot, we immediately fir'd, and kill'd fifteen or ſixteen of them.

them. Then, some of them who were
arm'd with bows and arrows, letting
fly at us, wounded one of our comrades, but very flightly. We were
not under the leaft terror, but fuffer'd
them to advance within the reach of
our piftols, which we then fir'd fo happily, that a dozen more were kill'd
and as many wounded. At the fame
time, we fix'd our bayonets on our
muskets, and fell upon them. They
defended themfelves as well as they
could with their clubs; and tho' they
had by this time loft upwards of forty
men, they yet did not once flinch,
but roar'd in a dreadful manner; and
their cries ecchoing to a great diftance,
the favages fcour'd thither from all
parts, fo that we immediately faw upwards of two hundred come to their
afliftance. Then judging it would be
difficult for us to refift fo great a number, we refolv'd to retire, which the
favages perceiving, advanc'd towards
us. Then drawing up in a kind of
fquare, we fought in our retreat for
the fpace of a quarter of a league, and
kill'd

kill'd a great many more of their people, without lofing fo much as one of
our own; for as we always kept clofe,
and prefented our bayonets towards
them, it was impoffible for them to
clofe in with us.

At laft we got to the long-boat, but
with much difficulty. As I was the
laft who was ftepping into it, and that
the favages, tho' continually repuls'd,
ftill purfued us; I was unfortunately
taken prifoner with three of my comrades; and all that thofe who were on
board the long-boat could do for us,
was, to charge their pieces as quick as
poffible, and fire upon the favages, tho'
to no purpofe.

In the mean time, they carried us
towards their habitations, howling ter-
ribly at the fame time; where being
arriv'd, their women danc'd about us,
and having ftript us to the waift, painted our breafts and backs with red and
blue colours. The fame night, the favages who had taken us made a great
feaft, at which we were very much
furpriz'd. But we were much more fo,
when

when several of them, after the banquet
was ended, came and felt about us,
some on our arms, others on our legs,
some on our thighs, and others again on
our shoulders; and at the same time, made
a present to the master of the hut,
where the entertainment was given. I
was afterwards inform'd, that those
who felt us in this manner, bespoke
such of our limbs as were most agreeable
to their palate, in order to eat us, after
knocking out our brains. Each of us
had a mat given him to lie upon in the
night; but the reader will easily suppose
that neither myself, or any of my companions, slept a wink, being fully persuaded this night would be our last.

Next morning, the bodies of those
who had been kill'd the day before,
were brought in a very ceremonious
manner. We then saw a great number
of women, sitting at the doors of their
huts, crying very mournfully, and
breaking into these words, which they
repeated often: *Stulli baba coobico somac
barahou, suhanahim, him him ! jartana
frebibachoo rabapinouficon, coortapa sallo-
orik,*

orik, him him! Which fignifies, as I
learnt afterwards: *my love, my hope,
charming face, eye of my foul, alas!
alas! nimble leg, fine dancer, brave war-
rior, late in bed, awake in the morning,
alas! alas!* After this fort of *Næ-
nia* or funeral fong, feveral favages
came out of their huts, with a forrowful and dejected air, and their
eyes caft on the ground. Obferving
a deep filence, they feem'd to be in
great affliction, and to look upon the
plaintive cries and groans of the women, as unworthy their courage.

In the mean time, the women got
up, and taking hands, began to dance
round the dead bodies, finging mournfully feveral *Threni* or funeral fongs.
This recall'd to my memory, what I
had read in † *Macrobius,*viz. that funeral fongs took their rife from the notion which men had, that the foul
when feperated from the body, took
its flight to heaven, the place of its
original, and of all the harmony which
preferves the univerfe. For this reafon,

† *In Somn. Scipi. L.* 2. *C.* 3.

fon, thefe favages fang in honour of
their dead, and danc'd alfo in cadence,
in order to imitate the regular and har-
monic motion of the cœleftial Bodies.

A little after, they beat on barks of
trees, and made a great noife, in order,
as I was fince told, to force the fouls
of the deceas'd to remove far from
their bodies, and unite with thofe of
their anceftors. After this, one of
the chiefs made a long harangue, in
which he celebrated the virtues of
the perfons deceas'd, and endeavour'd
to comfort the furvivors for the lofs
they had fuftain'd. Then they began
to dig a great many round graves, in
the fhape of wells, where the bodies
were buried in the fame pofition children lie in the womb ; to fignify, that
the earth is the common mother of all
men; which cuftom, *Herodotus* in his
fourth book relates to have been practis'd by the *Nafamones*. In the graves
were laid, fmall loaves, *fagamita*, tobacco, a pipe, a gourd full of oil, a
comb, and feveral colours, with which
the favages ufe to paint their bodies.

L   After

After the burial was over, a public
feaft was made, to which we were not
invited; but faw them bring in all the
dead dogs, that had belong'd to the
deceas'd favages, cook'd up and
drefs'd. The feaft being ended, one
of the chiefs who prefided at the ceremony, threw a ftick about fourteen
inches long among the young fellows,
which each of them endeavour'd to get
hold of; knocking at the fame time
their heads one againft the other, and
ftriking a thoufand blows with their
clench'd fifts. Another fuch ftick was
thrown in the midft of a company of
young women, who ftrove in the fame
manner as the men had done to get
hold of it, and kick'd and cuff'd one
another very luftily. This battle, or
rather funeral game, which lafted
about half an hour, after having enliven'd the hearts of all the fpectators,
and banifh'd from their minds the
mournful ideas of the burial; concluded with the diftribution of the prizes,
which were given to that man and woman

man who had gain'd the victory; and
this being done, they all withdrew.

All this while we were confin'd in
a hut, whence we could fee the whole
ceremony. We were taken out of it,
when all the favages arm'd with fticks
and bucklers drawing up round us, return'd us our piftols, and gave us to
underftand they were going to knock
out our brains; but that 'twas their cuftom, to return the prifoners part of
their weapons, in order that they
might revenge their deaths valiantly;
fo that, with thefe weapons, we were
allow'd to affail all fuch as fhould
come within our reach, and exert our
felves to the utmoft. We then defir'd them, fince that was the cuftom,
to return us our fabres; but this was
refus'd, the fabre being thought too
bloody a weapon. Thofe who had
wrench'd them from us, brandifh'd
them, and were very proud of their
booty.

And now each of us took powder
and ball out of his pouch, and charg'd
his piftol; but the favages had no no-

tion

tion of what we were about. Tho' we
had kill'd feveral of them with our
muskets and piftols, they fancied we
had hurl'd fire at them; and did not
imagine it was poffible for them to
receive the leaft hurt, with mere black
duft and little balls, unlefs fire was put
into the barils.

I then faid to my comrades, that
we muft firft fhoot the four favages
thro' the head who fac'd us, and had
got our fabres; that at the fame time,
we muft force them out of their hands,
and feize their fhields: that poffibly,
in cafe we defended ourfelves bravely; kept clofe together, and affifted
one another dexteroufly, we might
fave our lives, or at leaft lofe them
with honour. They promis'd to obferve what I recommended to them,
and to fight bravely to the laft gafp.

We then cock'd our piftols, and going up to the four favages who had our
fabres, fhot them thro' the head, each
of our piftols being loaded with a brace
and half of ball. They fell backwards,
when immediately we feiz'd upon their
fhields

fhields and our own fabres. Several other favages, running inftantly to
prevent our difarming thofe we had
laid on the ground, as they were lifting up their fticks to ftrike us, met
with the fame fate. We now threw
away our piftols, as being of no further
ufe ; when ftanding all four back to
back, we put ourfelves in a pofture of
defence. The favages furrounded us,
and we endeavour'd to cut as many of
them to pieces as we cou'd, and kill'd
and wounded a confiderable number.
Some of them taking up our piftols
which lay on the ground, thought to
ufe them as we had done; and fancy'd
they fhould kill us, by prefenting the
muzzels to our faces, and making a
noife with their mouths like the report
of a gun; but their experiment coft
them dear, and we cleav'd them down
the head with our fabres.

But now we began to be opprefs'd with
numbers and wearinefs. Several favages finding they could not knock us
down with their fticks, becaufe we
warded off the blows with fo much

skill, went and fetch'd their clubs,
tho' contrary to their cuftom. But
now we were fcarce able to hold out
any longer, and were going to be over-
power'd, when an unexpected fuccour
refcu'd us from danger.

Our comrades who had efcap'd in the
long-boat, carried the news of our
battle on board, and the fad fate we
had met with. The captain, griev'd
and exafperated at this accident, becaufe his nephew was among the prifoners; exhorted all the crew, moft of
whom were very brave fellows, to return back; and do all that lay in their
power, to refcue us out of the hands
of the favages. All the paffengers,
and the greateft part of the failors,
bravely offer'd themfelves for volun-
tiers in this expedition. The captain
told them, they muft not be terrified
at the number of the favages, they being forrily arm'd; and as they were
wholly ignorant of military difcipline,
would eafily be defeated.

Accordingly, a hundred men well
arm'd, with the captain of the fhip at
their

their head, got into the long-boat,
and going up the river, drew near the
huts of the favages; who feeing fo many men coming down upon them, took
to their heels, and fled into the wood.
In the mean time, our people advanc'd
and fet fire to their abandon'd huts.
Seeing this, we went up to our companions, who were overjoy'd to fee us ;
when we gave them a thoufand thanks
for their great friendfhip and generofity.

C H A P. XI.

*Whilft part of the crew is on fhore,
thofe who ftaid on board the veffel,
weigh anchor. The author, with
feveral* Portugueze, *is oblig'd to continue a long time in the ifland of*
Mahoonam. *They make an alliance with a nation of favages.*

THE captain having fent for
the hatchets and faws which
he had order'd to be put into the
long-boat, commanded the failors to
fell two great trees, that were afterwards

wards to be faw'd into planks to
refit our veffel. But while we were
thus employ'd, under the direction of
one *Ovielo* who was an excellent fhip-
carpenter; we faw two of our people
rowing towards us in the canoo, who
landing. brought us a moft melancholy piece of news. They told us, that
the thirty men whom we had left on
board the veffel, to guard it in our
abfence; finding the captain and all the
officers on fhore, had confpir'd together to feize the fhip and its lading;
that my casket of jewels was a ftrong
temptation; that they had weigh'd
anchor and fet fail: that as the captain
had invefted them equally with the
command of the fhip, during his, and
the officers abfence on fhore; they
had done all that lay in their power to
oppofe fo horrid a refolution; but fo
far from being heard, had been threatned with death: that they then jumpt
into the canoo, being refolv'd to come
to us, in order that they might not
be forc'd to joyn in fo black a
crime. This news threw us into a deep
consternation,

confternation, and as to myfelf, I very
much regretted the lofs of my casker,
which held all my treafure. We had
no manner of provifions, and all we
had to fhift with was our muskets,
two barrels of powder, and two bags
full of leaden ball, which had been
put into the long-boat; to ferve us, in
cafe our fight with the favages had
continued longer. The only courfe
we could then take, was to ftay in the
ifland, and endeavour to fubfift upon
what our guns could procure us. In
this fatal extreme, a council was call'd;
when it was refolv'd we fhould immediately kill what game we could,
which we fhould broil, and put on
board the long-boat; and this being
done, we fhould coaft round the ifland,
and endeavour to fettle in fome place
where we fhou'd have nothing to fear,
till fuch time as we might meet with
an opportunity for returning to *Europe.*
It being impoffible for us, as we had
only the long-boat, to go fo long a
courfe; nor even to reach any part of
the continent of *America,* which we
concluded

concluded lay at a great diftance from
us.

Accordingly we went a fhooting,
but kept clofe together for fear of being furpriz'd by the inhabitants. We
kill'd game enough, which we broil'd,
and feafted upon it very heartily that
evening. We fpent the night in the
wood, where, after appointing two
men to watch, who were to be reliev'd
every hour, we flept under the trees.
The next morning, we put the reft of
our game on board the long-boat, and
getting in her, coafted along the ifland
all that day.

About evening we went on fhore, in
a place which feem'd very agreeable,
where we thought to fpend the night.
A brook we obferv'd, had made us
pitch upon this place. We fed, as
we had done the day before, upon our
broil'd victuals, and afterwards laid
ourfelves down under the trees, keeping guard as ufual.

We flept pretty found, but the moment day began to appear, our watch
awak'd us, and call'd to arms. Four
favages

favages had pafs'd very near them, and advanc'd forward in order to view us. We awak'd inftantly, and taking our muskets, ran as faft as poffible; and furrounding the four fpies, took them prifoners. Immediately we gave them to underftand, that not a hair of their heads fhould be hurt; and that we were refolv'd not to injure any of the inhabitants of the ifland, provided they did not attack us: we offer'd them victuals, and having given them the higheft teftimonies of friendfhip, we defir'd them to tell their countrymen, we were their friends, in cafe they were ours; and would do them all the fervice that lay in our power. We endeavour'd to explain thefe particulars to them by figns, which they feem'd to underftand. The favages overjoy'd at our kind ufage, gave us alfo to underftand by other figns, that we needed not be under any apprehenfions from the natives. Upon this we difmifs'd them, after having given each of them the little knife we had lent them to eat with; having obferv'd that they had view'd
them

them feveral times with the deepeft attention.

However, as we did not think proper to rely entirely on their word, we ftill continued to keep guard. We advanc'd up into the country, but did not go far from the long-boat, being unwilling to leave it.

About noon, we perceiv'd a great number of favages coming towards us, carrying fruits and refrefhments of every kind. The moment we faw them, we faluted them as the four favages had faluted us; that is, by croffing both our hands over our heads, and fmiling gracioufly upon them. They return'd us the fame falute at a diftance, when coming up, they offer'd us their prefents, which we accepted, and at the fame time embrac'd them.

We fhew'd them our long-boat, and gave them to underftand that we came from a far diftant country; that our being oblig'd to ftay in their ifland, was a very great misfortune to us; and at the fame time intreated them to receive us as allies and brethren.

Then

Then making figns for us to follow them to their habitations which were not far off, we confented to it with pleafure.

Being come to their huts, the women and children began to dance about us; and foon after a kind of cake was given us to eat with meat and fruits : they alfo gave us a liquor to drink, which was agreeable enough. As we had a little brandy, we gave them a fup of it, which pleas'd them mightily; but when we found they would have drunk too much of it, we gave them to underftand, that to drink to excefs of that liquor was mortal; and that they muft take it down but very fparingly. They believ'd us, and accordingly their chiefs commanded the reft to leave off. The whole afternoon was fpent in finging and dancing. At night, mats were given us to lie upon, and we were lodg'd all together in a large hut.

As feveral of us had been wounded in the laft battle, the favages made figns that they wou'd heal them ; and immediately

immediately went and call'd a man,
whom they feem'd to look upon as a
faint, and treated with the higheft veneration. This extraordinary perfonage
vifited our wounded men, and then
fhut himfelf up alone in a hut, which
fhook in a moft violent manner for two
or three hours, to our great aftonifhment; we not being able to account
for it. He afterwards return'd to his
patients, rinc'd his mouth, fuck'd their
wounds; and apply'd a certain herb unknown in *Europe*, which in four and
twenty hours heal'd them completely.
This teftimony of the kindnefs of thefe
favages, remov'd all fufpicion from our
minds, and from that moment made us
confider them as our fincere friends.

The next day, they defir'd us to
hunt along with them, and for that
purpofe offer'd to furnifh us with bows
and arrows; but we gave them to underftand, fhewing them our muskets at
the fame time, that our weapons would
do as much execution as theirs. They
then view'd them attentively, and
feem'd not to comprehend how it was

poffible

poſſible for ſuch weapons, to reach things at a diſtance. But when they ſaw us actually kill birds with them, they were prodigiouſly ſurpriz'd; and ſuppos'd, as the other ſavages of the iſland whom we fought with had done, that fire was conceal'd in the barril of our muskets, which we had the art of hurling at pleaſure; but we clear'd up their miſtake at once, by ſhewing them our powder and ball; loading two or three pieces before them, and afterwards firing them. Our confidence on this occaſion, gave them the higheſt ſatisfaction; ſo that they look'd upon us as a ſett of men of a wonderful kind, and of a ſuperior underſtanding; and were fully perſuaded we had the greateſt affection for them.

At our return from hunting, we debated in conjunction with the ſavages, whether we ſhould build a hut large enough to hold us all; or whether we ſhould raiſe ſeperate huts for each, which the wives and daughters of the ſavages ſhould look after, and dreſs our victuals; and range them all in a
line,

line, in order to enlarge the village.
The women, whom we alfo advis'd
with upon this occafion, were, but for
what reafon I know not, unanimoufly
of the latter opinion. Accordingly,
we all fet our hands to the work; and
the inhabitants, overjoy'd to fee their
village fo much enlarg'd, work'd with
us, fo that in a month our huts were
completely built and furnifh'd.

We had among us one *Rodriguez*, a
Spaniard, who had fpent feveral years
in *S. Gabriel*'s land. He told us,
there was as great an affinity between
the language of the inhabitants of that
country and that of our iflanders, as
between the *Spanifh* and *Portugueze*;
that he underftood almoft every thing
they faid; and that in lefs than a week,
he would not only underftand their
tongue perfectly, but be able to fpeak
it fo well as to be underftood. As
we did not know how many years
we might be forc'd to refide in this
ifland; and wanted continually the affiftance of the inhabitants, with whom
we had contracted the ftricteft intimacy,

cy, we intreated him to apply himſelf to their language, ſo that he might be enabled to ſpeak in our name, and be our interpreter. He promis'd to do it, and indeed in a week's time he began to ſpeak the *Mahoonam* (for that was the name of the iſland) tongue; and the ſavages were overjoy'd to find themſelves able, by this means, to talk with us. As I myſelf had a great talent for languages, I took it into my head, for amuſement ſake, to learn that of *Mahoonam*; and for this pur-poſe, I deſir'd the *Spaniard*, who had gone thro' a regular courſe of ſtudies, to draw up a kind of grammar of it, and give me a few leſſons from time to time. I apply'd myſelf to it in ſuch a manner, that in a few months I began to have ſome notion of their language; and even ventur'd ſometimes to ſpeak to the ſavages in it, which improv'd me very much.

Aſſoon as our *Spaniard* was able to converſe with them, he had told them our country lay at a vaſt diſtance from theirs; and that we had ſcour'd up and

M   down

down the ocean for many years; that
we had been forc'd to put into their
island, in order to refit our veffel; that
upon our landing, we had been attack'd
by the inhabitants of the fouthern part
of the island, who attempted to murther us all; but that we had defeated,
and made a great flaughter of them.
That while this was doing, thofe to
whom we had entrufted our veffel, dif-
appear'd on a fudden; fo that we had
been forc'd to continue in their island.
The *Spaniard* related our battle and
victory, with fuch an air of vanity and
felf-fufficiency, as very much difpleas'd
us; we therefore defir'd him to add,
that what flaughter we had made was
involuntary; we having been abfolutely
forc'd to it upon their falling upon us
in fo unjuft and barbarous a manner,
and merely to defend ourfelves.

The favages liftned with the utmoft
attention to the particulars which
Rodriguez told them; the danger
to which we had been expos'd, and
the victory we had gain'd. Thofe,
faid they, whom you conquer'd, are a
wicked

wicked fett of people; and we are very glad you punifh'd them in fuch a manner. We have been at war with them for many years, and perhaps *Halaimi* (which is the name of the principal god thefe inhabitants worfhip, and is undoubtedly the *Hebrew* word *Eloim* corrupted) has brought you into this ifland, purpofely to affift us in extirpating that unjuft nation. Be always our brethren, and we will continue yours. Live among us, as tho' you were the children of our mothers and wives; and reft affur'd, we'll procure you every fatisfaction that lies in our power.

C H A P. XII.

The author falls in love with a pretty female favage. His converfation with her and her father, who cenfures the manners of the Europeans.

WE accuftom'd ourfelves infenfibly to this favage way of life, and began even to relifh it; all our time
M 2   being

being spent in drinking, eating, sleeping and hunting; so that we felt no manner of uneasiness, except that we wou'd every now and then wish to revisit our country; the dear thoughts of which, we could not possibly eraze from our Memory. However, in order to lessen my uneasiness in this particular, and bind myself in some measure to the country I was in; I devoted myself to a young she-savage, who was a pretty creature, of good sense; whom I should have married, had not our captain and all my friends, dissuaded me from it. She lov'd me to distraction; and I may say truly, that I spent many a delightful hour in her company.

Whether it were that her father, who was a man of very good sense, had taken a more than ordinary care of her education; or that nature had indulg'd her an uncommon share of reason, I never met with a woman who argued on all subjects, in so just and acute a manner. Neither the *Babilarian* women, whose minds,
tho'

tho' they are fo much cultivated; nor thofe of *England*, which are of fo delicate a caft, were, in my opinion, to be compar'd to that of my aimable favage.

I did all that lay in my power to pleafe her, and moft of our converfations turn'd on paradoxes with regard to gallantry; fubjects I ftarted, merely to amufe and flatter her. I remember fhe one day ask'd me, whether the women in *England* were handfomer than thofe of that ifland. Our *Englifh* women, fays I, are extremely fair, and 'tis in this their principal beauty lies, if we may be allow'd to give it that name: for this fairnefs, is, in my opinion, a very trifling advantage; and I will even own, that fince my being fo happy as to be acquainted with you, I begin to fufpect whether it may not be a real deformity.

Our *Englifh* women now abhor to fuch a degree the natural colour of their complexions, that they do all they can to change it. Hence it is, that they cover their cheeks with a deep

red;

red; and I imagine, that, in procefs of time, they'll paint their faces
black, the better to difguife the colour
of their skins. After all, if this mode
fhould happen to prevail in *Great-Bri-
tain*, our ladies will then acquire an
advantage, you enjoy naturally. 'Tis
a misfortune, that they're not able to
ftir out of doors, whenever the fun
fhines; or in cafe they are abfolutely forc'd to it, are oblig'd to employ a thoufand troublefome precau-
tions; whereas, the ftronger the fun
darts his rays upon you, the more
charms it lights up in your countenances, as it heightens its beautiful
black, and makes it ftill more lovely.
This fairnefs of our ladies, if it comes
to a certain degree, has fomething in
it vaftly flat and languid; and indeed
we always prefer a brown, to a fair
beauty, when the latter colour is too
predominant. By this 'tis plain, that
the colour which bears fome little re-
femblance to yours, or at leaft, comes
neareft to it, pleafes more univerfally
among us.

As

As we, fays I, like *Brunettes* more than fair women, our *Englifh* women alfo prefer men of a deep brown complexion, more than they do fuch as are extremely fair; a foft complexion denoting effeminacy, and being generally a fign of imbecility. With regard to the various kinds of ornaments, which the women in *England* employ to heighten their beauty; I can affure you, there's no man among us, but fincerely wifhes they were as unadorn'd as you are. Our *Englifh* women conceal a thoufand defects, under their vaft, and fplendid habits; which are of no other ufe, but to difguife the fhape, and impofe upon the eye. But they have fo little notion of their own intereft, that they wear large pieces of filk wrought in folds, which defcends from the waift to the foot; and enormous circles of whalebone cover'd with linnen, which makes them look like big-belly'd women, juft ready to cry out. They ftrut in the midft of thefe moveable hoops, which furround them perpetually, like children when you teach them to walk

M 4   in

in go-carts; and thefe they pufh forward, or backwards according as they
pleafe to direct their motions.

I beg pardon of our *Englifh* ladies,
for prefuming to relate the anfwer I
made to my pretty female favage's queftion. A lover always fancies his miftrefs exceeds all other women in beauty; and as mine was of a jetty black,
and cloath'd in no other drefs but the
plain fummer habit, which the favages
in thofe countries wear all the year
round; decency and good manners
oblig'd me to prefer her complexion
and habit, to thofe of our *European*
women. If any of thefe fhould happen to be fhock'd at it, I befeech
them to afcribe it to the fincerity of a
traveller, who is refolv'd not to difguife or omit the moft minute circumftance.

Abenouffakee her father, was, as I before obferv'd, a man of excellent fenfe;
but of that fenfe which nature herfelf
indulges, unrefin'd by the paffions. As
I frequently vifited his hut, attracted
by

by his daughter's charms, I us'd to difcourfe with him now and then; and
our converfations were perhaps not inferiour to *Plato's dialogues.* For what
reafon, fays he to me one day, as we
were walking together, whilft our *Portugueze* were hunting with the favages;
for what reafon, did you and the reft
of the *Europeans* leave the country
where nature thought fit to place you;
and hazard the few days you are allow'd to live, upon the ocean? Were it
not better to fpend them with your family, or in the company of your
friends; and employ yourfelf in hunting, that agreeable as well as ufeful
exercife? Had you devoted yourfelf
to fuch a way of life, you would not
have been expos'd to all the perils
and misfortunes, which an idle curiofity has made you undergo.

'Tis true, fays I, that the fole motive of my leaving my native country,
and going to fea, was a ftrong curiofity
to vifit diftant regions; and to know
the different nations which are difpers'd
up and down the earth. But then, as

I

I have undergone many hardships, and been expos'd to the greatest dangers in this voyage, I also have had the pleasure of seeing a thousand curious objects: I shall always thank providence, for having conducted me into the island of *Babilary* and that of *Tilibet*; of which I have related many particulars, that both pleas'd and surpriz'd you.

What you have told me, says he, of your own country, is equally surprizing, and has diverted me full as much. But, after all, I cannot conceive how men should put themselves to the trouble, merely for the pleasure of enquiring into the manners and customs of other nations, to build huge floating huts; and be so rash, as to brave storms and tempests, and undergo so many hardships.

I was young, says I, when I left my native country, and will own that I went abroad, merely out of a vain curiosity; but those who built the vessel, and the crew who were on board with me, were prompted by more substantial and rational motives. Their business,

buſineſs, ſays I, was to trade, and bring back goods from foreign countries, which being ſold at their return, would produce a conſiderable ſum of money. I continued to tell him, we labour'd all our lives, purely to get this money, and amaſs as much of it as we could; and made ourſelves truly miſerable, in hopes of being one day happy, from a perſuaſion we entertain'd, that money only could make us ſo.

What is this ſame money, ſays the ſavage, which has the virtue to make you happy, the moment you poſſeſs it? See, ſays I, ſhewing him a piece of gold and another of ſilver, which I had kept for ſome time in my pocket; 'tis this procures us the ſeveral neceſſaries of life, and furniſhes us with all the conveniencies and delights we can poſſibly wiſh for. The poſſeſſion of theſe two metals, regulates ranks and degrees among us; creates eſteem and veneration; and has even the wonderful faculty of beſtowing merit and good ſenſe.

Abenouſſakee,

Abenouſſakee, obſerving figures and characters ſtampt on my gold and ſilver pieces, fancied they contain'd a certain magical virtue; and therefore deſir'd me to lend him one of them to make an experiment with, and ſee whether it could really inſpire his ſon, who, he ſaid, was a very ſilly boy, with good ſenſe. I'll try, ſays he, whether you don't impoſe upon me; and if that piece has the power you aſcribe to it.

It would not, ſays I, have the leaſt effect upon him, tho' he had as many of them as would fill the largeſt of your huts. What, ſays he, interrupting me, have theſe pieces no virtue but in your country? No, ſays I; and the reaſon of it is, becauſe we, by agreement, aſſign to them certain ideas which it is impoſſible for you ever to entertain: as for inſtance, when a great number of theſe pieces are in a cheſt, we fancy it contains ſpacious fields, commodious edifices, ſplendid furniture, magnificent habits, honours, dignities, a croud of ſervants, beautiful women and delicious viands. One circumſtance which
will

will aftonifh you, is, that we no fooner
open the cheft, but we, whenever we
think proper, really find all thofe particulars in it. Then, by acquiring thefe
things, which are in fome meafure
worfhip'd in our country, becaufe they
are fo ardently thirfted after, we procure efteem; are rever'd, and courted
by every individual; and every one
cries up our merit, wit and fenfe.

Abenouffakee, who had not the leaft
idea of this ænigma, imagin'd I only
told him a fett of fictions, purely to
impofe upon his credulity. However,
when I afterwards clear'd up the paradox, he told me, that to him, our
manners appear'd very contemptible;
and that tho' gold and filver might
have been originally ufeful, thofe metals were yet of pernicious confequence,
by our unreafonable abufe of them;
whence he concluded, that fince we were
oblig'd to take fo much pains and labour; and fo idly made our felicity
entirely dependant on a thing that was
not in our power, we were unhappy by
choice, and deferv'd to be fo. Happinefs,

nefs, fays he, confifts in defiring nothing, but your whole life is fpent in
defiring. As for us, we enjoy all
things, becaufe we want nothing we
wifh for.

But as thofe men among you, fays
he, who poffefs a much greater quantity of money than the reft, fee themfelves efteem'd and rever'd upon that
account; does not this puff them up
with a ridiculous pride, and prompt
them to defpife all who are not fo
wealthy as themfelves? Yes, fays I,
this indeed is commonly the cafe. A
rich man is generally a very filly fellow,
unadorn'd with one fingle virtue or talent: but this is a trifle; for he fondly
imagines that his poffeffions fupply every
defect, and give him an indifputable fuperiority over the man of fenfe and merit, who tho' not in good circumftances,
yet does not fue for any favour at his
hands. If thefe two happen to be together, the one, tho' he condefcends to pay
the greateft civilities to the other, he yet
does not fpeak to him as tho' he were his
equal. But if the man of merit is fo
unhappy,

unhappy, as to difcover his indigence by the meannefs of his drefs, this is of worfe confequence to him, than if his reputation were fullied. Poverty, in the eye of a rich man, is the moft difhonourable of all qualities, and the moft ridiculous thing in nature.

Another aftonifhing circumftance, is, that a wealthy man, who was once poor, and long pining in mifery, as multitudes are, is generally the moft impertinent, the moft infupportable of all rich men. He forgets the meannefs of his extraction and his once low condition of life; but never his education, for this fhapes his manners and behaviour. In fine, thofe rich upftarts, whom we call men of fortune, generally diftinguifh themfelves from the nobles, and fuch whofe poffeffions are antient and hereditary; and are always difcover'd by the marks above-mention'd. Thefe falute thofe they meet, who always pay them the compliment firft, with a carelefs nod; and fmile at the fame time with an air of fatisfaction, or difcover an abfence of thought; they

they speak very loud, and very improperly: all their furniture is made after the last mode that prevail'd; they entertain persons of high birth and quality with the utmost magnificence, tho' they are forbid their tables; and are profuse to their mistresses only. As virtue never enriches the possessor, and that these men generally owe their fortune to guilt; they never pay homage to the deity, well knowing they are obnoxious to him, unless hypocrisy can be of any advantage to them; and then indeed they will address him, but 'tis merely to impose upon the public. They are asham'd of their own names, and generally shade it with a magnificent sirname; and endeavour to make the world forget what themselves or their fathers once were, by a particolour'd cloud of servants, who are for ever at their heels.

Explain, says *Abenouffakee*, interrupting me, what you mean by the word *servant*. Has money the virtue to increase the number of your children? Our children, says I, never wait upon their

their parents, unlefs they are extremely poor. All people in tolerable circumftances give money to men and women, whom they keep in their houfes,
and provide with neceffaries, to perform the very loweft and moft contemptible offices; thefe are oblig'd to
do whatever they are commanded; are
fubject to the whim and caprice of
their mafters and miftreffes, and dare
not difobey them. Are not thefe people, fays he, of another country, and
prifoners of war? No, fays I, they are
born among us, but wanting that thing
I juft now fpoke of, call'd money,
fubject themfelves to us; and become
in fome meafure our flaves, merely to
acquire fo fmall a portion of it, as may
be neceffary for their fubfiftance.

Is it poffible, fays *Abenouffakee*, there
fhould be men among you, of fo abject
and groveling a caft of mind; fome to
make themfelves flaves to their countrymen, and others to fuffer them to
be fo? I fee that money is your enemy,
fince it reduces you to a ftate of captivity, and fubjects you to fuch as poffefs

N   it.

it. It muſt be confeſs'd, ſays I, money is a kind of tyrant; and 'tis a great misfortune to us, that we ſhould be born with the want of the ſeveral neceſſaries of life.

Your country, then, ſays he, is either too ſmall for you, or you are overſtock'd with people, ſince it cannot ſupply them with food; and that ſome of them either cannot live in it, or are forc'd to ſubſiſt by the moſt baſe and unworthy methods. I anſwer'd, that our country was very fruitful, and could ſubſiſt twice as many inhabitants; but that there was a ſett of powerful men among us, who had ſeiz'd upon the greateſt part of our lands; and having left none for the reſt, theſe were oblig'd to work day and night for the former, in order to procure themſelves the common neceſſaries of life.

Abenouſſakee then enquir'd, whether thoſe potent perſons, who thus triumph'd, were more numerous than ſuch of their countrymen, as were forc'd to lead ſuch abject and miſerable lives. I anſwer'd, that the poor exceeded infinitely

nitely the rich in number. If this be
fo, fays he, your poor people muft
have little fenfe, or elfe are cowards,
to fuffer a number of rich men, who
are much fewer than themfelves, to
feize upon all, and leave them nothing.
The laws, fays I, prevent their doing
this. What are thefe *laws*, fays the
favage, interrupting me? Are they
men arm'd with muskets and fabres,
who ferve as a guard to the wealthy,
in order to maintain them in the quiet
poffeffion of their riches; and defend
them againft the juft pretenfions of the
poor.

The laws, fays I, are public rules
and maxims, receiv'd among us from
time immemorial, which are equally
rever'd both by rich and poor, becaufe
we confider them as the bond and fecu-
rity of civil fociety. Both parties
therefore unite to maintain them, and
fee them duly executed; fo that a poor
fellow, for inftance, who fhould rob a
rich man, would be punifh'd with the
utmoft feverity. Not only the rich
would call aloud for punifhment, but

all the poor would approve of it, and even fome of them would themfelves be the executioners upon thefe occafions. 'Tis no wonder, as you may perceive, that the rich fhould revenge an attempt like this; and call fuch an action, groveling, fhameful, and criminal, as it really is. But you poffibly may be furpriz'd, that the poor fhould condemn this action equally with the rich, fince it effects thefe much more. But two motives engage them to deteft it, in cafe they have the leaft probity or honour; and confequently to maintain the Great in the poffeffion of the riches they may have got, by what methods foever. The firft is, that were the poor man allow'd to feize upon the treafures of the rich; he alfo might be difpoffefs'd, by a rich man, or another who is as poor as himfelf, of the little he enjoys; and confequently, 'tis his intereft to fupport the law, which forbids every kind of theft. The fecond motive, is grounded on a famous principle of morality, which is look'd upon as the ba-

fis

fis of all civil fociety; and that is, not
to do to another, what we fhould be
unwilling to have done to ourfelves:
fo that the poor man, confcious he
himfelf fhould be very forry to be difpoffefs'd of what he might have got by
his labour; forbears, in order not to
vex the rich man, to rob him of any
thing, tho' of the moft trifling value.

We allow equally with you, fays
Abenouffakee, this moral principle of
all juftice, which is born with us, and
is ever imprinted on our minds, how
deprav'd foever we may be; but methinks 'tis not, according to your notions, and what you juft now told me,
fo pure and facred as according to ours.
Your way of life, and what you call
civil fociety, makes you obey it with
fuch partiality, as fullies its beauty;
fince, purfuant to your manners and
cuftoms, 'tis manifeftly more favourable to fome than it is to others. 'Tis
an eafy matter for a wealthy man to
fay, I am very rich, and fhould be
very forry to be bereav'd of my pof-

N 3   feffions;

seffions; confequently I muft not difpoffefs other men of their riches.
Whereas the poor man who wants every thing, can only fay thus: Had I
wealth, I fhould be forry to be difpoffefs'd of it; confequently I muft not
feize upon that of others. Obferve the
difference there is between the *I am* of
the rich, and the *Had I* of the poor
man; and you'll confefs that the principle is applied in a very different manner among you; whence 'tis plain, that
this morality is defective, becaufe 'tis
partial, fince it is not equal and uniform with regard to all men and all
conditions; the rich and poor being
oblig'd to argue differently.

Whatever you may fuggeft, fays I,
this law of nature is equally rever'd by
us all: by this, order is maintain'd in
all governments; every one fubmits,
and no one dares to complain againft it.
It muft indeed be confefs'd, that 'tis
not always religioufly obferv'd; for
the poor man frequently fteals the property of the rich; and on the other fide,
the rich man not only feizes fometimes
the

the poffeffions of the rich, but endeavours to force away whatever the needy man may have got by his labours.
But in this cafe, if the law be infring'd,
'tis immediately reveng'd; however,
with this difference, that the poor fellow never fails of being punifh'd according to the enormity of his crimes,
whereas the rich man fometimes eludes
the courfe of juftice.

Wherefore, fays the favage, interrupting me, is this fhameful diftinction
made? 'Tis, fays I, becaufe the opu-
lent are generally the arbiters and dif-
penfers of juftice among us, and commonly favour thofe who are wealthy
like themfelves; whence it often happens, that when a poor man is oppreft,
he chufes to ftifle his complaints rather
than publifh them to the world. However, thofe awful minifters of juftice,
whom we call magiftrates, naturally in-
cline to give each man his due, when nothing clafhes with the notions they have
form'd to themfelves of equity: but
then, on the other fide, as 'tis natural
to love one's felf beft; whenever it fo

N 4   happens

happens that their paſſions may be
gratified by ſwerving a little from
juſtice, they are apt to indulge
them. If, for inſtance, a pretty woman ſues for any thing at their hands,
the firſt motion infallibly pleads in her
favour; but happily, the ſecond ſometimes declares for truth and equity.
They are generally check'd by the
fear of infamy; however, there are
certain circumſtances where fear does
not take place, which is, when iniquity may be conceal'd : in this caſe, woe
to him who has only reaſon on his ſide;
and is deſtitute of all protection but
that of juſtice or innocence ! Were not
men, ſays I, aw'd by heaven, this e-
normity would be much greater than
it is; but our religion, whoſe precepts
agree with thoſe of the law of nature,
makes us look upon double-dealing or
prevarication in a judge, as the blackeſt of all crimes; ſo that, if a magi-
ſtrate ſtands but in ſome little awe of
the Divine Being, he never pronounces
againſt the dictates of his conſcience;
but ſometimes his conſcience is of ſuch

a

a caft, that one wou'd be apt to conclude he had none at all.

Here the favage ask'd me, whether
confcience did not comprehend all our
laws. As confcience, fays I, is not a
curb fufficient to reftrain fuch as are
prompted to guilt; and that thofe who
commit evil, eafily flatter themfelves
at the fame time that they are innocent;
we have a vaft number of laws, which
prohibit the commiffion of a multitude
of things, whence an infinite number
of decifions arife from innumerable cafes, which inflict different punifhments
on thofe who tranfgrefs them. Of
what ufe, fays *Abenouffakee*, are fo many enacted laws, fince you are inform'd
with that of nature, which is fo plain,
fo decifive? Our laws, fays I, are no
other than that of nature, extended and
applied to various kinds of particular
cafes.

But, fays I, notwithanding the wifdom of our legiflators, and the fagacity of our interpreters, there is among
us a certain furious wide-gaping monfter, which is protected and cherifh'd

by

by a croud of *long robes*, who feed
this monfter, and are mutually fed by
it; it laughs at juftice, devours the fubftance of families, and endeavours to
abolifh or elude all laws in general.

The name of this dangerous monfter
is *Chicane* or *Cavil*, a monfter infinitely
more formidable than injuftice itfelf;
for this, when it oppreffes us openly,
leaves us at leaft the vindictive right of
breathing our complaints. But this *Chicane* is fo envelop'd in its numberlefs
folds, and fo fubtile in its quirks and eva-
fions; that favour'd by certain formalities,
which are fo many chains we have been
pleas'd to bind juftice with; this monfter makes us lofe every thing thro' the
oracles of the judges, even the confolation of being allow'd to fay, they
were partial in their decifions. The
dreadful minifters of *Chicane* croud all
the courts of juftice; enflame them by
the perpetual fire they keep in thefe
places; and make them eccho inceffantly with their piercing cries, which yet
are not always loud enough to wake
the judges from their flumbers: an unhappy

happy circumftance is, that the old judges only fleep, and the young ones keep awake.

It muft be confefs'd, fays I, that juftice is more rever'd, and perhaps better adminifter'd among the favages, than by us. Upon my mentioning the word *favage*, which happen'd to drop from me unawares, *Abenouffakee* interrupted me, and enquir'd the meaning of it, and why I call'd him *favage*? The reafon is, fays I, becaufe you and your countrymen are not like us, polifh'd and civiliz'd; that you live in a ftate of independance, and follow merely inftinct; that you obferve but very few rules of decorum; that you have no notion of what we call good breeding, all which are laws of fuch mighty confequence among us, that we almoft put them on the fame foot with thofe of nature; in fine, becaufe you go naked, and are not like us, govern'd by kings aud magiftrates.

How great is your blindnefs, fays *Abenouffakee*! What! becaufe we content ourfelves with following inftinct;

ſtinct; and are unacquainted with all laws, but thoſe which nature dictates, you call us ſavages! You fancy your-ſelves more improv'd, more poliſh'd, and more civiliz'd than we, becauſe a thouſand arbitrary inſtitutions, to which you have ſacrific'd your liberty, pre-vail among you! As for us, who ſtill preſerve ours, and conſider it as the moſt valuable gift that nature has be-ſtow'd on man; we ſhould think it loſt, were we ſubject to that multi-tude of ſuperfluous rules, upon which your civil ſociety is grounded. What-ever you may fancy, methinks our ſo-ciety is much more civiliz'd than yours, becauſe 'tis more ſimple and equitable; we don't ſuffer the leaſt injuſtice or partiality in this ſociety; we think all mankind upon a level, becauſe nature has made them ſo, and as we don't preſume to change the order ſhe has eſtabliſh'd; we obey our fathers, and revere old men, who having more ex-perience, are conſequently more judi-cious than young men. Nature, you ſee, only, has eſtabliſh'd this preceden-cy

cy among us. We have a chief, who
always is elected; and the reafon of
fuch elections, is, becaufe we have obferv'd, that tho' all men are equal in
dignity, there is neverthelefs a vaft
difference among the feveral individuals, with regard to genius, talents,
bravery, and bodily ftrength.

As nature, fays he, herfelf made this
diftinction among her children, fhe
therefore dictates that we conform to
it; and confequently to fet at our head,
that man among us to whom fhe has
been moft liberal of her favours. Is
this, fays I, the rule you obferve, in
the afcribing of honours, and the diftin-
guifhing of ranks? With regard to all
your laws of decorum, as they are
fuggefted by caprice, they ferve only
to foment your pride and depravity,
and footh all your paffions. In the
manner you feem to live among yourfelves, what you call politenefs and good-
breeding, is in reality falfhood and dif-
fimulation. You lay one another under the greateft conftraint, purely to
deceive; and this affiduous care is a
continual

continual flavery, you reduce yourfelves to. You look upon a thoufand
particulars, as the moft important duties of life, tho' it be as juft to omit,
as comply with them.

Do you, fays he, pretend to be more
civiliz'd than we, becaufe you are
cloath'd? But were we born in a climate, that lay at a great diftance from
the fun, d'ye think we fhould not take
as much care to cover our bodies as
you do? We content ourfelves with
concealing that from fight which nature has appointed for the continuation
of our fpecies; and this we do to prevent our eye from growing too familiar with objects, which, were they
continually expos'd to fight, would
therefore be lefs pleafing. We are ignorant of fuch arts as owe their invention to neceffity, and the fantaftic ine-
quality of your ftations. For what
man among you, that cou'd fubfift
without labour, would give himfelf
the trouble to work? Thefe arts therefore you glory fo much in, are fo many teftimonies of the wretchednefs of
your

your condition; and as they produce arbitrary conveniences, or fuperfluous commodities only, we are far from envying them; we defire nothing but what we are acquainted with, and this alone is fufficient to make us happy.

In a word, fays he, we never fee a man among us fue to another for fubfiftence; work for him as a hireling, or wait upon him after a mean, groveling manner. Our women till our lands, which are in common; and the labour we beftow upon them, intitles us to whatever they produce. Our bows and arrows are an agreeable amufement; and give us an opportunity of fpending our lives without the leaft care or folicitude. We are ignorant of your art of building great huts on fea or land: we are very well fatisfy'd to live beneath our own, and never once entertain a thought of quitting the ifland we inhabit. We have only fmall canoos made of the barks of trees, with which we coaft the ifland, and go up and down our rivers. If our huts chance

chance to fall to the ground, they are
rebuilt with very little labour. All
things grow in our ifland, becaufe we
confider every thing as ufelefs that
does not grow in it. Obferve now the
difference that is between you and us,
and which may with the greateft propriety be call'd *favages*. Do you imagine, that the man who follows the
fteps which nature has pointed out, is
more favage than he who leaves them
to follow art? Are thofe trees in our
ifland, which without the leaft culture
or care, bring forth the delicious fruits
you eat with fuch a relifh, juft as they
come from the hand of nature, to be call'd
favage? Do you fet a greater value on
thefe plants, which will not bring forth
fruit unlefs they are drefs'd and cultivated? If you do this, I then indeed
will allow you to confider yourfelves
as fuperior to us.

I yet don't, fays he, tho' we
plead for plain and uncorrupted nature,
pretend to affert that we always keep
ftrictly to her facred maxims; or that
our manners are conftantly pure, and all
our

our cuſtoms irreproachable. We are
inform'd with the ſame paſſions as the
Europeans; and as theſe paſſions deprave
the rational faculties, they conſequently
corrupt nature. As for inſtance, we are
too cruel to our enemies. This is a vice
of long ſtanding, which has taken very deep root in our minds, tho' cuſtom
and prejudice conceal its deformity
from us; but Poſſibly we may one day
open our eyes.

I was highly delighted with the
great wiſdom which ſhone forth in
Abenouſſakee's diſcourſe; and tho' his
reaſons ſhock'd my vanity, I yet
could not forbear applauding them.
I was for ſome time ſo wrapt up in
thought, that I did not make a word
of anſwer to what he ſaid laſt, which
engag'd him to ſpeak as follows.
Don't fancy, *Gulliver*, that I'm angry
becauſe you call'd me ſavage; ſince in
caſe you had, out of reſpect for me,
forbore to employ that word, you always wou'd have thought me ſo; and
I ſhou'd never have had an opportunity
of undeceiving you in that particular.

O   I

I am senfible that felf-love prompts us to love our own country beft; and therefore I freely forgive you, for pre-ferring your nation to ours.

As we were thus talking, we found ourfelves infenfibly at the end of our walk, and thereupon went back to our huts, where we found our companions with feveral of the inhabitants return'd from hunting, loaded with game, which we fhar'd with them. The women drefs'd it, and I feafted in *Abenouffakee's* hut to which feveral of the hunters had been invited, as agreeably, as I could have done in *England* in the midft of my friends. The entertainment being ended, we all took the * *Calumet*, and regal'd ourfelves with it till very late at night.

C H A P.

---

* *A fort of large pipe, made of red, white or black marble, to fmoak in. The bowl of it is very fmooth, and is in the fhape of a battle-ax. The tube is fett with porcupine's quills &c; 'Tis fuppos'd by the favages to be of a myfterious nature, and is the em-blem of peace.*

C H A P. XIII.

Battle between the Kiſtrimaux *and*
Taouaous. *The latter, being aſſiſted
by the* Portugueze, *are victorious.
The author makes a ſpeech, to diſ-
ſuade the ſavages from putting the
priſoners to death. A peace is concluded between the two nations.*

ABout this time we were told, that
the *Kiſtrimaux*, or ſavages a-
gainſt whom we had fought upon our
firſt landing in the iſland, who had
long been at enmity with the *Taouaous*,
for ſo the ſavages among whom we liv'd
were call'd, had lately laid waſte ſome of
their lands; and were advanc'd in great
numbers, in order to ſet fire to their huts,
and to kill, or carry off all the *Taouaous*
they could meet with. We offer'd our
ſervice to our allies upon this occaſion,
and deſir'd we might be permitted to
aſſiſt them in repulſing their enemies,
who had already felt the fury of our
arms. The *Taouaous* having accepted
our offer with thanks, we order'd them

to

to aſſemble on the morrow, in order to
be taught the art of fighting, which
we told them, would give them a
great advantage over their enemies.
They agreed that our captain ſhould
head them, promiſing to obey all his orders, and ſubmit in the engagement
to ſuch of the *Europeans* as he ſhould appoint for officers under him. Our whole
army, the *Europeans* included, conſiſted
of nine hundred men. The firſt thing
our general did, was to exerciſe the
ſavages for ſome days; however, he
did not flatter himſelf, that it would be
poſſible for him, to make them as expert in military diſcipline as ourſelves;
when having done this for ſome days,
and thinking them ſufficiently inſtructed,
he led them forth againſt the enemy.
Our ſavages were arm'd with bows and
arrows, and hatchets made of a black
ſtone as hard as iron; and the *Europeans* with muskets, piſtols and bayonets.
We had not march'd a league, before
we arriv'd at the foot of a hill, where
our general, accompanied by his nephew and myſelf, went up to view the
enemy,

enemy, whom our fcouts faid were en-
camp'd in the plain. We difcover'd
them at about half a league diftance
from us, and judg'd, by the manner
in which they had pofted themfelves,
that they were ftronger than we; for
they had extended their wings to a
great length, in order to furround us;
having probably been inform'd that
our army was very inconfiderable.
They alfo had the advantage of the
ground; for a very thick wood cover'd
them on the left, and a large rivulet lay
on their right. Our general, after having attentively confider'd the pofture
of the enemy, chang'd that of his own
army, and drew it up in manner following. As it was impoffible to fall upon
them in flank; and that it was very eafy
for them to furround us, becaufe of their
great numbers, had we attack'd them in
front; he divided his army into three
battalions. The firft was commanded
by *Cuniga* a *Portugueze,* a man of great
bravery and moft confummate experience, who had ferv'd on the frontiers
of *Portugal* under the lord *Galway,* in

O 3   the

the laſt war of the allies againſt *France*;
this body conſiſted of two hundred ſavages, and twenty five *Portugueze.*
The ſecond battalion was commanded
by the captain's nephew, and was
form'd of the ſame number as that of
Cuniga. The third battalion conſiſted
of four hundred ſavages and fifty *Portugueze,* among whom I march'd, and
was commanded by our general.

We advanc'd in this order, and perceiv'd that the *Kiſtrimaux* had ſtill enlarg'd their wings. We halted, in order to ſee whether they would advance
and attack us; but obſerving they kept
their ground, we march'd towards the
enemy, within twice the length of a muſ-
ket-ſhot, when they began to howl in a
moſt dreadful manner. *Cuniga* and the
captain's nephew began the attack on
different ſides, and our general ſent
them reinforcements, whenever he found
it neceſſary. Seeing that his nephew's
battalion, was forc'd to fight in reti-
ring, he commanded me to reinforce
him with a detachment of a hundred
ſavages and twenty five *Portugueze.*

Our

Our fabres, and the fire of our muskets,
chang'd the fcene; for the captain's
nephew and his battalion taking heart,
he charg'd the favages with frefh fury,
and we made a great flaughter of them.
They did not flinch, tho' they labour'd
under the greateft difadvantage: on
the contrary, their courage feem'd to
break out with greater vigour, the
more we cut them to pieces. *Cuniga*
and his men perform'd wonders, and
that brave man made a great havock of
the enemy's left wing, whilft we repuls'd the right. The *Taouaous* difcover'd an uncommon joy, when they
faw us fight fo bravely for them and
their country : but to do them juftice,
they behav'd with extraordinary valour.

In the mean time, the general, who
now was under no farther apprehenfions of being furrounded, advanc'd forward againft the enemy. Then it was
that the battle was bloody. The *Kiftrimaux*, tho' they had loft a great
number of men, did not once offer to fly; but fought with fo much

O 4   intripidity

intrepidity and refolution, as would ftill have made the victory doubtful, had they engag'd the *Taouaous* only. We heard them cry out one to another, *Can, obami paru, nate fris mikio*; which fignifies, *Let us then die, fince we muft yield.* Very few efcap'd alive out of the battle, and we took a great number of prifoners.

After this victory, in which we had fo great a fhare, the *Taouaous* could no longer doubt but we were their fincere friends, and accordingly gave us a thoufand thanks. But whilft they were thus employ'd, in congratulating one another upon their good fuccefs; *Abenouffakee*, who had not left me during the battle, bid me obferve the cruelty of his countrymen, who, in cold blood, murther'd all the wounded among the enemy; and, at the fame time, obferv'd to me, that he was greatly fhock'd at their barbarity. In the mean time, they began to think of returning home; and it was neceffary to drefs the wounds of our foldiers, of whom there were great numbers.

I

I myfelf had been flightly wounded
in the fhoulder, with a hatchet which
had juft graz'd it. My pretty female
favage, would not fuffer any perfon to
drefs my wound but herfelf; and accordingly fhe went and gather'd fome
plants whofe virtues fhe knew, and
applying them to the wound, it was
heal'd in a very fhort time.

Night being come, we were order'd
to affemble in the large hut, where a
grand fupper was provided for us, to
which the prifoners were invited.
They eat as heartily as we did, and
did not feem the leaft dejected at
their hard fate. We all feperated after fupper, and agreed to meet in
the fame place on the morrow.

Being affembled the next day, one
of the chiefs advanc'd towards us,
and asked whether we would have
the prifoners burnt, or were for having their brains dafh'd out? He added, with a very polite air, that fince
we had contributed fo much to the
victory, they ought to beftow on us
the

the honour of having the chief hand
in punifhing the prifoners.

Saying this, he prefented our captain with a club and a torch, purpofely that he might fignify by his
choice, what kind of death the prifoners fhou'd die. The reader will naturally fuppofe, that our captain refus'd to
accept of this terrible honour. At that
inftant recollecting how I myfelf had
once been in the dreadful condition
of thofe unhappy wretches, I addrefs'd the affembled favages in thefe
words.

    " Is it poffible, O generous *Taouaous*,
" for men who boaft fo much wifdom,un-
" derftanding and virtue, to be fo inhu-
" man? Is it not enough that you have
" vanquifh'd your formidable enemies;
" humbled their pride; put them to
" flight; and cover'd with their de-
" feated battalions, the bloody plain
" where you behaved in fo gallant a
" manner? The flaughter is at an
" end; muft therefore a company of
" unhappy vanquifh'd people, who ef-
" cap'd the fury of your arms in bat-
                   " tle,

" tle, be now, after the victory is o-
" ver, fo many victims of your rage?
" Why did you not cut them all to
" pieces in the field, when they had
" their weapons in their hands, and
" were able to defend themfelves?
" How can you think it glorious, to
" put to death an enemy after you
" have difarm'd him? If, by fparing
" the lives of thefe unhappy men, you
" intended them merely to grace your
" triumph; why don't you make this
" triumph ftill more lafting, by ex-
" tending your mercy to thofe you
" conquer'd; who, fo long as they
" draw breath, will, in fpight of
" themfelves, be forc'd to publifh
" your glory and their own defeat?
" How many advantages will your
" clemency on this occafion procure
" you? The fate of arms is various
" and inconftant: and therefore, in
" cafe your enemies fhould one day be
" victorious, and thofe of your nation
" fo unfortunate as to fall into their
" hands; you then may propofe an
" advantageous exchange, and pro-
" cure

" cure their liberty; confequently the
" faving of their lives, will in fome
" meafure be faving your own. But
" I am fenfible, O generous *Taouaous*,
" that your magnanimous hearts will
" look upon this confideration as tri-
" fling; your great fouls muft be mov'd
" by more nobler motives, and more wor-
" thy objects. Let then your generofity
" now appear, in an action which is fo
" worthy of it. Don't imagine that
" the abolition of this barbarous cuftom,
" fo repugnant to virtue and good fenfe,
" is fufficient; or that 'tis enough barely
" to fave the lives of fo many unfortunate
" warriors, who are not in a capacity to
" annoy you. Go ftill farther; give
" them their liberty, and generoufly fend
" them back to their countrymen, who,
" ftruck with the heroifm of this action,
" will be forc'd to own, that your cou-
" rage is great, but your virtue ftill grea-
" ter; and will by this action, be no lefs
" prompted by gratitude and efteem,
" to fue for your friendfhip. Can any
" thing be more valuable than peace ?
" War fhould never be undertaken
                      " but

" but in the view of obtaining it: Now
" peace, which generally is the price
" of blood ; may, on this occafion, be
" procur'd by your forbearing to fhed
" it. This liberty you are fo jealous of,
" which is fo often hazarded in war,
" will be fecur'd to you for ever, if
" you indulge it to thofe who are now
" in your power. In cafe your ene-
" mies fhould be fo injudicious, as not
" to applaud fo magnanimous an acti-
" on; they at leaft will be oblig'd to
" fuppofe, that you have them in the
" higheft contempt, fince you are not
" afraid of increafing their numbers,
" by fending thefe back alive: and
" this confeffion, at the fame time that it
" fills them with confufion, will tran-
" fmit your glory to lateft pofterity.

As foon as I had ended my fpeech, *Abe-*
nouffakee, for whom his countrymen had
the higheft veneration, rofe up, and turning towards them, faid, that he had long
condemn'd, in his heart, this barbarous
cuftom I then exhorted them to abolifh:
that nothing could be more contradictory to the virtue they profefs'd ; that
'twas

'twas a people's glory, not to oppreſs,
but vanquiſh a nation; that the de-
ſtroying them any otherwiſe than in
the field, was baſe and groveling : and
that 'twas inhuman to make warriors
ſuffer a cruel death ; warriors who
were taken in battle, and reduc'd to a
ſtate of ſlavery, merely becauſe they
fought valiantly: that, as they ow'd
their victory to the bravery of the *Europeans*, it was but juſt, at leaſt on this
occaſion, that all the priſoners ſhould
be given them, to be diſpos'd of as
they thought proper.

Immediately a murmuring ſound was
heard among the ſavages, who began
to debate upon my ſpeech, and *Abenouſ-
fakee's* diſcourſe. The women, being of a more cruel and revengeful
temper than the men, did not much
reliſh my arguments, but inſiſted ſtre-
nuouſly for the antient cuſtom, and
were unanimous to have the priſoners
put to death. However, notwithſtanding all they could ſay, *Abenouſſakee's*
advice prevail'd; and it was reſolv'd
that they ſhould all be put into our
hands,

hands, to be difpos'd of as we fhould
fee fitting. Immediately they were taken out of the hut in which they were
confin'd, when fuppofing they were
going to be put to death, they firft
ask'd for their hatchets, according to
the ufual cuftom, in order to revenge
their deaths. Finding themfelves afterwards deliver'd up to the *Europeans*,
they look'd fternly upon us, and began
to revile us in a moft outrageous manner. They faid, by way of bravado,
that had not the powerful dæmon who
was propitious to us, fill'd our long
tubes with a liquid and impetuous fire,
they would eafily have cut us all to
pieces; and that we were a company
of mean-fpirited wretches, fince we
had employ'd more art than bravery in
the fight.

One of the chiefs of the *Kiftrimaux*,
who was among the prifoners, recollecting he had feen me, fpoke as
follows. " 'Tis thou, who fome
" time fince efcapedft the punifhment
" thou defervedft, which fhould have
" been as cruel a one as I cou'd poffibly
" have

" have inflicted, had not the dæmon
" who protects thee, refcued thee out
" of my hands: I would have burnt
" thee at a flow fire, and have taken
" care that no part of thy body fhould
" be exempt from pain. I now defy
" thee to be as ingenious in tormenting
" me, as I would have been in tortu-
" ring thee, hadft thou continued my
" prifoner. But before I die, I and
" my companions may poffibly have
" the fatisfaction to fee thee perifh.
" Yes, 'tis on thee, moft odious fo-
" reigner, we'll revenge our deaths,
" fince 'tis to thy bloody and infer-
" nal weapons, we owe our deftructi-
" on.

We were all aftonifh'd at this inhuman fpeech; infomuch that I began almoft to wifh, I had not fpoke
fo much in their favour; when our
captain advancing towards this chief,
with an air of fweetnefs and humanity, which feem'd to furprize him,
fpoke to him as follows. " Brave iflan-
" ders, we have defended our gene-
" rous allies, and are now to deter-
            " mine

" mine your fate; but you are very
" little acquainted with our difpofiti-
" ons. We deteſt the cuſtom of put-
" ting a naked and defenceleſs enemy
" to death, much more to torture him.
" Not one among you ſhall die by our
" hands. So far from ſentencing you
" to a grievous puniſhment, we are
" unanimouſly reſolv'd not to enſlave
" you, but will ſend you back into your
" own country, equally free as when you
" came from it. Go and tell your coun-
" trymen that we know how to conquer,
" but better how to pardon ; or rather
" that we conquer merely for the ſake of
" peace. Tell them, that when we are
" under arms, they will find us formida-
" ble as ever; but that when we have
" laid them down, they'll diſcover us to
" be humane, tender conquerors, who
" are incapable of abuſing their victory.
" Go ; you are free ; but remember,
" that we neither fear or hate you.

This diſcourſe, intermix'd with pride
and humanity, rais'd the admiration of
all the priſoners, who, looking upon us
as extraordinary perſons, that were e-
qually mild and formidable, were ſtruck

P   dumb

dumb for fome time; till their Chief bowing, look'd upon us with a countenance, glowing with efteem and gratitude, and deliver'd himfelf in thefe words.

" Magnanimous foreigners, your un-
" parallel'd generofity, which engages
" our affections, becaufe you have re-
" ftor'd us to our liberty, is a fecond vic-
" tory you obtain over our nation ; as
" you manifeftly fhew, that tho' you
" exceed us in valour, your humanity is
" ftill greater. Don't imagine we
" fhall be fo ungrateful, as ever to
" forget this generous action; nor
" that our refentment for the evils
" you have made us fuffer, fhould rife
" to that height, as to make us endea-
" vour to leffen the merits of it. As
" your hatred is at an end, it alfo ex-
" tinguifhes ours; and your generofity
" ftifles all our refentments. I and
" my companions will go and infpire
" our countrymen, who are no ways
" dejected at their defeat, with fenti-
" ments as magnanimous as yours. I'll
" exhort them to pardon, for your fake,
" the *Taouaous* your allies.

" This, anfwer'd the Captain, is
" our

" our firft and greateft wifh. Since
" we have vanquifh'd you, and re-
" ftor'd you to your liberty, nothing
" is now wanting to complete our
" glory, but to fettle a peace between
" the two nations, and reconcile you
" to the generous *Taouaous*, whom,
" prompted by an inveterate hatred,
" you unjuftly confider as your ene-
" mies. We offer our felves as medi-
" tors, and will ufe our utmoft endea-
" vours, to conclude a lafting peace be-
" tween the two nations.

Then fetting the prifoners at liberty,
we treated them with all poffible magnificence. We carefs'd their Chief;
and paid him all imaginable honours,
and did whatever lay in our power
to engage their efteem. We now
perceiv'd that reafon began to refume
its throne, in the minds of thefe barbarous and inhuman favages; and we
then found, that where the light of it
is not totally extinguifh'd, there is ftill
room left for virtue.

And now the prifoners went away,
and three or four days after return'd in
quality of embaffadors, with a confiderable

rable prefent; being at the fame
time invefted with full powers to conclude a peace, not only with us, but
alfo with the *Taouaous* our friends,
which at laft was refolv'd upon, and
folemnly fwore to. Great rejoycings
were made on this occafion; and I obferv'd, that they treated each other with
the greateft candor and integrity.

The *Kiftrimaux* told us, that if we
wou'd come and fee them, they would
receive us with due honour; but we
thank'd them for their invitation, and
did not think proper to promife them a
vifit. The prefents they made me, were
much more confiderable than thofe
which were given to the reft; they
having been inform'd of the fpeech I
had made before the affembly in their
favour; and that I had firft mov'd to
have their lives fpar'd. Their prefents
confifted in furs, baskets finely wrought,
and fruits of all kinds. After this
they return'd back to their village,
highly fatisfy'd with the civilities they
had met with, and the good fuccefs
of their embaffy.

End of the Firft Volume.

THE

TRAVELS

OF

Mr. *John Gulliver,*

Son to Capt. *Lemuel Gulliver.*

Tranſlated from the *FRENCH,*
By *J. Lockman.*

VOL. II.

LONDON:

Printed for SAM. HARDING, at the
Bible and *Anchor,* on the Pavement
in St. *Martin's-Lane.* MDCCXXXI.

(i)

THE
CONTENTS.

CHAP. I.

CHAP. II.

A 2   CHAP.

CHAP.

C H A P.

T H E

THE

TRAVELS

OF

John Gulliver, &c.

CHAP. I.

The author and all the Portugueze, *embark on board a* Dutch *veſſel. The young ſhe-ſavage who was in love with him, throws herſelf into the ſea. He meets with Capt.* Harrington, *who relates his adventures in the iſland of the* Crump-back'd. *A Ship is built and a forge ſet up.*

UST after the departure of the *Kiſtrimaux,* ſix of our companions whom we us'd to ſend every day in a canoo upon diſcoveries, came and told us they had ſpied a veſſel at

A anchor,

anchor, at about three leagues from them; that after looking at her thro' their glaſſes, they had row'd up towards her; and ſeeing ſhe carried *Dutch* colours, had gone on board her at once, when being introduc'd to the captain, they told him our caſe; upon hearing which, he had promis'd to take us all on board, provided we would bring him ſome proviſions, which he now began to want.

Overjoy'd at this news, we ſent back the canoo, to deſire the *Dutch* captain to wait for us; and to inform him, at the ſame time, that we were all going to hunt in a body, in order to get as large a quantity of proviſions as he could wiſh for. But now the ſavages hearing we intended to leave them, were deeply afflicted. We told them we were indiſpenſably oblig'd to return into our own countries, to comfort our wives, our relations and friends, who very poſſibly might think we were buried in the waves; that we would never forget the friendſhip they had

ſhewn

ſhewn us, and at the ſame time deſir'd them to think ſometimes of us.

Theſe worthy ſavages, tho' they were very much griev'd and vex'd at our departure, did yet immediately begin to hunt for us, and kill'd a prodigious quantity of game. Their wives broil'd part of it, ſo that they were continually bringing proviſions in their canoos to the ſhip; they alſo brought us water. In a word, five days after, we bid adieu to our beloved allies, and all got into the long-boat.

The *Kiſtrimaux* hearing of our departure, came to bid us farewel, and brought us alſo proviſions, inſomuch that the part of the ſea where we were, ſeem'd almoſt cover'd with canoos. When the long-boat was got within a quarter of a league of the ſhip, the *Dutch* captain ſent to enquire, whether the ſavages would be frighted at the report of the cannon, he being deſirous of having them fir'd in token of rejoycing. Before we gave him an anſwer, we inform'd the chiefs of the *Kiſtrimaux* and *Taouxous* of his deſign, when

A 2   commu-

communicating it to their respective nations, they told us it would please them mightily; and that since we had been so kind as to give them notice of it, it wou'd not terrify them. We therefore sent word to the captain, that we thank'd him for the great honour he intended us; and that the savages who were in our company, would be diverted with the firing, which at the same time, we told him would oblige us very much.

The answer was no sooner carried back, but immediately a discharge was heard like the noise of thunder. 'Twas a great pleasure for us to view the countenances of the savages on this occasion, some of whom, rais'd almost to extasy, stood like so many statues; whilst the rest, being greatly terrified, tho' acquainted before-hand with the nature of the explosion, seem'd resolv'd to fly back into the island. At last we got on board, and were receiv'd by the *Dutch* with all imaginable civility.

I cannot forbear taking notice of the tears and sighs, with which the lovely

A   daughter

daughter of *Abenouſſakee* bemoan'd my departure. The day we ſet ſail, ſhe ſtole out of the hut, in which her father had confin'd her, when ſhe came to me, and made me the ſevereſt reproaches. The famous *Dido* of *Carthage*, was not in deeper deſpair when *Æneas* abandon'd her; nor ever was my heart more deeply afflicted. I regretted the iſland I was now leaving, no leſs than the long ſtay I had made in it, had made me regret my native country. To footh my miſtreſs's affliction, I aſſur'd her, ſhe ſhould always live in my memory, and promis'd to reviſit her in a little time; but nothing could calm her tranſports, for when ſhe ſaw the long-boat go far from the ſhore, ſhe leapt into the ſea and was drown'd. This ſight forc'd a flood of tears from my eyes, and I verily believe I ſhou'd have died, had not the reproaches of the *Portugueze* captain and my friends, made me bluſh for ſhame; and convinc'd me that the weakneſs I then diſcover'd was very unbecoming a true ſon of *Neptune*.

A 3   The

The *Dutch* captain being inform'd I was an *Englishman*, told me there was a countryman of mine on board, who was a person of great wisdom and experience; that it muſt be a great pleaſure to me to meet with ſuch a man, eſpecially, as he was a perſon of great merit, who beſides had liv'd in ſeveral unknown regions, of which he related wonders. At the ſame time he ſent for this *Englishman*, in order to bring us together.

But, gentle reader; what words can paint the joy and ſurprize I felt, when I ſaw this *Englishman*, and found it was my worthy friend, Capt. *Harrington*! We embrac'd each other with the utmoſt tenderneſs, and could not forbear burſting into tears. We were unable to utter a ſyllable, becauſe we had ſo many things to ſay; and were ſeiz'd with the moſt violent tranſports. However, at laſt we both broke into ſpeech at the ſame time, when we aſk'd one another, how it was poſſible for us to be actually together again? What kind providence had preſerv'd our lives

at

at our fhipwreck. I anfwer'd firft, and
gave him a faithful account of every
thing I had met with. I told him how
my canoo had brought me on fhore in
the ifland of *Tilibet*; in what manner I
got away from it, by the happy arrival
of a *Portugueze* veffel, which was come
to take in water; the manner how we
came into the ifland we were now leaving; and how we had been forc'd to
ftay above a twelvemonth in it, by the
departure of our fhip, our failors having weigh'd anchor whilft we were on
fhore. I alfo related to him the finifter
accidents we had met with in that
ifland; the dangers to which we had
been expos'd; the victories we had
gain'd, and in a word, the life we
had led in it.

Captain *Harrington* having liftned to
me in fuch a manner, as plainly fhew'd
he was touch'd with this relation of
my adventures, fpake thus: Let me
alfo, deareft *Gulliver*, acquaint you with
all that has befallen me fince our fad
feparation. When the violence of the
ftorm had forc'd us to leave our fhip,

and

and make all the hafte we cou'd into
the long-boat, we enquir'd for you;
and not finding you, were refolv'd to
row back to the fhip in order to take
you in. But a fudden flurry drove us
at fuch a diftance from it, as made it
impoffible for us to reach her, tho' we
ply'd our oars with all our ftrength.
And I'll affure you, that notwithftanding the imminent danger we ourfelves
were in, we yet were greatly afflicted
for your lofs.

In the mean time, the fea grew fome-
what calmer, and having row'd for
feveral hours, we at laft difcover'd
land with our glaffes, which at once
reftor'd us to our hopes we till then
had loft. We now ply'd our oars
ftrongly, in order to reach the fhore
we faw at a diftance; and were almoft
come up with it, when our boat, which
had ftruck feveral times upon the
fhelves, and was very crazy, open'd on
a fudden againft the point of a rock,
which reach'd almoft to the furface of
the water, tho' we had not the good
luck to fpy it. Immediately it was full
of

of water, and finking to rights with the whole crew, they were all drown'd. As for myfelf, having by good fortune got hold of a plank, I fav'd myfelf as well as I cou'd, when I exerted myfelf in a furprizing manner in order to reach the fhore: At laft I got to it, but was almoft opprefs'd with wearinefs, and the weight of my cloaths; but much more fo with the grief which then feiz'd me.

In this deplorable condition, being almoft parch'd with thirft, I walk'd about three leagues, to look for a fpring; when after having rambled about to no purpofe, night came upon me, fo that I was forc'd to lie down in a plain, but did not get a wink of fleep; for the pain I felt, and the dread I was in of being devour'd by wild beafts, wou'd not fuffer me to clofe my eyes. The next morning at day-break, I fet out, and happily met with feveral trees which bore a fruit very like a cherry, but much better tafted. I eat of it with the higheft pleafure, becaufe it at the fame time fatisfied the

cravings

cravings both of hunger and thirſt. I
walk'd on, but in great pain, and
came to the banks of a pretty large
river, the current of which ran vaſtly
ſtrong.

I walk'd up towards its head for
about two leagues, and at laſt perceiv'd
ſome peaſants working in the fields. I
went to them, and by a thouſand humble geſtures endeavour'd to excite their
pity; but the peaſants, inſtead of being
mov'd at my diſtreſs, burſt into a loud
laugh every time they turn'd their
heads to look at me. However, after
they had giggled their fill, they by
ſigns bid me go to a village which was
not far off. I obey'd, and was no
ſooner arriv'd at it, but all the inhabitants running out of their houſes, ſurvey'd me as a very odd ſort of human creature, and laugh'd very heartily at the ſame time.

I cou'd not poſſibly gueſs at the
meaning of all this; however, having
obſerv'd they were all crump-back'd,
I ſuppos'd they might poſſibly be ſurpriz'd at my ſhape, and to ſee I was
                                    not

not hump'd like themfelves. I was not out in my conjecture, for being carried into a houfe, all the fellows began to ftare at me, and laugh in my face; but I obferv'd that a woman who was among them, furvey'd me very ferioufly, the reafon of which I afterwards found. In the mean time, the mafter of the houfe, who was a man of great gravity and prudence, but more crooked than the reft; gave, as I was fince told, his family to underftand, that it was ungenerous to infult a poor, deform'd ftranger in that manner; but they continued their ha, ha, ha's, at fuch a rate, that he himfelf, notwithftanding his grotefque gravity, cou'd not forbear laughing by intervals. Having made figns that I was hungry, they gave me a piece of cake, and a glafs of liquor, but fo ill tafted, that I chofe rather to drink water.

After this wretched meal, which plainly fhew'd they confider'd me in the moft contemptible light, I was left alone, and advis'd not to ftir out, for fear of being infulted by the populace. In the evening, they gave me a piece
of

of pye-cruft that was but half-bak'd;
and afterwards carried me into a kind
of garret, where I found a miferable
kind of couch. I laid myfelf down
upon it, but had no other covering
than my cloaths, which I had dry'd a
little.

The next morning, I went and
thank'd, as well as I was able, the
mafter and miftrefs of the houfe for
their very great civility; upon which
they ask'd me by figns, whether my
native country lay at a great diftance
from theirs. I gave them to underftand,
that I had crofs'd feveral feas, and was
come from a far diftant country. Then
the mafter told me, by figns, that he
had heard ftrangers were arriv'd in the
fouthern part of the ifland, who were
fhap'd pretty much like myfelf, and
that they alfo came from a very remote
country; that the next day he would
inform himfelf better of thefe particulars, but cou'd not do it before, becaufe his daughter was juft going to be
married.

And

And indeed, the young lady's humble fervant came a moment after to pay her a vifit. He was a little fellow, who tho' he had a large protuberance both before and behind, he neverthelefs affum'd the fmirking air of a gallant; and feem'd to entertain a very good opinion both of his perfon and underftanding. The young gentlewoman he was to marry had but a fingle hump, which was fituated between the two fhoulders; but then it was fo fharp-pointed, and fhot out to fuch a length; that in viewing her behind, it fhaded every part of her body the crown of her head excepted. Our two lovers were mighty fweet upon one another, and feem'd inchanted with their refpective beauties. Every one congratulated them on their approaching felicity, and were particularly ftruck with the bride's lovely fhape. They gave me to underftand, that her father had admitted me into the houfe, purely that I might ferve as a foil to the bride and bridegroom's exquifite fhape. As for my own part, in fpight of the deplorable
condition

condition I was in, I yet could not forbear laughing every now and then, to fee fo many crump-backs of both fexes got together, befides I was willing to pay them in coyn, for having rallied me fo feverely the night before, at a time when I was fo little able to play upon them again.

And now they went out of the houfe in order to celebrate the marriage. I defir'd to be prefent at the ceremony, but this favour was denied me, for fear my out-of-the-way fhape fhou'd occafion immoderate laughter, and difturb the folemnity. I therefore was order'd to ftay at home with the bride's mother, who a little after fat down at her toilet; and with the affiftance of her Abigail, made herfelf as fpruce as poffible. She had lock'd herfelf and her waiting-woman in the room, and as I did not know what to do with myfelf, I peep'd thro' the key-hole. I firft obferv'd two artificial humps of a decent fize lying upon the toilet. The lady ftript as low as the girdle, and order'd her woman to clap on her back and
breaft

breaſt the two humps abovementioned,
which ſhe fix'd to her ſhift with great
nicety and skill. I then found the reaſon, why ſhe had not laugh'd the night
before, when the reſt were ſo merry
upon me: ſelf-love, or rather a conſci-
ouſneſs of her own defeᴄt, having forc'd
her to be ſerious.

The new married-couple being return'd home with all their friends and
relations, great rejoycings were made;
and after the banquet was ended,
which was very ſplendid, they oblig'd
me to dance, in order to divert the company. I was as good as a *Punchinello*
to theſe delightful creatures, and indeed
my dancing made them laugh very
heartily. Some of them, who were
more polite and humane than the reſt,
came to me, and deſir'd me, by ſigns,
to excuſe their laughing, ſince it was
impoſſible for them to refrain from it;
they told me however, that tho' my
ſhoulders were even, and my breaſt flat,
I yet ought not to be ſo much dejeᴄted,
ſince nature does not indulge a fine ſhape
to every one; and that it is not in our

power

power to be otherwife than fhe has made us. So true it is, that nothing is really deform'd or ridiculous in itfelf; and that whatever appears fo to our eyes, is fingular and uncommon only by comparifon. However, the lady of the houfe, who had always forbore laughing, defir'd the company to fpare their raillery, and not ufe me with contempt. We always have an affection for thofe who refemble ourfelves, tho' the fimilitude be in our imperfections. The next day, they gave me a country fellow to conduct me to the fouthern part of the ifland, where the ftrangers abovemention'd like myfelf, were faid to be. I then took leave of the family, and thank'd them for all their favours; and fetting out with my guide, he accompanied me two leagues, and pointing out to me the way I was to go, left me. I travell'd feven days, and at laft, after having loft my way, and fuffer'd very much from hunger, thirft, fatigue and uneafinefs, I at laft came to the place to which I had been directed.

1

I was agreeably furpriz'd to meet
with feveral, who were friends and
neighbours to our country, *viz. Dutchmen.* As moft of them underftood *Englifh,* I told them my ill fortune, and
begg'd them to let me ftay among
them. They receiv'd me with great
civility, and told me, there were an
hundred and fifty of them, who, like
myfelf, had met with foul weather, and
been oblig'd to run-a-ground upon that
coaft; that they had not during the
fix months they had liv'd in it, once
left the coaft where I then found them,
and had always ftood upon their guard;
that hitherto they had been unmolefted;
and that the only incivility they had
receiv'd from the inhabitants, who
appear'd very ugly and ill-fhap'd,
was, to have been frequently laugh'd at
by them; whence they judg'd that they
were a prefumptuous, arrogant, wag-
gifh, malicious people; qualities commonly found in the deform'd.

And now, faid they, we are perhaps
condemn'd to fpend the remainder of
our days in this melancholy condition,

we having nothing left but a long-boat,
which is fo crazy, that we dare not
venture to fea in it. We have a few
able fhip-carpenters among us, but thefe
cannot refit her, becaufe there is no
iron in this ifland, and confequently it
will be impoffible for us to fell any timber. And tho' we were to do this
with fharp ftones, like the inhabitants of
the country; of what ufe would our
little planks be to us, fince moft cf the
iron of our boat is broke to pieces, and
too old to ferve again?

This difcourfe, which made me almoft defpair of feeing my country more,
gave me very much uneafinefs; but, I
at laft fet my mind at eafe, and refolv'd
to live like thofe I was got among; and
fpend all my days in hunting, eating
and drinking. How many country-
Efquires, fays I, in *England*, lead the
very fame life? What do they elfe?
and yet they are highly fatisfy'd with
their courfe of life; whilft on the other
fide, the inhabitants of cities, who fpend
their time quite differently, have them
in the utmoft contempt; and look upon
them

them as a fett of men, equally brutifh
with the beafts they declare war againft;
much after the fame manner, as the
inhabitants of this ifland defpife us, and
think our fhape and way of life equally
ridiculous. After all, fince I am reduc'd to this unhappy condition, 'twill
be in vain for me to repine at it.

I therefore went a hunting with all
my exil'd companions ; and cuftom
which makes all things familiar, made
me infenfibly take pleafure in an exercife, I before almoft thought unworthy
a rational creature.

One day, as I was returning from
the chafe, being got into a pretty deep
valley, I perceiv'd certain cracks,
by which mines are generally found.
I immediately ran to my companions,
and telling them of it, engag'd them to
come the next day and break up the
ground; in order to fee whether we
fhould not meet with iron, in the place
where I had feen thofe cracks. We
had not digg'd above a foot, before we
were agreeably furpriz'd to fee a fine,

B 2   round

round mafs of oar. Having look'd fome time about it, we alfo had the good fortune to find an excellent lime-ftone of great ufe in melting iron. Upon this happy difcovery, we refolv'd fome time after to build a little furnace. Having no caft-iron to build the vaults with, we made them of ftone. We made a pair of bellows out of fome of the planks of our boat, which we put together; cover'd them with skins, and faftned them with wooden pegs. The nofe of this clumfy pair of bellows was made of a piftol-barril. The difficulty was to make the bellows play, and as we had no water near the furnace, we were oblig'd to fix them in fuch a manner, that we might be able to manage them with our hands, as the fmiths do in *Europe.*

Having a great quantity of wood, we made as much charcoal as was requifite for lighting our furnace. We dug a proportionable quantity of iron out of the mine, and after the ufual labour, we caft a fow of about three hundred

dred weight. This operation was fo
much the more furprizing, as we had
nothing to work with but wooden
pokers.

Having caft our fow, we made it into
hammers, fuckers, anvils; and continued to melt the iron, that we might be in
a condition to work foon at our forge.
For this purpofe we built a chafery,
where we employ'd our cleats, and
our bellows; we laid a bottom of caft-
iron, and made bars of different fizes,
wedges, hatchets, faws, pincers, vices,
nails, and every thing neceffary for
building a fhip. A lockfmith in our
company, was of great fervice to us in
fhaping feveral pieces of iron, and making the fteel for our different tools.
Our anchors coft us a vaft deal of labour, however we at laft finifh'd
them.

We afterwards fell'd feveral trees;
thefe we faw'd, and with our tools
wrought them into mafts and yards.
We faw'd the timber into planks of
different fizes, when our carpenters,
who were very good workmen, began

B 3   to

to build the veffel, and made fuch difpatch, that in a few months fhe was almoft compleated. But now we were
in want of cables, tar, and cloth to
make fails with. To procure thefe,
we gave feveral pieces of our caft and
wrought iron to the inhabitants, who
came in crouds to admire our work,
and were now fo accuftom'd to fee us,
that they no longer burft out a laughing. We, I fay, barter'd feveral pieces of our iron, for ropes and cloth, of
which they gave us great quantities ;
and likewife tar made of a fine turpentine,
which diftill'd from lofty fir-trees fituated in the north part of the ifland.

Our veffel being completely built, we
caulk'd her tight, and likewife tarr'd our
ropes, which we made into cables of all
fizes. We fet up our mafts with their
top-mafts and fhrowds, and fix'd the
yards with the feveral geer. At laft,
after above a years labour, we launch'd
our fhip, and call'd her the *Vulcan*, becaufe fhe ow'd her original to the forge,
which we had fo happily built in a country where there never had been any before. 'Twas

'Twas then the curiofity of the inhabitants increas'd to a prodigious degree. One of them ofter'd us a confiderable fum, upon condition that they might fhew our fhip for money, in that part of the ifland where fhe then lay, which we agreed to. Crouds of people flock'd daily to the fight, and their aftonifhment was not inferior to their curiofity, and a confiderable fum of money was gain'd by it.

C H A P. II.

The emperor of the ifland of the Crump-backs *comes to fee this veffel. Their departure. A fea-fight, in which they are victorious.*

THERE was among us, continued Capt. *Harrington,* a young fellow who had a great talent for learning languages. This man having made a little progrefs in that of the country we were in, had been of great fervice to us in the trade we had been oblig'd to carry on with the natives; in order to purchafe fuch things as were neceffa-

B 4   ry

ry for us before we left the island.
He was our interpreter in a visit we
then receiv'd from an envoy sent by
Dossogroboskow, emperor of the island,
the LXXVII of that name; a monarch
who had reign'd with glory upwards
of thirty years.

The envoy told us, that his *Independance*, (which is the title of honour given to their emperors,) having heard of
the prodigious canoo we had built, desir'd we would carry it to him, in order for his viewing it; that for this
purpose, he would send us as many camels, as might be necessary for making
the carriage of it to court the easier.
We answer'd by our interpreter, that
his *Independance* desir'd an impossibility;
and that in case he wanted to see our
canoo, he must give himself the trouble
to come to the coast, where we would
endeavour to receive him with all
the honours due to so great a
prince.

He answer'd, that he must be oblig'd
to take the dimensions of the great canoo, in order to satisfy the emperor,
who

who he faid would never condefcend to come and fee her, unlefs he were firft fhewn the impoffibility of conveying her by land. Immediately he went on board our veffel, and having taken all her dimenfions very exactly, and calculated her burthen, he promis'd to make a faithful report of the whole to his *Independance*; and endeavour to demonftrate to him, that there was no poffibility of conveying her by land. He fet out, and return'd fome days after, to acquaint us, that on the morrow, the emperor and his whole court would come to fee the canoo; and therefore we muft prepare to receive him in a manner fuitable to his exalted dignity.

Unhappily we had no cannon, which was a great difappointment to us, fince it would prevent our making a figure on fo glorious an occafion. The envoy told us, that as foon as his imperial majefty fhould be advanc'd within an hundred paces of us, all we had to do, was to fall proftrate with our faces to the ground, in teftimony of adoration;

adoration; that after this we ſhould riſe; and that our chief, or the inter-preter in his name, and in the name of us all, ſhould make him a ſhort com-pliment, to declare the admiration with which his auguſt preſence fill'd us; and the deep ſenſe we had of the ſingu-lar honour he condeſcended to do us. At the ſame time, he gave our firſt captain, whoſe name was *Van-Land*, a kind of ſpeaking-trumpet; and told us, that whenever the emperor gave audi-ence, thoſe whom he indulg'd that ho-nour, were not allow'd to approach his ſacred perſon nearer than the diſtance of an hundred paces; and conſequently that they muſt uſe a ſpeaking-trumpet in diſcourſing with him; and that his chancellor always deliver'd his anſwers thro' the ſame inſtrument.

He told us farther, that whenever the emperor ſhould come forward, in order to view the great canoo, we muſt retire an hundred paces to the left: that however, he would ſend his mini-ſters and courtiers to entertain us. Having acquainted us with theſe whim-
ſical

fical formalities, we ask'd the envoy, if, in addreſſing any of the prince's miniſters or courtiers, any titles of honour were beſtow'd upon them, ſuch as your *lordſhip*, or your *excellence* : he replied, that 'twas cuſtomary among them to beſtow titles of honour upon perſons, not from the qualities of their minds, but from ſuch as ſuited their ranks and dignities. As for inſtance, ſays he, in addreſſing a miniſter of ſtate, we ſay your *Affability*; a military man, your *Humanity*; a commiſſioner of the treaſury, your *Diſintereſtedneſs* ; a judge, your *Integrity*; the Brachmans who attend upon the emperor, your *Knowledge*; the ladies, your *Rigour*; the young noblemen, your *Modeſty*; and all the courtiers in general, your *Sincerity*. Our interpreter got theſe ſeveral titles by heart, and promis'd to obſerve them, as far as his memory wou'd give him leave.

The next day, the emperor having mounted a huge camel; preceeded by a large body of life-guards, and follow'd by a numerous train, arriv'd about three in the afternoon. Being come within

an

an hundred paces of us, he ftopt; upon
which we immediately fell proftrate,
according to our inftructions. We
then rofe up, when our interpreter taking the fpeaking-trumpet, made a
compliment to his *Independance,* which
lafted five minutes. The chancellor's
anfwer, which was very polite and
eloquent, took up thirty feconds; and
this being done, we drew off to the
left, in order to make room for the
emperor, who getting into our canoo
with fome of his favourites, fet out
towards the fhip; but as his *Independance* was very fat and unweildy, all the
courtiers were forc'd to lift him into
the boat, but he had like to have tum-
bled into the fea. He did us the honour to ftay two hours on board; and
his courtiers having view'd her one
after another, were in the higheft admiration at fo uncommon a
fight.

The emperor was look'd upon as
one of the fineft fhap'd princes, that
had ever fat upon the throne of that
ifland. He was very tall and corpulent.
His

His ſhoulders were vaſtly broad, between which there aroſe a perfectly convex hump, that quite eclips'd
his ſhoulder-blade, and ſham'd all
the camels of his train. Another
natural protuberance he had before, fell down to his ſtomach, and
was almoſt contiguous to his prominent belly. This, in the eyes of
his ſubjects, diffus'd a majeſtic gravity
over his whole perſon.

Our interpreter diſcours'd with ſeveral of the courtiers, who told us very
politely, that they ſhar'd with us in
the joy we muſt have felt, in having
had an opportunity, of adminiſtring a
new pleaſure to their auguſt ſovereign.
But now the emperor having ſeen and
examin'd the veſſel at leiſure, and applauded our great art and skill, return'd into the canoo, when mounting
his camel, he departed with his whole
train. Before he left the place, he
ſent our captain his picture, ſet with
diamonds and emeralds, which was
very like his majeſty, except that the
artiſt had flatter'd him a little, by
drawing

drawing his protuberances a little larger than the life.

In the mean time, as we cou'd not leave the ifland before a month; and that each of us had not above five or fix charges of powder left, it was refolv'd we fhould husband our provifions till we embark'd ; and keep our powder to knock down game two days before we fet fail, in order that we might not be forc'd to broil it. Accordingly we made a refolution to live upon fifh till we fet out; but then we were unprovided with nets, which was a great difappointment to us; however, we fupply'd the want of them in the following manner.

I went into a neighbouring wood, and cut eight very ftrait branches, which I made into poles of ten foot in length. I afterwards got our lockfmith to make five or fix hundred little hooks, all of them very fharp pointed. Thefe hooks, being baited with pieces of flefh, were fix'd to my poles; and I fet them on the ftrand when the tide was out, knowing it would be cover'd with water at the

return

return of it. I waited for this, in order to fee whether the waves would not carry away my poles, but had the fatisfaction to find they kept tight and firm, and indeed I had drove them in very ftrong. Three hours after it was ebb, when I faw all my poles loaded with fifh of different fizes. I then went and call'd feveral of my comrades, and defir'd them to help me in bringing along the great cargo of fifh I had catch'd. They were agreeably furpriz'd to find I had had fuch good fport. We repeated it for feveral days till we fet out, and catch'd fo much fifh, that we carried great quantities on board with us.

Having put fufficient ballaft into our veffel, and being prepar'd to embark, a general chafe was order'd for three days together. Fortune was fo favourable, that we kill'd a great number of wild oxen, deer, and feveral other animals, all which we carried on board the veffel; and at laft, a favourable gale fpringing up, we weigh'd anchor and fet fail for *Europe.*

A

A week after, by an obfervation, we computed we had ran an hundred and thirty leagues. We were not in want of a compafs, our mate having given us an excellent loadftone, he had happily fav'd from the wreck, and with this he touch'd a needle which our lockfmith made. But unluckily we had not one great gun on board; and having no other arms but our fabres, bayonets, muskets and piftols, as our powder was gone, the latter confequently could be of no ufe; fo that we were very un-eafy left we fhould be oblig'd to fight. However the firft engagement we met with, procur'd us the very thing we wanted, as the reader will prefently find.

We had now gone on in our courfe for about two months, when we dif-cover'd a pirate of *Achem* who gave us chafe. We crouded all our fail in or-der to get clear of her, but to no pur-pofe, and fhe came up with us. We then prepar'd to put ourfelves in a pofture of defence, and join'd in opinion with the captain, the pilot and the mate, that

that we ſhould endeavour to grapple
with her, ſhe being a ſmall veſſel, and
her crew very inconſiderable.

Accordingly we did ſo, and after
having ſtood a few broad-ſides, which
did us very little damage, we got to
windward of the pirate, and ſoon
grappled with her. Immediately we
boarded her, thoſe at the head puſhing
forward with their drawn ſabres, and
the reſt with their bayonets fix'd upon
the muzzel of their pieces. The barbarians, who were much inferior in number
to us, aſtoniſh'd and confounded at this
bold action, were moſt of them cut to
pieces; ſo that we got poſſeſſion of
their veſſel, which we clear'd of the
proviſions, goods, powder and whatever
tackle and rigging might be of ſervice
to us; and were overjoy'd to find
twenty four pieces of cannon on board
her; and this being done, we put the
pirates on board their own ſhip, not
thinking it proper to encumber our
veſſel with ſuch priſoners.

'Tis now, ſays Capt. *Harrington*,
about two months ſince this happen'd;

Vol. II.   C   and

and as by taking this prize, we have got
India goods of great value on board,
such as callico's of *Bengal* and *Surrat*,
and *China* silk, we are resolv'd to sail
for the south-sea, and there carry on a
private trade. Happily, chance carried
us near the island on which you was
cast; and a calm having detain'd us in
the road, you spy'd us, and implor'd our
succour. Let us ever, my dearest *Gulliver*, bless providence, whose ways are
unsearchable; and always put our greatest confidence in it, tho' we should be
opprefs'd with numberless misfortunes.

I now, says he, have told you all my
adventures, since we parted, by which
you find I have led a very melancholy
life; however, my fortunate meeting
with you, has restor'd me to all my
joy. In the mean time, let me know
why you seem to regret the place you
lately came from. Are you dead to
those impressions, which a love of liberty, and the desire of seeing again
one's native country, inspires all other
men with? Has the continual series
of ill fortune, which has attended
you,

you, caſt a deadly damp upon your mind?

I cou'd not then forbear telling him the violent paſſion I had felt for *Abeno-uſſakee*'s daughter, and how I was tortur'd, when I ſaw her, overcome with the blackeſt deſpair, leap into the ſea, at my leaving her. Capt. *Harrington* did all that lay in his power to comfort me, and told me very obligingly, that he had two daughters in *England*, who were look'd upon as very pretty women; that in caſe we had the good fortune of reviſiting again our native country, I ſhould take my choice, and at the ſame time promis'd to ſettle half his eſtate upon me; that he was oblig'd to me for refcuing him from ſlavery in the iſland of *Babilary*, which, he ſaid, was ſuch an obligation, as it wou'd be impoſſible for him ever to repay.

C H A P. III.

The author goes on shore on Estate's-
land. *Description of the different
islands of* Terra del Fuego. *Islands
of poets, geometricians, philosophers,
musicians, and actors.*

THE discourses I frequently had
with Capt. *Harrington*, allay'd,
in some measure, my anxiety; reason
began insensibly to resume its throne,
and the deep anguish which sat brood-
ing over my spirits, was now a little
abated. Two days after our being on
board, a gale sprung up, which tho' not
a very favourable one, we yet weigh'd
anchor. We spread our sails, and
ply'd to windward. The wind afterwards blew very favourable, so
that in about six weeks we entred
the streights of *Magellan*, between
Terra del Fuego and that of the *Pata-
gons*. 'Tis well known that *Terra del
Fuego* was discover'd in 1520 by the
famous *Fardinand Magellan*, who took
it

it for a large ifland; but mariners have
fince difcover'd that this land does not
confift of one fingle ifland, but of a
confiderable number, which lie very
high, but are little known to this day.
The inhabitants, if we are to credit the
Spaniards, are giants; but other nations, who have gone into the fouth-
fea thro' the ftreights of *Magellan*, inform us, that thofe iflands are inhabited by people, who, tho' very robuft,
are but of the ufual ftature; that they
live like fo many beafts; and tho' they
inhabit a very cold climate, they yet
go naked, and dwell in the holes of
the mountains.

In my opinion, they all have impos'd upon us; and I'm perfuaded
thefe people are as much civiliz'd, as
the nations of the fouthern part of
America have been in all ages, who
are feperated from them only by a
very narrow *Streight*. Be this as it
will, the difcoveries we made in our
paffage thro' the ftreights of *Magellan*,
may be of fervice to correct the miftake we have hitherto been in with

regard

regard to thofe iflands, whofe inhabitants were fuppos'd to be wild, unpo-
lifh'd, untractable men. However,
'tis certain that fome of them at leaft
are peopled by men who are far
from meriting the name of favage,
as will be fhewn in the fequel.

Our crew were for putting into
Eftate's-land, the moft fouthern of all
the iflands. It was formerly difcover'd
by the *Dutch*, who have given fuch a
general and confus'd idea of it, that
we may conclude 'tis but little known
to them. Curiofity prompted us to fee
whether that ifland were really barren
and uninhabited, as was reported; or
whether it were poffible to make a
fettlement upon it, and carry on a trade
there. We coafted feveral iflands, and
being got near that of the *Eftates*, were
very much furpriz'd to fee a boat rowing towards us, fill'd with people
in *European* habits, who drawing near
the fhip, fpoke to us in *Dutch*, and in-
vired us to caft anchor in their port.
They guided us through the midft of a
multitude of rocks which form'd a
kind

kind of bulwark round their ifland, that wou'd have barr'd our entrance, had we not made ufe of the long-boat. 'Twas then *January*, and the feafon was vaftly hot; but they affur'd us 'twas very cold in thofe parts in *June* and *July*. We went up a little bay, which form'd a pretty fecure road, and caft anchor in a nook on the left.

So far from finding the ifland barren and uninhabited, we faw a very fruit-ful populous country. I am fure my eyes never beheld fuch handfome men and women; and I can affirm, that I did not meet with fo much as one per-fon who was the leaft deform'd. A *Dutch* veffel, as we were told, ha-ving caft anchor at that ifland in 1673, but upon what defign I cannot tell; found the country fo lovely and fruitful, the inhabitants fo kind and po-lite, and particularly the women fo beau-tiful, and fweet-temper'd, that the crew cou'd never be prevail'd with to quit fo delightful a place, which abounded with every thing that could be wifh'd; a place where love, the ftrongeft of all tyes, kept

C 4 them

them in fpight of themfelves. Accordingly, they thought no more of their
country and families, but marrying feveral women of the country, (polygamy being allow'd both by law and cuftom) they
had children by them, which increas'd
their affection for that charming fpot.

The reader will fuppofe, that we
met with a hearty welcome ; and indeed I never fpent my time fo agreeably in any place before or fince; infomuch that we were tempted to imitate
the *Dutch*, who at the fight of this
country, had forgot their own. But
our captain, and the reft of the officers,
being of an age not to be enfnar'd by
female charms, eafily refifted the temptation. As for myfelf, I muft confefs
I fhould have been captivated, had
not the judicious advice which Capt.
Harrington gave me, check'd my natural
fondnefs for the fair-fex. He told me,
that the beauty of a woman ought never to tempt us to engage in fuch tyes
as were lafting; that I ow'd myfelf to
my country and family; that my father might poffibly be dead; and that
I

I was bound to affift my brothers and fifters, who were ftill very young.

During my ftay in this ifland, I one day faw the natives croud about the port, and embark haftily on board a great number of little veffels. I enquir'd the reafon of that, of a young man, whofe name was *Wanottef*, born in that ifland of *Dutch* parents, who gave me the following anfwer. You are to know, fays he, that this ifland is furrounded with feveral others, with whom we trade, and this trade is of feveral kinds. In the ifland of *Foolick*, fituated five leagues from hence to the north-weft, will fhortly be open'd a celebrated fair, which is kept every year about this time. To give you an idea of the curious wares which are fold at this famous fair, I muft firft tell you, that the moft confiderable inhabitants of that ifland are all poets, who pretend to be infpir'd by heaven. They affirm themfelves to be defcended from one *HEROSOM*, an illuftrious poet of great antiquity, fon to the fun and moon, whofe celeftial defcendants, they fay, are inceffant-

ly

ly indulg'd the influence of thefe two
powerful planets. They adore this
HEROSOM, and pay him a moft
folemn worfhip. Like him, they
fpend their whole lives in writing
verfes of every fpecies, all which
they vend in a grand manner at the
fair abovemention'd.

I then ask'd *Wanouef*, whether this
trade were advantageous and profitable. Of little profit, fays he, for the
ifland in general is very barren, and the
inhabitants miferably poor; but then,
happily for them, they defpife riches;
and the poetical traffic, which is the
only one, produces fufficient to maintain the people, and defray the fmall
expence of the nobles, or in other
words, the poets. As the kingdom is
elective, the monarch is always chofen
from among thefe; but the electors are
themfelves chofen out of the body of
the people, otherwife the grandees
would eternally fquabble about the
election; each of thefe would aim at
the crown, becaufe there is not one
among

among them, but thinks he himfelf beft deferves to wear it.

Don't the grandees, fays I, fometimes foment great troubles in the State? Very often, fays he; the government is obnoxious to frequent revolutions, occafion'd by the ambition of the Great, who are vain, haughty, jealous, fickle, factious, and reftlefs. About twenty four years ago, one *Hoftoginam* was chofen king. His reputation at that time was very great among the people. His juft, fagacious, fublime mind, and his great wifdom and extreme politenefs, gain'd him every voice. However, he did not fpeak his own tongue with the utmoft purity, which was the only objection that cou'd be made to him. The language of the grandees of this kingdom is vaftly difficult, becaufe they are oblig'd to fpeak in cadence, rime, and meafure; and to ufe a peculiar ftile, which is very different from that of the vulgar.

But *Hoftoginam*, notwithftanding this defect, was elected king. In the beginning

ginning of his reign, the people had no
reason to be diſſatisfy'd with their
choice, for he held the reins with the
moſt conſummate prudence, and govern'd with the utmoſt policy and moderation; he had the moſt tender regard for the grandees, whoſe frailties he
flatter'd, and conceal'd all their faults;
but as to the people, he was now become
their idol. However, this learned and
judicious prince, experienc'd the viciſſi-
tude of all ſublunary things. As he was
a prince of great underſtanding, and an
enemy to novelty, he attempted to aboliſh the worſhip of *HEROSOM*, whom
he affirm'd to be a mere man; and ſaid,
he did not deſerve that altars ſhould be
erected in his honour. He publiſh'd a
proclamation for the aboliſhing of this
worſhip; but this was look'd upon as the
moſt barefac'd impiety, and diſguſted the
nobles no leſs than the common people.
The former call'd a parliament, repre-
ſenting the whole nation, who were of
opinion, that as *Hoſtoginam* was convicted of a deſign to ſubvert the antient religion of the country, they therefore ſhould
ſummon

fummon him to revoke his fcandalous
edict, and immediately recognize *HE-
ROSOM* as god. *Hoftoginam* refus'd
to comply, and oppos'd the confpirators
with a fmall number of his faithful
fubjects, who had approv'd his innovation; and were as incredulous, at
leaft, as himfelf, with regard to the
pretended divinity of the father of po-
efy. This occafion'd the utmoft confufion, and 'twas in vain that *Hoftoginam*
relied upon his feeble authority, and
the love of his fubjects; for by this
time it was grown very cold.

That of the grandees, which now
was more powerful and in greater credit in the ftate, refolv'd to enquire into
the genealogy of *Hoftoginam*, and affirm'd he was not one of the poetical
defcendants of *HEROSOM.* 'Tis not
known, whether this accufation was
well or ill grounded. But be that as
it will, this pretended difcovery was
made a handle to ruin him, and accordingly he was try'd and declar'd to
have forfeited his crown. As feveral
perfons of great authority were his
friends,

friends, some of the grandees voted to have him put to death; however, this cruel motion was unanimously rejected, and *Hostoginam* was only banish'd to a royal palace, situated on the banks of a river which flows by the capital city. Here he spends his life with his old friends, men of equal merit with himself, who still adhere to him in his misfortunes; a rare example of fidelity, of which there are few instances in history.

In the mean time *Bastippo,* who had the chief hand in dethroning the prince, was rais'd to the throne, and crown'd with the utmost solemnity. This prince would have been rank'd among the most illustrious that ever reign'd in the island, had he been more politic, and behav'd with greater moderation. But he had no manner of regard for the grandees; so far from it, that he endeavour'd to lessen them; treated them with contempt upon all occasions, and went such lengths as to use several of them ill.

But now the friends of the ejected monarch, took advantage of the discontent of the grandees, and form'd a conspiracy confpiracy againſt him, in which they engag'd thoſe very perſons who had rais'd him to the throne. The inſurrection became univerſal, inſomuch that the new king was forc'd to quit the iſland, for otherwiſe he would have fallen a ſacrifice to the vengeance of the grandees. Ever ſince that time, the government has ſunk to a kind of anarchy, the people not having yet agreed to elect a new king.

I was extremely pleas'd with theſe particulars, and ask'd *Wanouef*, whether the fair of the iſland which drew ſo many merchants to it, abounded with commodities. Yes, ſays he, of all ſorts. One ſhop is full of tragedies, another of comedies; here we meet with operas, (the words I mean,) cantata's and paſtorals; there epic poems; here, ſatyrs, epiſtles and elegies; there tales, fables, epigrams and ballads. Some ſhops are ſtock'd with every ſpecies of poetry, from the epic poem and tragedy, down to the ballad and riddle. There are alſo manufactures of all prices, but nothing ſells ſo cheap as ſpiritual ſongs.　　　　　　　Have

Have all the merchants, fays I, who
buy thefe feveral particulars, a good
market for their wares. That's as it
happens, fays he. As moft of the
buyers who retail out their goods
again, are no judges of their value;
they are often impos'd upon, and
oblig'd to fell that for a trifle, for
which they paid a great price. Befides, the trade thefe retailers carry
on, is not very confiderable; for the
goods they purchafe at *Foolick* fair, are
always fearch'd before they are fhipp'd
for the other iflands, and what is
moft grating, are fometimes confifcated
by the infpectors.

But, fays I, interrupting him, are
there no orators, philofophers and
geometricians in this ifland? If there
are any, how is it poffible for them to
fubmit to a poetical government? We
formerly, fays the *Dutchman*, fwarm'd
with them, but they have been drove
out, as fo many difturbers of the peace,
becaufe they contemn'd the pofterity of
HEROSOM, or the children of the
fun and moon, tho' they are defcended
from

from the earth and air. Thefe were
for ever exclaiming againft poetry; they
depreciated the beft manufactures, and
put the moft celebrated artifts upon
the fame foot with thofe contemptible caper-merchants, whofe art, faid
they, is equally difficult and unprofitable.

The orators are happily retir'd into a
very fruitful country, where neverthelefs
moft of them are either over-grown with
fat, or reduc'd to fo many skeletons. But
the philofophers and geometricians have
been forc'd to inhabit a dry, barren
country, in which nothing is found but
bitter fruits, and is befides choak'd up
with briars and brambles. 'Tis here
the geometricians fpend the day in
drawing figures on the fand, and in
demonftrating clearly to one another,
that one and one make two; and
the night in obferving the cœleftial motions, infomuch that one would think
they were fo many inanimate Beings. A deep filence reigns through-
out the whole ifland; and they meditate fo intenfely on curves, obtufe an-

Vol. II.   D   gles,

gles, *trapeziums*, and other mathema-
tical figures, that one wou'd conclude
their minds were moulded into thofe
fhapes.

As for the philofophers, fome employ themfelves in weighing the air,
others in meafuring the feveral degrees
of heat, cold, drynefs, and moifture;
in comparing two drops of water, and
examining whether they are exactly
alike; in hunting after definitions, that
is, in fupplying the place of a word by
feveral others equivalent to it; in difpu-
ting on the nature of exiftence, on in-
finity, on modal entities, the origin of thought, and fuch like topics,
which they look upon as highly worthy the employment of the human mind.
They take a particular delight in
raifing vaft edifices, call'd by them
fyftems. Thefe they begin at top, and
fhore them as well as they can, till
fuch time as the foundations are laid;
but very often, while this is doing, the
building falls to the ground, and bu-
ries the architect under its ruins.
Some of them are perpetually talking
of

of *Vortices*, and the *materia subtilis*; others about absolute accidents and substantial forms; whence it is, that such as have had the curiosity to visit our island, purely for instruction, return almost as ignorant, as those who never came among us. In fine, this country is always cover'd with a perpetual snow; the roads are very bad, and travellers frequently lose their way in them.

Tho' the inhabitants of *Foolick*, says I, would not permit philosophers, orators, and geometricians to live among them, I presume they had not the same antipathy to musicians, since their art bears such an affinity to poetry. Musicians, says he, don't live in the poetical island, but inhabit one that lies very near it, where they are suffer'd to spend their days in peace and tranquility, provided they pay tribute to the king of *Foolick*. Their island is vastly agreeable, and no other sound is heard in it, but that of voices and instruments, which form a perpetual concert: the parterres of their country-houses are so

dispos'd,

difpos'd, that they look like pieces of mufic prick'd upon paper: all their gardens are fo many mufical compartments, where all kinds of airs are found at fight; fo that it may be juftly affirm'd, that the groves, the trees, and flowers are really fung in this country. Their houfes in general are hung with operas, cantata's, interludes, and fonatas; the people always fing their words; and the moft common trifling things are exprefs'd in recitativo, and the moft melting airs. They are fubject to a monarch whofe fcepter is in the fhape of a cylinder; this he always holds in his hand, and therewith checks their flights, and whimfical maggots. In fine, they are all voice or all ear; infomuch that they feem not to make the leaft ufe of their other fenfes, much lefs of the rational faculties: however, we are affur'd they would be very reafonable creatures, were it poffible for good fenfe to be prick'd down like mufic. They buy up vaft quantities of the commodities of *Foolick* fair, but of the very worft
sort;

fort; but then they have the art of fetting the moft wretched performances, in a very advantageous light, by their learned fophiftication; befides, what they gave but a very trifle for, they vend at a very high price.

Another fort of men, who inhabit an ifland which is not very far diftant from it, follow almoft the fame method, and are no lefs gainers by it. The people I mean are players; a polite and aimable fett of creatures, whofe fole aim is to pleafe. They travel into all the iflands round about them, where they build ftages, and fpend their whole lives in fpeaking in public. Their government is far from being regular, and is a kind of anarchy. We are affur'd, that they underftand perfectly the art of giving elegance to flat verfes; ftrength to low and trifling thoughts; fublimity to rants; and grace to the moft trite circumftances. In a word, I don't know whether it would be poffible for the inhabitants of *Foolick* to fubfift, did

not

not the players and muficians, confume
the greateſt part of their commodities.

C H A P. IV.

*Sequel of the defcription of the iſlands
of* Terra del Fuego. *Iſland of
phyſicians, and that of gluttons.*

AFter this account, which I thought
amuſing enough, but dare not
quite affirm it to be matter of faƈt, as I
know it only by hear-fay, the *Dutchman*
continued to relate the following particulars, which I ſhall ſet down with the
fidelity of an hiſtorian. Since I, fays
he, have mentioned thefe feveral iſles to
you, I muſt not omit a very famous
and wealthy one, which alfo is one
of thofe that the *Europeans* have improperly call'd *Terra del Fuego.* 'Tis that
of phyſicians. It produces nothing but
manna, rhubarb, caſſia, fena, and ſuch
like medicinal plants. All the artificers
are either apothecaries, or makers of
ſiringes, inciſion-knives and lancets.
All its waters are mineral, fo that
the

the foil yields nothing neceſſary to the ſuſtenance of the body, or the convenience of life.

However, the people are very rich, and enjoy an affluence of all things. As the inhabitants of the other iſlands fancy they want their aſſiſtance, they go thither in crouds, and carry great ſums of money along with them, but generally return from thence, naked and pennyleſs, in caſe they are able to return, for ſeveral of them die there. And indeed their plains are ſo many wide-extended church-yards, the air thereof being very dangerous, particularly to foreigners, notwithſtanding the ſalubrity of the plants. The inhabitants of *Foolick*, affirm there is a ſubterraneous paſſage in this iſland, which leads to hell by very ſhort paths, and that the ſprings of *Acheron* and of *Lethe* are found in it.

The goverñment of this iſland is like that of antient *Rome*. The phyſicians who preſide in the adminiſtration repreſent the patricians; and the ſurgeons, who compoſe the ſecond body

D 4 of

of the republic anſwer to the plebeians. Both of them aſſemble daily
in a gloomy palace, hung with black
velvet. 'Tis here all their conſulta-
tions are held, but with this difference,
that the former, who compoſe the
higher houſe, form their eſſays and diſcourſes on the living, and the latter on
the dead.

Theſe two bodies hate one another,
as cordially as the ſenate and people
of *Rome* us'd to do; the former has alſo its conſuls, and the latter its tri-
bunes. The firſt are perpetually endeavouring to humble and depreſs the
laſt; but as theſe are more numerous,
and powerfully protected by the
prieſteſſes of the goddeſs of *LOVE*,
who is greatly rever'd in this iſland,
they maintain their ground with great
vigour, and defy the empty efforts of
their adverſaries, tho' they at the
ſame time look upon them as their
maſters.

The former, finding the latter began
to triumph over them, publiſh'd ſome
years ſince a large volume in quarto,
intitled,

intitled, *The murthers committed by the furgeons*; containing a lift of thofe they either maim'd or butcher'd during a century. The furgeons, by way of reprifal, publifh'd a lift of thofe whom the phyficians had difpatch'd in the courfe of ten years, which we are told fwell'd to twenty volumes in folio, on a very fmall letter; with the fignatures of the feveral Relations of thofe they affaffinated in the margin. The publication of thofe twenty volumes, occafioned by their inteftine feuds, has prejudic'd them in the minds of feveral inhabitants of the neighbouring iflands, who confider them as man-flayers. However, they ftill maintain their reputation, and people yet confide in them, the reafon of which is, that the love of life is ftronger than a thoufand arguments or experiments; befides, the cure of one fingle perfon, obliterates the remembrance of a million they have fent out of the world.

After all, it muft be confefs'd, that fometimes, 'tis not their fault, if a patient does not recover; however,

ever, the world is fo partial, that they would have them cure every one that comes under their hands, as tho' life and death were abfolutely in their power, and it were poffible for them to change the decrees of fate. Thefe people have a kind of *Alcoran* or *Tal-mud*, the precepts of which they fol-low to a tittle; their ftatutes not al-lowing them to deviate from it. Lord have mercy upon thofe whom this *Al-coran* or *Talmud* fentences to die !

Befides thefe furgeons who are for ever rebelling againft the phyfici-ans; this ifland is infefted by another kind of refractory mutineers, who are equally abhorr'd by both. Thefe are your quacks, that practice phyfic in a fraudulent manner, who are treated like our pedlars that fell with-out a licenfe; when thefe are catch'd in the fact, their ufual punifhment, is, to be forc'd to fwallow down all the aloes, mercury, and pills that is found in their houfes. Further, we are told, that thofe phyficians exclaim againft celibacy, which they are fup-pos'd, pos'd to do either from a confcientious, or political motive, in order to attone for the injury which their art does to nature.

The men who contribute chiefly to the wealth of this ifland, are the inhabitants of a neighbouring one, lying weft-ward, whofe government is wholly hierarchical, that is, entirely fuperintended by the priefts of the god *BELLY*, call'd in their language *BARATROGULO*. This ridiculous deity is reprefented in his temple under a monftrous fhape. 'Tis a fhort ftatue, but vaftly corpulent and unweildy, whofe prominent belly is four ells from fide to fide. Its goggle-eyes are very large, in comparifon of its head, which is narrow, flat, and earlefs; its jaw-bones appear very wide, and are arm'd with fharp-pointed teeth; and in its mouth, which is made to gape continually, by means of a fpring conceal'd in the ftomach, is heard a noife made by the chattering of the teeth.

The

The God is feated before a table,
on which the fuperftitious people are
continually placing, in a moft devout
manner, viands and dainties of all kinds,
to feed the priefts of this temple, who
boaft a moft delicious corpulency, and
double chin; and in fhort are the very
picture of the canons in our cathe-
drals. One very odd circumftance is,
that they are what we call *Ventriloqui*;
for always when they are confulted, they
never give their anfwers by the mouth,
but by the belly. In a word, they are
heavy and indolent, and are generally
found with victuals before them. 'Tis
here thefe devout drones treat of all
affairs relating to religion or government; here they frequently chaunt the
praifes of the God they worfhip; nor
are they afham'd to affert, that the god
BELLY is the inventor of all arts
and fciences; and that he firft taught
men to labour in order to procure themfelves the neceffaries of life. But tho'
they won't give themfelves the trouble
of fetting a pattern to others, they yet
earneftly exhort the common people to
be

be laborious, and difpenfe none but the rich from working.

To conclude, the chief trades that are exercis'd in this ifland, are all relative to feafting and good cheer, and it abounds with cooks of all forts. The priefts, elect annually a doge or dean, who is chofen out of their chapter: however, this dignity is beftow'd on the moft deferving; and he who eats the greateft quantity, and gobbles it down fafteft, has the honour of being elected. The country abounds with pafture ground, which feeds a multitude of cattle, and is ftor'd with game of every kind. But notwithftanding this, a dangerous diftemper reigns perpetually in this country, which, had it not been for the conftant ufe of rhubarb, caffia, manna, fena, antimony, and the fyringe, would have long fince made a dreadful havock among the inhabitants, and been particularly fatal to the god who is the object of their worfhip.

Is it poffible, fays I, interrupting him, for thefe indefatigable eaters not to fall a prey to their voracious appetites?

tites? But then, why don't thefe glut-
tonous wretches ; thefe flaves to fenfuality, prefer a falutary regimen, to
the frequent ufe of naufeous potions,
which phyfic adminifters?

To prevent, fays he, their exceffive
corpulency from throwing them into
mortal difeafes, and efpecially apo-
plexies, they ufe an excellent prefervative four times a year; which is the
getting able furgeons to take down
their fat. Thefe, by flight incifions in
the moft mufculous parts, by corrofive
topical remedies, by repeated rubbings,
and the ufe of a catholicon, diminifh
their enormous fize; and thereby difpenfe them from the dreadful neceffity
of being abftemious.

With regard to the preparation of
purgative remedies, which they are
often oblig'd to take, to remove the
obftructions and fuffocations with
which they are opprefs'd, 'tis done
in fuch a manner, as no way inter-
feres with their fenfuality. Manna,
milk-thiftle, and fcamony, or bind-
weed, are boil'd in their broths; they
have

have a cullis of rhubarb, a fricaffee
of julips, pidgeons cook'd with fena,
pills tofs'd up in a ragout, a rump of
beef larded with caffia, a fhoulder
powder'd with mineral and vegetable
kermes; fallets made of the flowers
of the peach-tree and follicle, feafon'd
with antimoniz'd falt, foluble-tartar, oyl
of vitriol, and vinegar of fquills; *colo-
quintida* pies bak'd with quinces, and the
cruft made of *ricinus vulgaris* or indian
pine-nuts; cheefes and hams impregnated with *Epfom* falt, *fal armoniac*
and *polychrefton*; and laftly, preferves of elder, fweet-almonds and
province rofes. All thefe are fo learn-
edly prepar'd, and fo wonderfully
feafon'd by their cooks, who have
great skill in pharmacy, that they
are purg'd without knowing it; and
perceive it only by their ftrong reach-
ings; their breaking wind both ways
more frequently, than ufual; and their
copious and violent ftools, which
they forward by a few dofes of
tobacco. Before they go to reft,
they frequently drink a broth made
of

of henbane, mandrake and *ſtramo-nium*, this throws them into a ſound ſleep, and regales them with viſionary banquets.

CHAP. V.

The author narrowly eſcapes being de-vour'd by bears in the iſland of Le-tatiſpons. *The reception he meets with from the inhabitants. He lives among them. His converſation with* Taiſaco.

AFter we had reſided ſome time in *Eſtate's-land*, where we refreſh'd ourſelves, and ſeveral of our crew who were ſick recover'd their health, we took leave of the *Dutchmen* who had receiv'd us ſo courteouſly. Theſe gave us plenty of proviſions, and made us promiſe to call upon them at our return from the *South-Sea*, in order to bring them ſeveral things they wanted, which we hop'd ſuch of our *European* veſſels would furniſh us with, as carry
on

on a private trade on the coafts of
Chili and *Peru.*

We then fet fail the 17th of *Auguſt,*
1718, and directed our courfe to the
ſtraits of *Magellan,* which we paſs'd
very happily, and as the current
ran vaſtly ſtrong, in a ſhort time.
After leaving *Cape Victory* to our ſtar-
board, and then the iſland *Madre de
Dios,* being got off cape *Diego Cal-
lego,* it blew ſouth-eaſt, upon which
we refolv'd to make a little to ſea-
ward, in order to attempt to diſcover ſome iſlands, in that part of the
Magellanic ſea, in which our geographers
have not placed any. I hinted this to
our captain and the chief officers, and
at the ſame time took notice, that it
was inglorious for the *Europeans,* not
to have made any diſcovery in thoſe
parts, for thefe fifty years laſt paſt.
Alas! I foon had reaſon to repent my
giving this fatal counfel.

Being in about the 45th degree of
fouthern latitude, and the 269th of
longitude, we diſcover'd an iſland
Vol. II. E which

which appear'd to us large, and worthy of being vifited.

We did not wonder that the *European* veffels which go to *Chili* and *Peru*, had not yet difcover'd it, becaufe they ufually coaft along that pacific ocean; and are in no danger of ftorms, thefe being as rarely met with as rocks in thofe parts.

Being come within two leagues of that land, call'd, as I afterwards found, the ifland of the *Letatifpons*, we caft anchor, and our captain with fome *Dutch* officers, feveral of our *Portugueze*, Capt. *Harrington* and myfelf, got into the long-boat, and were row'd fafe to fhore. We firft found a folitary place, cover'd with tufted trees; but afterwards perceiv'd a little beaten path, whence we concluded that the ifland was inhabited. We follow'd the track, keeping clofe together, and went near half a league up it without meeting either man or beaft. I got a confiderable way before the reft, having a brave young *Portugueze* in my company, who lov'd walking

ing as much as myfelf, and was no lefs
impatient to gratify his curiofity. We
left the path, and going up a pretty
fteep mountain, the better to view the
country, we left our company behind
in the valley.

We were fcarce got to the top,
when we faw feveral bears of an enormous fize coming down on the left fide of
the mountain. Our companions feeing
them, did not dare to advance forward,
or ftay till they were come up, and
therefore thought it would be beft to
go back. We were then for coming
down the mountain, as they did, but
were intercepted by the bears. Their
number and fize, notwithftanding that
we were arm'd with fabres and muf-
kets, terrified us very much. In this
dreadful dilemna, recollecting I had
heard, that the way to efcape thofe
fierce creatures, was to fall upon
one's belly, and lie motionlefs on the
ground, and not difcover the leaft
fign of life, I refolv'd to do fo, and
bid my companion do the fame, which
he did accordingly. The bears came

up to us, and finding we did not ftir, they went away without doing us any harm. In the mean time, our companions, who ran as faſt as their feet would carry them, feeing us at a diſtance extended on the ground, in the midſt of thoſe cruel beaſts, and ſuppoſing we were kill'd, return'd on board; ſo that we were left in an unknown country, abandon'd to grief and deſpair.

I faid to *Silva*, for ſo was the young *Portugueze* call'd, that it would be proper for us to remove from that dangerous place, and follow the beaten road. We trac'd it for five hours, without meeting ſo much as one human creature or a ſingle habitation. At laſt, about ſun-ſet, we met a man who ſeem'd to be about eight and twenty. He wore a cap made of red morocco leather, ſhap'd like a cone, the ſides whereof were ſett off, and faſtned with a claſp; a kind of ſurtoot made of green ſattin deſcended almoſt to his feet; under which ſurtoot he wore a red waiſtcoat, and
breeches

breeches and stockings of the same
colour, which were tied together.
We made him a very low bow, and
going up to him, gave him to understand by the most expressive gestures,
that we were two unhappy strangers,
who stood in need of his succour.
But how great was our surprize when
he spake *Spanish* to us, and told us,
we had an *European* air! he ask'd us
what part of *Europe* we were born in,
and what chance had brought us into a
country so little known to the rest of
the world. We answer'd him in the
same tongue, that one of us was a native of *England* and the other of *Portugal*; and then acquainted him with
the long voyage we had made; the
reason of our landing in that island;
and the fatal accident which had separated us from the rest of our comrades.

Unhappy travellers! says he, be
not dejected because you are forc'd to
stay in this island, for you are got
among a most beneficent people, whose
chief law is hospitality, and assisting
the wretched. Follow me, says he;

I'll

I'll carry you to a village that is not
far from hence. Supprefs the grief
and anxiety that appear in your countenances; I'll take you into my own
houfe, and depend upon't my wife,
my children and grand-children will
be overjoy'd to fee and fuccour you
to the utmoft of their power.

Overjoy'd at this compliment, we
return'd our unknown patron a thoufand thanks for his generous offer; but
cou'd not think how it were poffible
for fo young a man to have great grand-
children. In the mean time we walk'd
towards the village, and in the way,
ask'd our guide whether he were born
in *Spain* or *America.* I was, fays he,
born in the village to which you are
now going; and don't wonder if I
fpeak *Spanifh*; for I was in *Chili* about
threefcore and ten years ago, and
there learnt the *Spanifh* language. I am
glad you was not born in a country, the
natives of which, fir'd with an infatiable thirft of wealth, deftroy'd a million
of fouls in *Chili,* which was once the
fineft fpot upon earth, but is now wild,
and

and very thin of inhabitants, and fubject to the *Spaniards*, who govern it with a rod of iron. 'Tis a great happinefs for us that we are fecur'd from their tyranny; and, we thank Heaven, that the moft valuable metals in our ifland are copper and iron. But, the advantages we enjoy are vaftly preferable to imaginary riches; we breathe a pure air; our fruitful foil produces wholefome food, which enables us to live to a great age; and our lives are unruffled with cares and infirmities. In other countries, people die of age; here, my countrymen, after having liv'd a long term of years, die with youth; but this is a paradox, you will comprehend and admire, after you have liv'd fome time among us.

We arriv'd at the village, which, it being dark, we entred privately. Our guide, whofe name was *Taifaco* as we afterwards found, going thro' it, carried us to his houfe, which was large, and immediately prefented us to a boy drefs'd in black fattin clothes, whom we took to be about ten or twelve

E 4   years

years of age, for whom he feem'd to
have the higheſt reſpeᴄᵗ. This boy,
who had a magiſterial air, and whoſe
judgment feem'd to be ripe, receiv'd
us with great civility; and after *Taifaco* had told him our caſe, he gave
orders that we ſhould be well us'd.
At the ſame inſtant the whole family
came about us. *Taifaco* pointing to a
woman, who look'd to be thirty, told
me ſhe was his wife; and daughter to
the perſon, to whom he had juſt before
preſented us. We bow'd to the
ground, and begg'd her to indulge us
her proteᴄᵗion, and honour us with her
favour. Her husband, who was
pleas'd to be our interpreter, told her
we were *Europeans* that had been
abandon'd on the coaſt by our companions, thro' the dread they were under
of being devour'd by the wolves of the
foreſt of *Arisba*, who had oblig'd them
to run to their canoos. She anſwer'd
with the utmoſt politeneſs, that ſhe
thank'd her husband for the honour he
procur'd her; that ſhe was deeply
affeᴄᵗed with our misfortunes, and
would

would do all that lay in her power to make us happy. At the fame time *Taifaco* bid his daughter come forward, who feem'd to be about five and forty; who curtzing very modeftly, prefented her children to us, the oldeft whereof feem'd to be of the fame age as his grand-father, and older than his great grand-father.

Silva and I gaz'd one upon the other, but cou'd not poffibly conceive this genealogical order; upon which *Silva* whifper'd in my ear; Thefe people have a mind to be merry with us; they certainly take us for a couple of ftupidly-credulous fellows; I wonder how long they intend to joke upon us in this manner. Being more us'd to furprizing incidents, and having much more experience than he, I defir'd him to fufpend his judgment, till we knew more of the matter.

Then *Taifaco* carried us into a room, where fervants were waiting to bathe us, and give us clean linnen and filk robes after the fafhion of the country. This pleas'd us mightily, we being fo dirty,

dirty, that we were afham'd to appear
in fo frightful a pickle before the ladies. We were bath'd in perfum'd
waters; and being drefs'd, we waited
upon the company, and a moment after
were told dinner was ferv'd up.

Immediately they open'd the door
of a large dining-room, that was finely
illuminated. The grand-children
walk'd into it firft; then the fons and
daughters; afterwards the grand-father
and grand-mother; and laft of all, the
young great grand-father, who taking us
by the hand,fat down firft at table,placing
me at his right hand, and my companion
at his left. As the children walk'd
into the dining-room before their fathers and mothers, and had not offer'd
to let us go in before them, I fuppos'd
they had done this by way of compliment, a circumftance that no ways furpriz'd me, as I knew it was the cuftom
in feveral countries.

Taifaco, who fat next me, interpre-
ted to me in *Spanifh* moft of the particulars that were mention'd at table.
Among other things, they difcours'd of

a

a wedding, which was to be celebrated fhortly, between a man of thirty and a woman of threefcore. They pitied this woman mightily for marrying a man of that age, fince he, according to the courfe of nature, muft feel a decay for thirty years together. They alfo fpoke of a man of threefcore, who was going to marry a girl of five and twenty; and faid, fhe was either too young or too old for her intended hufband, who, they affirm'd, ought to have made choice of a woman of threefcore and ten, or a girl of fifteen. What a paradox was this to us, who were unacquainted with the fingular prerogative the inhabitants of this country enjoy'd!

Now, tho' I cannot exactly tell what it was we eat, nor give any manner of idea of the tafte of the victuals, I yet fhould be heartily forry the reader fhould not know that we far'd delicioufly. But 'tis certain we eat no flefh; for as thefe people believe the tranfmigration of fouls, they never kill any animals but fuch as are noxious;

and

and thefe, they never dare to feed upon.

'Twas in this entertainment that I was inform'd of their notion on this head; for having ask'd *Taifaco* what kind of victuals we had eat of, which had fo exquifite a tafte; he told me, that our repaft confifted wholly of the herbs and roots of the country, which are of a fingular kind, and were drefs'd after a peculiar way. We, fays he, don't imitate the *Spaniards* and other *Europeans* in their cuftom of eating animals; a fatal cuftom, which, in fome meafure, has made the fhedding of human blood familiar to them. Are not brutes endued with fouls? What right has man to divorce them from their bodies, and make their fubftance fubfervient to the nourifhment of his own, fince the earth indulges him with a liberal hand, a numberlefs multitude of roots, herbs and fruits, which he is allow'd to feed upon.

Silva liftned to this difcourfe with a difdainful air, and difcover'd his ignorance

rance by an awkard fmile. As he was
wholly uninform'd by education, the
prejudices he had imbib'd in his infancy, completely refuted, as he imagin'd, *Taifaco's* doctrine. As to myfelf, who had ftudied philofophy very
young, and paid no regard to vulgar
and national ideas, unlefs they agreed
with that reafon which heaven has im-
planted in the foul; methoughts our
patron's doctrine deferv'd to be refuted
in another manner.

I firft explain'd to him the two
fyftems eftablifh'd among us with regard to the fouls of brutes. The firft,
fays I, which is but little follow'd, does
not allow them the leaft intellectual
fenfation or knowledge. According to
thofe who follow this opinion, brutes
are inanimate Beings, entirely dead to
pleafure and pain, to fear or love.
You fee that according to this fyftem,
the charity you have for them is very
ill plac'd; and that 'tis as lawful to
put them to death, as to fell trees, to
cut up herbs, or pull up plants. But
as this fyftem, which confiders brutes

as

as so many machines, is patroniz'd by none but a set of whimsical people, who are wholly unattentive to the voice of nature; I never take advantage of this, to justify the custom we have of killing and eating animals. The opinion which prevails most univerfally at this day, and which indeed appears the most rational, is, that brutes are endued with souls, but of an inferior kind to those of men, as it neither reflects or resolves; is fix'd by objects; govern'd imperiously by its passions; and absolutely sway'd by all its impulses. 'Tis manifest then, that brutes are vastly inferior to men, since the soul of these thinks, reflects, compares, and resolves; has a full power over all its actions; the faculty of distinguishing between virtue and vice, and the liberty of chusing which it thinks proper.

Tho' I were to grant you all this, says *Taifaco*, I yet cannot see how any inference can be drawn from thence, to favour the privileges you ascribe to yourselves, of killing and feeding up-

on

on animals. If brutes, fays I, are fo
much inferior to us, they are of a different fpecies from ourfelves, and confequently we are not bound by any
obligations to be tender of their lives.
For this very reafon, fays *Taifaco*, you
ought to fpare them. 'Tis mean to
take advantage of the weaknefs of the
brute creation, and opprefs them merely
becaufe you are ftronger than they.
Why do you treat them thus, fince you
yourfelves would be very unwilling to
be us'd in that manner by them ? You
hate thofe cruel beafts, that rufh'd upon you near the foreft of *Arisba*, and
had like to have torn you to pieces;
we likewife look upon them as our
enemies, and therefore don't fcruple to
kill them whenever they come in our
way ; it being natural to kill one's ad-
verfary : But is it juft to entertain the
fame opinion with regard to harmlefs
and innocent animals, who never do
the leaft injury to man ; and efpecially
the feathery creation, whofe plumage
is as delightful to the eye, as their
harmony is to the ear ?

I

I anfwer'd, that as all animals in general had been created for the ufe of
man, it confequently was lawful to
kill and eat them; that providence had eftablifh'd a regular fubor-
dination among the feveral fpecies of
animals, which was the reafon why
fome ferv'd for food to others; that
the fouls of brutes perifh'd with their
bodies, whereas that of man was immortal, fo that, properly fpeaking,
they refembled us only in the organi-
zation of their bodies. Then *Taifaco*
attempted to prove, according to the
Pythagorean principle, that the fouls of
brutes don't perifh with their Bodies;
but all his arguments appear'd to me
mere fuppofitions, wholly unfupported
by proofs; and indeed, I puzzled him
very much, when I prov'd to him, that
the fyftem of the tranfmigration of
fouls, was inconfiftent with the wifdom
of the creator.

C H A P.

C H A P. VI.

Queftions propos'd to the author, and his
anfwers. He is told that the inhabi-
tants of the ifland of Letalifpons *en-*
joy the happy prerogative of growing
young again.

HAving difcours'd on this fubject
till fupper was ended, we rofe
up from table, and were defir'd to
walk into a flower-garden, the moon
fhining very bright, in order to breathe
the cool and fragrant air. The inhabitants of this country, are, by an exprefs law, enjoyn'd to walk an hour
after meals. Being firmly perfuaded
that this exercife is a great friend to
digeftion; they look upon this inftitution as a very wife one, as indeed they
do all the reft, moft of which relate to
the prefervation and prolonging of
life.

The ladies having defir'd us, with
great civility, to relate fome of the adventures we had met with in our tra-

Vol. II.   F   vels,

vels, I gratified their curiofity by *Tai-faco*'s affiftance, who always was my interpreter. They liftned with plea-fure to the account I gave them of what had befall'n me in the ifland of *Babilary*, and ask'd me a thoufand que-ftions about it. They enquir'd particu-larly, whether the indolence and effe-minacy, into which the fuperiority of the females had plung'd the other fex, was not prejudicial to thofe very wo-men, who triumph'd over them.

Thofe men, faid they, who are of an effeminate caft, are not men; furely, they muft perform the feveral functions of their fex in a moft wretched manner; and we may prefume their country is not very populous. I was furpriz'd to find thefe ladies hit at once upon the very circumftance in which the govern-ment of *Babilary* is defective; and this gave me a moft advantageous idea of the fharpnefs, as well as folidity of their underftandings. I anfwer'd, that indeed their ifland had been very thin of inhabitants ever fince that revolution; but that the ambition of the women

was

was fuch, that they look'd upon this
difadvantage as very trifling, and imagin'd they might eafily remedy it, by
the privilege they affum'd of divorcing
their husbands, whenever age, conftitution, or behaviour rendred them obnoxious. This privilege, fays I, which
the women have arrogated, keeps their
husbands in awe, and obliges them to
fhew them as much refpect as if they
were fo many lovers. But then, the
only advantage they reap from all their
complaifance and affiduity to pleafe
their wives, is, to fufpend for fome time,
the divorce with which they are perpetually threatned, the fatal period whereof
happens after a certain number of years.
For very few of thefe are fo conftant,
or have the courage to keep their huf-
bands when once they grow in years;
nay, their very old women are mighty
fond of changing their husbands.

The ladies cou'd not forbear fmiling,
when the youngeft of *Taifaco*'s grand-
daughters, who feem'd to be about fourteen, defir'd her grand-papa to ask me
at what age women generally married

F 2   in

in *Tilibet.* I forbear repeating the expreſſion ſhe employ'd on this occaſion:
words which raiſe a bluſh in our language, are indifferent in theirs: they
having no ſuch thing as an indecent
phraſe among them. *Taiſaco* interpre-
ted her queſtion exactly, and I anſwer'd
it, by telling him that their women generally married at three years of age.
Heavens! ſays ſhe, with ſome warmth,
had I been a native of that country, I
ſhould have been a wife theſe eleven
years! Oh, ſays I, I have ſeen ſome of
your age that had buried four husbands,
but then they were far from boaſting ſo
many charms as you are miſtreſs of. How
happy, ſays ſhe, wou'd thoſe women
be, if, as they are ripe ſo ſoon, it
were poſſible for them to live as long as
we do, and afterwards revive in all the
bloom of youth.

'Twas then *Taiſaco,* who before had
not given me the leaſt light into this
matter, told me, that in his country,
men and women generally liv'd to
an hundred and twenty years of age;
that their vigour did not decay till their
ſixtieth

fixtieth year; after which, fo far from waxing old like the reft of men, they grew young again, and returned to the bloom of life. We cannot fay, continued *Taifaco*, whether the inhabitants of this ifland, are a peculiar kind of creatures, to whom the eternal fovereign of the world, has indulg'd this happy prerogative; or whether we owe it to the purenefs of the air, the falubrity of the plants and fruits; the regular and undifturb'd life we lead, or our laws, which prohibit us either to ufe too much exercife; to be too fedentary, or give ourfelves a prey to the paffions. However this be, 'tis a wonderful advantage we have enjoy'd from time immemorial; an advantage which gives us a fuperiority over all other nations. Look upon me, fays he; I am turn'd of fourfcore and ten, and my father you fee there, is one hundred and nine.

Silva, upon hearing what he laft faid, fix'd his eyes attentively upon this little great grand-father of one hundred and nine; and examin'd his features

fo

fo narrowly, that he at laſt diſcovering in his juvenile and even blooming countenance, ſome almoſt imperceptible furrows, which time had made; he then whiſper'd me in the ear, and made me obſerve it alſo. His skin ſeem'd a little ſhrivel'd, and was not fluſh'd with that vital juice, which is ſeen in a young countenance; he look'd like fruit gather'd over night, which in the morning loſes the bloom it boaſted upon the tree. The compariſon we made between him and his great grandſon, plainly ſhew'd this difference. Tho' *Taiſaco* himſelf had a healthy, freſh and vigorous complexion, neverthelefs, when it was narrowly ſurvey'd, it plainly appear'd to be a little worn. He reſembled in one ſenſe to ſuch of my countrywomen, as are fond of pleaſing in ſpight of years; ladies who have the art of putting off twenty years every morning, and of reſuming them every night when they go to bed.

I don't wonder, ſays I to *Taiſaco*, that the air you breathe, the eaſy and unruffled

ruffled life you enjoy, and the regular
courfe of diet you obferve, fhould
make you live longer than the reft of
men; for thefe feem to do all that lies
in their power to fhorten their days.
What furprizes me, is, to find that old
age, with refpect to you, is but a kind
of eclipfe, which you retrograde as it
were; and recover the feveral years
you had loft, by returning back to the
flower of youth and even childhood itfelf.

Light, fays *Taifaco*, is an emblem of
our life; it dawns every morning in
our hemifphere; it increafes infenfibly
as the lamp from which it flows rifes
higher; and after the fun has been at
the meridian, it leffens imperceptibly,
and returns to the fame degree, the
fame point, where it appear'd at its
rifing. You wou'd not, fays he, be
furpriz'd at any of thefe things, did
you not confine the power of the e-
ternal fovereign of the univerfe, and
imagine, that nature obferves the fame
laws in all places: but this regularity
and uniformity, you afcribe to her,

fuppofes

Renders God
Barren and impotent?
by Reducing nature
to a System of Regular
laws

ſuppoſes her barren and impotent. As for inſtance, had we never ſeen any but our own people, we could not have be-liev'd there were men in the world, who died of age.

What! ſays I, interrupting him, don't all animals and plants die of age; and is not this ſufficient to make us conclude, that human creatures ſub-mit to the ſame fate? We, ſays *Taifaco*, make a great difference between old age, and what we may call antientneſs. Animals and plants die, like us, of antientneſs; but not of old age, unleſs ſome cauſe changes this uſual courſe of nature. 'Tis ſo with men, whenever they don't obſerve the laws of health, which have long ſince been eſtabliſh'd in our country; if we labour too im-moderately, or are over ſedentary; if we don't curb our paſſions, which light up and nouriſh a conſuming fire in our bodies; we then always die, re-cent, as it were, or old, but never of antientneſs.

We then heard the ſound of a kind of violin, upon which all the company return'd

return'd into the room, where we had
fupp'd. *Taifaco* inform'd us, that his
countrymen always danc'd every night
after fupper; and this, he faid, was
not the moft inconfiderable of their
laws with regard to health; and added,
that the ladies would be mightily diverted to fee us dance after the *European* manner. *Silva* and I anfwer'd,
that we would not make the leaft
fcruple to oblige them in that particular, but defir'd them to begin, in
order that we muft firft fee the nature
of their dances, and be encourag'd by
their example. Then the youngeft of
the family open'd this kind of family-
ball, in which all danc'd fucceffively;
now fingle, now in couples; fometimes
four, and by and by all together; and
ever with the utmoft regularity and
grace. It now being our turn to dance,
I defir'd the violin to play again a
certain air which pleas'd me, the movement whereof was in the nature of a
jig; and the whole company were
mightily pleas'd. As for *Silva*, he
danc'd a double ftep, and was more
                              applauded

applauded for the lightnefs of his heels than his air.

Then the ladies took their leave and withdrew. As for *Silva* and I, *Taifaco* carried us into an apartment, confifting of two rooms, the furniture of which was plain, but very neat, and the beds were mighty foft. This, fays he, is your abode, where I wifh you may enjoy the fweeteft flumbers. Sleep in peace, amiable ftrangers, and banifh every gloomy reflection from your minds.

Having made this compliment, he faluted us civilly, and bid us good night. As *Silva* and I were very much tir'd, after returning thanks to providence for its great care of us, we went to bed, and immediately fell into a found fleep, and did not awake till late the next morning.

C H A P.

C H A P. VII.

Taifaco *explains to the author the laws of health eftablifh'd among the* Leta-lifpons.

THE refin'd aliments we had fed upon fo heartily the night before, for we were very hungry, did not at all difturb our reft in the night. We had now been awake fome time, when *Taifaco* came to us, and after having ask'd us in a very obliging manner how we had flept, he order'd breakfaft to be brought up; and when this was over, he propos'd our taking a walk to a very agreeable place, where he affur'd us we fhould meet with a great deal of pleafure.

Immediately we left our apartment and follow'd him. The firft thing he made us obferve, was the rural beauty of feveral houfes we faw in the way. We, fays he, never build cities; I am told there are fome in *Europe* which are of a vaft extent. As for myfelf,
who

who have only seen those small ones,
which the *Spaniards* have built in *Chili*;
I suppose that the great cities in *Europe*, are rather a confus'd heap of prisons and dungeons, than a range of
edifices built in a commodious manner.
How is it possible for you to be calm
and undisturb'd, when you're surrounded with such a numberless multitude
of men? Are you not incessantly pester'd
with visits and affairs; frequently those
of other people? Methinks cities are
to men as cages to birds. The celestial fire which animates our bosoms,
will not be pent up; it pants after the
cooling breeze and embowering shade;
'tis there it has leisure to meditate with
freedom, and is more secure from those
prejudices which the passions suggest.
In large cities, the numberless vices,
so far from being palpable, must insinuate themselves in all places unperceiv'd. There virtue must be obscur'd, and generally be destroy'd by
deprav'd examples. A country-life
is made up of exercise and action.
That which whets the appetite,
strengthens

ftrengthens the body, and makes it more robuſt. Our laws are therefore very prudent in forbidding us to build cities. Were we to imitate the *Europeans* in that particular, we probably ſhould ſoon loſe the privilege which is indulg'd us, of living a long courſe of years, and the happy advantage of growing young again.

Taifaco then enquir'd into our laws of health. We anſwer'd, there were none eſtabliſh'd among us; and that our Legiſlators had never once thought of ſearching any method of prolonging our lives; ſo far from it, that moſt of our laws were calculated to ſhorten its period, by the difficulties they brought upon us. Beſides, ſays I, we value and eſteem a man who ſleeps little, works much, leads a life of ſeverity, defies the inclemencies of the weather, heat, cold, hunger, thirſt; and who feeds upon nothing but juiceleſs food, which heats his blood and prejudices his health.

You don't then, ſays *Taifaco*, conſider life, as the foundation of all happineſs,

pinefs, and health as the greateft advantage man can boaft? Did the eternal fovereign of the univerfe indulge you life, that you fhould make fo bad a ufe of it? Have you no more regard for this cœleftial gift? We, fays he, who look upon life as the greateft bleffing, do all our endeavours to prolong it, and to detain the foul, as long as poffible, in the body it actually animates, for which purpofe we have excellent Precepts.

We then asked, what was the general purport of thofe laws, and whether they were very numerous? They don't, fays he, include above four or five articles, which I'll explain to you in a few words. The firft law relates to the air we breathe. By this important article, we are exprefly commanded to live in that place, whofe air agrees beft with our conftitutions, whether it be our native air or not. For the air we firft drew, cannot be wholefome, unlefs it has that degree of temperature which agrees with our conftitutions. We have thermometers, barometers,

rometers, hygrometers and anemome-
ters, by which we difcover the quality of the air that furrounds us; and
to find out that which fuits us ftill better, there are skilful men among us,
who, by obferving attentively how
thofe who confult them breathe, pronounce infallibly what kind of air their
conftitution requires. 'Tis prov'd, that
the fermentation which is found in all
fluid fubftances, is owing to the air :
judge then the great influence the air
has over us, fince it enters not only at
the mouth, and the reft of the natural
conduits ; but alfo pervades the outward pores of the skin. And indeed,
when we compare the changes which
air produces in the animal œconomy,
with thofe which food occafions; we
find that fuch as are caus'd by the
former, are much more confiderable. We
are, in general, commanded to breathe
a wholefome air ; for which reafon,
we, as I told you before, are efpecially forbid to build cities, where vapours neceffarily arife, which are clogg'd
with heavy corpufcles, capable of cor-
rupting

rupting the whole mafs of blood. Too
fharp an air, like that of high mountains, may be very pernicious; becaufe, as the column has not height
enough in thofe places, and confequently renders the preffure of
the air very weak, it fwells the
lungs, and makes one breathe fhort.
I fhall here, for the fake of the curious
reader, obferve, that in this country,
water is us'd in barometers, and not
mercury; agreeable to the opinion of
the learned *Boyle*, who tells us, he had
found by experiments, that the weight
of the atmofphere is much more fenfible
in the barometer, when water, than
when mercury is us'd for that purpofe.

The fecond article, fays he, relates
to food. I have already told you,
that chymiftry has taught us the art
to refine our aliments, and reduce
them to a kind of quinteffence. We
are not indeed abfolutely forbid to
feed upon herbs, roots, pulfe and
fruits, fuch as we receive them from
the hand of nature, after having
drefs'd them in a proper manner; but
then,

then, we are commanded not to eat too much, nor to feed upon too great a variety, fince this makes fermentation more difficult; we then digeft flower; and the chyle, being compofed of too great a number of heterogeneous particles, cannot eafily complete that perfect mixture, fo requifite to nourifh every part of the body. With regard to liquids, we never drink cold water, but always mix it with hot. I know that 'tis more agreeable in the midft of fummer, to drink not only cold water, but fuch as is cool'd with ice; but we find that ice, inftead of quenching the thirft, rather inflames it; that it's chill clofes the pores of the palate, and ftops the falival fprings, whence the radical moifture flows which tempers the warmth of the blood.

The third article relates to bodily exercifes. By our laws we are commanded to proportion our exercife to the food we eat; fo that if we eat little, we don't do much work; and on the other fide, if we labour much, we eat a large quantity. From

this judicious harmony between labour
and food, 'tis that we are so seldom troubled with diseases; and are enabled
to enjoy the singular prerogative which
nature has indulg'd us, of returning to
the bloom of life. The motion of the
muscles, excites the natural heat;
assists the circulation of the blood;
helps the distribution of the aliments;
prevents and removes all obstructions,
and increases perspiration.

The fourth article relates to sitting
up a nights and sleep. The laws forbid our inverting the order which nature has prescrib'd, and command us
to rest in the night, and work in the
day; and to let the proportion between
them be as three to one. For if sleep be
necessary to relax the fibres, and ease
and refresh the body, when it has been
fatigued with the labours of the day;
'tis certain, that nothing contributes more
to weaken it than too much sleep, this
wasting the spirits more than exercise.

The fifth article, says he, relates to
the irregular impulses of the soul,
which are as contrary to health, as
moderate

moderate bodily exercife is advantageous to it. To prevent the fatal effects
of thefe, we are taught from our infancy to curb the paffions, and fupprefs
felf-love from which they always flow.
As anger acts more upon the body than
the other paffions, 'tis punifh'd with greater feverity; for 'tis on thefe occafions
that the exafperated foul, uniting all
its ftrength in an inftant, drives the
blood and fpirits to the extreme parts,
and fires the heart, whofe fyftoles
becomes fo violent, by the impetuous
efflux of animal fpirits, that the blood
being thus hurried into the arteries, inftead of entring the veins, extravafates
in fome meafure, and occafions that in-
ftantaneous flufh which is feen in the
countenance of a very angry man. The
very contrary happens in fear, for then
all the fibres in general are contracted,
and the blood is brought back again
towards the heart through the arteries;
whence it is, that people under any
terror are pale. As therefore, there
is fo great a mechanical tye between foul
and body, the impulfes of the former

G 2   act

act upon the whole mafs of fluids, and thereby invert the natural oeconomy. We have therefore great reafon to controul our paffions betimes, fince they have fo mighty an influence upon the conftitution; and to make the practical ftudy of moral precepts, the grand article in our education. Above all, we exhort our youth to indulge themfelves in the pleafures of love with moderation, fince excefs, on thefe occafions, is very fhameful and prejudicial.

But you, *Europeans*, fays he, on the contrary, only oblige your young people to ftudy feveral languages; and beftow much more care in cultivating their genius, than in moulding the heart, and eradicating the paffions; nay, you often prejudice their health, by forcing them to ftudy immoderately. Upon pretence of making them imprint deep in their memories, the traces of a numberlefs multitude of words and grammatical rules, you fhake the tender and delicate fibres of the brain; and when their memory is overcharg'd, it blunts the imagination and weakens the

judg-

judgment; and the knowledge which
you generally inftill into their minds by
dread, according to the * *Spanifh* cuftom, cafts fuch a damp upon the mind,
during the reft of their lives, as quite iner-
vates it. 'Tis not that we defpife learning, but then we apply ourfelves to it
with moderation. A medium is no lefs
enjoyn'd us with regard to the ftudy of
the fciences, than food; fince too clofe
an application to books, extinguifhes
the native heat, and interrupts and di-
verts the courfe of the animal fpirits.
The head, which is the feat of the foul,
and the palace of fcience as it were,
being thus heated by the uninterrupted
action of the fibres, and the habitual
tenfion of the nerves, ceafes to diftri-
bute the vital fpirits, which all flow
from it, into the feveral members;
whence a dangerous weaknefs and de-
jection arifes, and a kind of ftupor,
which haftens our diffolution.

G 3   C H A P.

* *The* Spanifh *proverb is,* La fciencia por lo
fangre entra, *that is,* knowledge enters by the
blood.

C H A P. VIII.

Learning of the Letalifpons. *Reflections on latin verfe and rhime.*

WE were equally pleas'd and attentive to the judicious and ufeful maxims which *Taifaco* fet before us; but were furpriz'd to find him a fort of phyfician, arguing clearly, and with the greateft propriety on the animal œconomy. However, we did not fuppofe there were any phyficians in this country, fince the inhabitants liv'd to fo great an age. *Taifaco* obferving our furprize, told us, that indeed there were no perfons among them who made a trade of curing others, every man being his own phyfician, in which, fays he, we imitate the example of all the brute creation, who in all their infirmities have recourfe to nature only; that befides, his countrymen were feldom indifpos'd, and never but when they infring'd their laws of health; that they always confulted their own reafon

and

and experience on thefe occafions; and
as every man was thoroughly acquainted with his own conftitution, which
he ftudied thoroughly, they cur'd
themfelves with the greateft eafe.

As he had mention'd the degree of
application they beftow'd on the fciences, and the efteem they had for letters, I ask'd him which fciences they
cultivated moft. He anfwer'd, that in
general they cultivated all, but that
they fet the higheft value on mathematicks and phyficks ; that generally,
they preferr'd to the ftudy of the fublime fciences, thofe of the polite arts,
fuch as mufic, poetry, eloquence and
painting; becaufe, as thefe arts amufe
the mind agreeably, and footh the
fenfes, they confequently were of advantage to preferve health and prolong
life.

Our poetry, fays he, is not like that
of the *Spaniards*, whofe verfe, notwithftanding the fublimity and majefty
of their language, has a tedious, difa-
greeable cadence, which proceeds from
the affected grandeur and monotony of
G 4 their

their words. Befides, rhime, tho' 'tis
thought a beauty, and is, as I have
been inform'd, the characteriftic of the
verfe of moft *European* nations, 'tis yet in
my opinion a contemptible invention,
and a childifh affectation. What can
be more ridiculous, and even more
tirefome to the ear, than that periodical
return of fimilar fyllables, plac'd regularly at the end of every line, with the
fame meafures and the fame paufes?
If nothing pleafes the fenfes more than
variety, how could men be fo filly as
to imagine that the ear would be delighted with uniform and fimilar
founds? Rhime muft certainly be a prodigious reftraint to a poet, and can never produce any thing that is capable
of giving ftrength or grace to a difcourfe, or of moving the foul. I
formerly could not forbear laughing,
to fee the heroes of the *Spanifh* tragedies die in rhime. But the moft abfurd
circumftance of all, was, to fee at the
fhifting of a fcene, the perfon who
came laft upon the ftage, and cou'd not
poffibly have heard the verfe that was
repeated

repeated the inftant before he appear'd, rhime neverthelefs to the laft verfe, which had been fpoke in his abfence, juft as tho' he had heard it. To fay the truth, fays he, I have no notion of your *European* tafte, nor the folly and extravagance of your Wits. Our verlification is purely metrical, and confifts of long and fhort fyllables, whence there refults a variety of harmonious founds, which, by the different degrees of their flownefs or rapidity, exprefs and excite, at one and the fame time, the foft or impetuous impulfes of the foul.

Such, anfwer'd I, was the verfe of the *Greeks* and *Romans*, nations of great renown in antient times, from whom we borrow'd all the arts and fciences which now flourifh among us. Tho' their languages are now dead, and the latin only makes a figure in our colleges and fchools, (we generally learning it in our infant years, purely to forget, or make no ufe of it the remaining part of our lives;) we yet have men among us, who, not only cultivate, and devote a
confiderable

confiderable part of their time to ftudy
the rules and genius thereof, but alfo
take a pleafure in compofing admirable
verfes in that language, tho' no body
reads them. Thefe verfes are much
more nervous, and boaft a finer grace
than ours: and a circumftance which
proves their genuine merit and beauty,
is, that fome poets among us write in
that language; tho' they are fure not
to be underftood.

'Tis great pity, fays I, that the tafte
for this harmonious verfe fhou'd be loft,
and that, by a fatal effe't of our ignorance, we fhould be forc'd to prefer to
it our vulgar, harfh, and uncouth founds.
The language of the antient *Romans*,
was, about an hundred years fince,
fpoke and writ by all the learned and
witty in *Europe*; who by means of this
common tongue, could mutually
communicate to one another their
feveral lights, and difcoveries. But
the vain and empty defire of being read and underftood by the ignorant, made them negleƈt that language; the applaufe it obtain'd, being
too

too little to fatiate their boundlefs vanity. Hence it is that they can't now
underftand one another without an interpreter, or are oblig'd to while away
their time in learning feveral vulgar
tongues. This abufe, fays I, is ftill
more fenfible with regard to *England*,
than any other nation in *Europe*. Our
† dry and almoft inharmonious tongue,
is hardly underftood out of our
own iflands; and yet our Literati ftill
write in it; fo that one would be apt
to conclude, they either were afraid, or
difdain'd to let foreigners fhare with
them in their riches. Poffibly too they
intend to force, in fome meafure, the republic of letters to adopt their tongue, or
in other words, to rank it among the learned languages, and put it upon the fame
foot with thofe of *France* and *Italy*,
which for fome years have boafted this
noble prerogative.

C H A P.

† *The* Englifh *reader will call to mind on
this occafion, that our author is writing a romance.*

C H A P. IX.

Defcription of the village of the Cerebellites, *and of the four Harpfi-*
chords. Admiffion of a new Cerebellite.

WHILE we were difcourfing in
this manner, we almoft got infenfibly to a village, which is very famous in this country, and call'd by the
inhabitants *Scaricrotariparagorgoolao*. I
was very much furpriz'd to view the
places which lie round about it, they
having fomething very whimfical in
them. I obferv'd on high mountains,
meadows that were water'd by feveral
pumps, and vineyards on the banks of
rivulets; fountains on the craggy tops
of rocks; cafcades every ftep we went;
and lone fummer-houfes built in a very
particular tafte, expos'd to every wind
that blows, on the top of which a numberlefs multitude of loud-founding
weather-cocks and moon-dials were
plac'd.

What

What you now fee, fays our guide, is the celebrated village of the *Cerebellites* of our nation. It was a very difficult matter for him to defcribe this kind of men, whom he at laft confefs'd pafs'd all defcription; however, we comprehended that the *Cerebellites* were very like thofe we call in *Englifh*, maggotty fellows, and the *French*, *Calotins*, a fett of people, whofe fruitful brain, notwithftanding the fire which confumes it, is productive of the moft odd and extravagant whims. 'Tis now, fays he, the fourteenth day of the moon, a day with them facred to mirth; you muft fee their exercifes and amufements. However, thefe people are neither fools or madmen; or if we muft give them that name, they are at leaft very witty madmen, and of a moft amiable caft of mind. To fay the truth, were it not for this fpecies of jovial creatures, whom providence has difpers'd up and down our globe, for the pleafure and delight of wife men, methinks we fhould lead very melancholy lives. And indeed I believe

there

there is no country but has its *Cerebellites*. Let us, fays he, firft go this way, for they generally meet in the large fummer-houfe which you fee to the left.

Being got there, *Taifaco* prefented us immediately to the prefident of the affembly, who was fhort of ftature, lean, and active; and his bald pate was cover'd with a *calot* or fcull-cap, made of a metal more refplendent than thofe of the reft of the company. All the *Cerebellites*, overjoy'd to fee two foreigners, fpectators of their periodical games, were wonderfully polite, and feated us in the moft honourable place, a little after which a kind of ball was open'd.

That which chiefly engag'd my attention, was the *Orcheftra* or mufic, compos'd of four harpfichords, which did not play in concert, but one after another. The firft, to the mufic of which they danc'd, was made of latten wire, at the end of which a great number of little bells, of a due proportion between the feveral fizes, were hung, whofe

whofe clappers being put in motion
by a light and skilful hand, gave a
fhrill and harmonious filver found,
and the cadence thereof was highly
worthy a *Cerebellite* ear.

The concert was follow'd by a ball,
compos'd of one family only. The
great grand-father fung the firft treble,
his fon the fecond treble, his grand-fon
the bafe, and his great grand-fon the
counter-tennor.

The bell-harpfichord was not employ'd in this concert, its found being
too fhrill to accompany the voices; but
another was us'd, made like ours, except that the ftops, inftead of making
the jacks jump up and down, and fhaking the latten wire by their motion;
turn'd, by fecret fprings, a certain
number of fmall wooden wheels, cover'd with a kind of rofine, each of
which turning about, made the cat-
gutt ftring found, which was contiguous to it, much after the fame manner
as our crowds, that have a wheel inftead
of a bow.

I

I thought this harpsichord infinitely superior to those of *Europe*, on which, such as are skill'd in this instrument know, the player can neither increase, diminish, or hold on the sound; but that they always have a harsh and grating kind of sound, tho' play'd upon by the finest finger. This on the contrary was vastly sweet, in proportion to its loudness: the performer could with great ease, make a close shake, hold on, diminish or swell the sound; so that methoughts I heard one of *Corelli*'s or *Vivaldi*'s concertos, perform'd by two *Violoncelli* or four string'd base, and four *Italian* fiddles.

I have lately employ'd a famous musical instrument-maker in *London*, to make a harpsichord after the above-mention'd model, and don't doubt but all the harpsichords in *Europe* which have hitherto been us'd, will then be as much despis'd as the guitar, the lute, and theorbo; instruments which are now as much out of date, as the persons who delight in playing upon them. However, I
thought

thought proper to make fome little improvement in that inftrument, by the advice of a perfon who is one of the fineft players in *England.* Inftead of that multitude of wheels, each of which by turning about, moves its correfpondent ftring; he hinted to me, that it would be better to reduce them all to one, and of a fize proportionable to that of the harpfichord, which is always to turn by the motion of the player's foot. So that, as in the harpfichord of the *Cerebellites,* the little wheel runs to the ftring; here, on the contrary, the ftring will always go after the great wheel; which is much more fimple, more natural, and eafy for the performer.

This concert, in a grave ftyle, was follow'd by a little burlefque one, that gave me the higheft delight, and was perform'd by the third harpfichord, the form thereof was intirely new. Fifteen pigs of various ages were plac'd in fo many different cages or holes. Under each of the ftops of the harpfichord, long needles were fix'd perpen-

Vol. II.   H   dicular,

dicular, the points whereof were directly oppofite to the pig's backs.
Now, according as the mufician apply'd his skilful fingers to the ftops of
the harpfichord, the needles always
run into the pigs, which being of different fizes, broke into plaintive notes,
fome fqueaking a third, others a fixth,
fome a fifth, and others again an octave.
The hogs which were to roar out the
bafe, were of a tolerable bulk, and
feem'd to grunt *Howhn*, as the little
pigs fqueak'd *Howihn* moft delicioufly.
And in order that the found which
each of thefe fweet animals breath'd,
might end clearly and regularly, and
not be rugged and uncouth to the ear,
there were pedals or lower keys in
this kind of organ, which, by means of
feveral thongs that were fix'd tight to
the pig's fnouts, made them ceafe their
harmony, whenever the player prefs'd
the ftops with his foot. I have fometimes been at concerts in this tafte,
when the harmony has not been fo
beautiful, nor the voices altogether
fo fweet. The inventor of this inftru-
                                    ment

ment informs me, that he is now tuto-
ring a fett of cats, and teaching them
to fing; a hint he borrow'd from an ingenious *Cerebellite,* who writ a book on
this fubject.

But a circumftance which gave me
the greateft pleafure, and at the fame
time the higheft idea of the *Cerebellite*
genius, was, the fourth harpfichord,
of which we *Europeans* have no notion.
The long life which the inhabitants of
that country are indulg'd, gives them
an opportunity of aiming at, and at-
taining perfection; whereas 'tis the
very reverfe among us, life being fhort,
and art long. This inftrument, which
indeed is made fomething like the
harpfichord, and therefore went by
that name, tho' it does not any way relate to mufic, is call'd in their language, *Tir-a-flook,* that is, an ocular
harpfichord, or *Tir-a-crac,* as much as
to fay, dramatic harpfichord; and is
never us'd but at the reprefentation of
automatonic comedies, or puppet-fhews.
A *Cerebellite* who was wonderfully well
skill'd in this art, by the fwift motions

and

and different sweep of his nimble fingers, which he press'd upon different stops, exhibited and mov'd up and down upon a stage, that rose up at one end of the harpsichord, several figures like to our puppets; and enliven'd them by the situations, postures, attitudes and various gestures, which his intelligent fingers communicated; and by an agreeable kind of squeak he gave them, disguising and modifying his own voice, an hundred different ways, to my great surprize.

The poet, who writ the piece represented by the dramatic harpsichord, was present. This virtuoso, says *Taifaco* to me, is a noble soul, who does not labour in the view of acquiring a chimerical glory, for this he despises. All he proposes in these kind of pieces, is, to exhibit to the public a polite and at the same time an useful entertainment. As some little satyrical pieces have been levell'd at him, with regard to the motives which prompt him to cultivate the muses; our poet, enflam'd with a truly philosophical bravery,

very, has taken for his device an afs
eating of thiftles, with this motto, *Let
them prick, fo they do but feed me*:
to fhew, that he fcorns the biting fatyrs which his poems draw upon him.
Thefe poems, tho' laugh'd at by the
public, are yet excellent in the opinion
of his appetite, which never fails to
applaud them.

After thefe diverfions, we were told
that a *Cerebellite* was going to be matriculated; a perfon, whofe numberlefs
fhining actions, and works of wit, had
merited him a place in that illuftrious
body. 'Twas affirm'd, that this worthy
profelyte had follicited this honour very earneftly; it being granted to thofe
only who fue for it in the moft urgent
manner. The new member, puff'd up
with a haughty modefty, and affuming
the air of a rafh philofopher, advanc'd
into the midft of the affembly, and
throwing himfelf at the feet of the
prefident, firft took an oath to obferve
all the ftatutes of the fociety, which
were reduc'd under three heads, in-

H 3   cluding

cluding the whole of human life, *viz.*
thoughts, words and actions.

With regard to thoughts, he promis'd folemnly, firſt, to follow always
the firſt, and never to regard the fecond; the *Cerebellites* maintaining that
the fecond thoughts are not preferable
to the firſt. 2dly, Never to think as
the reſt of the world do; but always
to hunt after fomething new, fingular
and bold. 3dly, Not to confider taſte
as a part of the judgment, but a *fixth
fenfe.* With refpect to words, he promis'd, 1ſt, To fpeak much, and for
that purpofe to treafure in his memory
a great number of tales and ſtories,
without regarding whether they were
fmart or trifling. 2dly, To accuſtom
himfelf ever not to think, till immediately after he has fpoke. 3dly, To
exprefs himfelf always in a new and uncommon manner. Laſtly, with regard
to actions, he oblig'd himfelf to defpife
what we call cuſtom, ufe, decorum;
and to prefent the public, once a year
at leaſt, with fome agreeable fcene.
After taking this oath before the prefident,

dent, the candidate receiv'd from his hands the honourable badge of his dignity, which was a fcull-cap of fhining-metal. He then made a fpeech by way of thanks, in which I was affur'd that, according to cuftom, he had wittily fatyriz'd the fociety into which he was then incorporated.

I thank'd my guide, for making me fpend the day fo agreeably, and faid to him, that 'twas a great pity, the *Cerebellites* in *England*, had not fuch affemblies, and did not form a particular body: that indeed the *French*, a nation bordering upon our ifland, had form'd a kind of order or regiment of thefe: but then, that they generally enlifted people againft their wills, which was contrary to the rights and privileges of a people; that they had no correfpondence with, and hardly knew one another; that few of them wou'd take a jeft, efpecially if they were perfons of fome rank; and that they confider'd the fuffrages, and letters of affociation with which they were honour'd, as fo fo many perfonal fatyrs: that however,

H 4

ever, nothing could be more ufeful than
thofe letters call'd *brevets* or *commiffions*,
fince they might be of fervice in check-
ing the ftupid pride of fome *French-
men*, and curbing their mad fallies;
that the dread of being malicioufly incorporated in this burlefque regiment,
often prevented their making themfelves ridiculous in a notorious and
public manner; infomuch that this filly
fociety was to them a fchool of wifdom,
or rather a prefervative from folly.

C H A P. X.

Manners and government of the Letalifpons. *Their notions of fovereign power.*

AS I ever had the curiofity, in
what country foever fortune
caft me, to enquire into the particular
cuftoms of the people, and the form of
their government, I fuppofe that the
reader will expect fomething here on
thofe heads, with regard to the *Letalifpons.* We have hitherto feen, that
this

this people make the prefervation of
life the chief article, and wifely confider it as the bafis of all happinefs.
The extreme care they take of their
health, prompts them to fhun every
thing that may ruffle the mind, whence
it is, that they are never feen in a paffion. They neither hate, perfecute, or
tear one another to pieces, by malicious
afperfions, or barbarous calumny. Not
a man among them, has one enemy,
becaufe no one offends his friend or
neighbour; and if thro' frailty or inad-
vertency a man fhould happen to let
drop fome fhocking expreffion, 'tis immediately pardon'd and atton'd for.

I remember, that having told them
one day, how in *England* an offended
perfon loft his honour for ever, in cafe
he did not revenge the affront he had
receiv'd; they anfwer'd, that among
the *Letalifpons,* difhonour always reflected upon the offender, who by his
injury had committed an act of injuftice; and that in order to remove the
witnefs of it, he, properly, ought to
wifh the deftruction of the injur'd perfon,

fon, were it lawful to defire fuch a
thing. They cou'd not conceive, that
men, who boaft a rational foul fhould
draw their fwords, and expofe themfelves, not only to kill another for
fpeaking a bare word, and fometimes
for a nod, or wink; but alfo to venture their being run through the body,
to revenge the affront they receiv'd.
Were it not for this, fays I, we fhould
infult one another frequently, but the
fear of revenge, makes us more polite;
and it has been obferv'd, that fear prevails much more among fuch as wear at
their fides an inftrument with which
they may punifh injuries, than among
thofe who by their profeffion, are forbid to ufe this flaughtering weapon.

Your mutual refpect, fays he,
flows wholly from cowardice, and if
you fpare one another 'tis thro' fear;
but wou'd it not be much more lauda-
ble, were reafon and equity the motives
of it. But fince revenge is fo familiar
to you, how came you to have fo little
notion of it? To kill an enemy is not
revenging one's felf, 'tis downright
cruelty;

cruelty; to revenge, is properly making the offender uneafy, and forcing
him to repent of the injury he has
committed; but in cafe he is kill'd,
how will it be poffible for him to repent? He then is fecur'd from anguifh
of every kind; whereas the revenger
is left in a ftate of uneafinefs, expos'd
to remorfe, and the dread of punifhment.

Let not the reader be furpriz'd at
this odd way of reafoning. The *Letalifpons* abhor to fhed not only human
blood, but that of the meaneft and
moft groveling animal, as was before
obferv'd. However, the love of their
country, and the neceffity of felf-de-
fence, rouzes their courage, and infpires them with a fpirit of intrepidity,
when any of the neighbouring nations
attack them; they looking upon it as
lawful to kill thofe who would murther them. But then they never, in a
time of peace, and when they are in
their country and with their families,
wear offenfive weapons to force either
awe or refpect. The only ufe they
make

make of arms is to kill wild beafts, or
repulfe the enemies of their country.

Marriages are here conducted after
a different manner from ours, where
the girls are always a clog to
the family, and the handfomeft, in
cafe they have but fmall portions, can
hardly meet with husbands. In this
country, pretty women are always
purchas'd, and are as good as an eftate
to their fathers. Such as are but tolerably handfome, are generally taken
without a fortune; but as for thofe
who are very ugly, and of a deprav'd
and ftupid caft of mind, they frequently
ruin their unhappy fathers, who are
bound by the law to get them husbands.
In a word, a high regard is always had
to good fenfe and wit, whether in the
beautiful or ugly.

Further, a young man always pur-
chafes cheaper than one advanc'd in
years; fo that a handfome, witty, young
fellow, fometimes gets a lovely, witty creature, without paying a far-
thing for her. The qualities on each fide
are always weigh'd, and they ever have
regard

regard to the circumſtances of the man
who marries.

The *Letaliſpons*, are not, like us,
fir'd with an inſatiable thirſt of riches,
neither do they deſpiſe them, but only
blame thoſe, who from a philoſophical
principle, ſeem not to concern themſelves about wealth, and wholly diſre-
gard it. To deſpiſe riches, is, in their
opinion, deſpiſing the opportunity of
practiſing ſeveral virtues. Poverty
gives occaſion to exerciſe our courage and patience only ; whereas affluence, on the contrary, gives us an
opportunity of diſplaying our temperance, our modeſty, our diſintereſtedneſs and generoſity.

They conſider beauty, whether in a
man or woman, as a very valuable jewel ; not becauſe of the pleaſure which
exterior charms may give, but in con-
ſideration of the cloſe tye that is between ſoul and body. Their general
notion is, that an ugly, ill-ſhap'd perſon, has a rankled ſoul ; and that thoſe
of a handſome man, or a beautiful woman, are commonly of an amiable nature,

unleſs

unlefs education happens to change the
ufual courfe of nature; which makes me
call to mind the faying of *Socrates*,
who fpeaking of himfelf, fays, that the
uglinefs of his body was a fign his foul
was of the fame caft ; but that he had
in fome meafure leffen'd the deformity
of the latter by his great care and pains.
However, they don't look upon this as
an infallible rule ; but think that thofe
who give their honeft countenances the
lie, are more guilty than other people,
becaufe they deceive the eye, by be-
traying the publick promife which nature had drawn on their countenances.
As deform'd and mifhapen Perfons
don't impofe upon any one, they are
therefore thought to be lefs guilty.

The *Letalifpons* adminifter juftice with
great integrity and uprightnefs. One
very particular circumftance, which
may poffibly appear incredible in *Europe*, is, that law-fuits never occafion
the leaft animofity between the con-
tending parties. Thefe mutually confider each other, as perfons who vary
in opinion on a doubtful fubject. Each
defends

defends his right without the leaft malice or rancour. The parties are even
bound by the laws to eat together, at
leaft on the two days which immediately precede the final fentence; and
the cuftom is, that he who lofes his
caufe, always vifits the perfon who
gains it, to congratulate him on his
good fuccefs.

The government was formerly mo-
narchical, and the crown elective; but
within thefe hundred years, 'tis a republic; however, this change was not
occafion'd by the fubjects rebelling
againft their lawful prince, or the
inconftancy and ficklenefs of the
people; but from the impoffibility of
finding a man who fhould afpire to the
throne, juft and rational, and worthy
of being rais'd to it. As I could
hardly think this was the genuine caufe
of that revolution, *Taifaco* one day
told me, he was furpriz'd I found it
fo difficult to comprehend a thing that
was fo natural in itfelf; but to give
me a better idea thereof, he thus fet
before me the troubles and inconve-
niences,

niences, which, in his opinion, attended upon royalty.

Tho' the advantages of sovereign power, says he, may seem so glorious and inviting, they yet are weak and unstable. 'Tis true indeed, that the vulgar are dazled with the splendor of sovereign power; 'tis a continual series of honours and respect; an absolute power, on which the happiness or unhappiness of a great many men depends: a vast profusion of riches and magnificence: the soft enjoyment of all things that highly delight the senses: for these we envy kings, but then compare such frivolous advantages with the substantial misery which is inseperable from royalty, and you'll find that a king is very much to be pitied, and that his condition is perhaps of all others the most unhappy.

What an assemblage of uncommon talents and superior qualities must center in that man, who would act the part of a king to advantage? If it be a hard matter to govern one's self, how difficult must it be to superintend a numberless

berlefs multitude of people; to fteal
upon their affections, and awe them at
the fame time; to correct the abufes of
men, without fhocking the prejudices they may have imbib'd; and to
rife to great power, without becoming odious? A king ought to be
a better man than thofe over whom
he reigns, and the model of all
the virtues. But then, how fhall
he reconcile thefe with politicks?
How fhall he become formidable to his
enemies, and not opprefs his fubjects?

In cafe he be a pacific prince, they'll
charge him with being weak and indolent; if he be of a warlike difpofition,
his neighbours will take umbrage, and
his fubjects will fuffer for it. Are the
gratifications he taftes, capable of ba-
lancing the fatigues he undergoes? His
pleafures are vaftly inferiour to thofe
which a private man enjoys. They
croud upon a monarch unfought: he
does not purchafe them like the genera-
lity of the world, by agreeable cares:
he is infenfible of thofe things which

Vol. II.   I   give

give them the greateſt reliſh, I mean
difficulty and reſiſtance; he is altogether unactive in his inſipid pleaſures;
he ſlides, he ſlumbers.

With regard to the pleaſures of the
mind, a king never taſtes thoſe of praiſe
and approbation in a pure and unaffec-
ted manner. He is ſenſible that ſuch
perſons as are moſt laviſh of their in-
cenſe, are not at their liberty, nor
dare to refuſe it him. He is not
ſure of ſucceeding in any one thing,
unleſs it be in breaking his horſe; for
in all other exerciſes, every thing
bends to him, and acknowledges his
ſuperiority; his horſe only is neither a
flatterer nor a courtier.

The grandeur of a monarch lays
him under the utmoſt conſtraint. In-
ceſſantly depriv'd of the liberty of viſi-
ting foreign countries, he is, in ſome
meaſure, a priſoner in his kingdom,
and a captive in his court, where he
is almoſt perpetually ſurrounded with
an importunate croud of courtiers,
who watch all his motions, and ſtun
his ears; ſome with ſuing for places,
and

and others with thanks for favours indulg'd. He can never taſte the ſweets
of friendſhip, which ſubſiſts only between
equals. All the ſervices which are done
him, are the effect of cuſtom, of
ambition, or conſtraint. And indeed,
the moſt wicked princes are as well
ſerv'd as the beſt; the ſame reſpect
is paid them, and they are honour'd
with the ſame ceremonies and elo-
giums.

But the moſt unhappy circumſtance
of ſovereigns, is, that truth never ap-
proaches their ears. They generally
ſee by other men's eyes; and frequently thoſe they make uſe of on theſe
occaſions, are aſſiſted by ſeveral other
eyes, on which they rely, and are deceiv'd by them. Hence it is, that they
often reward vice, and abuſe or
neglect virtue.

I anſwer'd *Taiſato*, that the reſt of
the world did not conſider ſovereignty
in this light, but look'd upon the king
as the happieſt man in his dominons:
that ſometimes one ſingle man, purely
to acquire the glory and happineſs of

I 2   reigning

reigning over a little ſpot, made a conſiderable part of the univerſe tremble, and deſtroy'd a million of men, half of whom fought on his ſide, and the other half on that of his rival; that 'twas a maxim among ambitious conquerors, that a crime ceas'd to be ſo, when a crown is obtain'd by it: that all our hiſtories were fill'd with relations of monarchs, betray'd and dethron'd; of rebellious ſubjects, who had uſurp'd the ſovereign dignity; of tyrants, who had ſacrific'd to their grandeur, all the tender ſenſations of nature and of honour; and had maintain'd themſelves upon the throne, merely by blood and ſlaughter: that the luſt of empire had formerly overthrown the mightieſt republic in the world; that one man had the ambition of governing alone half the ball, and had ſucceeded in his attempt; and that ſome of our monarchs had been puff'd up with the ambitious thoughts of giving laws to the whole world.

Hence,

Hence, fays I, you may conclude, that fovereignty does not appear fo unhappy in our eyes as it does in yours. We are fo much dazled with the fpendor of a crown, that it appears in a quite different light to us. There is no man among us, but would willingly facrifice all he holds deareft, to the glory of reigning, could he flatter himfelf with the hopes of ever mounting fo high. The happinefs of the kingly ftate is look'd upon as fo certain, that to exprefs the felicity of a man, we generally cry, that he's as happy as a prince. We look upon the care which is infeperable from the regal dignity as nothing; 'tis in our eyes the moft defirable object in the world, becaufe we are infenfible how weighty a crown is, when worn with honour.

I 3   C H A P.

C H A P. XI.

The story of Taifaco *and* Amenosa.

ONE day as I was discoursing with *Taifaco*, under an embowering shade, where we breath'd the most delicious fragrance, I enquir'd what had engag'd him formerly to leave his native country and visit *Chili*; whether he was prompted to it by traffic, or a curiosity like to that which had made me abandon mine, purely to enquire into the manners and customs of distant nations? I was not, says he, engag'd by any of these motives; love only made me tempt all the dangers of the ocean.

About eighteen years since, I fell in love with a maiden, whose name was *Amenosa*. Her youth and beauty had enchanted my soul, and her father was look'd upon as one of the wealthiest men of the island. I was so happy as to please her; she listned to my melting vows, and we both should have

then

then been happy, had not the meannefs
of my condition, which my lovely
charmer overlook'd, made her father
defpife me ; for when I defir'd his
confent to marry her, he gave me a
haughty refufal, and told me I was
poor. When I found that my narrow circumftances were the fole caufe
of my ill fuccefs, I refolv'd to try
all lawful methods in order to better
my fortune. Tho' this was my fix'd
refolution, I yet was in doubt feveral
days, what courfe to take. 'Tis very
eafy to form a refolution of amaffing
wealth, but nothing is more difficult
than to ftrike into the methods
which procure it.

I was in this perplexity, opprefs'd
with grief, and abandon'd to defpair,
when I one day met on the fhore of
the fea, into which I was refolv'd to
throw my felf, an intimate friend of
mine, whofe name was *Hafco*. The
moment I perceiv'd him, I wou'd have
turn'd another way; but *Hafco* immediately advancing, ftopt me, and having ask'd me with the moft indulgent

tenderness, why I thus abandon'd my
self to sorrow, and mus'd in solitude;
he besought me, in the most soft and
passionate terms, to lay open my whole
soul to him. I gratify'd his amicable
curiosity, when he said : Had heaven
indulg'd me as much wealth as the father of the lovely *Amenosa* possesses, I
would with pleasure have divided it
with you, in order to make you happy, and give the charming creature to
your arms ; but you know how little
my father left me, so that all I have
to offer you, is barren advice. I have
heard, continued *Hasco*, that eastward
lies a country which abounds with
gold, whence all that comes into our
island is brought; but that about an
hundred years since, a sett of extraordinary men, arm'd with thunder and
lightning, had conquer'd it, and cut
to pieces, or struck dead with their
thunder, most of its inhabitants, which
had ruin'd the trade we us'd to carry
on with that people, and made gold
less plenty among us. Were you, says
he, not so dear to me, I wou'd advise
you

you to vifit that rich country; poffibly,
heaven might fmile fo far on your
wifhes, as to point out the methods to
you, of amaffing vaft fums of gold ;
but then the dangers to which this
painful voyage would expofe you are
fo great, that as I am your fincere
friend, I cannot poffibly perfuade you
to undertake it.

Alas ! fays I, the moft dreadful dangers cannot intimidate my foul; thrice
happy to fuffer ten thoufand hardfhips,
could I at laft but merit my dear,
dear *Amenofa !* I thank you, O beft of
friends ! for what you have hinted
to me : heaven, which now relents,
becaufe of the numberlefs evils I fuffer, moft certainly infpir'd you to give
me this advice. 'Tis enough, I'm determin'd to fet out. *Hafco* finding my
refolution fix'd, endeavour'd to divert
me from it ; efpecially fince he himfelf had fuggefted it to me ; however,
perceiving me inflexible, he fpoke thus :
fince you will venture your life, and I
am the caufe of this fatal defign, I am
refolv'd to accompany you, and fhare
all

all the dangers of your voyage. 'Tis
but juft, fince I firft fet you upon this
projeċt, I fhould be an eye-witnefs of
the fuccefs of it. 'Twas in vain for
me to oppofe his heroic generofity,
whereupon we prepar'd to fet out together.

The evening before our departure,
I went to *Amenofa*, to bid her farewell, and acquaint her with my departure. She was feiz'd with the deepeft
forrow at the news, and curs'd ten
thoufand times the love of riches,
fince they were the caufe of our diftrefs, and would perhaps prove my
deftruċtion. She employ'd all the en-
dearing arguments fhe could think of,
to divert me from undertaking fo dangerous a voyage; but I told her it was
not fo hazardous as fhe imagin'd; and
footh'd her with the hopes, that providence would indulge me a fpeedy
return, and then tore myfelf from her,
after we had mutually fwore to love
one another eternally.

The next day I went to the place
where *Hafco* promis'd to meet me, and
finding

finding him, we walk'd together to
the fea-fide, where we went on board
a canoo which we had got ready for
that purpofe, and ftor'd with provifions.
We lie about threefcore leagues from
Chili, and had happily made the greateft part of our courfe, with a wefterly
wind, when a ftorm arofe on a fudden,
which expos'd us to the greateft peril.
We lower'd our fail, and row'd with
all our ftrength, to ftem, if poffible,
the violence of the waves. Our canoo was thrice under water; but the
bark of which it was made, being very light and tough, we, by jumping
thrice into the fea, and fwimming back
to our canoo, kept it from finking, and
turn'd it right again with great dexterity; but while we were thus employ'd,
an impetuous wave, which fwell'd
mountains high, wrap'd us round, and
wafh'd off my companion whom I never fet eyes on fince. Alas! in lofing
him, I loft a kind and moft generous
friend, at a time when I moft wanted
his affiftance. As for my own part, I
held the canoo faft, which I turn'd
over

over, as I had before done feveral times.
The extremity I was then in, made
me not fo fenfible of the lofs I had
fuftain'd, as I was afterwards; and my
whole endeavours were to keep myfelf
from being fwallow'd up by the
waves.

But now, the wind fell and the
waves were hufh'd. Tho' I was prodi-
gioufly fatigued, I neverthelefs row'd till
night, when it blew a pretty brisk gale,
upon which I fet up my fail, and took a
little reft. I ran fo many leagues in the
night, that I difcover'd land the next day
about noon. Three hours after, I had
the good fortune to get on fhore on a
point of land, call'd cape *Acchamqui*,
above *Angud*. I walk'd till night,
without meeting one human creature,
this part of the country being defolate
and barren. In the mean time, I eat a
few roots, that were not very well
tafted, and fome wild fruits, which I
found upon the coaft; and pafs'd the night
on a tree, but had very little fleep.

The next day, after coafting a long
time northward, I met about dusk with
some

fome of the natives, who ftruck with the oddnefs of my habit, came up and ask'd me a great many queftions, concerning the motives of my coming into their country. Our language differs but very little from that of this people, our country, if we are to credit tradition, having been antiently peopled by a colony fent from the moft fouthern part of *Chili*; fo that we underftood one another very well. I anfwer'd very politely, that I was a *Letalifpon,* who had been invited by curiofity to vifit a nation we were defcended from, and with whom we formerly had been ftriƈtly united, before they were conquer'd, and their country invaded by thofe blood-thirfty foreigners.

At thefe words tears ftood in their eyes; they gave me a general account of the numberlefs evils thofe mercilefs conquerors had made them fuffer, and afterwards carried me to their houfe, where they treated me with the utmoft humanity. They told me, I was at liberty to live with them fo long as I pleas'd; that as their anceftors were
antiently

antiently fo nearly related to the *Leta-lifpons*, they look'd upon me as one of their countrymen; but then they advis'd me not to difcover myfelf to their tyrants, for fo they call their *Spanifh* conquerors: for thefe, faid they, will poffibly imagine that your country is as fruitful of gold as ours; in that cafe, they'll oblige you to guide them to it: then facrifice your wife and children, to force you to difcover your treafures, and afterwards murther you. Prevent all this from befalling you, by concealing yourfelf, till fuch time as you have catch'd our air, and learnt our cuftoms, and may feem to be a native of this country.

I thank'd them for their advice, and ask'd whether the *Spaniards* were the fole proprietors of their gold mines, and were only allow'd to approach them? They alone, fays he, reap all the benefit. They have unjuftly feiz'd thofe things which heaven had allotted us; and not contented with this, they alfo wou'd force us to bury our felves in the bowels of the earth, to

administer

adminifter to their avarice ; however,
they have not yet fucceeded in this part
of their tyranny.

I then began to think, that I had undertaken a painful voyage to no purpofe ; and therefore refolv'd to return
back into my country, and do all
that lay in my power, to get poffeffion
of *Amenofa* ; or, in cafe fate ftill oppos'd my wifhes, to die at her feet.
Accordingly, after I had fpent fome
time in this houfe, and repos'd my felf
after my great fatigues, I took leave
of the whole family, and fet out for
Acchamqui, where I had left my canoo.

I had fcarce walk'd fix leagues, before I met feveral *Spaniards* a hunting,
who feeing I was a foreigner by my
drefs, ftopt me, and asking me where
I was born, I thought proper to tell
them that my native country lay at a
great diftance from theirs. I did not
confider that I betray'd my felf, in
anfwering them in the fame language
they fpoke to me, *viz*. the *Chilian*.
They ask'd me whether my country
was rich ? I reply'd no, and that I
my

my felf was an emblem of its poverty.
An unexpected ftorm, fays I, threw me
unhappily on this coaft, and I am endeavouring to return to my own country.
I would have proceeded on my way,
but the chief of the *Spaniards* ftopping
me, fpoke to me as follows. Stranger,
I am pleas'd with your perfon ; come
to my houfe, and I'll give you a cre-
ditable employment in it ; and whenever you think proper to return back
into your country, you fhall have leave
to do it, and I'll give you a reward that
will far exceed your expectations.

I turn'd pale at his propofal ; being
afraid that he intended to fend me to
work in the mines. The *Spaniard* obferving my confufion, bid me fear nothing ; forget, fays he, whatever the
natives of the country may have told
you to our prejudice ; and rely entirely
on my word, and I'll do all that lies
in my power to make you happy.
Had I the leaft defign upon your liberty, I could now force you to follow me ; but I fhall content my felf
with intreating you to do it.

Thefe

These kind expreſſions ſtole upon my heart, and notwithſtanding I was prejudic'd againſt his countrymen, I yet thought my ſelf oblig'd to hazard my life and liberty, and ſacrifice them to the hopes of getting gold. I imagin'd, that in caſe the *Spaniard* was as good as his word, I ſhould ſoon be in a condition to merit *Amenoſa.* Upon this I bow'd very low to *Don Fernandez de la Chirade,* for that was the *Spaniard*'s name, as a token that I accepted his offer; upon which he immediately order'd one of his ſervants to mount me on his horſe.

We got to his houſe about evening. 'Twas a magnificent edifice, built on the ſea-ſhore. On one ſide of it lay a meadow a of a prodigious extent, cover'd with a never-fading green, and ſurrounded with hills crown'd with tufted trees. On the other ſide, was a view of the ſea, which ſometimes rais'd its tempeſtuous waves to the clouds, but generally was ſmooth as a mirrour. The furniture of this houſe was vaſtly rich. Gold dazled the eye in every apartment, and the moſt trifling part of the moveables, were made of that precious metal.

My mafter, (for tho' I was not his
flave I yet was his dependant,) made
me fit at table with him. Seeing it
was cover'd with viands of various
kinds, I rofe up, and refus'd to touch any
thing; and at the fame time, begg'd
Fernandez to let me eat after the manner of my own country, and abftain
from the flefh of animals. He indulg'd
my requeft, upon which I immediately
went into the garden and there gather'd
roots, herbs and pulfe, which I cook'd
and eat before him. Supper being ended, he took me afide, and faid, that as
none of the *Spaniards* who waited upon him, underftood the *Chilian* language, he was very glad he had met
with me; and that he would fooner
truft me than the natives, becaufe of
the great averfion they bear to his
countrymen: that fuch of the natives as
were his domefticks, fought every opportunity to injure and betray him:
that, as he was perfuaded I had not
the fame motives to hate him, I therefore fhould fuperintend their behaviour;
and that he hop'd my zeal and fidelity
would

would fecure him from all their plots:
that as I fpake their language, it gave
me an opportunity of gaining their
efteem; of difcovering their defigns,
and keeping them to their duty. I promis'd to act honourably, and be ever
faithful to him; and indeed I kept my
promife, which won his heart fo entirely, that he unbofom'd himfelf to
me without the leaft referve.

I not only was appointed to infpect
the conduct of all the natives of the
country that were in his fervice, but
was alfo trufted with the keys of his
treafure; fo that I was happy, were it
poffible for a man to be fo, who is far
remov'd from the woman he idolizes,
and a country he pants to revifit. Befides, I daily beheld a fpectacle, which
was yaftly fhocking to a *Letalifpon*; I
mean, that I faw *Fernandez* and the
reft of the *Spaniards*, inhumanly murther the moft amiable animals, and
afterwards feed upon them. I wou'd
fometimes employ prayers and entrea-
ties, in order to prevent the flaughter
of thofe creatures; but they, inftead of

K 2   being

being mov'd with my compaſſion, would laugh in my face; and ſo great was my anguiſh, upon this account, that nothing but a thirſt of acquiring gold, which love only had inflam'd me with, could have prevail'd with me to reſide among them. However, heaven, by a moſt ſingular and unexpected accident, reſtor'd me to my country, and crown'd all my wiſhes, as the reader will ſoon find.

Some of my countrymen who go out in canoos had found the body of *Haſco*, on the coaſts of their iſland, thrown thither by the tide. They had view'd it; and as he was very like me in the face; of the ſame age and ſtature; not to mention that I was much better known than he, and that my departure had made much more noiſe, they had taken the disfigur'd corps of my dear friend for mine. Immediately a report of my death was ſpread over the whole iſland. My mother, who lov'd me tenderly, was deeply afflicted at the news, and going to *Amenoſa*'s father, ſhe broke out into a thouſand reproachful expreſſions, and ſaid he was guilty of my death.

death. He did not endeavour to apologize for his conduct, but feem'd very forry for her lofs, and did all that lay in his power to comfort her.

But the moment *Amenofa* heard the fad fate I had met with, fhe fhut herfelf up alone in her chamber, and would have kill'd herfelf; when happily, the dread which is almoft infeperable from her fex, ftopt her trembling arm, as fhe was going to ftab herfelf with a dagger. They broke open her chamber-door, to prevent the fatal confequences of her defpair, and forc'd the weapon out of her hand; but then it was impoffible for them to tear away her forrows, which made no lefs impreffion upon her father, who lov'd her with uncommon tendernefs. Thou art no more, deareft *Taifaco*! fays fhe, overwhelm'd with grief, thou art no more! my father's favage, obdurate, heart; and my foft, my tender one, have been thy death; they alfo will kill me, and I'll follow thee. May my foul, after it has wing'd its flight, meet in the fame region with thine, and inform a

body

body like to that it now animates! Heaven is too juſt and equitable, to ſuffer us to be for ever ſeperated from one another; 'twill certainly unite us together, to reward thy courage and my conſtancy.

Amenoſa, after having thus given vent to her grief, was for ſome time plung'd in a deep melancholy, and did not once open her lips. However, ſhe deceiv'd her father, and all her ſpies; for afterwards aſſuming a leſs gloomy air, ſhe told them, time might poſſibly heal the wound which my death had made in her heart. This her father believ'd, and therefore did not guard againſt the tranſports of her deſpair, which however, at laſt, broke out in the following manner. After having meditated ſome time, on the kind of death ſhe ſhou'd chuſe, ſhe reſolv'd to throw herſelf into that part of the ſea, where ſhe imagin'd I had been ſwallow'd up.

With this reſolution ſhe ſteals from her father's houſe, and runs to the ſea-ſhore, in order to put her fatal deſign

in

in execution. But now, the death fhe
is going to die, makes her fhudder.
What! fays fhe, does my coward
mind oppofe the generous refolution
my heart has taken! ah! my heart
fhall triumph on this occafion, and
I'll conceal from it all the horrors of
this death, fince it terrifies me fo.
Immediately fhe ran to a canoo which
lay on the fea-fhore, and jumping into
it, boldly cut the rope that faftned
it to the ftrand; hoifted the fail;
and laid hold of the oars, in order to
drive into the main ocean. Then, with
a flood of tears, covering her head, fhe
laid herfelf down in the canoo, and
abandon'd it to the mercy of the
waves, equally wifhing for, and dread-
ing death.

The wind blew pretty ftrong weft-
fouth-weft, which was very favourable
for *Chili*; when the canoo, after having
happily made its courfe for twenty
eight hours, and gone in a direct line,
as tho' it had been fteer'd by the moft
experienc'd pilot, was met the next
day by a *Chilian* woman who was fifh-

K 4　　　　ing,

ing, and got three or four leagues from land. This woman, furpriz'd to fee a canoo purfue its courfe, without any hands on board, ply'd her oars, and being come up with it, was much more aftonifh'd when fhe faw a young woman on board, in a fwoon, and half dead. She ftept into the canoo; took her in her arms, and endeavour'd to recall her to life. *Amenofa* recover'd from her fwoon, fix'd her eyes upon the woman, call'd upon me, and then clos'd them again. My lovely maid acquainted me with part of thefe particulars, and the reft were told me by the woman we are now fpeaking of; who hooking her canoo to *Amenofa's*, carried her to her houfe which ftood on the fhore, at a little diftance from ours.

She had known me fome years, her husband being a hunter, whofe houfe I often went to, purpofely to ranfom fuch creatures as he caught in his gins and fnares. I came accidentally into it, a few hours after *Amenofa* was brought thither.

But

But heavens! how great was my
aftonifhment when I beheld the darling
of my foul! furely I never felt fuch
emotions either before or fince; but
my joy was mix'd with hope and fear.
I was in raptures to meet with her
again; but then the deplorable condition I faw her in, was more painful
than her dear prefence was ravifhing.
Is it then you, fays I, adorable *Amenofa!* What chance has brought you
hither? Alas! to what a wretched ftate
are you reduc'd!

Amenofa, ftruck with a voice, which fhe
knew to be mine, open'd her lovely eyes,
which were almoft clos'd in death, and
looking upon me with a furprize equal
to her dejected condition; Do I then,
fays fhe, deareft *Taifaco*, behold fo fweet
an object? Yes, fays I, you fee your tender, your faithful adorer. Cheer up, and
be not troubled, but take a little fuftenance to fupport nature. My prefence
feem'd to revive her; and a foft joy
diffufing itfelf over her countenance,
leffen'd its deadly palenefs. 'Tis univerfally believ'd, fays fhe, in our ifland that
you

you are no more, but was buried in the
waves. How blefs'd am I to fee you
again, at a time when I thought of
meeting you only in the fhades below!
For this I ventur'd amid the winds and
waves, in order to be entomb'd, as I fuppos'd you had been, in a watry grave.

Tho' I before thought it wou'd be
impoffible for me to love with a greater excefs of paffion, I yet at that inftant, found it more violent than ever.
I return'd thanks to heaven, for its
goodnefs in fo happily preferving the
object of all my wifhes, and earneftly
befought the good woman of the houfe
to take the utmoft care of my *Amenofa.*
At the fame time I defir'd her, not
to reveal any of thefe particulars, and
promis'd to reward her very handfomely for her care and fecrecy.

Amenofa recover'd a few days after,
infomuch that my happinefs would now
have been complete, had I been at liberty
to return with her into my own country;
but my condition of life, my duty, and the
beneficence of my patron the *Spaniard,*
were tyes I could not eafily break.

However,

However, I had this comfort, that I was at full liberty to visit my mistress every day, and feast my eyes with her numberless beauties; and should then have made her my wife, were not children expresly forbid by the laws, to marry without the consent of their parents.

In the mean time, *Don Fernandez* fell dangerously ill, and knowing that his dissolution was at hand, and that it would be impossible for him to recover, he prepar'd himself to die, pursuant to the dictates of his religion, and a little after rewarded all his servants. As I had a great share of his esteem, he bequeathed me an hundred pound weight of pure gold, three thousand pound of silver, and some other things of value; desiring me, at the same time, not to forget him, after which he expir'd, to the great grief of the *Spaniards* and *Chilians*, who had so long experienc'd his great virtue. Thrice happy region, did all his countrymen but resemble him!

I then thought of revisiting my native country with my dear *Amenosa,* persuaded

perſuaded it would be impoſſible for her father, when I reſtor'd him his only daughter, whom he ſuppos'd to be dead, and ſaw the treaſure which was left me, to refuſe her to my ardent wiſhes. Accordingly, I provided a ſufficient quantity of fruits, herbs, and roots, and order'd them to be dreſs'd ; and after thanking the good man and his wife for their great care of *Amenoſa*, and rewarded them for their ſervices, we both embark'd on board a large canoo, which I had order'd to be built for that purpoſe. I hir'd two ſkilful rowers, for our greater ſecurity, and deſir'd the good woman, for decency ſake, to accompany *Amenoſa*, promiſing to make her ample amends ; and gave her my word, that the ſame canoo ſhould carry her back ſoon. She agreed to my propoſal, and we prepared to ſet out.

As we were juſt going to put off from ſhore, we ſaw at ſome diſtance ſeveral *Spaniards* running towards us, who made ſigns for us to wait their coming up. As we were ignorant of their

their defign, and fufpected they poffibly wanted to plunder us of our gold
and filver, we did not think proper to
comply with the fignal. Finding this,
they fir'd upon us; but we were out
of the reach of a ball; and a furious
lionefs rufhing out at the fame time,
they were obliged to fly. However,
we immediately cut the rope which
faftn'd the canoo, and made off as
quick as poffible from the fhore. The
lionefs being almoft famifh'd, plung'd
into the fea, and fwimming after us,
was upon the point of rufhing into our
boat, when I laid her over the head
with my oar, and hit her fuch a blow
that fhe duck'd; but coming up again,
our watermen feconded me fo well,
and we ftruck her with fo much violence and dexterity, that fhe plung'd
into the water, and we faw her no
more. *Amenofa* herfelf had taken up
an oar, and affifted us in keeping the
lionefs off.

Our voyage was fuccefsful. As it
was a dead calm, we could not put
up the fail, but were oblig'd to make
our

our way with the oars, which kept us
five days out at fea. At laft, we got
on fhore in our dear country, and I
immediately carried *Amenofa* to my
mother, who receiv'd us with the
utmoft joy and aftonifhment. Is it
poffible! fays fhe, clafping me in her
arms, for you to be alive! How many
tears and fighs have you coft me!
Your happy return reftores me to life,
by affuring me you are ftill living.
And you, lovely *Amenofa*, go and be
happy in the tender embraces of a father who ftill bemoans your lofs with
tears. Both of you fhall afterwards
relate, by what happy turn of providence, we enjoy the inexpreffible comfort of feeing you again.

The next day my mother was to
carry *Amenofa* to her father, but I refolv'd to vifit him firft. The inftant
he faw me, he cried out, Is it you,
Taifaco, or your angry ghoft that is
come to torment me? I have atton'd
for my crime by the lofs of my dear
daughter, whom I refus'd to beftow on
fo much virtue. She plung'd into
those

thofe waves which fwallow'd you up.
The fharp pangs I feel at the remembrance of this fad accident, is torture
fufficient, and therefore do not heighten
my forrows: O guilty thirft of riches,
'tis thou art the wretched caufe of all
my misfortunes! Unhappy father! thou
ftill enjoyeft the treafures, but thy daughter is no more. 'Twas thus my prefence awak'd his anguifh, and aggrava-
ted his forrows. I endeavour'd to calm
his foul, by telling him I was *Taifaco*,
who was fuppos'd to be buried in the
waves, and with whofe death he reproach'd himfelf.

Both your daughter, fays I to him,
and my felf, are ftill living; inform me
only whether fhe fhall live to be mine
only. At thofe words he embrac'd me
with an air of tranfport, and affur'd
me that no man breathing fhould poffefs her but myfelf. I then related to
him all my adventures at fea; the riches
I had got in *Chili*; in what manner his
daughter had got fafely there; and
how I had brought her from thence,
accompanied

accompanied by a woman of that country.

He was now in the higheſt raptures,
and impatient to bleſs his eyes with
the ſight of *Amenoſa*, when my mother
brought her. The moment ſhe ſaw
him, ſhe fell on her knees, and begg'd
him to excuſe the grief ſhe had brought
upon him. He took her affectionately
in his arms, and after ſhedding a flood
of tears, ask'd pardon, for the dangers
to which he had in ſome meaſure expos'd her, by oppoſing her innocent deſires; then taking our hands, made us
claſp with a mutual embrace, in preſence
of the witneſſes; and my mother, doing
the ſame, we were that inſtant married,
according to the cuſtom of the iſland,
which requires no other ceremony.

Amenoſa, ſays he, and I, have been
married threeſcore and nine years, and
nothing has been able to interrupt our
felicity. My eſtate, and that of her
father, with whom we live, has made
our family one of the richeſt and moſt
flouriſhing in the whole country. Such
were the motives and ſucceſs of my
voyage to *Chili*, whither poverty and
deſpair

despair had drove me, and whence I return'd rich and happy.

C H A P. XII.

The author going a fishing in a canoo with his companion, meets a French *vessel, which takes them in, and brings them back into* Europe.

DUring the three months I had now liv'd among the *Letalispons*, to pass over the *tædium* and uneasiness, which will almost inevitably prey upon a man who resides in a foreign country, whose language he does not understand; I had a strong desire to revisit my native country. Besides, *Silva* and I could not accustom our selves to feed always upon roots, which was our only sustenance; and tho' they were tofs'd up with great delicacy, we nevertheless loath'd them.

We one day told *Taisaco*, that the diet we fed upon in his country was too severe; that the monks and hermits in *Europe* men of the greatest

ſanctity, tho' they made a vow never
to eat fleſh, did nevertheleſs make no
ſcruple of eating fiſh; that as the element which the fiſh inhabited, was different from that we liv'd in; as we
had no correſpondence with them, and
that they were not, ſtrictly ſpeaking,
inhabitants of the earth, 'twas a ſort
of ſuperfluous charity to ſpare their
lives; that in caſe we continued to eat
after the *Letaliſpon* manner, and feed
only upon roots, we ſhould ſoon die;
becauſe we had been accuſtom'd to a
quite different diet from our infancy.

I ſhould be very ſorry, ſays *Taiſaco*,
did our roots, which are ſo benefici-
al to us, prejudice you in any manner. You very juſtly make a difference, between thoſe animals which inhabit the earth, and ſuch as live in ſeas
and rivers. Tho' the latter are inform'd with a ſoul; and are, no leſs
than we, the work of the creator, they
yet are not our brethren, like the former; for they breathe a different air,
and we have not the leaſt ſociety with
them; for which reaſon, we don't
think

think it a great crime to kill and eat
them. However, few among us go
thefe lengths; whether it be from a
fort of fcruple of confcience, or becaufe that kind of food does not appear wholefome to us. But as your conftitution is different from ours, and you
cannot poffibly accuftom your felves to
our diet, you are at liberty to catch,
and eat fifh. You may take my canoo in which I fometimes recreate my
felf when the fea is calm; and in cafe
you are fo ingenious as to make nets,
and know how to ufe them, you may
go up a little bay hard by, where you
will meet with fhoals of fifh. But
then fport at a confiderable diftance
from the fhore, for fear left any one
fhould fpy you, and be offended at the
fight.

We thank'd *Taifaco* for his goodnefs and condefcenfion in fo readily complying with our frailty and
weaknefs. On the morrow at day-
break, *Silva* and I took the canoo on
our fhoulders, which being made out
of a bark of a fingle tree, was very

L 2   light,

light, together with a fail and oars;
when making for the creek, we got to
it without much fatigue. The night
before we had made a fweep-net with
packthread, which *Taifaco* was fo kind
as to give us. We row'd a confiderable diftance from the fhore, as he had
defir'd us to do; and the wind blowing fair, to fpare our felves the trouble of rowing, we hoifted our little
fail, and without any other affiftance
got about four leagues from the fhore,
and even out of the bay.

Juft as we were going to caft our
fweep-net, we perceiv'd a large veffel,
at about three leagues diftance from
us. As my eye was more us'd to the
fea than *Silva's*, I fpy'd her firft, and
faid to him, that fince heaven, probably,
now gave us a favourable opportunity
of returning into *Europe*, it was our
duty not to negleét it. As we both
had our muskets on board, we fir'd together, in order to make the greater
report, as a fignal. In the mean time,
fhifting our rudder and our fail, we
took a quarter wind, and made for
the

the veſſel. We ſtill continued firing, in order that they might know what we wanted, and found they underſtood us; for we ſaw them ſhift about a little to the larboard, and ſail towards our canoo, and in an hour's time, we got ſo near, as to ſee ſhe carried *French* colours.

I was very ſorry to leave the iſland of *Letaliſpon*, without bidding adieu to *Taifaco*. He will ſurely, ſays I, conclude we are loſt, and that muſt certainly afflict him very much. But what ſhall we do in this dilemna! Shall we let ſlip ſo fair an opportunity? *Silva* thought that inſtant of an expedient, which was, that we ſhould firſt get on board the veſſel; and then ſhift the ſail, and fix the rudder in ſuch a manner, that the canoo might get alone into the bay, which did not lie far off; that the wind had chopp'd about, and ſtood fair for *Letaliſpon*; that this being ſo, we ſhould run no hazard in writing a letter of thanks to *Taifaco*, and therein acquaint him with our departure; that as he would not

L 3   fail

fail to fend after us in the bay, the
meffengers would find both our canoo,
and the letter. I was pleas'd with the
hint, and having pen, ink and paper
about me, I drew up the following
letter, while *Silva* continued rowing
towards the fhip.

To the moft excellent and virtuous Taifaco.

" THE ftrong defire, dear *Tai-*
" *faco*, we have of revifiting
" our country, forces us to leave you;
" and to take this happy opportuni-
" ty of going on board an *European*
" veffel we have now met with. We
" wifh it may be in our power to re-
" turn on fhore, to thank you for the
" numberlefs favours you have in-
" dulg'd us ; but cannot tell whether
" the captain of the fhip on which
" we are now preparing to go aboard,
" will allow us time for it. However
" this be, we earneftly wifh this let-
" ter may come fafe to hand, and that
" we may fucceed in our attempt. Be
" affur'd that we fhall ever entertain
" the

" the higheſt ſenſe of the numberleſs
" obligations by which you have bound
" us; nor ever be ſo ungrateful, as to
" blot the remembrance of them from
" our minds; but ſhall publiſh to the
" whole world, that wiſdom and vir-
" tue have choſen the iſland of *Letaliſ-*
" *pons* for their reſidence.

John Gulliver, Francis Silva.

We fix'd this letter in ſuch a manner, that it might eaſily be found, and
not be blown away. In the mean time,
after turning our rudder and ſail, we
left the canoo, and ſtept into one be-
longing to the veſſel, on which we
ſoon got aboard. The reader will
ſuppoſe that we met with a hearty reception, the *French* being extremely polite and curteous to foreigners. We firſt
went and paid our compliments to the
captain; told him our names and our
country; and afterwards gave him an
account, how we had been forc'd to
live ſix months among the *Letaliſpons.*
The captain told us, he was going directly for St. *Malo,* whence he came

L 4   about

about eighteen months before, and that I should easily meet with an opportunity of embarking from thence for *England*, and *Silva* for *Portugal*.

We found they had carried on a private trade in the *South-Sea*, for which reason I ask'd the captain whether he had not heard of the *Vulcan*, a *Dutch* vessel. He answer'd, that she set out a month before him from the port of *Coquinbo*, and had met with pretty good success. I likewise ask'd him, whether he had known one Captain *Harrington* who was on board her; he answer'd yes, and at the same time prais'd him to the skies, and assur'd me he was on board her in perfect health, and was gone for *Europe*. I was over-joy'd at the News, and had now a much greater desire of returning to *England*, since it would give me an opportunity of seeing again so worthy a friend.

The *French* are as incredulous as the *English*, with regard to incidents of an extraordinary and wonderful nature; so that it was with the greatest reluctance,

luctance, that I was forc'd, by the
officers and chief perfons of the crew,
to give an account of the furprizing
adventures I had met with. *Silva,*
whom I had acquainted with the mi-
nuteft particulars of my ftory, having the higheft opinion of my veracity, did not doubt but that every
thing I told him was fact; and had mention'd them to the captain and fome o-
ther officers; fo that they themfelves
were vaftly urgent with me to relate
the whole my felf. But when I had
gratified their curiofity, they at firft
took me for an enthufiaft, and perhaps
a liar. However, after they were a
little better acquainted with me, and
plainly perceiv'd that I was neither
filly or crack-brain'd, but a fincere lover of truth, they began to judge o-
therwife. They firft liftned to my adventures purely for amufement fake;
they were afterwards prompted by curiofity; and then conviction mix'd with
aftonifhment fucceeded their incredu-
lity, efpecially when I told them, that
Capt. *Harrington,* whom they knew in
Coquinbo,

Coquinbo, to be a man of great probity
and veracity, had himſelf been an eye-
witneſs to my adventures in the iſland
of *Babilary*. They were very merry,
(the *French* being famous for raillery
and extempore wit) on the political
government of the *Balibarians*. And as
in relating what had happen'd to me
in that iſland, I could not omit telling
them, that the women of this country look'd upon me as a very handſome young fellow, as my readers have
heard; the officers were very waggiſh
upon that occaſion. I muſt confeſs
they were not to blame : however, no
one ought to be offended at the applau-
ſes which a man beſtows upon himſelf,
when his relation is ingenuous, and is
not dictated by pride or falſhood.

As I had not met with any thing re-
markable from my leaving *England*
till I came into the ſea of *China*, as
was before obſerv'd, nothing extraordinary happen'd to me in my return to *Europe*. To amuſe myſelf on
board, as I had no money to play, I
drew up an account of my travels in
Engliſh ;

Englifh; and a *French* gentleman, with whom I had contracted a friendfhip, and who underftood our language tolerably well, engag'd himfelf to tranflate it; and his pockets being as empty as mine, he found this employment an excellent remedy againft the hyp. When we had finifh'd our refpective tasks, he defir'd my leave to publifh the work, as foon as he fhould be got to *Paris*, which I agreed to.

We arriv'd at St. *Malo, Nov.* the 8th 1720, and on the 20th following, I embark'd for *Portfmouth*, and arriv'd fafe in that harbour.

End of the Laft Chapter.

CON-

CONTINUATION

BY THE

TRANSLATOR.

FROM the time of my good
friend Mr. *John Gulliver*'s return
into *England, viz.* fince the year 1720,
I have correfponded regularly with
him by letter. He was no fooner got
home, but he acquainted me he had
found his father, his mother and all
the family in good health; that his father was then writing an account of his
travels, with a defign to publifh it; that
as it was near printed off, he would
immediately fend it to me, but in the
mean time earneftly defir'd me not to
fhew the tranflation I had made of his
travels, to any perfon, till fuch time
as his father's were made public. Some
time after he wrote me word, that he
had been fo happy as to meet with his
dear

dear friend Capt. *Harrington*, and was upon the point of marrying one of his daughters.

About the clofe of the year 1726, he did me the pleafure to fend me the two printed Volumes of the *Travels of Capt.* Lemuel Gulliver, before any copy of them was publifh'd in *England*, and defir'd me to tranflate them, which I accordingly did. The fuccefs which this work, printed at *Paris* in 1727, met with, is univerfally known; and how delighted both the *French* and *Englifh* were with the bold and grotefque pleafantry of that piece. I only wifh that the work I now offer to the public, may excite their curiofity as much. The * original will be publifh'd in *London*, the fame day this tranflation appears at *Paris*. No doubt but a comparifon will be made between the travels of the father and thofe of the fon. If the reader fhould
find

* *This is mere banter, for the work is fuppos'd to be written originally by the pretended tranflator.*

find lefs fire, lefs genius and delicacy in this, than in the former *Gulliver*; thefe defeéts may poffibly be compenfated, in fome meafure, by the gaiety of the images; and the ufefulnefs of the moral couch'd under them, notwithftanding the incidents are lefs aftonifhing.

The author having lately tranfmitted to me a letter concerning his travels, written by one of his friends, I thought it might not be improper to tranflate and publifh it. 'Tis with pleafure I undertake any thing that may be of fervice to my friends.

A letter from Dr. Ferruginer, to the author of thefe Travels.

I am, dear Sir, infinitely oblig'd to you for giving me the perufal of your travels in manufcript, the incidents whereof I take to be as true as they are extraordinary. I am not one of thofe

thofe fcepticks, who look upon every thing as fictitious, which happens to vary from their manners, or clafh with their prejudices. Had thefe never feen any Negroes, I fuppofe that the relations of fuch as have been on the coafts of *Senega* and *Guinea*, would fcarce have gain'd credit with them, or perfuaded them there were ever fuch men in being. To give my humble opinion, nothing can be a ftronger indication of a weak mind than fcepticifm.

We learn from hiftory both facred and profane, that there were antiently giants; and travellers affure us, that *Terra Auftralis* is now inhabited by men of a prodigious ftature; and notwithftanding this is notorious, yet very few people wou'd credit what your father has related of the giants of *Brobdingnac*, or thofe diminutive creatures the *Lilliputians*. But then, will any one prefume to affert, that the battles of *Hercules* and the *Pygmies*, are fabulous; that *Paulus Jovius* was miftaken, when he affures us there were feveral of thefe in the north parts of *Ruffian-Lapland*,

Lapland, and eastern *Tartary*; that the *Samojeds* a people subject to the *Czar,* are not such as they are describ'd; in a word, that the savage *Americans* impose upon us, in asserting that men of exceeding little stature, are found to the north of their continent? I lately read in a faithful description of *America,* that a young she-savage, born among the *Eskimaux,* being taken and brought in 1717 to the coast of *Labrador,* where she continued three years, affirm'd; that to the north of her country, were whole nations of people, the men whereof were hardly three foot high, and the women much shorter.

'Tis certain, that such of the learned as have read *Ctesias, Herodotus, Pliny, Solinus, Pomponius Mela, Orosius, Manethon,* are much more inclin'd to give credit to the wonderful particulars which are related of remote countries, than the vulgar ; whose minds being clouded with ignorance and prejudice, are therefore suspicious and diffident. When a man, for instance, has read in those

thofe grave and venerable * authors,
that there are nations of *Cynocephali* or
men with dogs heads; *Acephali*, or
headlefs men; *Enotocetes*, as *Strabo*
calls them, or men whofe ears are of
fuch a length and breadth, that they
wrap themfelves up in them; (fome
authors call them *Fanefii*, and others
Satmales;) *Arimafpes*, or people with
but one eye; *Monofceles*,or*Sciopodes*,that
is people with one leg and a foot only.
When he reads in the fame writers,
that in fome countries, women never
bear children but once in their lives;
others, where all the children are
born with white hair; that fome nations are born nofelefs; others without
either mouth or *anus*, and confequently
never eat as we do, but fupport nature after a very odd manner; a man,
I fay, who has heard of all thefe
particulars, is never furpriz'd, but
eafily believes the moft aftonifh-
Vo l. II.　　M　　ing

* *See* Ctef. Fragm. *l.* 7. *c.* 2. Solin. *cap.* 44.
Pomp. Mel. *l.* 1. Auguft. Serm. 3; ad Fratres
in Eremo.

ing particulars. For this reason § *Pliny* obferves with great judgment, that many things were thought impoffible, till experience prov'd the contrary.

But tho' a man were fo rafh, as to doubt of thofe particulars, which men of the greateft learning and under-ftanding have tranfmitted to us; he yet cou'd fcarce prefume to contradict the modern relations of the *Weft-Indian* iflands, which confirm the teftimony of thofe antient writers? Thefe inform us, that there are in our days, men whofe ears are of fo monftrous a length, that they reach below their fhoulders; and take a pleafure in lengthning thofe of their children, by fixing weights to them: that in fome † countries, the breafts of the men are fo large, that they defcend as low as their thighs, fo that when they run, they are oblig'd to tye them round their bodies; that

---

§ *Lib.* 7. *cap.* 1.
† Joan. de Laet. Ind. Occident. *lib.* 17. *cap.* 7. Sir Walter Rawleigh's defcription of *Guyana.*

that in *Guyana*, there are men without
heads; that in other countries, some
people never take any sustenance; that
others have but one leg, and are besides
splay-footed; that others are incredi-
bly tall and corpulent; such as the
king of *Juda*, who having not long
since desir'd the *French* who trade on
that coast, to get a suit of cloaths
made for him in *France*, cou'd never
draw that on which they brought him,
tho' they had made a tun the standard
of his measure.

Let us now take notice of the curious incidents mention'd in your own
travels. With regard to the manners
and customs of the island of *Babilary*,
every one knows, that anciently, in several parts of the world, the women
were inform'd with a masculine bravery, and the men weak and effeminate.
We find in the description of *America*,
that formerly among the *Ilinois* and
the *Sioux*; in *Jucatan*, *Florida* and *Loui-
siana*, there were men who wore female apparel all their lives, and led a
womanish life; like to those priests of

M 2 *Cybele,*

Cybele, or *Venus Urania,* mention'd by
* *Julius Firmicus,* who always wore a
female habit; took the utmoſt care of
their beauty and dreſs; painted their
faces, and employ'd every art to preſerve the delicacy of their features,
and the freſhneſs of their complexions.
Thrice happy, that they did not meet
with the fate of ſome of thoſe effeminate, male *Americans* abovemention'd,
who were devour'd by the maſtiffs
which the *Spaniards* let looſe upon
them! †

The cuſtom of ſome antient nations
is well known, whoſe men us'd to go
to bed the moment their wives were
deliver'd. On this occaſion, they receiv'd the compliments of their neighbours; and thoſe men-in-the-ſtraw were
attended by the very woman who juſt
before cry'd out. This was alſo the
cuſtom of the *Iberians,* an antient people of *Spain;* of the inhabitants of the
iſland

* Jul. Firm. lib. de error. prof. Relig.
† Lopez de Gomora. Hiſt. Gener. de las
Indias.

ifland of *Corfica*; of the *Tibareni*, a people of *Afia*; and is, as we are inform'd, ftill preferv'd in fome provinces of *France* bordering upon *Spain*, where that ridiculous ceremony is call'd *faire couvade*, or to *brood over the young*. 'Tis alfo practis'd by the *Japoneze*, the *Caraibes* and *Calibis*. Can it therefore be fo fuprizing, that women fhould ape the other fex, and reverfe thofe laws which to us appear natural?

Why therefore fhould I wonder, when I read in your relation of the ifland of *Babilary*, that the men thereof are wholly feminiz'd; efpecially when you inform us of the origin of this cuftom, which arofe from the ignorance, idlenefs and effeminacy of its male inhabitants? My furprize is lefs, to find that the women fhould govern there; fhou'd act a male part, and bear arms, like to the *Menades* or *Bacchantes*, who follow'd *Bacchus* into the field, that is, *Dionyfius* king of *Lybia*; or thofe female-warriors of antient ftory, who firft feated themfelves on the banks of *Tanais*, and afterwards extended their empire from the

M 3   river

river *Caicus* to the extremities of *Lybia*.
By how many exploits did thofe illuftrious *Amazons* fignalize themfelves?
What mighty heroines were *Thaleftris*
and *Penthefilea!* How glorious were
the battles which they fought againft
Hercules, *Thefeus*, *Achilles*, and laft of
all againft *Pompey* in the *Mithridatic*
war when they were almoft extirpa-
ted! Further we are affur'd by all relations, that there are now women, in
America, on the banks of the river *Mara-
gnon* or of *Amazons*, who boaft the
fame martial fpirit; and if we may
give credit to an *Italian* writer, a
miffionary in *Colchis*, mount *Cauca-
fus* is to this day inhabited by
Amazons

Is not the infurrection of the *Babilarian* women, againft all the male inhabitants, fomething like the confpiracy of *Hypfipyle*, and the women of
Lemnos, who, according to antient
hiftorians, murther'd all their husbands
in one night? Did not the *Babilarian*
women, do, in fome meafure, as much,
fince they, by their bravery and cun-
ning,

ning, trampled on the fuperiority which
the men of that ifland had fo long enjoy'd ?

However, as the male fex is naturally the ftrongeft, this ufurpation of the
females would feem very odd, did not
hiftory inform us of feveral inftances
of the fame nature.

" The *Lycians*, fays *Herodotus* in his
" firft book, are partly govern'd by
" the *Cretan* laws, and partly by thofe
" of the *Carians* ; but they have this
" cuftom, which is wholly peculiar to
" themfelves, *viz.* that they take their
" mother's name ; and if at any time
" one man enquires of another what
" family he is of, he has recourfe to
" that of his mother for his extracti-
" on, and thence deduces his genea-
" logy. When a woman of noble
" birth marries a plebeian, their off-
" fpring is enobled ; but if a man of
" high extraction and quality, marries
" a foreigner, oi a woman that was
" once a harlot, their children are
" plebeians.

M 4   " The

" The *Lycians*, fays *Heraclitus* of
" *Pontus* in his firſt book, have no
" written laws, but are wholly go-
" vern'd by cuſtom. Their women
" have maintain'd a fuperiority over
" the men ever fince they were a
" people.

" The *Lycians*, fays *Nicholas Da-*
" *mafc*; ΛΥΚΙΟΙ, revere the women
" more than they do the other fex.
" Children are always nam'd from their
" mothers ; and the females only fuc-
" ceed to eſtates.

This *Gynecocracy*, or government of
women, was not confin'd to the *Lycians* only. The *Scythians* and *Sarmatæ*
were fubjeƈt to women ; and where-
ever the *Amazons* extended their con-
queſts, they infpir'd the women with
a defire of triumphing over their
husbands. *Ifis*, according to *Diodorus
Siculus*, had eſtabliſh'd this cuſtom a-
mong the *Egyptians*. *Ifis*, fays he,
was become fo glorious in this
country, that their queens were moſt
honour'd, and bore a greater fway than
the kings. In all their marriage contracts,

tracts, wives were allow'd a full power over their husbands, who were oblig'd to take an oath to obey the former in all things.

Among the *Medes* and *Sabæans*, the women commanded alfo over the men, and their queens always led them to the field, which † *Claudian* expreffes as follows.

———*Medis, levibusque Sabæis*
Imperat hic fexus, Reginarumque fub armis
Barbariæ pars magna jacet ———

The children of the *Garamantes*, a people of *Afric*, paid the utmoft fubmiffion, and were vaftly fond of their mothers; but had fo little regard to their fathers, that they fcarce feem'd to own them for fuch. One would have concluded, that the children were in common, and equally related to all the men of the nation; becaufe thefe, according to their notion, could not difcover who were their true fathers, or at leaft be pofitively certain who were really fo. 'Twas

† *In Eutrop. Lib.* 1.

'Twas the cuſtom, ſays *Strabo*, a-
mong all the people of *Spain*, particularly the *Cantabrians*, for the huſband to bring a portion in marriage ;
daughters always ſucceeded in wrong
of the male iſſue, and were entruſted
with the care of marrying their brothers. We are farther told, that the
Biſcayans, who deſcend from the antient *Cantabrians*, ſtill preſerve a ſhadow of this cuſtom, in their marriages and inheritances.

* *Plutarch* relates, that a foreign lady,
who liv'd with *Leonidas* the *Lacedemonian*,
ſaid one day to the wife of the latter,
whoſe name was *Gorgo*, by way of reproach, as a circumſtance which ſham'd
the wiſdom of the *Lacedemonians*; that
the *Spartan* women only (tho' ſhe was
miſtaken) had an abſolute authority
over their husbands; and that *Gorgo*
reply'd with a haughty tone, that none
but the *Spartan* women deſerv'd that
preeminence, becauſe they only brought
men into the world.

I

* *In Lacon. Apoptheg.*

I know that thefe *Gynecocracies* were of a different kind, and that the women abovemention'd exercis'd their authority varioufly. However, we may infer in general from thence; that it is no new, or ridiculous thing, for men to fubmit to a female government, and for the latter to prefide wholly in the adminiftration.

Further; every one knows, that in moft of the negro nations of *Africa*, in all parts of *Malabar*, in feveral countries of *India*, and particularly in *America*; 'tis an eftablifh'd cuftom for the heirs in the collateral maternal line, to fucceed to the throne, in prejudice of the direct line; fo that children never inherit their father's eftates. In order, fays *Owington* in his defcription of *Malabar*, that the crown may be more certainly preferv'd in the royal family, the king is always fucceeded by his fifter's fon; for this reafon, the king's fifter ufes all her endeavours to have a numerous iffue; infomuch that any man who offers himfelf as a voluntier upon thefe occafions, is always well receiv'd.

He

He alſo relates, that on the coaſts of
Malabar, whenever the king marries; a
bramin or prieſt, has the firſt fruits of
her majeſty on the wedding night, in
order that the people may be convinc'd,
that the ſon ſhe will be deliver'd of, is
not of the blood-royal; which is the
reaſon why the king's ſons never ſucceed
him, but thoſe of his ſiſter.

Agreeable to this cuſtom, *Nicholas
Damaſc:* relates, that the *Ethiopians* paid
the utmoſt honour to their ſiſters; that
the kings never nominated their own
ſons their ſucceſſors, but thoſe of
their ſiſters; and in caſe theſe were
barren, or their children died, they
then elected that man king, who was
moſt fam'd for gracefulneſs, valour and
fine accompliſhments.

It muſt indeed be confeſs'd, that *Gynecocracy* in the iſland of *Babilary* is carried
to the higheſt pitch; its men being ſo
much ſubject to the women, that they
are in ſome meaſure their ſlaves. Women indeed have govern'd kingdoms
and headed troops; and armies have
conſiſted wholly of women, ſuch as
thoſe

thofe of the *Amazons*; but that which
furprizes me in your ifland of *Babilary*,
is, that women only fhould fill up the
feveral places of truft, and manage the
whole civil power and the revenues.
After all, this is a natural confequence
of *Gynecocracy*; and when we read that
women have govern'd kingdoms and
fought battles, are we to wonder they
fhould be minifters of ftate, magiftrates,
authors, and academicians?

Another difference between the *Gynecocracy* of *Babilary*, and that which
was formerly eftablifh'd among the nations abovemention'd, is, that the huf-
bands of the latter were neither weak
or effeminate; fo far from it, that the
fuperiority of their women, feem'd to
infpire them with greater bravery.
Tho' the *Scythians*, the *Garamantes*,
and the *Spartans* were fubject to women, they yet always had the reputation of being inform'd with a martial
fpirit. 'This was, becaufe their women never went into the field; and
that their men, notwithftanding the female fuperiority, only bore arms. But
I

I am perfuaded, that where women only form the military power, their men
muft neceffarily become foft and pu-
fillanimous. And indeed, we don't find
that in thofe countries where the *Amazons* govern'd, the men ever exerted
themfelves in any warlike exploit.

After all, 'tis as natural for women
to be brave, as for men to be effeminate; when one party is active, 'tis no
wonder the other fhould be fupine and
indolent. Our women are timid, weak,
and fluggifh, becaufe our men are bold,
ftrong and active.

I have read in a relation of *Siam*,
that the language of that country has
the fame perfection you afcribe to the
Babilarian tongue, which, like the *Englifh*, does not admit the ridiculous diftinction of mafculine and feminine
genders, in inanimate things; nor
has even genders to diftinguifh the
fexes. When, for inftance, the *Siamois*,
would afcribe a certain quality to a
woman, which ftanding alone, is underftood of man only; they join the adjective *young* to it. As for example, inftead

ſtead of ſaying the empreſs, they expreſs it thus, the *young* emperour; to denote the wife of a miniſter, they ſay the *young* miniſter, and ſo on. 'Tis plain, this muſt ſooth very agreeably the vanity of their women, ſince they have always the epithet *young* beſtow'd upon them, tho' they are never ſo far advanc'd in years.

Paſs we now to the *Oligochroniſm* or ſhort life of the inhabitants of your iſland of *Tilibet.* I muſt own I have not found any thing ſo ſingular, in either antient or modern writers. However, methinks this is ſomething like what is related of the inhabitants of the weſtern Peninſula of *India*, who, we are told, are ſooner ripe than we, and conſequently have a more early decay. In this country people marry at five or ſix years old, and at that age a maiden is made a wife.

In my opinion, the inhabitants of that iſland, argue not only ſuitable to the length of their lives, but alſo agreeable to the idea the antient philoſophers had of the duration of ours.

'Tis

'Tis well known, that *Cato* of *Utica*
anfwer'd thofe who would have prevented him from killing himfelf, that
they could not reproach him with a-
bandoning life too foon. Neverthelefs, he was then but eight and forty;
but he look'd upon this as an advanc'd
age, fince the greateft part of men feldom live fo long. 'Tis generally faid,
that the life of man is of threefcore and
and ten, threefcore and fifteen, and
fourfcore years. However, as men
die oftner at twenty or thirty, than at
the ages abovemention'd, methinks it
would be more natural, to fix the period of man's life at the former term
of years, rather than the latter, fince
it is fo feldom attain'd. May we not
infer from hence, that we begin to live
too late; or in other words, don't enter upon the ftage of the world foon
enough, and are too late entrufted
with the management of our eftates
and public employments? If men
would but change the ufual methods
of education, and accuftom children
early to bufinefs, politicks, and dome-
ftick

frick cares; and not make them trifle
away their bloom in fruitlefs ftudies;
their life, which, as things are now
manag'd is fhort, would then be much
longer.

By the laws of antient *Rome*, no man
could enjoy a poft in the civil government, till he was five and thirty. *Au-
guftus* thought proper to retrench five
years, and declared that thirty fhould
be the ftated age; but had he not
better have retrench'd ten? 'Tis certain that we are as much men at
twenty as at threefcore; for the mind,
after this age, enlarges its views no
more; the only advantage is, we gain
experience, and the paffions abate in
their violence; but 'tis falfe to affert,
that the foul difplays itfelf afterwards;
that the mind enlarges its views, or the
judgment grows ftronger. Collect the
moft renow'd actions of heroes antient
and modern, and you'll find that
the greateft part of thofe exploits were
perform'd by men who had not yet
feen thirty. *Alexander, Hannibal, Scipio,* the prince of *Conde,* immortaliz'd

V o l. II.   N   their

their names before they were come to
that age. The moſt famous works of
wit, were ſtruck out by young writers.
The longer a man lives, the more he
learns; but he decays in fire, emulation, courage, vigour, reſolution, beauty, and ſprightlineſs. Methinks the
calculation of your *Tilibetan* is very
juſt, when after having computed the
time we loſe in infancy; what we trifle
away in a tedious education; that
which ſleep bereaves us of; and the tedious hours of ſickneſs, ſorrow, ſpleen,
and old age; he concludes, that ſuch
among us as attain to the moſt advanced age, have not lived twenty
years complete.

The contempt in which the *Tilibetans* have ſleep, recalls to my mind a
beautiful paſſage of *Plutarch*, who compares it to a collector of the revenues.
" In like manner, ſays he, as thoſe
" men always ſteal half the money that
" paſſes thro' their hands, ſo ſleep robs
" us of half our life. " This paſſage,
Sir, proves two things. Firſt, That
in *Plutarch's* time men us'd to ſleep as
they

they do now; and, Secondly, That collectors were then in as good repute as they are in this age.

With regard to the different iflands of *Terra del Fuego*, which you fay were defcrib'd by a *Dutchman*, give me leave to obferve, that tho' this may be ftrictly true, yet his relation feems of the fame caft with the true hiftory of *Lucian*, I mean fabulous and allegorical. However, tho' you don't warrant the truth of it, I yet am pleas'd with you for illuftrating your travels with thofe fictions, which are far from leffening the character you have for veracity.

But one circumftance, which, fo far from appearing fictitious, feems to agree with reafon and experience, is, the *Palineacy*, or return of the *Letalifpons* to the bloom of youth. This happy ifland, was certainly worthy of being confecrated to *Hygeia* and *Panacea*, daughters of *Efculapius*. I am no longer furpriz'd at the long life of thofe people, when I call to mind the antient anchorets, who tho' they fubfifted wholly on roots, herbs, and

dates

dates, did neverthelefs live a century, as St. *Jerom* tells us of St. *Paul* the hermit, and St. *Anthony*. This regimen was alfo obferv'd by the famous *Lewis Cornaro*, a noble *Venetian*, who was robuft and vigorous at fourfcore and fixteen, when he publifh'd his book *Of the advantages of being abftemious*, on which I one day intend to publifh a commentary, which every man may make ufe of, agreeable to his *Idiofyncrafy*, or particular conftitution. I fhall therein difcover the truth of thefe words of *Celfus*, * *Ignavia maturam feneSutem, labor longam adolefcentiam reddit*; and fhall apply to the human body, what *Virgil* fays of *Fame*.

† *Mobilitate viget, vires acquirit eundo.*

I fhall be fure not to omit the admirable laws of health, obferv'd by the

---

* *Lib.* 1. *c.* 2. *That is*, Sloth haftens old age ; activity keeps us long in bloom.
  † *Swift from the firft; and every moment brings New vigour to her flights, new pinions to her wings.*   Dryd.

the *Letalifpons*, they being, in my o-
pinion, preferable to thofe of the
twelve tables.

If any one fhould look upon the account you give of the periodical revigo-
ration of thofe people as chimerical, I
fhall refer them to the learned difler-
tation of Dr. *Begon*, of *Puy* in *Vellay*,
printed in 1708. This excellent author, mentions feveral perfons who actually grew young again, and particularly a marchionefs, whofe *menſtrua*
return'd in her hundredth year, after
they had left her fifty; and in her
hundred and fourth year, (the time
when he writ his book) as ftrongly as
in the flower of her age. 'Tis well
known, that the famous *William Poſtel*,
at the age of an hundred and four
years, recover'd the full ufe of his
reafon, tho' it had before been confiderably weakned ; that his wrinkles
faded away, and his white hair turn'd
black; in a word, that he grew young
again; and would not have been
known by his friends, had not they
themfelves feen this wonderful meta-
morphofis

morphofis. Now is it not natural to
fuppofe, that the very change which
fome perfons have undergone, may
happen to a whole nation.

To conclude, I am highly pleas'd
with the exactnefs of your geography.
This circumftance will be confider'd as
a beauty by all who are acquainted
with the fituation of the different parts
of our globe; and your ftrict regard to
truth will do you the greateft honour.
I am with the utmoft efteem, &c.

F I N I S.

LILLIPUT:

BEING

A NEW JOURNEY

TO THAT

CELEBRATED ISLAND.

CONTAINING

A FAITHFUL ACCOUNT

OF THE

MANNERS, CHARACTER, CUSTOMS, RELIGION,
LAWS, POLITICS, REVENUE, TAXES, LEARNING,
GENERAL PROGRESS IN ARTS AND SCIENCES,
DRESS, AMUSEMENTS, AND GALLANTRY

OF THOSE

FAMOUS LITTLE PEOPLE.

From the Year 1702 (when they were first discovered
and visited by Captain Lemuel Gulliver, the Father of
the Compiler of this Work), to the present Æra 1796.

By LEMUEL GULLIVER, Jun.

Designed to shew—" *Virtue* her own feature, *scorn* her own image,
and *the very age* and *body of the time* its *form and pressure.*"

SHAKESPEARE.

LONDON:

PRINTED FOR T. CHAPMAN, FLEET STREET,

1796

DEDICATION.

TO THE MOST NOBLE
FRANCIS,

DUKE OF BEDFORD, MARQUIS OF TAVISTOCK,
EARL OF BEDFORD, BARON RUSSELL
AND HOWLAND.

MY LORD DUKE,

IF it is ever necessary for *virtue* to oppose a shield against the poisoned shafts of *calumny* and *envy*, it should be either of *satire* or *ridicule*.

In the Pagan mythology, we read, " That one of the furies (Tisiphone) became enamoured of *Cythæron,* an amiable youth ; but fearing to affright him by her *natural form, voice,* and *manner,* she employed a third person, or *in the third person* addressed him. *He* disdainfully rejected her suit ; on which she threw one of her snakes at him (*perhaps only a letter of invective*), which, twisting round his body, strangled him."

A   Had

Had *Cythæron* uplifted the buckler of *satire* or *ridicule*, the serpent would either have glanced harmlessly aside from its highly-polished and well-tempered front, or forcibly rebounding, have spent its venom on the breast of the enraged, disappointed, malicious jaculator.

If, on the perusal of the few following pages, YOUR GRACE should discover the meritorious attempt (though of a feeble arm) to raise the guards of *satire* and *ridicule*, protective of assailed integrity, against the gall dipped ebon arrow of a *sublime modern Tisiphone*, the exertion will not pass without your praise : The ambition of,

My LORD DUKE,

Your GRACE'S

Most respectful admirer,

Fellow-subject, and citizen,

CONTENTS.

CHAP.

the

LILLIPUT,

&c. &c.

CHAPTER I.

The Author's Birth, Parentage, and Education.

MY father, during his refidence at *Blefefcu*, became enamoured of *a nun*; her name was *Adeline Belciglia*, fhe favoured him, and *I* am the iffue of the amour (at leaft, it has hitherto been fo reported). My mother was of courfe obliged to confefs herfelf to the vifitor of her convent, *Father Rambellius*: Youth, beauty, and tears, obtained his pity (fomething more, perhaps) however, he preferved her character, by his care and fecrecy, and during the remainder of her life was, as my father had been, the neareft and deareft to her heart.

B   To

To their care and caution, the reader owes
the gratification, which, no doubt, he will
receive, in the perufal of the following
pages.

For want of a cradle, as foon as born, I
was popped into a relique cheft, two feet four
inches long, which had, as was faid, contained the afhes of the firft abbefs of the
nunnery, a pure virgin, though at her deceafe upwards of ninety years of age. In
this depofitary of fuppofed innocence was I
enclofed for the firft eight years of my exiftence, for the firft two years of which, a
muflin bandage was always enfolded many
times round my head, fo as to cover my
mouth, that my infantine cries might not be
heard; and I was often fed by phyfical aid,
when I appeared any ways uneafy, left my
artlefs murmurs fhould caufe difcovery. I
grew to my manfion, beyond it I could not
lengthen, which, as it has fince proved, was
of great advantage to me during my fojourn
in Lilliput, being, on account of my diminutive fize, lefs an objeƈ of jealoufy in that
fufpicious country, than my father had been,
whofe gigantic height and finewy qualifica-
                                                tions,

tions, the perufers of his travels remember to have been continual fources of inconvenience.

The day after I had reached my eighth year my mother died, and the good Rambellius, with truly pious fraud, took me and my narrow home in his arms to his cell, under the pretence of obtaining a fimilar farcophagus to contain the bones of my *virgin mother*, that there might be a pair of chafte examples ever before the religieufe, to fix their ideas the right way.

Arrived at the monaftery, he clofed the door of his cell, and turning my houfe topfyturvy, emptied me on a large oak table; then, with tears in his eyes, thus addreffed me:

I.

" *Now* first to day and day-light giv'n,
 " Poor little orphan'd boy!
" Sad child of chance, yet heir of heav'n,
 " Ah, whither canst thou fly?

II.

" Without or shelter, means, or friend,
 " The world's thy utter foe;
" If short thy stage, thou'lt wish its end,
 " For all thy wealth is woe!"

He

He then preffed me to his bofom, and kiffed
me. I do not recollect that I then underftood
the meaning of his words, as I fince have
from reading fome of the manufcripts he left
me ; but I put both my hands on his pallid
care-worn cheeks, and wept on his beard.
He wiped his eyes, and, looking upwards,
continued—

III.

" Thou fhalt be mine, I'll guard thy youth,
  " My cell fhall be thy home ;
" And I will give thee holy truth,
  " Bless'd fortune for the tomb.

IV.

" So, chearly boy, dry up thy tears,
  " And dread nor care or ftrife ;
" Here rest in peace, 'till rip'ning years,
  " Befits for active life.

V.

" *Then* try the world, and mayst thou find,
  " Kind fortune still thine own ;
" If not, and thou'rt to grief consign'd,
  " *Sad child, my duty's* done !"

He again embraced me, placed me by
him, and gave me refrefhment, adding the
ftory

ſtory of my life to the then paſſing moment.
I liſtened with attention, and gave him in
return my promiſe of aſſiduity, and profiting
by, as far as my abilities would permit, his
kind aſſurances of education, and fitting me
for the world. *I* was not diſappointed; *he*
fulfilled his part; and often in the progreſs,
he has ſaid, *I* was a grateful pupil.

We lived together till I attained my twen-
tieth year, when a dreadful revolution in
Blefeſcu, overturned as well the church as
ſtate.

My kind patron was among the early victims to anarchic frenzy; he was butchered;
and I, alas! had the wide and unknown
world before me: All my treaſure the few
manuſcripts he had given me but a ſhort
time before his end.

From thoſe manuſcripts, among which were
my father's travels, I ſhall occaſionally endeavour to amuſe my reader. *For myſelf!*
I am no longer to be conſidered as the virtuous
eléve of *good Rambellius,* but,

GULLIVER, *Junior*

" without or *friend,* or *relative,* or *home.*"

B 3   CHAP.

CHAP. II.

Blefefcu—-Author's Departure therefrom— Voyage to, and Arrival on the Coaft of Lilliput.

---

*M*ASSACRE reigned uncontrouled through-out the once fine and flourifhing king-dom of *Blefefcu*; perfons of all ranks and either fex were engaged in the general havoc; fave *that*, here and there, an indivi-dual philofophically beheld the horrid ftorm, and in filence wept the lofs of friends, and ruin of his country.

It was my good fortune to be known to one of the latter defcription. I had often been at the villa of the *noble Mediocritas*, in company with my patron, to whom I now fled for fhelter. He received me with open arms, but dared not refcue me from diftrefs by per-mitting me to refide under his roof, as I had been the inmate of a religious houfe, without himfelf incurring the danger of death, from the municipal authority then governing, as a

man

man *yet tainted* with *goodnefs* and *the remains of religion.*

All he could he did for me; he put a thou-fand pieces of gold into my pocket, and ad-vifed me to feek the coaft of *Lilliput.* The advice was taken, and I flowly withdrew from him with thanks and tears.

I repaired to the *foreft of Balono,* and *there,* having previoufly purchafed a fmall ftore of provifion, I fecreted myfelf fome days, my time wholly occupied in reading my father's account of that beautiful country, and ftudy-ing, by the help of a grammar and diction-ary which I had of the language, to become fome proficient therein.

Vanity is an ingredient thrown into every mortal's compofition; of courfe, *I* had my fhare. I muft firft confefs it *here,* even *here.* I thought that my father wanted fome perfpi-cuity in not furnifhing himfelf with a pair of fpectacles, whofe magnifying powers would increafe the tiny race of Lilliput to the fize of common mortals; by that means he could have gained numberlefs advantages, and have obtained confiderable knowledge. I was fo
fully

fully convinced of *this*, that I repaired to *Balono*, and completed the purchafe. I bought alfo a few more bifcuits and a faufage or two, for which that place is famous, then hafted to the fea-fhore, determined, like my *father (here vanity* was again predominant), to wade over without delay. The moon fhone, and I dafhed into the wave. Attempting too much, we often fink into contempt and ridicule. I was in danger of worfe than either of *thofe*—of *drowning!* I had forgotten, or *vanity* had made me forget, that my *father* was fix feet high, and the waters of the paffage were up to *his chin*. *I* was, as before ftated, only two feet four inches, fo that my firft purchafe fhould have been a *cork jacket*. After fwimming about for almoft half an hour, though only an hundred yards from the ftrand, I regained it. Fatigued, almoft exhaufted, I again fought the wood, and in a hollow tree patiently waited the return of the fun to dry my clothes, that I might, unfufpected of attempt at efcape, revifit the town to buy a cork jacket, before I again fet forward.

Night

Night is the time for contemplation and ftudy; I was fo damp and cold I could not fleep; my voyage occupied my mind.

I was abforbed in thought till a guft of wind roufed me. How, thought I, will it fare with thee *Gulliver*, fhould the wind blow hard, when thy little frame is on the face of the waters? How, without rudder, fail, or compafs, wilt thou fteer thy way, though kept by cork above the wave? Thy little feet will not be within four feet of the bottom, and thou mayeft be carried about like a float on a fifhing-line, the whirligig of every gurglet in the ftream. Prudence, or vanity, inftantly replied, " A *fail* is within thy power, and purchafe; at leaft, that which will anfwer as well for thy aquatic tour—a *large umbrella.*" I was fatisfied, I flept, and awaking, found the long-rifen fun had dried me thoroughly. I walked to the town, bought my fail, and at nightfall again hafted to the beach. Clad in cork, I launched in; and was fo fortunate as to preferve my paffage on fhallows, till I was one third over the river, before I had occafion to think of my fail. The waters now rofe on me; I was

above

above my middle; I hoisted my *umbrella*, and boldly pushed forward. The wind was fair, buoyed me up, and carried me on. I kept my way, chearly, steadily; holding my sail by turns with either hand, and by turns paddling with either: But I was compelled to hold it so low before me, that I could not see what ground I made, though I was certain I was at a quick rate, by the frequent blasts of wind that forced me on. All of a sudden a violent storm of hail, as I thought, assailed me; with difficulty, the wind still blowing fresh, I lifted my sail so high as to peep under it, *when*, to my pleasure and surprise, I perceived the storm of hail, as I had apprehended it to be, was a broad-side, fired at me from a Lilliputian man of war, then within two yards of me. I took in my canvass a little, which, it seems, was understood as my signal for striking; on which they put out all their boats, and in about two minutes I found myself overwhelmed by near four hundred of them climbing on my back. Fortunately I was now within my depth; I put my feet to the ground; and with one exertion furled my sail. Sorry am I that I

did

did fo, for the wind and report of it occafioned upwards of fifty of the poor little
wretches to fall off me into the water; nine-
teen of whom never more faw friends, or
wives, or children. The reft, the moment
they beheld my head, fled with confternation
to their boats, and regained the fhip. I
boldly fought and gained the fhore. The
fhip returned to port making fignals, which
I have fince learned, were for the reft of the
fleet to do the fame; imagining that the
Blefefcudians had begun an invafion of their
country, long threatened, by me, who was
fuppofed the van fhip of their fleet, the
Commerci Baloni, the Blefefcudians' largeft
man of war.

CHAP.

CHAP. III.

Arrival and reception at Dopb'r.

I WAS *now* fafely landed, far beyond the reach of curfed democracy; and, compofedly, happily walked on to a hillock, on which, feating myfelf, and looking downwards, I faw the Lilliputian

" Crows and choughs, hanging the midway air,
" Shew scarce so gross as atoms."

Then cafting my eye over the water I had paffed, I enthufiaftically exclaimed, with horror!

" I look back upon thee, oh! thou country,
" That girdlest in these wolves."

I took a bifcuit from my bag, ate it with gratitude, and thanked heaven for my efcape. Soon after I fell into a fweet flumber, and awoke quite refrefhed and ferene. I got up, clapped *my fpectacles* on my nofe, and walked into *Dopb'r.* Thinking that I might poffibly

hire

hire fome ftate machine, or ammunition wag-
gon, large enough to carry me to *the capital*;
having alfo plenty of wealth about me, and
my time my own, expedition was unneceffary.
My fortune too, being, as I fuppofed, equal
to the royal treafury, I thought, like other
great travellers, I might be *pleafurably expen-
five*; and that *that* would be a ftep towards
aggrandizing myfelf in the eyes of my new
countrymen.

I had not proceeded above twenty yards,
when I found the ufe of my fpectacles, without which I fhould infallibly have trod to
death two fine children, of about ten years
of age, who were carelefsly playing at marbles
in the high road, down which I was obliged
to pafs, the footpaths being only three inches
wide.

Dopb'r is a well built clean town, has a
beautiful fort and caftle on the fummit of a
monftrous mountainous rock, nearly fixteen
feet above the level of the river, to which I
walked, and ftooping low, fpoke to a centinel who was parading the upper parapet
(and, as I have fince learned, watching my
motions) as lowly as I could, to know if I

C   might

might obtain a vehicle for travelling. I
found I had not mifpent my time in the *wood
of Balono*, for he anfwered me readily,
" *What money have you ?*" " Why ?" faid
I : " Becaufe," he replied, " if you have
money enough, you can command every thing
here." I put my hand in my pocket, and
produced a piece of gold. " I perceive,'
faid he, " you are *civilized*, and worthy to
fpeak to *our governor*; I'll call him." He
then founded the great bell of the caftle,
which was nearly the fize of (and muft have
been a wonderful work for thefe little people)
thofe which are hung round the necks of
fquirrels in *Blefefcu*. Inftantaneoufly appeared *the governor*, with his fuite; I pulled
off my hat incautioufly, for down fell the
governor and his train on their faces ! I perceived my error, and thinking to amend my
rafhnefs, uttered, in rather an animated tone,
" *Fear not*." Inftead of the effect intended,
a battery was difcharged full on me ; luckily,
only one ball hit me, about the fize of a
mofs feed, but which, ftriking my nofe,
though it occafioned a little pain, forced me
to laugh aloud. The walls were inftantly
lined

lined with mufquetry; I then waved my
hand gently; this anfwered better than my
voice had done ; they grounded their arms ;
a buz, like the humming of a fwarm of bees,
fucceeded, and up rofe the governor and his
attendants. I made fignal for an amicable
parley; it was granted. I requefted,

" 1ft. A lodging in the great hall of the
caftle, while I ftaid with them ; and

" 2dly. That I might, if poffible, be provided with a carriage to convey me to the
capital."

The governor *fhook his head!* I thought
I had afked too much ; recollecting myfelf,
I again put my hand in my pocket, and produced *another piece of gold—the governor
fmiled!* I now perceived the centinel had
fpoken honeftly, and that in Lilliput, as well
as in Blefefcu, *gold* was the currency for
convenience. I laid the two pieces on the
tower of the caftle, and withdrew to the great
gate, bowing and courteoufly fmiling all the
way. I did right; flings were immediately
brought, the money was lifted off the turret,
and a dozen foldiers conveyed each away,
with feeming tranfport. The gate, foon

after

after, opened, and I crawled into the court, where the garrifon were formed to receive me. I feated myfelf; my ear was then juft one foot from the ground; this was an evidently pleafing mark of fuavity and condefcenfion in me. The governor boldly approached, and, exalting his voice, faid,

" What we can we will for your convenience, provided you faithfully narrate why you vifit Lilliput; if amicably, welcome; for the ftate is fond of power-promifing allies."

I whifpered (that I might not again fhock him with my voice)—

" That I had fled from anarchy and *Blefcu*; was rich, and, as he muft obferve, mighty; poffeffed of talents and ftrength; and that if I could be conveyed to the capital by art, as I did not love walking, I would throw myfelf and all I poffeffed at the feet of his fovereign."

He believed my affurances; the guards filed off, the hall-door was opened, and walking ftatelily in himfelf, he beckoned me to follow.

CHAP.

CHAP. IV.

In continuation, with the Author's manner of travelling, and first Week's Journey towards the Capital.

———————

THE resident governor, whose name was *Tomazza Beſtanza*, was a well-made man, and full nine inches high without his ſhoes, ſo that by ſtanding on his chair of ſtate, and I ſeated, our ears were nearly on a level. We very ſoon became friends, and he promiſed me that he would give orders for a carriage to be built for my conveyance ; and that the gold I had depoſited in the tower, ſhould be ſolely expended in furniſhing me with a table, during the time neceſſary for the apparatus being got ready for my departure, which would be ſome days, as they muſt diſmount, at leaſt, one of their batteries, to furniſh timber for my carriage ; and ſcour the country for relays of bullocks to draw me. I offered him more money, but he would not take it, ſaying, " The

C 3   former

former fums were fimply depofits in truft,
till he knew the pleafure of *Magno Vilpi
Tico*, the chief governor, and which would
be duly returned me, if my fervices were
accepted; for that *the Lilliputians* always
paid, inftead of receiving from their allies."
I could do no lefs than repeat my affurances
of gratitude and fincerity, and we parted;
each feemingly well pleafed with the other.

In about two hours my dinner was ferved
up, and a really fumptuous regale it was;
confifting of twelve delicately flavoured fifh,
fomething lefs than minnows, two fine grown
roafted lambs, in a porcelain plate, and fix
large turkeys ftewed in an elegant fmall filver
bafon; vegetables of all forts anfwerable, in
little enamelled faucers. The fruits were
delicious, and I obferved (which fhews hor-
ticulture muft be in great perfection with
them) a melon, nearly as large as a Blefefcudian current.

I was very hungry, yet reftrained my
appetite, left I fhould create aftonifhment, fo
only eat the fifh, one of the lambs, and three
turkeys. The dinner over, delicioufly flavoured wine was brought me; this was from
the

the chief governor's store, who muft be, from the fample I had, a perfect judge, if not a lover of the juice of the grape. I own I was here a little bold—I drank nine bottles (about a pint). I had no fooner finifhed my repaft, and the table cleared, than, preceded by a band of mufic, re-entered the governor, leading his lady and family; I had pulled off my fpectacles during dinner, but perceiving ladies enter, I haftily rofe to pay my devoirs. On a fudden there was a great buftle, and the attendants flocked round the women; but Beftanza, unmindful of them, ferioufly proceeded on to me, and inquired, " How I liked my fare?" I thanked him, " Well, and begged to know what was the occafion of the feeming confufion I had imperfectly feen?" He courtlily fimpered, " Nothing! a mere trifle! only that two of the children, frightened at your rifing, had fallen into fits." I begged his pardon for the unintended accident, and refeated myfelf; he defired me not to think of it, for that as he meaned them for foldiers, they muft learn, while young, to defpife danger like himfelf. I thought on the clofe

of

of his fpeech ; he looked hard on me, and
crefted himfelf, as much as to fay, " An't I
a *brave fellow?*" Order being reftored by
the removal of the children, the ladies were
prefented : I kiffed their arms, and bowed ;
they courtfied ; I clearly faw though that
they winced and drew back, as my mouth
approached them. A fpirited converfation
enfued, in which they bore their parts till
day clofed, when they withdrew, and left
me to repofe.

Thus five days paffed : On the fixth, a
meffage from the governor, by a herald,
informed me, all was ready for my departure, whenever I chofe to fet forward ;
and that, at the time I fhould name, he
would, properly mounted and attended,
efcort me to the out-pofts of his conftabulary.
I named the following morning. On awaking
at funrife, the bells of the caftle were tink-
ling like fheep-bells at a diftance, and the
artillery going off by royal falutes, almoft as
loud as tolerable pop-guns. I looked into
the yard, where my equipage was waiting
with all the pomp and circumftance of am-
baffadorial fplendour. The carriage was
about

about three feet two inches long, and two feet broad, placed on forty-eight wheels, four inches and a half high; to it were faftened thirty bullocks, by pairs, (that is) fifteen in length; to each pair a driver; they were beautiful cattle, about the fize of well-grown cats. I was fo intent on my new ftate, that the governor was within a foot of me befote I faw him: He affifted me to my carriage. I feated myfelf thereon as gracefully as I could; bowed to the ladies, and fmiled on the hofpitable, admiring, affembled croud; and unfurling my umbrella over my head, which added confiderably to the effeft of the cavalcade, I sat off—the governor leading the way in full martial difplay, amidft the found of bells, of cannon, and fhouts of the multitude: To compare a moufe to an elephant, fomething like the majeftic Catharine's Ruffian fnowy trip from Mofcow to Peterfburgh.

CHAP.

CHAP. V.

Obſervations on the Road.

IT was the laſt day of Auguſt that I ſat *off* from *Doph'r.* The harveſt was begun, and general induſtry pervaded the face of the country. My ſpectacles and ſenſes informed me it was a productive and a rich one; but ſince my arrival in the capital, I have been told, by ſome who ought to know, (being the greateſt grain-holders) that it was a very bad one. Nothing particular occurred on the road, till I arrived at *Shrino-becketto,* the end of my firſt day's journey. *Here* I alſo halted, on purpoſe to view and contemplate a religious pile I had often heard of during my reſidence with *Rambellius.* It did not anſwer my expectation: I imagined I ſhould have found an eſtabliſhment equal to ſome I had ſeen in *Blefeſcu.* I was diſappointed. I inquired for the reſidence of, and to be introduced to, the *ſuperior.* I was chagrined, on being told, they had not ſeen him a long while;

while; that the monks were abolifhed; the chapels and fhrine deftitute of votarifts; and the trifling emoluments of this once gorgeous cathedral, a church coloffus, were now diftributed among a few mendicant almsmen, called (excepting the fuperior) *Queerftrums*, &c. who prayed for almoft nothing, fo of courfe feldom prayed; that *the fuperior* was of the mendicant order himfelf, and begged about, fomewhere in the neighbourhood of *Flubndubnna.*

Once more feated in my caravan, away I went, and in the courfe of the day arrived at *Chtmhaa. Here* they build fhips of war. As I had heard much of the Lilliputian navy, I refolved to vifit the docks and ftores; and muft own I was amply gratified. With fome labour I took a *three-decker* on my knees, and was indulged with a review of their manœuvering their watery manfions and bulwarks, in which their abilities are beyond competition, and furpaffing imagination. In fhort, they feem to have no dread of that element; fo that I fhould really think they were primarily *nautilæ*; and ftill further indulging a philofophical hypothefis, conclude,

that,

Evolution!

that, from some volcanic emotion, this little island was raised above the face of the waters—that the aboriginals, by degrees, lost their shelly coats, and, from being *natives* of the deep, became *only amphibious.* My equipage ready, on I drove for the metropolis—arrived there about seven in the evening, and found apartments, or rather, a street laid into one apartment, ready for me, near the court.

CHAP.

CHAP. VI.

Arrived at the Capital—Vifit from a Minifter.

---

*A*RCHITECTURE muſt have been a
ſcience earlily ſtudied by theſe minimæs
of mankind, to have ariſen to ſuch perfection
as my manſion fully illuſtrated.

I was lodged in the wideſt ſtreet of the
ſuburbs, oppoſite to the reſidence of the
royal guard ; and though in a baby-houſe,
compared with Blefeſcudian palaces, I had
abſolutely elbow room. I ſlept like a traveller after a journey. My firſt buſineſs of
the morning was to unlade myſelf. *My
money*, conſiſting of nine hundred and ninety-
eight broad pieces of gold, I ſtored by ſcores
in piles againſt the walls of my apartment;
before them I placed a pair of piſtols, with a
bag of powder and bullets, I had carried in
my belt and pockets, together with a broad
ſword given me by the worthy *Mediocritas*—
not forgetting to take care of my faithful
preſervers, my *umbrella*, my *cork-jacket*,

D though

though, at that time, unconfcious they would
lead me to honour.

Thus, a perfeᾰ piᾰure of Mammon, was
I fituated, when a vifitor was announced. I
put on my fpeᾰacles; through their medium
he appeared about five feet nine inches high.
He was thin, pale, and of a countenance far
from pleafing; his nofe offended me; it
feemed to have quarreled with his mouth
and chin, and was looking to the forehead
for proteᾰion; however, he fmiled, waved
a lady-like hand, and we feated. He then
produced, and offered me, a letter: I read
as follows:—

  " To Magno-Vilpi Tico.

  " Noble Renommoc,   *Doph'r.*

  " On the 24th ult. arrived here, from
 " Blefefcu, a powerful *drol*, as I take him
 " to be, from his worth *in gold*. As wealth
 " is the *fummum* at *Flubndubnna*, I have
 " done him honour, and forwarded him, in
 " a manner, that, I hope, will prove agree-
 " able to you, and convince him of the
 " grandeur of Lilliput. He left in the gar-
 " rifon two enormous ingots of gold; I beg
       " you

" you to inform me what I am to do with
" the fmail remnant that will remain, after
" the fees of office, due to you and us, are
" fatisfied.

" I reft your faithful deputy,

" Tomazza Bestanza."

How fully I was prepoffeffed with the juf-
tice of Lilliputian government, this letter
explains, without comment. I returned the
fcrol, bowing as gracioufly as my manners
inftructed. Then thus he—
" You feek afylum in Lilliput ?'
" I do."
" You have fled from Blefefcu ?"
" True !"
" *We* are at war with *Blefefcu.*"
" I know it !"
" *You* may be a fpy."
" I am rich."
" Enough ! ! !"
He fhook my hand—
" How do you mean to beftow your
wealth ?"

" I wifh

" I wifh to do good to the ftate I live in;
yet reap the juft advantages *due* from my
abilities and talents."

" You fhall be *a Drol!*"

" I beg pardon, *noble Renommoc!* (for
fuch the letter has informed me is your defcription) I am not qualified; I am a ftudious
man; I have no drollery about me."

He laughed, then—

" Excuse me! you are unacquainted with
the idioms of our language: *A Drol* is not,
as you fuppofe, *always* and *totally a buffoon*;
but is *any man* of wealth (no matter whence
his extraction) who *I* recommend to notice.
I only take him with me to court—a ribbon
of any indifferent colour, red, blue, yellow,
or green, is thrown acrofs his fhoulder, and
away he goes, a *perfect Drol.* From thenceforward he may fay, act, and do as he
pleafes; even run in debt, and fet creditors
at defiance—a kind of political adjective :
But *intereft, intereft,* you know, always joins
him to *me, the fubftantive.*"

" Sir, I comprehend; but fear *I am too
unworthy.*"

" Say

" Say no more!—you are rich. I fhall be
glad to fee you at the receipt of cuftom.
Adieu!"

We parted : If I had not felt, I fhould
have thought it impoffible he could have had
fuch mufcular ftrength ; for though he only
grafped my little finger, yet I felt the fenfation for half a minute. He retired bowing ;
his eyes fixed alternately on me and the
ftored wall of my chamber.

Materialism

D 3   CHAP.

CHAP. VII.

A little Ride in the Streets—Change, and another morning Vifitor

---

WISHING a breath of ars, I ordered my equipage. Inftead of my thirty bullocks, only fix were harneffed. I was angry : My valets fhook their heads. " What may this mean ? I want to go to the national depofitory of wealth ; I fhall not get there to-day !" (A low bow)—" The Sovereign *only, here,* travels with eight oxen." I fubmitted ; and flowly on we went—reached my defideratum—entered a circular veftibule, and fat down. Prefently up came to me a queer little fellow, and vociferated—

" Are you bull, or bear ?"

I felt—I am afhamed : How ! I caught him between my finger and thumb—

" Neither bull, bear, lion, or tiger !"

I let him go—I was forry.

" Sir, (faid he) I beg your pardon ; I
thought

thought you might be come to raife the ftocks."

I thought he was farcaftic on my fize, and feized him again—

" Reptile, If you are again impertinent, I'll raze your bank!"

He trembled in my fingers. I let him go— and he continued—

" I am broker for *Magno Vilpi Tico,* and I humbly thought you had inftructions "—

" Inftructions !—for what ?"

" Bubble !"

" Bubble !" (faid I) and repairing to my carriage, drove home, not comprehending his meaning.

I dined about feven, (as I thought, *evening*) ; but *another morning vifitor* was announced. He was the reverfe of *Vilpi Tico*— rubicund, rude, and rough.

" *Blefefcudian,* you are welcome ; have you bought in to-day ?"

I did not underftand him, fo was filent.

" Damn it, (faid he) why did not you buy ?"

" What ?"

" *Stock.*"

" What's

" What's that ?"

" *Ideal wealth* for *gold,* but current *here*—gold is of no ufe!—*paper*! *paper credit*!—*ftocks*!—*funds*!—I'll teach you!"

I bowed attention.

" All the wealth of *Blefefcu's here*—all the wealth of *Dnallob*—all the wealth of *Aidni*—all, *all in paper*—gold's of no ufe—we *eat with paper, drink with paper, love, game, build, buy, fell*—all with paper!"

" Sir, I fhall require inftruction."

" Enough; you fhall—I'll fend to you. Good *morning.*"

Away he went with his " *good morning,*"—(8 o'clock). I called for light; fhut my chamber, and took out one of *Rambellius's* manufcripts, which I had never before opened, and read—

CONTEMPLATION ON ADELINE.

I.

" If thou wert virtuous as thou'rt fair,
" How rich a prize thoudst prove;
" To me no jewel half so rare,
" As thy unblemish'd love!

But

II.

" But—as it seems !   *   *   * !
    " *   *   *   *   *   *   * !
    " *   *   *   *   *   *   * !
      " *   *   *   *   *   * !

III.

" Perhaps, remov'd from this terrene,
" Some other world you'll grace ;
" And perfect *there*, as *here*, be seen,
" In *form*, and *voice*, and face !

IV.

" If to that star my loosen'd soul
" Shou'd wing its last long flight—
" The essence, guiding its controul,
" Wou'd be thy charming light !

V.

" Then—if thou *there*, with *virtue* bless'd,
" Mayst own me just as *here;*
" I'll pray that Heav'n will doom my rest
" Eternal in *that sphere!*

As I concluded the laſt ſtanza, ſleep weighed down my lids ; I fell into ſlumber, and dreamed. I thought I ſaw Adeline and Rambellius treading the ſtarry pavement. They ſmiled on me, and were about to ſpeak, when my attendants rouſed me, and announced a meſſenger from *Vilpi Tico.*

CHAP.

CHAP. VIII.

The Balance.

THIS *vifitor* was no lefs a perfonage than *Nave Npnaee.* After the ufual ceremonies of congratulating me on my fortunate efcape from Blefefcu, he informed me, that he came immediately from Vilpi Tico, whofe confidential fecretary he was: That an account of the treafure I had depofited at *Dopb'r*, had been juftly remitted to Vilpi Tico, who by him had fent the fame to convince me, without delay, of the juftice and liberality practifed in the Lilliputian Government.

THE ACCOUNT.

	Copars.
" Received—by 2 Blefecudian ingots, in Lilliputian currency - - - }	1152

	C.	
" Disbursed—Expences of the Drol's journey - - - }	24	
" Do. do. at *Dopb'r* - -	40	
" Fees to deputy governor -	150	
" To bailiffs, subalterns, &c. -	50	
" *Fees to chief gove nor* -	885 $\frac{1}{4}\frac{7}{8}$	

{	Copars -	1149 $\frac{1}{4}\frac{7}{8}$	1152
	Due—balance	1 $\frac{1}{4}\frac{1}{8}$	
{	Copars paid	1152	1152

By

By this account it appeared I had *two copars* to receive. He pulled out a purfe almoft as long as himfelf, whereon was embroidered, " *Money received for fees—money to be allowed for overcharges.*" The *firft end* appeared quite full, *the other* almoft empty. I obferved my two copars came out of the *empty* end. When he delivered them, he bowed very low, and long kept his hand extended, bending in a kind of fupplicatory attitude. I had heard in *Blefefcu* that minifters' fervants, *now and then,* took perquifites ; fo that I might not appear ignorant of *good cuftoms* and manners, I withdrew from my pocket the *two copars* again—popped them into his hand, and thus fettled the value and return of, and from my two impounded ingots, whofe remains *thus ftood* at *nibil.*

Carefully placing my gift in the ftuffed end of his purfe, Mr. Secretary began :

" It is my way always to be methodical : *Thus* our firft bufinefs well concluded, and, as I hope, to mutual fatisfaction, we will proceed. I am to inform you, that *Vilpi Tico* will efteem your company, at the receipt of cuftom, a favour. He is now in confult

with

with *Dunheldafhio* and others, on important matters, and wifhes your advice therein. We can go in my carriage, now at your door."

" Sir !" (faid I).—He corrected himfelf —

" Excufe me ; but really I am fo ufed to practife the offer I made you, as a little trap to inferiors, indicative of humility and courtefy, that I overlooked the impoffibility." (Lifting up his eyes at me)—

" Vanity ! vanity ! all is vanity !"

" Pray be compofed (I returned) ; it was a mere *lapfus linguæ.* Only let me know how far from hence I am to go, and I will be there before you ; at the fame time deem myfelf much honoured by the invitation."

He led me to the window, and fhewed me the archway through which I was to pafs to the council-houfe. I then faw him to his carriage—returned to my chamber, a little to decorate myfelf—locked up my ftores—ruminated on *my balance* ! and fet forward.

CHAP.

CHAP. IX.

Attends the Council—Defcription of fome of the Members—Converfation—Confultation— Propofes Taxes—-and Plan for reducing Provifions.

I WAS foon there, and as foon admitted. *Vilpi Tico* advanced, and introduced me to the affembled junto, whofe names he thus announced:

"The myfterious *Dralpont*."

"The fublime *Pekrub*." *Burke*

"The loquacious *Vile-grin*." *Grenville*

"The rebel-hunter *Sevrefe*." *Graves*

AND

"The ductile *Efor*." *Rose?*

Befides *thefe*, there were my friends *Dun-beldafhio* and *Nave-npnaee*. They were fitting at a table covered with green cloth, with numbers of papers before them. *Efor* carefully clofed the door, ftopped the key-hole with his finger, and fo ftood during the

E   meeting.

meeting. *Dralpont* beckoned me; I fat me down on the floor clofe to him; filence en-fued. *Sevrefe* then came up, and, on a long flip of parchment, took notes of me from the crown to the toe. While this was doing, *Pekrub* put on an enormous pair of fpectacles, and ftood up, ftaring me all the time full in the face: I fhall never forget him; he appeared for all the world juft like a darning-needle, with two collateral eyes to it. *Vile-grin* whifpered *Efor*; but *Dunbeldafbio* and *Nave-npnaee* attentively, in filence, watched *Sevrefe's* countenance, who, having finifhed his obfervations, fpake—

" I have carefully run over the lines of this *foreign drol's* countenance, and, according to my approved *ariftocraticilian rules*, he is neither *leveller*, or *fpy*; even *I* find no fault with him."

Then cringing and bowing to each, he paffed down the room, and made his exit!

" What may *this* mean?" thought I; but *patience!* He had hardly cleared the door, when, with open arms, *Pekrub* flew to me, and, Stentor-like, exclaimed—

" Oh

" Oh, most illustrious Blefescudian drol!
" Clear'd, thus fully clear'd of democratic suspect,
" Sleep in *my bosom*!!
" Oh, thou son of Gulliver! my dear friend
    " Gulliver!
" Yes, we were friends! friends! friends indeed!
" In rant, and cant, sublime hyperbole."

" Pardon me, noble auditors, for this enthufiaftic burft! ye know my tender nature!"

" Blefescudian, I have wept your woes!
" Blefescudian, I have written on your woes!
" Blefescudian, I have eat on—drank on!
" Blefescudian, I have slept on! and,
" Blefescudian, *am pensioned* for your woes!!!

Down he fell quite exhaufted. *Dunbel-dafbio* burft out into laughter, and *Dralpont* blufhed. The reft feemed unmoved as at common converfation.

The voice of *Vilpi Tico* now drew my attention.

" I fent for you, *Gulliver,* folicitous of your opinion and council; we want money, and our fupplies muft be fo artificially created, that though the people fenfibly feel, they may infenfibly pay. Our ftock of corn is

E 2   exhaufted

exhaufted nearly, and the mob are clamor-
ous; yet *I*, and *one more*, will continue *war*;
war, though multitudes are againft it, muft
be continued. You, who have feen and
known, in its days of luxury and riot, mil-
lions raifed from chaff in *Blefefcu*, advife *us*
now, and accept both minifterial power and
influence."

" Noble renommoc," I replied, " it appears to me that the ftate of Lilliput is over-
run with wealth—its primary and principal
fault; that *the taxes* are not half equal to
your power of enforcing; that from the la-
bourer to the merchant, the mafs have too
much liberty; and that the *refplendency, neceffary elegance*, and eafe of ariftocracy, is
fullied and debafed by thofe general errors.
National poverty, debt, and *taxes*, can only
render the mafs fubmiffive; mention, therefore, your requifites, and as far as my fhal-
low capacity can afford, I'll adminifter pro-
pofitions for the fupplies."

" In few words then, 1ft. Aliment made
from corn muft be fparingly allowed at home,
that the armies, fleets, and allies, may be
plentifully ferved.

" 2dly.

" 2dly. Money muſt be had for the troops.

" 3dly. Money for the navy.

" 4thly. Money for allies.

" 5thly. Money for *us* !"

I conſidered for ſome time, repeating to myſelf the *wants* before mentioned; then thus replied—

" If the ſoldiers of Lilliput are to be confided in, I can ſuggeſt *requiſitions* which will amply furniſh your loan; but I have read, and underſtand that—"

Here he cut me ſhort, ſaying,

" The armies of Lilliput are not *now*, as at the time of your father's viſit to us, merely feathered, and muſqueted citizens, ſolely called out, and ſuppoſed to act for general defence againſt a *foreign foe* ; *diſcipline, barracks*, and *private tuition*, have made them equal to your deſires ; ſo point out the means, and I'll adopt."

I then propoſed—

" 1ſt. That inſtead of aliment made from corn, *filings of ſteel* ſhould be uſed for *farina*, mixed up with water, in which a certain quantity of *nitre, ſulphur*, and *charcoal* were diſſolved ; this would be palatable

E 3   enough.

enough. But as, perhaps, the mafs might not at firft like it, or be at the trouble of the experiment, the foldiers, on home fervice, having little to do, might be employed in making it, baking in barracks, and delivering out a fample or two, gratis, on their pikes.

" 2dly. A tax of feven hundred copars on the entrance door of every houfe, to which fhould be affixed a padlock, to enclofe the owners from feven in the evening till funrife; to be collected daily by armed watchmen appointed for that purpofe. This tax would alfo operate to prevent tumultuous nightly meetings.

" 3dly. That as, from convenience and cuftom, men hitherto have buttoned their coats before, in future they fhould pay a tax of feven hundred copars each for fo doing, or be compelled to button them behind.

" 4thly. That numbers of diffipated people having tricks of whitening their heads, and cramming them with greafe, they fhould now ufe inftead lamp-black and fifh-blubber, or pay for the exemption feven hundred copars each.

" 5thly.

" 5thly. Fine weather. This tax, though uncertain in its produce, muft raife an immenfe fum, by levying one hundred copars on every one who fhall leave the city in funfhine, to be received by toll-tickets at the gates of the metropolis."

I was convinced the above would, on computation, aggregate at leaft one hundred and eighty million copars, and as they fimply ftruck at luxuries and frivolities, could not, except the change in corn aliment, be grumbled at ; and even if it fhould, I trufted, the method I had propofed for the delivery of the fample, and the padlocks mentioned in the firft tax, would obviate all difficulties, and filence every murmur.

While fpeaking, I put my plan on paper ; he took it from me, carefully folded, and placed it in his bofom. The affembly rofe ; each came up to me, and rapturoufly kiffed the *bind lappet* of my coat *(they could reach no bigher)* ; then all went away excepting *Vilpi Tico, Pekrub,* and *Vile-grin,* who, as foon as we were together, burft out as it were with one voice—

" You

" You muſt go with us to *Elſac Sinwrod*, and be preſented to *Log-Ereg* ; order your equipage, in full diſplay, as when you ſat off from *Doph'r :* We'll attend you ; be ready by ſun-riſe.

" Adieu!"

" Adieu!"

" Adieu!"

We then ſeparated ; they, as I ſuppoſed, to their official duties ; *I,* to my home—wondering at the paſt!

CHAP.

CHAP. X.

*Amufement, and mifcellaneous Matter—Jour-
ney to* Elfac Sinwrod—*Introduced—Finds*
Log-Ereg *fick—Attends Confultation of the
Phyficians.*

ON reaching my manfion, I ordered for
the morning's excurfion ; and wifhing
a relaxation after the bufinefs of the day,
determined to vifit fome place of public
amufement. On inquiry, I found a celebrated tragedy and mufical piece were to be
reprefented in the evening, with the ftrength
of all the capital performers at the New
Theatre, which, for diftinction's fake, was
named the King's Company. Thither I went.
Six boxes were laid together for my reception, fo that I was commodioufly feated.
Here my fpectacles were truly of ufe ; for
without them I could not have diftinguifhed
the performers. The houfe is fo ridiculoufly
large, compared againft their pigmy organs
and dimenfions—a reflection here ftruck me,
which

which I often found myfelf juftified in bringing home to thefe diminutives—to wit, that
their general ideas are far beyond their
powers of execution. I heard as imperfectly
as I fhould, without artificial aid, have feen ;
for, excepting fome rants in the tragedy,
and full pieces and choruffes of the farce, I
might as well have been at a pantomime.
However, I could not help making a few
criticifms. Before the curtain drew up, one
half of the audience began clapping their
hands, and hallooing; the other half made
violent groans and hiffes. I was fimple
enough to conclude this proceeded from the
difference in opinion of the favourers of the
feveral pieces about to be reprefented : That
the groaners were the *tragedy admirers*, and
the hallooers the lovers of *farce ;* and the
difturbance a conflict for which fhould be
firft brought on. I mentioned this to a little
old man with one eye, who had introduced
himfelf to me immediately on my entrance,
and who I perceived (by a fmall glittering
badge he wore on his left breaft) was a perfon
of rank. He fimpered, and thus put me
right :

" This

" This is a political conteft : *The clappers* are determined to have a tune adapted to their opinions—*the hiffers* that they will not be infulted by it. But the clappers will have it, as numbers are (gratis) fent here by *Sevrefe*, nightly, for the fole purpofe of infifting on it."

As he faid, the tune was played ; plaudits enfued ; and up drew the curtain. The dreffes and fcenery were fplendid and appropriate ; yet, though the tragedy appeared very complex, (comprehending elementary ftorms, battles, banquets, fupernatural appearances, and murders ; and, at times, great numbers came on, and went off the ftage); I could only difcover two performers who had any bufinefs in the drama. Varieties of paffions agitated their countenances, and their action was exactly fuited. I wifh I could have heard them diftinctly ; for I have no doubt I fhould have been completely gratified. As it was, I could only diftinguifh their voices were exactly toned alike ; this I mentioned to my old neighbour, who told me—

" They were brother and fifter."

For

For the reft, who, or what they were, or
what was their refpective interefts in the
fcene, I know not—

" They had neither action, or utterance, or
" The power to stir mens' minds."

The tragedy concluded, the farce began.
The principal or leading character feemed to
be that of a romp or hoiden. It was, I
confefs, moft admirably performed by a
little female, with a remarkably loud voice
and large mouth : In truth fhe was fuperlatively vulgar. My old friend feemed charmed
with her; this I thought a good opportunity
of obtaining fome ftage information, fo thus
addrefſed him :

" You feem much to admire the actrefs
now fpeaking."

" She is my intimate friend!"

" Blefs me, Count !"—(for I had heard
him titled by a fruit-woman, to whom he
had been whifpering).

" She is my intimate friend!" (he repeated) and that vulgarity you now admire her for fo juftly perfonifying, conftitutes
her

her private merits, and has raifed her to the envied fituation of miftrefs, friend, and companion of *Arcelanc*, Log-Ereg's third fon. *Clarence*

I was fatisfied, I faid, nor liftened more; I wifhed the play over—grieving within my-felf, to find the vices of *old Blefefcu* regene-rated in *Lilliput*. The curtain fell, and my neighbour addreffed *me*—

" How do you pafs your evening ?"

" I fhall return home to repofe."

" Pho! (faid he) go with me; I'll in-troduce you to fome choice fpirits—men of genius, rank, fafhion, and fplendour."

I thought I could not do better—confented to accompany him : He led the way. I faw him into a fuperb *vis-a-vis*, and ordered my equipage to follow.

From external appearances, he made good his promife. We were ufhered into a mag-nificent faloon.

The company confifted of about twenty perfons, of all ages, from twenty to extreme fenectitude. They were at play. And much hurt that I could not contrive to throw a few mains, I told them, " It was always my cuf-tom to do at Rome as Rome does; and

F   therefore,

therefore, though I could not manage their
box, (from its petitenefs) fo as to play with
diftinct fairnefs, yet I would bet." The
groom porter gave me change for five ingots,
and I fat down to the table. The fight of
my three thoufand five hundred copars, (the
amount of their currency, and which I placed
before me), feemed to electrify the whole
company with joy. I could fee their eyes
gliften, and each was anxious for *my* wager.
As my old chapron (whofe name I now found
to be *Ekud-Rat)* had informed me the affembly would confift entirely of people of diftinction, I much wondered at this defire for
my money ; which wonder was not a little
increafed, on perceiving him enter the lifts,
and become one of the moft greedy. I began now to fufpect I was with fharpers of
fafhion ; and correcting my *dafh*, betted cau-
tioufly. I foon found they difcovered the
alteration in my mode ; and, in five minutes,
inftead of every mouth being opened at me,
I could fcarcely obtain a bet.

The company by degrees left the table—
all, excepting *Ekud-Rat*, myfelf, and two
others, who were called *Nadirefh* and
Calxboffer.

Calxbosfer. In about an hour, 2000 of my copars were become the property of *Calxbosfer,*
1000 of old *Ekud-Rat,* and the remaining
500 of *Nadirefh.* *Ekud-Rat* obferving the dif-
femination of the coin, remarked, " *It was
very late—time to retire,*" and withdrew. I
did fo alfo, and left the other two to decide
the fuperiority of fortune together.

By the time I reached home, it was broad
day ; I therefore, inftead of going to repofe,
dreffed myfelf for my journey ; and till the
arrival of my ftate friends, who were to accompany me to *Elfac-Sinwrod,* amufed myfelf with taking notes of paft occurrences, and
rummaging my little bundle of manufcripts.
I came to one tied with narrow black ribbon;
it was fuperfcribed—

" *Found in Adeline's cell after her death.*"

I opened it; it contained numbers of poetic
fcraps, on different flips of paper. They were
not paged, fo I determined to read them in
the order they were placed. The firft confifted of the following ftanzas :

" My

I.

" My love was brave, was young, was gay,
" Wou'd laugh and sing both night and day ;
" He lov'd but me, with artless flame ;
" My bosom glow'd, and own'd the same.
" We meant in holy bands—But now !
" Ah what avail'd our fruitless vow !

II.

" The morn was fix'd, we thought no wrong,
" I smil'd, and chear'd him with my song ;
" With lightsome tread, then sought the shrine,
" His trembling hand fast lock'd in mine.
" We meant in holy bands—but now!
" Ah what avail'd our fruitless vow!

III.

" Opposing sires, appris'd, we found
" Enclosing ev'ry altar round ;
" Our hands, by force disjoin'd—I fell—
" Such woes who feel can only tell.
" We meant in holy bands—but now !
" Ah what avail'd our fruitless vow !"

I now took up the second ; the ink seemed
discharged in part, as if tears had fallen on
it. It consisted of this single stanza :

SECOND.

" Thus reft of all—no friend to cheer !
" List to my sighs, or wipe my tear !

" Who

" Who wou'd give a home to me!
" Lovelorn child of misery!
    " Where cou'd I fly?"

THIRD.

The third contained the two following ftanzas, which clearly proved to me I had now poffeffion of my fad mother's hiftory:

I.

Forc'd by a father's stern command,
To yield to hated age my hand,
    Or take the mystic veil—
Tell me, fond youth—O teach me how
To love thee still, yet keep the vow,
    Which soon these lips will seal!

II.

At morn, at noon, at vesper pray'r,
Thou, thou alone, shalt be my care;
    To thee I'll pour the song,
Sacred, fervent, and sincere;
And many a sigh, and many a tear,
    Each cadence shall prolong.

Pekrub, *Vile-Grin*, and *Vilpi Tico* now entered my apartments. I tied up my port folio, all but the packet I had begun perufing, which I again fecured with its narrow black ribbon, and placed carefully in my bofom. I made

F 3   my

my devoirs, and we propofed to fet forward.

I leaped on my car, then politely lifted
up my companions, who were fo terrified at
the immenfe heighth they were from the
ground, that I was compelled to mitigate their
fears, and take them into perfonal protection :
So, placing *Pekrub* and *Vile-Grin* on each knee,
holding them carefully round the waift, and
with *Vilpi Tico* feated between my thighs, Jehu-
like, off we rattled, and in about three hours
reached *Eſſac-Sinwrod.* The attendants faid
it rained fmartly, but I could not perceive or
feel it.

I own I was proud of my fituation; (and
furely, reader, if vanity ever was, it was in me,
at that time, pardonable). View my fituation!—The *protector, the supporter,* and *abfolute mafter* of the three great ftate props of
Lilliput!—What would many a Blefefcudian
fenator have given for my place ?

Nothing material occurred on the road,
fave that, as we paffed a common called *Wolf-
nou-Hbtea, Pekrub,* on beholding fome gib-
bets (whereon I imagine malefactors had
been expofed) exclaimed,

"Oh

" Oh *Blefescu! Blefescu!*—Oh !"

Whether he uttered the ejaculation from dread for himself, or for the love of Blefescu; or that some of his friends had been or expected to be there, I know not; but I felt that he trembled on my knee.

Vile-Grin uttered not a syllable, till we were entering a town called *Korbloc.* It was market-day, and there were a prodigious quantity of hogs. The moment he heard their gruntings, he held his nose, and screamed out,

" Brutes !—swinish multitude !—beasts !— swinish multitude !"

And so kept on till he had cleared the town. I thought, by this, (but delicacy kept me from inquiry) that he was probably of the Jewish persuasion.

Vilpi Tico and myself had all the conversation: It consisted merely in his asking me, " How I had passed my evening ?" which I recited, together with the manner of *Ekud-Rat* drawing me to the gaming-house, my losing my money, &c. He laughed heartily, and prayed me to be cautious in future, saying,

" As for *Ekud-Rat,* he is an old turn-coat debauchee,

debauchee, faved, by rank only, from contempt : But *Nadirefh*, and *Calxbosfer* are two deep ones—*fo* deep, that they are the only enemies I dread. *Calxbosfer* is adored by the populace, and, by way of diftinction, called *Ebt-nam-fo-ebt-elpoep*. He hankers after my place, and sticks fo clofe to my fkirts, that I am fometimes almoft frightened into quitting : But then *Nadirefh* would take *Vile-Grin*'s, and *Pekrub* might lofe his penfion, and I be called to account for paft matters ; therefore, as my enemies, guard againft them."

I thanked him for his ufeful intelligence—promifed to avoid play, and be careful of " *the deep ones.*" We now reached *Elfac Sinwrod.*

We drove ftraight up to the great gate of the palace. Two foldiers carefully took down each of my companions, who walked *fans ceremonie* into the hall, I following.

We were inftantly fhewn to the *auguft prefence.* He was feated on an ivory fopha, inlaid with gold, wrapped up in an Indian brocade ; his head bound, and reclined on a pillow, voluptuoufly fringed with the fineft oriental pearl. Indeed the whole apartment bore

evidences

evidence of eaſtern magnificence, which I much wondered at, and never could account for, as this nation never had the leaſt intercourſe with *India,* its *European peculators,* or *murderers.*

Vilpi Tico advanced, and whiſpered ſomething in the royal ear, and I diſtinguiſhed,

" Hah! how! propoſed good taxes?— Good! good!—Like him—like him—Speak to him."

Vilpi Tico now advanced to me, and led me to make my bow, which I did, (of courſe low enough, being on preferment). I waited anxiouſly, expecting ſome queſtion of conſequence to be propoſed to me, and had prepared my tongue for a courtly reply; inſtead of which I only heard articulated—

" Sick, ſick, ſick—Got a blow, ſad blow, bad blow—blow on the head."

He then ſank on his embroidered bolſter, and ſeemed perfectly apathetic.

Three or four grave looking men, dreſſed in black, drew round, and ſhaking their heads, requeſted me to retire : We did ſo, into an antichamber, when the ſenior looking ſaid to me—

" Have

" Have phyfic or furgery made any part of your ftudies ?"

I replied, " Monaftic education was general, therefore they formed part of my attentions."

" Here then (faid the fecond) is the Sovereign's cafe reduced to paper. Confider it well; and, when we meet together in the prefence to-morrow, give us your opinion."

They left me. I opened the fcroll to perufe it, but was interrupted by the entrance of the domeftics of the bedchamber, who fhewed me to an apartment fit for the Perfian Sophi.

CHAP.

CHAP. XI.

*The Cafe—Prefcribes Cure—*Log-Ereg *recovers*
—Rewarded, and placed near the Perfon—
Vifits the Farm—Improves it—Made Head
of the Agricultural Society—Ball at Court—
Victory—Rejoicings—Made a Norab.

IN the courfe of three months, from an ob-
fcure individual in Blefefcu, I was become
an efteemed financier and phyfician in Lilliput. To fay truth, I flept but a fhort time,
delighting myfelf in idea with the honour I
might arive at ; and once had *the vanity* to
think I might, at laft, eclipfe and fuperfede
even *Vilpi Tico.* However, I checked that
fallacious fancy ; and, the fun breaking into
my chamber, arofe to ftudy THE CASE the
doctors had left with me. It was as follows :

THE CASE.

" As *Log-Ereg* was walking on the parapet
of his caftle, and mufing on the contents of a
packet received from *Envina,* he ftumbled
againft a battering ram, and fell on a war-
pike,

pike, which had been incautioufly left there
by a fentinel. It pierced his head a little
above the left ear, entered half through, and
broke off, leaving full as much out, as within
the fkull. On being called in, we propofed
extracting it : This he abfolutely objected to.
We, fearful left a fatal hœmorrhage might en-
fue, defifted. We confider a perfect cure impoffible, while the offending matter remains.
The patient's fituation is, by turns, from *fever*, to *torpor*, to *delirium*. The delirium (as
if fympathetic from the caufe) is a perpetual
raving of *war* ! *war* ! *war* !—How farther to
advife in this cafe, and promife perfect recovery, is not within our fkill; therefore we
fubfcribe our names for your affiftance.

> " *Abno.*
> " *Mahlta.*
> " *Wifhkan.*"

I had read of many ftrange and furprifing
cures in the philofophical tranfactions of Blefefcu, fuch as " *men recovering, and being perfectly well, after lofing their lungs,*" &c. To
fuch, the prefent cafe was a bagatelle, on the
                                    fcore

fcore of danger. The principle I determined to act on was, to avoid either of two extremes, the one of which is almoft always the unhappy patient's death warrant, *viz.* " The cold methodical fear of exercifing reafon and genius againft formal practice, in the regular bred man of phyfic." The other, " The rafh adminiftration of drug and inftrument, without or reafon, or genius, by the empiric." *I* determined boldly to unite the fcience I poffeffed with invention ; for, " as the patient had refolved againft extraction of the fpear," it was clear to me, without going out of the common road, a cure could not be effected. I was certain that " the delirium" proceeded from the point of the weapon, pricking and irritating the fenforium every time he moved or refpired. I deliberated—a thought, a fortunate idea rufhed into my mind ; I felt convinced I was right, and hurried to the prefence-chamber.

The doctors were already affembled; *I* advanced—the head was unbound, and the wounded parts tenderly examined. I told them—

G " It

" It was very eafy, without extracting, fo
far to effect a cure, as that the pike fhould
not be troublefome or dangerous during the
patient's life, though he fhould attain the
age of Methufelah."

They fmiled farcaftically. Wrapped up in
confidence, *my vanity* urged me to fay, rather
above common tone,

" There *is not* occafion for extraction."

In few words, they gave up the point, and
it was left to me to perform my operations,
ad libitum.

I proceeded.

The metal whereof the inftrument was
formed, was perfectly flexible. I only employed a fmall hammer, mallet, and pincers;
inftead of drawing out, at one fmart blow,
I drove the fpear clean through his head, fo
far, that about half an inch was prominent
at either fide; then, with my pincers, I
bent both extremities in form of a hook, and,
with my mallet and hammer, rivetted them
clofe to the fkull, immoveable.

At the firft blow, the doctors fhrieked and
turned their backs; and all the attendants
fled in confternation, thinking I had mur-
dered

dered their mafter, excepting one old crabbed looking man, who carefully watched my movements. My patient, in a few minutes, fhook his ears, jumped up, and cried out with extacy—

" Well! well! quite well! Great doctor! good doctor! fine doctor! great financier! Know farming too? See my farm! manage my farm!"

I bowed, and begged him to keep himfelf, for fome time, quiet. He complied; and I, putting up my inftruments very methodically, retired—the old man, I have before mentioned, following me.

As foon as we were alone, a tear, which he was afhamed to let drop in public, left it fhould mingle with thofe of hypocrify, fell on the floor; he embraced me, and with honeft fervour exclaimed—

" By * * *, you are a brave fellow! you have faved my dear mafter! you have faved Lilliput! and I'll ferve you. I'll never forget you; by * * *, I wont."

Reader, I muft here digrefs to fhew in the treatment this old man once experienced,

that

that *ingratitude* is a weed, natural to the foil of every court, from *Lilliput* to *Brobdignag*.

His name was *Whol-tru*.

Sometime before my arrival in *Lilliput*, *Log-Ereg* had been very ill, fo ill, that his life was defpaired of; and different factions contended to difplace him from royalty, and appoint a regency in his ftead. Each pulled as intereft led; fome were for nominating the heir-apparent; others, for the queen confort. This old man, loyally, wifely, immoveably, ftood alone, well knowing,

> " There's but a little space
> " Between the prison, and the grave of princes."

And would not fuffer innovation. *Log-Ereg* recovered, and retained his crown.

As is natural to fuppofe, *Whol-tru* was now the firft man in the cabinet. However, not to be prolix, he chanced to differ in opinion with *Vilpi Tico*, about deftroying a fwarm of lice and caterpillars that infefted the country. Each perfevered; and *Log-Ereg's* mind having been poifoned againft his preferver, not only preferred *Vilpi Tico's* mode, but gave *Whol-tru*

tru to underſtand, he muſt conſider his opinions, in future, as only ſecondary to the new favourite, and his favoured ſyſtem. Conſcious of his rectitude, the juſt pride of ſuch a poſſeſſion, impelled *Whol-tru* to throw up the important poſts he held; he retired in diſguſt, and, as the author of this anecdote informed me, never returned to court, till a ſecond illneſs threatened his maſter's life. Then, forgetting the paſt, he again ſhone forth—

 " A precious jewel in a rugged caſe."

The perfect recovery I had completed was now announced. I enquired for my friend *Whol-tru*. He was gone: Satisfied that his duty was performed, he retired to learned leiſure, and I never more ſaw him, till near my departure from Lilliput; though, whether he remembered me or not, will be ſeen hereafter.

I was now ſummoned to a private audience. As I paſſed along I could ſcarcely avoid treading on the crouds that were crouching round me; and, but for my ſpectacles, certainly ſhould have *extinguiſhed* ſeveral *diſ-*
   G 3   tinguiſhed

tinguifhed perfonages. Among others, three *drols*, who were very anxious for preferment, jumped on the fore-leathers of my fhoes, and were abfolutely bold enough to climb up my legs; their names were, *Oro-Bluff*, *Truc-on Wo*, *Chieters-Fled*.

I fhould not have perceived them but for a ludicrous circumftance; my fmall-clothes were open at the knees, and *Oro-Bluff*, in fcrambling up to be firft at my ears, abfolutely miftook his way, and found a paffage into the feat of my breeches. A tickling obliged me to put my hand there, when, out I drew the great little man! After a hearty laugh, he was well fatisfied; and affured me, fince he had firft gained my ear, he was fully recompenced for the difgrace of groping in the dark. The others were both purfuing his route; decency prevented my fuffering it; fo I gently put them on the ground, and pacified them with promifes. They kiffed my fhoe-latchets, and walked off contentedly.

Arrived at the cabinet-door—the firft object that ftruck my attention was, my old examiner, *rebel-hunter Sevrefe*, fitting on a little black

black ſtool; in one hand a key, in the
other an alarm bell: He knew me, ſo without ringing or inquiry, opened the portal of
the ſanctuarium.

I ſubmiſſively aſked of his health; he ſaid,
" Never better; ſlept well—dreamed of a
victory."

I was fearful the delirium was not quite
removed, but ſoon diſcovered no other ſentiment filled his mind than that I found him
originally impreſſed with, and that, *ſick* or
well, " *war*" was his ruling paſſion.

Before him lay two ſheep-ſkins; he rolled
them up, and put them into my hand,
ſaying,

" Read, read, reward, honour, honour
the phyſician."

And ſmiled.

I did as he bade me: *The firſt* was my
ordination to the rank of *nŏrăb*; the title,
Glulplew; which, Blefeſcudianized, ſignifies
Plug-well—alluding, as I ſuppoſed, to the
ſervice I had rendered him.

The ſecond was the grant of a penſion of
five thouſand copars on another iſland he
governed.

I was

I was satisfied with the first distinction, and took the liberty of thus remonstrating to the second :

" That I did not desire it; and that as a stranger, and a man who had done no service in *that island*, I had no right to accept or demand it."

" Pho, pho !" said he, " take it, take it; only use I make of that country—tax 'em, tax 'em every year, to pay places and pensions—proud, proud set, forced to keep 'em poor."

I submitted, pocketed my pension, and thenceforward ranked as *Norab Glulplew*.

As soon as I had impocketed the gifts, he waved me to sit by him, saying,

" *Cousin*, what is your opinion of my persevering in this war, and of war in general ?"

" Sir," said I, " the laws of war, that restrain the exercise of national rapine and murder, are founded on two principles of substantial interest :

" 1st. The knowledge of the permanent benefits which may be obtained by *a moderate use of conquest*. And,

" 2dly.

" 2dly. *A just apprehension lest the desola-tion which we inflict on the enemies country, may be retaliated on our own.*"

" *Good tax-maker, cousin; good doctor; bad politician,* bad as old *Whol-tru.* Know-ing in agriculture ? *come,* wont talk of war; go to my farm—come, go.*"

I perceived *my* ideas *on war,* accorded not with *his.* He led the way, and we visited

THE FARM.

The hoards of grain were astonishing, and must have been the produce of many years ; but the poor cattle that stood round hanker-ing after the stacked hay shocked me; they were so meagre, and seemingly exhausted by labour and want of food. Yet, and which hurt me most, I perceived several women at-tempting to draw milk from the dry kine, into little pails like thimbles, decorated with the royal insignia. We went next into *a barn,* where, instead of thrashing the corn as in Blefescu, many naked wretches were picking the grains out singly from the ears ; this, I learned, was to prevent both waste and

and purloining. The ſtock viewed, we paſſed over ſome fields ; I obſerved—

" The ſoil was naturally good, but required dreſſing."

" Know that, couſin ; know that—coſts money ! manure coſts money ; got a great family ; can't afford it : But I ſee you don't underſtand farming."

I did ſee, and very clearly too, that as in my ſentiments *on war,* ſo, *on farming,* I had ſpoken too freely for a courtier, and drew in my horns ; adding,

" That if his highneſs would commit the trial to me, I made no doubt, I could conſiderably improve the land, without any expence to him."

" Take it, take it," was his reply ; " make good your word—give you *Cralſini's* place ; put you at the head of my agricultural ſociety."

I engaged for the taſk, and we returned. On our way back, ere we reached the palace, I heard the cannon firing, the bells ringing, and preſently, out of breath with running, up came *Vilpi Tico, Vile-Grin,* and *Pekrub.*

Vilpi

Vilpi Tico prefented a packet; we altogether entered the caftle, and I had the honour of being prefent at the reading the difpatches.

The Contents.

" Noble Drol,

" I have the pleafure and honour to ac-
" quaint you, that as I was cruizing on the
" 31ft ult. in lat. 30. l. 40. I difcovered
" land to the fouthward; which, by the
" charts I fortunately had with me, I found
" to be the ifland *Rockica*. I called a coun-
" cil of war; at which it was determined,
" we fhould immediately attempt the con-
" queft. Accordingly, we prepared for bom-
" barding; threw the fhips as clofe to land
" as the fhore would permit; and for two
" whole glaffes fired without intermiffion,
" both fhells, bombs, cannon, patereroes,
" piftols—in fhort, we fired away all our
" ammunition. Yet fuch was the cool in-
" trepid conduct of our antagonift, that
" though we diftinctly heard tremendous
" falls of ftone repeatedly after our firing,
" not a fhot was returned. Panting for
" glory, we refolved to force them to de-
" fence

" fence, or furrender; we manned all our
" boats, and fword in hand (favoured by a
" charming fog) we marched up to the walls
" of the very city, (as we then fuppofed.)
" Fortunately for his majefty's glory and
" fervice, and for the fafety, thus preferved,
" of many brave fellows, the city walls were
" rocks, the native barriers of the ifland.
" We climbed them dauntlefsly, and found
" every thing as we could wifh—perfectly
" peaceable and quiet; not a human foul to
" be feen, or the fmalleft veftige either of
" the animal or vegetable kingdoms.

" I truft you will conclude I lofe no time
" in fecuring poffeffion of this immenfe and
" valuable conqueft. I further deem my-
" felf fingularly happy in the trifling lofs
" we have fuftained, which I fubjoin here-
" unto, though adding fo fplendid a gem to
" the territorial grandeur of *Lilliput*. I
" muft beg leave to mention the very gallant
" conduct of my Lieutenant *Eggro Gul-peo-*
" *plo*, who, in a brave effufion of loyalty,
" at one ftroke killed Tomazza Talko, for
" feditioufly faying, ' The ifland was not
" worth powder and fhot.' Alfo the conduct
                                        " of

" of a young midshipman, named *Clereyo*;
" he being the first who discovered the
" rocks to be the only opponents to our
" progress.

" I have the honour, &c. &c.

" BANG-FRANCO.

" KILLED,
" As before mentioned—Tomazza Talko.

" WOUNDED,
" Eeggro *Gul-peoplo*; bit on the forefinger
" by a rat, into whose hole he had thrust
" his hand in *search of honey.*"

George —

The dispatches read, up jumped *Log-Ereg*,
saying—

" There *cousins!* there's war for you!
there's an island! there's a conquest! there's
a kingdom! No rebels in it, no rebels—
worth having—no grumblers. But, come;
go Vile-Grin, go; tell *Remdor-Ectrol*, we'll
have a *ball*, a *dance*, a *feast* to-night—lights,
guns, music, drums—go, Vile-Grin, go."

Electer ?

H   Then

Then putting the manufcript clofe to his
eye, out he went ; I, and the other attendants
following.

THE BALL.

By the time I had dined, it was time to
drefs for the gala. I might as well have
ftaid away; being obliged, from the etiquette
of *full drefs*, to decline the ufe of my fpectacles. The company were all affembled
when I entered; the floor glittered to my
optics, juft like a bank fpangled with glow-
worms; and they were confufedly moving
about, like emmets when their neft is dif-
turbed. Being unable, from the circumftance
of not having my glaffes, to mix with them
conveniently, I withdrew to a corner of the
hall and fat me down, to fcrutinize and remark what my eyes would permit. I could
fee the boards were painted curioufly, with
flowers in chalks, and at great expence, from
the ftyle of the finifhing; and could further
difcover the principal action of thofe who
were moving about, was to fcuffle them out
with their feet. As my eyes were attentively
fixed

fixed on the ground, fomething glittering came towards me—I laid my hand down flat, palm upwards, and it ftepped into it. I held it to my face, and was ftruck of a heap at my conduct—it was no lefs than the *Peffrinc-fo-Kyro*! a good little woman as ever lived; but fo fmall, that the diamond blaze fhe were totally eclipfed her perfon—till, fo dif-covered, I put her down as delicately as I could, apologized, and fhe fmiled, faying,

" Pray dont think of it *Norab Glulplew*; you know I come from the country of *Bra-vados*, and at my father's court, fear is faid to be unknown."

So courtefying, off fhe went. Fearful of more miftakes, for want of my ufeful lunettes, I made my bow of depart, and retired to reft.

H 2   CHAP.

CHAP. XII.

*Goes a Hunting—Gets into the Queen's good
Graces—Overtures made to him by an old
Woman—Plan laid to difgrace him—Pays
Attention to a young One—Sued for Crim.
Con.—Counfellors—Gets his Caufe—Hates
Law—fweats his Purfe.*

PHILOSOPHERS of all ages have deno-
minated temperance, a virtue.—In the palace of Lilliput, it was carried to the *ne plus
ultra* of perfection. Nothwithftanding the
jollity of the evening, by fun-rife, the court-
yard was full of hounds, of huntfmen, and
the attendant courtiers, who had been honoured by invitation to the fport. I, among
the reft, made my appearance; but as no
horfe could be found ftrong enough to carry
me, I was obliged to wa!k—no great hard-
fhip, as I could traverfe the whole foreft in
about forty Blefefcudian minutes. I was
honoured fingularly, being entrufted to lift
Log-Ereg on his fteed; they then all galloped
off.

off. I followed flowly, taking great care not
to get before the dogs, left I fhould firft
roufe the game and fpoil the fport. That I
might not do fo, I turned down a long ftrait
walk that led to the top of a very pretty hill,
from whence there was a delighful view of
Elfat-Sinwrod. On the fummit I found two
men waiting with a covered cart; I inquired,
" What was in it?" They told me, " *The
fport of the day.*" I thought they jeered me,
fo looked within, and fure enough it contained a fine ftag. I now civilly afked, " If
they had fpoken the truth; or what they
kept that poor brute caged for?" " Why,
mafter, we always catch him up, out of the
enclofure where he is kept, every night before
Log-Ereg hunts. This ftag is a great favourite; why he has been tormented fcores
of times, and will be many more. I dare fay
he'll foon give the dogs a flip, and we fhall
find him again fafe enough, in fome old barn
or other."

While they were fpeaking the horns and
hounds were heard at a diftance—they opened
the door of the cart, and away, pall mall,
fcampered the deer. " Ho!" thought I,

H 3 " *this*

" *this* is Lilliputian hunting—fport! fport
for the mighty man of Lilliput." It was
the firft trifling thing I had witneffed in the
country; and being againft my tafte, I again
walked down to the entrance of the foreft,
threw my hat on the grafs, and laid myfelf
under the fhade of a clump of oaks. Something prefently pattered by me; looking
round, I faw the poor diftreffed ftag—my hat
was in his way; he attempted to clear it with
a fpring, and fell into the crown : I gently
put the lappet of my coat over it, till I could
get at one of my fhoe-ftrings to halter him
with, which I foon did, and thus mercifully
preferved him, for fome *other* days' innocent
amufement. Up came the hunt, *Log-Ereg,*
and all, pleafed with their fport; *Log-Ereg*
moft, who exclaimed—

" Fine chace, fine chafe! But got away
as ufual—*have him again* !"

I well knew what *that* meant by the countrymen's information ; fo fitting up, and politely holding my hat, with its contents, I
aftonifhed the affembly. Laugh and jeft went
round, all huzza'd, were highly entertained,
and I was entreated, if not too labourious,

to

to carry the ſtag in my arms to the palace,
that the female part of the royal family
might be amuſed with the fight, and recital
of my dexterity. I complied : The horns
founded, as if for the death ; *I* marched firſt,
carrying the ſtag by the horns ; the dogs
were whipped back ; and horſemen and all,
in grand nimrodical diſplay, entered the court
we departed from.

The queen and female royal family were
out to receive us. I held the game at arm's
length in one hand, and with the other lifted
Log-Ereg off his ſteed, who inſtantly preſented me to his gracious conſort.

If the nod and caſual ſimper of a king
pleaſed me, what ecſtacies muſt I have felt at
her majeſty's ſmile of approbation, which extended from ear to ear ; and *who*, on my
being ſolicited by many to narrate my manner of taking the deer, &c. moſt affably
ſaid—

" No, no, not now ; I ſhall have a ſelect
party this evening, and I beg Norab Glulplew
will be of the company."

I bowed aſſent.

Arrived

Arrived at my apartments, my valets informed me, an old lady was waiting; having been entirely abftracted from female *private* fociety (the reader can eafily guefs why) fince my arrival in Lilliput, I was at a lofs to conjecture the occafion of fuch a vifit I haftened to her; fhe waved all ceremony, and thus introduced herfelf—

" *Norab Glulplew*, you *muft* know me!"

" Forgive me, madam; but really the fimilitudes in the Lilliputian ladies, that *general equal mixture of pure red and white in their faces*, confounds me fo, that *I often miftake one for the other.*"

" Ho! ho!" fhe replied, rather coarfely, " not know me! not know *old Berlengwelfen!* ho! ho! there's not a fcraper, a lick-fpittle about the court in want of a place, from one to a thoufand copars a year, who does not know *me—all* come to me—all *muft* come; elfe no place, no penfion, no fecret favourable whifper, till they *toucba me.*"

Her manner evinced fhe wanted me to *toucba* her—but, as I wanted nothing, I would not underftand her, fo only faid,

" Indeed

" Indeed, madam !" and hefitated.

She, as keen fighted, faw the fineffe, and cocking up her nofe, walked off in a huff; faying, as fhe parted—

" Perhaps the time is not far diftant, when *Norab Glulplew* may know the ufe of *toucba old Berlengwelfen.*"

Candid reader, didft thou perceive any thing in my conduct at the ball, which could fubject me to cenfure ? Wait with patience but a little, and the wickednefs of this old bargain-hunter fhall appear. And oh, all ye, who tread the glaffy polifhed floors of courts, remember, from the example I fhall place before your eyes, how flippery the footing that ye move on, and how ftrongly fcandal is reflected from it. But of this no more at prefent.

To proceed : At the private party all the females of royal birth, and many ladies were affembled ; I faw even my old vifitor *Berlengwelfen*, whofe head was piered juft above the back of her majefty's chair. Among the men, I faw alfo my fuitors, *Oro-Bluff, Truc-on Wo,* and *Chieters-Fled.* At requeft, I recited my manner of taking the deer—

which

which gave general fatisfaction. Converfation now grew general; the *Pefrinc-fo-Kyrc* *or h*
fingled me out for a chat ; proud of the honour, I leaned very low to accommodate her,
and fhe began—

" Pray *Norab*, what opinion had the Ble-
fecudians (at the time of your efcape) of
the peace my father condefcended to give
them ?"

" Firftly, madam, that he preferred pock-
eting the money for his own ufe, which the
Lilliputians improvidently had fent him for
the exigencies of war. And fecondly, that
he was fearful of his own people's infurgency,
had he continued it."

" Pray Norab, I expect a candid anfwer,
did not the daring conduct and *unprecedented*
bravery of *Ecnirp-fo-Kyno*, aftonifh and intimidate the enemy ?"

" I dare fay, madam, it would, if they
had ever heard of it."

" Heard of it, Norab !"

" You faid, madam, *you expected a candid
anfwer.* I believe they are fo ignorant of his
prowefs, as never to have feen his face in
battle ; and he fo fortunate, as never to have
                                        feen

feen *the giving* or *receiving* an enemy's fire
or wound."

" Ah! flander—ha!"

So faying, fhe abruptly left me; and I
could obferve fevere difpleafure on her brow,
for fhe had drawn within an inch of my nofe
to queftion me. I was furprifed, but much
more at feeing *old Berlengwelfen* make up to
me, and with a malicious fneer, utter—

" You *now know old Berlengwelfen !*"
And immediately walked off. I did not underftand her; but got up, to get rid of the
cramp, which the contracted attitude (I had
thrown myfelf into to talk to *Peffrinc fo-
Kyro)* had occafioned in my neck. I joined
the company. Nothing material occurred
during the evening, except that, instead of
mixing with the general group, or amufing
themfelves with cards or dancing—*Oro-Bluff*,
Truc-on Wo, and *Chieters-Fled*, together with
old Berlengwelfen, formed a party quarré of
clofe converfation ; and if any one attempted
to join them, moved to another part of the
room. My eyes told me reft was neceffary :
I retired.—

" Suffi-

" Sufficient for the day is the evil thereof."

While at my breakfaſt, *Chieters-Fled* was announced : He held in one hand a piece of ſkin, with a red ſeal at the end of it—in the other, a piece of written paper ; which pre-ſenting, he ſaid—

" *This* is a copy of the original procefs, which I here ſhew you (holding up the red-ſealed ſkin) iſſued againſt you. As a ſtranger to the laws of Lilliput, I adviſe you to apply to counſel immediately."

" Noble drol," ſaid I, " I am ignorant of any fault or error."

" I was defired," he replied, " by *Oro-Bluff*, to deliver you *this*. I know no more. Adieu !"

Away he went. I peruſed the ſcrol a dozen times, but could not make any thing of it ; I only underſtood ſomething at the conclu-ſion, of " *appearing in eight days.*"

I wondered what it meant ? what it could be about ? what cenſure I had fallen under ? To be ſure, I did not dread the confe-quences, for had I been difpofed to oppofi-tion or violence, I was a hoft within myfelf ;

I could

I could have pocketed all the judges of the land, and by fquatting on my breech, have exterminated every jurifprudential promul-gator of Lilliput. But as I had accepted title and profit, and ranked a fubject of that little realm, I confidered myfelf bound, by every moral tie, to pay due refpect and fub-miffion to its laws. I therefore inquired for the ableft counfel, and was recommended to *Enifker.* I wrote to him, requefting his at-tendance; which done, I followed the avoca-tions of my day as ufual. I expected fome one or other would have mentioned the cir-cumftance *to me,* but no notice was taken; every thing was pleafant as heretofore—all fmiles, bows, and careffes. Indeed I thought *Log-Ereg* more affable than ever, for he put me in mind of my promife of " *improving his farm.*"

About noon, the next day, Enifker was announced : Without ceremony he *thus* en-tered on the bufinefs—

" Norab, I have confidered your cafe, and I am afraid we muft (though its hard on us) admit *their* evidence, and reft *our* defence

I and

and *chance of a verdict* on *other* grounds, which *I* will fuggeft."

" Learned fir," faid I, " you *have con-fidered my cafe!* how can that be? *I* know it not myfelf! *I* am ignorant of the charge againft me!"

" Very likely; the Lilliputians poffefs præ-fcience in the higheft degree, and always know more of their neighbours' affairs than of their own. But *this matter of your's* has been the fubject of a fortnight's converfation (as likely to happen)—fpies have been planted over your every motion; and, I doubt!— But we muft make the beft on't. Meet me in the hall of juftice, in *Flubnduhna*, on the morning after next, and we'll do what we can. Adieu!"

" Pray, worthy counfellor, may I entreat to know the nature of my offence?"

" Oh, pho!" faid he, " did not I tell you?—(it's of no moment though) but as you wifh it, *it's for crim. con. with Peffrinc-fo-Kyro*. Adieu!"

Away he went; and fo did I, to a folitary walk—amazed, confufed. " *Crim. con.*" I repeated,

repeated, " *crim. con.*" ridiculous! impoffible! However, the laws fhall not by me,
be even fuppofedly infringed, without my
fubmitting to, and undergoing as ftrict a
fcrutiny, as the fmalleft mite of Lilliput.
Notwithftanding my confcious innocence, the
imputation made me afhamed of facing the
court, till I was exculpated; and I had refolved to return and fhut myfelf up in my
apartment, when *Chieters-Fled* walked up to
me, and faid,

" *Glulplew,* I give you joy; you have
acted wifely: I underftand you have retained
Enifker, and mean to plead guilty. Never
fear, he'll bring you off—he'll touch up the
paffions—dead hand at *crim. con.*"

I ftopped him fhort, rather angrily, faying—

" I truft, *drol,* my innocence wants not
the glofs of falfe rhetoric ; and I fhall incon-
teftibly prove myfelf above the villainous
breach of honour and hofpitality, which malice has attributed to me."

" I fincerely wifh, *norab,* for the honour
of our rank, you may. But how ? how will
you counterpoife the evidence of *Berlengwel-*

sen, as to *the attitudes you were difcovered in,
and the fcreams of Peffrinc fo-Kyro?*—circumftantial! Though l'm your friend, egad,
the *circumftantial* is ftrong againft you; and
in *thefe cafes,* you have a bad chance—your
judge is a very *Scipio.* The moment you fee
him, you'll know he never could love in his
life; fo be guarded—ufe all your artillery of
defence. But come, the morning wears, let's
to the levee."

   " Excufe me, compeer; while I am under
the imputation of fuch flagrant vice, I am
difqualified from advifing the monarch of
Lilliput. No! patiently will I wait in folitude
the event, and then—"

   " What monftrous affeftation!"

   " All that I can fay is, fimply, that you
and I differ widely in fentiment; yet, before
we part, know that *the attitudes* I was in,
were to accommodate the *peffrinc*; and *her
fcream,* for fhe fcreamed but once, was occafioned by—"

   " Hold, hold, pray fay no more! I may
be called on, *forced* to give evidence againft
you and *this* confeffion, *unextorted!* For
heaven's fake make the beft on't—*fave the
lady—*

lady—honour demands *that*; and take all the blame on yourfelf. At moſt 'twill not exceed a fine of ten thouſand copars. Sorry for you; very ſorry. Adieu! Good morning."

I was glad to be rid of him, ſo followed my original intention; returned to my apartments in the caſtle, took my dinner alone, ordered my equipage, and ſat off for Fluhnduhna.

THE TRIALS.

" The *charge* was prepar'd! the lawyers were met!
" The judges all rang'd!—a terrible ſhew!"

About nine in the morning the firſt cauſe was called on; it was for the ſame offence as that wherewith *I* was charged. The names of the parties were *Ardwbo* againſt *Mabgnib.* *Enifker* was employed for *Mabgnib.* His guilt was acknowledged; and it was ſo manifeſt, that I put him down in my mind for the penalty of ten thouſand copars, mentioned by my friend *Chieters-Fled.* But now *Enifker* roſe; he began.—His peroration ſhewed, in the moſt vivid colours, the flagrancy of

I 3   the

the crime his client had been guilty of. I
trembled for him; and applauded, from my
inmoſt ſoul, the honour of the advocate, who
thus, in virtue's cauſe, rendered up a villain
he had been retained to defend, a proper ſacrifice to juſtice. But, oh! how deceived!
with ſubtilty of logic—with the eloquence
of Cicero, and fire of Demoſthenes, he ſoon
aſſailed the injured huſband; and with di-
greſſion, *truly poetic*, on *beauty*, *health*, and
joy, and *luxury* of *uncontrouled love*—all which,
he contended, the lady had a right to enjoy,
as fully as if ſhe had been an inhabitant
of the once ſacred, afterwards voluptuous,
groves of Daphne. He ſo tickled the ears
of the auditors, and ſo agreably deluded
them with ſpecious oratory, that the hufband's caſe ſeemed to be little more confidered, than as debarring the vigorous youth
from *his* adulterous miſtreſs—*her*, from her
approved gallant.

A fine of one thouſand copars only was
the puniſhment. And *Eniſker* was congratulated on his triumphant reduction of expected damages.

The

The fecond caufe was a profecution againft a poor, forlorn, ragged wretch, whofe very appearance would have drawn—

" The iron tear down Pluto's face."

Sicknefs had prevented him from labour; and the tears of ftarving infants compelled him, againft inclination, to allay their momentary piercing cries, by committing a robbery of twenty-one copars. It was proved againft him : He bowed his head in the agonies, the complicated agonies of fhame, remorfe, and parental feeling, of fubjugated man, to the punifhment pronounced againft him—

" Perpetual banifhment, from home, from wife, from children !"

I could not help ejaculating—

" Fortune, kind fortune! travel with thee, *thou* hardly-dealt-by victim of juftice! And if not in this world, may fome propitious ftar receive and reftore thee to thofe thou lovedst and fuffereft for."

The third caufe appeared to me of great magnitude. A merchant, having occafion to leave Lilliput on affairs of confequence, entrufted

trufted a friend and neighbour to receive fuch
of his outftanding debts as fhould (during his
abfence) come to hand. He did fo; and in
gaming, and other follies, diffipated all.
Thefe facts were alfo fully proved. According to the rigourous fentence paffed on the laft
unhappy delinquent, I thought that death,
without doubt, would be the prefent culprit's
lot : But, it was determined to be only a
breach of truft. The folly of the unfufpect-
ing deluded, who was left to his action of
debt for reprifal againft a pauper, and might
mourn in prifon, with his ruined family, the
fatality of trufting (without redrefs) a robber,
the moft deteftable of fociety.

Now came on my caufe. I drew clofe to
Enifker, whofe pleadings of the day lay all before him. The counfel for the plaintiff rofe :
He told the court the moft dreadful tale of
treacherous feduction conceivable; and declared, *I* was the hero, againft whom he demanded reftitution moft ample, even beyond
the forfeiture of my whole perfonal fortune—
fome characteriftic ftigma, whereby all, who
in future fhould fee me, might know and remember, no man, let his *magnitude* be what
it

it might, was above the reach of the law ; and that although the fplendid talents of his worthy friend *Enifker* had moderated the penalty in *Mabgnib's* cafe—*here* they would not, could not avail, his train of evidence was fo clear, his witneffes fo unqueftionable ! So concluding, he hemmed, wiped his brow, and called up *old Berlengwelfen.*—

" You know *Peffrinc-fo-Kyro ?*"

" I do."

" You know *Norab Glulplew ?*"

" I do."

" Was you at a *gala* on ——? and were they *there ?*"

" They were."

" Tell us what you know, and faw tranfpire there, relative to the matter now before the court."

" I had miffed the *peffrinc* from her ftool of ftate ; and on walking down the room in fearch of her, I found her in earneft debate with *Norab Glulplew.* She was clofe to him, and he was half extended, leaning on his hand. I feemed not to notice them ; but accidentally looking down him, from his chin to his feet, I perceived, about the centre, a motion,

motion, which fhocked me. I turned my
head, and blufhed. At that inftant the
peffrinc fcreamed violently. I turned my
head again : She was hurrying from him in
terror, and he was rifing confufedly."

Here fhe clofed her evidence, and was
leaving the court; when *Enisker,* jumping
up, *thus* ftayed her :

" Stop, ftop a little, if you pleafe, Mrs.
Modefty, you blufhing lady ; and be fo good
as anfwer *me* a few queftions, as pat and
glibly as you have told your tale for my friend
Trafec-rob (which was the name of the plaintiff's counfel): And let me try if I cannot
fhake and purge this courtly evidence of
your's a little.—

" Pray, at what time of the evening did
this happen ?"

" About twelve."

" An apt time, I confefs : Had you been
drinking ?—was you drunk ?"

" Sir, I am a lady, and a court lady ;
and I fha'n't anfwer fuch an affronting
queftion."

" Oh, you fha'n't ?—we'll fee that. Noble and upright judge (addreffing himfelf to
the

the bench), will you direct an anfwer to my queftion ?"

The JUDGE.—" Why really, *Mr. Enifker*, I do not fee what your queftion, if anfwered, can benefit your client ?"

ENISKER.—" I beg your reverence's pardon; it is of great moment. I am coming to an explanation of *the motion*, and if fhe was inebriated, your worfhip knows fhe of courfe faw double; and, in *thefe cafes*, you are well convinced, *every motion* is of confequence."

JUDGE.—" I beg your pardon, I perceive it; you are right. Witnefs, you muft anfwer the queftion."

" Now, madam, was you drunk or not ?"

" No; not drunk."

" Was you merry, elevated ?"

" Little bit."

" *Little bit*! Are you a Lilliputian? where do you come from ?"

" *Grub-neck-lem*." *Mecklemburg*

" What are you ? Mind, you're on your oath !"

" Tale-bearer and general obferver for my mafter and miftrefs."

" And

＂And an't you—come, mind and keep up to the truth, or dread the confequences; ar'nt you a *general fpy* over all the houfehold ?＂

＂*Little bit.*＂

＂Very well, that will do fo far, Mrs. *Little bit :* Now for *this motion*—where was it? what was it like?＂

＂It was about the norab's centre, and feemed like a crocodile buried in fand, heaving to liberate itfelf.＂

＂Pleafe now to lay afide your blufhing, and tell us—fhould you, fuppofe you had been in the *peffrinc's* place, have been frightened?＂

＂*Little bit.*＂

＂Did any thing tranfpire after the motion and the fcream?＂

＂I don't know; I fhut my eyes, and walked away.＂

＂You may go.＂

Chieters-Fled was now called up; his evidence was an exact recapitulation of what I had told him of the occafion of the fcream. *Enisker* thought it unneceffary to crofs-queftion him, and the evidence clofed.

Trafec-

Trafec-rob now rofe again, and thus en-
larged on the evidence, in fubftantiation of
my guilt :

" Moft perfpicuous judge!—and ye, upright determinors and auditors! I am fatisfied the evidence you have heard, leaves no
doubt in your minds of the defendant's
guilt—*that guilt*, heightened too by its commiffion, under the very roof of protection
and friendfhip. If thefe were *all*, fufficient
would be before you for your fevereft cenfure! but, gentlemen, we muft—we are
bound to look a little further. Suppofe
progeny to have been the confequence from
this unnatural embrace! how could it have
been nurtured in infancy? If brought up,
how afterwards fupported? Next imagine—
dreadful imagination!—imagine it to have
arrived at years of maturity! whether male
or female, equally indifferent in confequences—it might ' have peopled all the ifle
with Gullivers.' There, gentlemen! there!
This hypothefis carries me warrantably on
to fhew you—the fire, and his probable iffue,
would, in twenty years, occafion a famine
in the land! I perceive, by the eye and

farcaftic

farcaſtic ſmile of my *honourable friend*
Enisker, he is preparing the flowers of
rhetoric, wherewith to counteract the fever
of truth, theſe truiſms muſt inflame you
with. He trembles ; I know he trembles
for his client, notwithſtanding the ſeeming
ſecurity on his brow : I know he is trem-
blingly alive for him. Therefore, gentlemen, be not ſwayed by ſeductive oratory :
Conſider the ſolemnity of the charge before
you ; and take care that the ſeal be not
torn from the marriage bond with impunity !
Then, gentlemen, think of ' peopling all the
land with Gullivers !' Think of your wives
and daughters, in ſuch enormous hands !—of
your ſons, in the arms of ſuch ſtreaming
concubines ! Think of famine !—enerva-
tion ! !—death ! ! ! Gentlemen, I have
done : My client, and, I may ſay, my
country, repoſes his, and its honour, in and
to your ſacred care. I wiſh them not in
better hands ; and leave them to you, confident of your verdict."

It was now *Enisker's* turn : In a low
voice, he addreſſed the court—

" When-

" Whenever it is left to me to reply, my learned and far more ingenious brethren of the robe endeavour to anticipate my argument, and invalidate my powers, by holding me to your view, *gentlemen determinors*, as ' *the very knight errant of rhetoric.*' Gentlemen, regard them not! I ufe no flowers, no tropes, no ftudied paufes, no high founding phrafe, no quotations from the ancients or the moderns. No; ' *I am a plain blunt man*, and that they know full well'—*that*, and no more. ' But were *I Trafec-rob, and he Enisker*,' then fhould you obferve what he imputes to me. I beg your pardons—I'll proceed; but fo accufed, my duty to my client obliged me to vindicate myfelf from *Trafec-rob's* infinuations.

" Gentlemen, I fhall call no witneffes, but truft to the adamantine coat of innocence my client is enveloped with, to bear him dangerlefs through this ftorm of afperfion, raifed by envy, hatred, malice, and all uncharitablenefs. And when I have proved to you, as I fhall, that the imputed villainy was *unaccomplishable*; you will, in juftice, grant him, not a verdict only—but direct a

K 2			profe-

profecution againſt his malevolent traducers. Gentlemen, the only evidence noticeable, was the good lady *Berlengwelſen's*—*Mrs. Little bit!* What did ſhe prove? ' That ſhe ſaw a motion,' and ' heard a ſcream!' *Politics* I conſider as indecorous diſcourſe in halls of juſtice, where not immediately pertinent to the cauſe: *I abominate, I never uſe them. Here,* Gentlemen, I avow to you, *politics* may be mentioned : It was *a political ſcream,* and *no other.* I ſhall not deſcant on it at preſent ; for *a ſhort bill of twenty thouſand ſheets,* is filed in another court, the anſwer to which, *oré indubitabilé,* though *here* inadmiſſible, will, *in ten or fifteen years,* deliver the innocence of *Norab Glulplew* down to poſterity. *The motion* is all I ſhall beg your attention to. Thirteen Lilliputian women, gentlemen, exude the effluvia of one Blefeſcudian : The baron had been converſing with that number. You all well know how unavoidably, incompreſſibly, and naturally ſuch motions ariſe, when the olfactories are touched by that ſubtle virility-exciting effluvia : We admit it. What follows ? ' *The crocodilian-like movement.*' But did

did the witnefs *fee the crocodile ?*—did it (in
the fportfman's phrafe) *break cover ?* No!
What damage then could arife ? In thefe
enlightened times, we laugh at the idea, of
women being impregnated by fouthern gales.
But you may as well believe *that poffible,* as
my client guilty. For I will tell you, that
the miafmata of a prolific miafm could not
find a lodgement. *Proportions* are phyfically
demonftrative of my affertion ; and you muft
all know, if a miafm could not lodge, what
would a miafmata produce ? Not *the race* to
be dreaded from *Trafec-rob's* figurative language ; it could but produce a fingle limb—
a head without a body, or a body without a
head, or disjointed limbs without or head or
body. If you believe this, gentlemen—if
you are convinced *the crododile never broke
cover* ; you will pafs over my learned oppo-
nent's argument, and, rejecting his allegory,
give a verdict to my plain unvarnifhed truth
and facts. *Gentlemen,* I am not afraid of
your decifion !"
    Down he fat. *The determinors* (twelve in
number) paufed for about ten minutes. In
            K 3   the

the interim, not uneafy at the confequences of what their determination might be, I was confidering how much I fhould give to *Enisker*, for his trouble and exertion of ability. I faw on the back of the caufe-paper marked " *Drawho* againft *Mahgnib*," the fee " 1000 copars." *He* was reprefented as poor—*I* was known to be rich : So put my hand in my pocket, took out two ingots, folded them up, and wrote on the back—

> " *Ecnirp-fo-Kyro*
> " againft
> " *Norab Glulplew.*
> > " *Enisker* 1500 copars,
> > " *for defendant.*"

Inftead of any Solonic obfervations, I wrote the following addrefs—

" TO ENISKER.

I.

" Unparagon'd ! illumin'd *being !*—hence !
  " Leave treach'rous logic—quit th' imperious gown !
" Such studies, sure, must give the good offence ;
  " Such dreadful merit, virtue must disown.

                     " Can

II.

" Can sordid fees, to palliate vice prevail !
" Can gold entice thee to *the murd'rer's aid ?*
" With rhet'ric's sweets to gloss the vilest tale !
" Or blast the innocent—because thou'rt paid !

III.

" Oh stain ! oh blot ! indelible disgrace !
" To learning's son, or whom the arts adorn,
" Or science lifts—to struggle for *that race,*
" Where knavery bears the palm, and virtue yields a
thorn !

IV.

" That goal be their's, whose deity is gain !
" The philanthropic path of life be thine !
" No longer member of the snarling train,
" Ah ! leave the courts, and visit nature's shrine !

V.

" *There* see mankind in every devious shape—
" Descant, reflect, and let no change escape ;
" Laugh with the gay, the poor and unbless'd bless,
" And, Cicero-like, retire—to mental happiness !"

The determinors now called our attention,
and delivered their verdict. It was simply
as follows :

" *Not Guilty—no ground for the prosecution.*"

I made

I made my bow to the bench and deter-minors, and hurried home as faſt as I could (being ſomething angry at the reflection at-tempted to be thrown on me), to avoid the crowd of friends who were ruſhing forward to congratulate me.   I paſſed the day alone, and next morning went to *Elſac Sinwrod*.

CHAP.

CHAP. XIII.

*Returns to Court—Dreſſes the Farm—Break-
faſt at Court—Berlengwelſen turns Gold-
finder ; gets into a Scrape—Gulliver relieves
her—Virtues of the Royal Family—Council
—Bad News—Gulliver deputed to view the
State of the Army and Navy—Diſcourſes
on Ways and Means—Places and Penſions
—Pekrub's Agitation thereat—Return to
Fluhndubna.*

I DROVE boldly up to the palace as uſual,
armed with the ſentiment, that,

> " Virtue needs no defence,
> " The ſureſt guard" being " innocence."

Had I been a *field-marſhal,* returned from
a *perilous retreat,* I could not have received
a more flattering reception. As proof, *Log-
Ereg* immediately named me *drol of his
camera ;* and ſhaking my hand, ſaid—

" Fine weather ! ſuit the farm ! go about
it, hah ? When ſet about improving it ?"

I re-

I replied, " Whenever he pleafed ; but that having juft efcaped the clutch of the law for an imputed offence, where I could not, fuppofing I had had the grofs and wicked intention, have been guilty, my proceedings in this bufinefs muft be prudently regulated : I had therefore to defire fome preliminaries might be agreed on, before I undertook the job."

" I hear, I hear—go on, I'll grant."

" Firft then, I begged orders might be iffued, forbidding any woman to lurk or lay hid in the hedges, while under my immediate care; which, as there were twenty fields, I could not well go through the tafk of improving, in lefs than as many days. This alfo, to prevent impertinent curiofity.

" 2d. That I fhould be exempt from profecution for a nuifance, by any of his fubjects, during the progrefs of my labour, arifing from vapour, noxious fermentation, &c.

" 3d. That as the late trial had occafioned much converfation on my limbs in general, that no one (excepting fuch as could not write and read) fhould be allowed to work

on

on the farm, while under my courfe of ma-
nurage; becaufe, as it was impoffible to conceal every thing while either flooding the
meadows, or dreffing the arable land, *fome
catch-penny bookfeller* might thus, without my
knowledge or concurrence, obtain, with ac-
curacy, *dimenfions*; which, improperly treated
of, might injure the morals of the young
and wanton.

" Thefe agreed to, I was his fervant to the
beft of my abilities, and would the next day
begin at fun-rife."

Notices to the above effect were immediately publifhed, and ftrictly enforced. I was
permitted to retire early, and never had before experienced two fuch gracious fmiles as
the royal pair honoured my adieu with.

Whether the anxiety I had experienced,
or whether fate, to reward me for the paft,
occafioned the circumftance I fhall next mention, I know not; but I willingly believed
the latter: And though I had the gripes ter-
ribly all the night, I perfevered in retention,
and fat intereft before eafe; confident too,
that—

" There

" There is a tide in the affairs of men,
" Which, taken at the height, leads on *to fortune.*"

With great difficulty I held till break of day, and never did I fo anxioufly expect the fun-rife.

" At length the morn unbarr'd her golden gates."

I hurried to the firft field, and beftowed the blefling of compoft in the moft luxuriant manner. And fo happily was I prepared, fo ready for the tafk, that I was returned to my apartment before a watchman was awake.

BREAKFAST AT COURT.

" *Care* keeps his watch in ev'ry old man's eye,
" And where *care* lodges, sleep will never lie."

By times I had an exprefs invitation to breakfaft ; the meeting was laughable—for though the old couple were as familiar as ufual, yet all the young ones looked very queer. Some were holding handkerchiefs, and fmelling-bottles to their nofes, fome ftopping

ping their's with rue; while the reft were cramming every crevice they could find with paper, to exclude the fumette arifing from the well-dreffed field, which lay in front of the apartment. Two of them reached, which the royal papa was very angry at, and mama frowned horribly. I was vexed for being the occafion, though it produced me a fine compliment from old Berlengwelfen. Genuine chara&er is difcoverable by the fmalleft accidental circumftances. That fhe was a perfe& courtier was by this trifle demonftrated. Under pretence of letting in frefh air, fhe threw up one of the windows, thruft out her head, and withdrawing it, with a deep fniff, exclaimed—

" Oh, heaven! how fine! more better, more wholefome than civit!"

So fweet is flattery, let the fource it fprings from be ever fo foul, I almoft forgave her for the attempted injury. The cataftrophe proves it was mere flattery—for in about ten minutes, the gale was fo highly tainted, that every foul, excepting *her majefty* and *Berlengwelfen*, vomited heartily. I was truly vexed for the poor girls, and could not help faying

L   fo

so to *Log-Ereg*, as I held the fourth bason to him : But he stopped me short, saying—

" Never mind ! ugh ! good ! fine ! save physic ! save physic ! ha ? and get great crop !"

The young ones were obliged to withdraw, and I was left with only the *majestic pair* and *old Berlengwelsen.*

" Pleasure never comes sincere to man,
" But lent by heav'n upon hard usury ;
" And when Jove holds us out the cup of joy,
" Ere it can reach our lip, 'tis dash'd with gall
" By some left-handed god."

While assisting *Log-Ereg*, I perceived I had lost a ring from my finger, which was given me by *Rambellius* at our parting, and which I had resolved never to go without. I could not help expressing my sorrow aloud. *Log-Ereg* looked *solemnly* on the ground—her majesty cast up her eyes *pitifully*—and old Berlengwelsen cried—

" Was it dimunt ?"

I told them " *it was*, and of some value, having belonged to an old usurer in Blefescu, who gave it at his last gasp to *Rambellius*, for

for extreme unction; and that *he* had given it me, as a memento of his friend-ship."

"Where, where could you lose it?" said Log-Ereg.

"Did you bring it here *to give me?*" said her majesty.

"We muſt hunt for it," said old Ber-lengwelſen.

"I believe, madam," said I to the laſt interrogatory, "on recollection, the ſearch muſt be mine *only*; I have a notion I dropped it in the field to-day. I'll look, however, in my apartment; and if not there, I dare ſay, in my buſineſs of to-morrow, I ſhall find it." So ſaying, I took my leave.

In vain did I hunt for my ring; and gave up the ſearch, hoping I ſhould find it *on the morrow*, where I had dropped my other treaſure.

Preſently a meſſenger came from the *great lady*, requeſting my acceptance of two diſhes, dreſſed after her country's faſhion. Highly flattered, I returned my lowlieſt duty, with thanks.

I beg-

I begged to know of the clerk of the kitchen, " of what compofed ? and how they were called ?"

He told me one was named " *bumſblub-ber*," the other " *pan-jottles*."

The firſt, made from ſea-fiſh, which had been left by the tides on the ſtrand, and to which, the ſearchers after theſe delicacies, were directed by the noſe, as the heat of the fun ripened them.

The other was of the fleſh of ſheep, which had not undergone the torturing pang of the butcher's knife; but dying, delicately ſtarved, were dreſſed (as ſome ſorts of fowl are) trail and all, which the delicious and tempting thickneſs of the gravy plainly ſhewed.

Complaiſance had compelled me to eat ſome few mouthfuls of each before he had finiſhed his explanation—my ſtomach heaved —but I had lived long enough at court to know, diſguiſe of ſentiment leads to prefer- ment ; ſo praiſing my *jottles* and *blubber* to the ſkies, I diſmiſſed the cook.

I ſtaid at home all the reſt of the day ; the loſs of my ring vexed me, and *Rambel-lius*

lius was uppermoſt in my mind. To diſpel
ennui, I took from it's manſion (my boſom)
the little bundle, tied with the narrow black
ribbon. The firſt paper that ſtruck my eye,
was thus labelled :—

" COPY of my EPISTLE,

" to

" *ADELINE,*

" On diſcovering at confeſſion our connexion.

" RAMBELLIUS."

I.

" Oh ! that no paſſion-ſwelling chord uprais'd *my* head!
  " That to a reckleſs ear !
" Slumb'ring on apathy's inſenſate chilly bed,
" Each humaniz'd effect—were, as unto the dead :
   " Then nor ſweet hope, or grief, or fear,
    " Fell diſappointment's fang ;
" Or poverty's ſoul-melting, ſad, unaided tear,
    " Would cauſe this heart a pang.
" But feeling *all,* unable to redreſs,
" What bane can equal *mine ?* who *would the wretched*
  bleſs?

II.

  " Thou, Adeline ! ar't now *the theme!*
  " Sweet viſion of my pray'r-bleſs'd dream !
  " On thee, when midnight's awful bell,
  " Commands each *cloiſter'd* from his cell,
    L 3   " I ſadly

" I sadly think, and turn to find,
" Within the volume of my mind,
" Some page of comfort, that, when next we meet,
" May bid thy sorrows fly—sweet smiles thy cheek
    regreet.

III.

" No more *Rambellius* shall you see,
" Cloth'd with terrific bigotry ;
" No solemn farce, no scaring aid,
" Priestcraft's vile trick---poor black parade !
" Shall anathematize thy pleasures past---
" I'll come and whisper *peace---love,* that shall ever last.

IV.

" At first, I'll not condemn thy tears,
" Or deep-breath'd sigh assuage ;
" Sorrow's sooth'd form such beauty wears,
" As portraits gain by age.
" Thy care-pale cheek, thine eye down-cast,
" And cold damp nerveless hand ;
" Thy hectic, throbbing, snow-drop'd breast,
" *My* ev'ry sense command.

V.

" What other graces can adorn
" That female frame, whose heart's love-lorn ?
" What other graces man desire,
" Who wastes from mem'ry's mart'ring fire ?
" That *I* so pine, my *signet* shews,
" And that *thou* long hast wept my woes.

                                        " Wept

" Wept them ! till, fatal similars ! thine own,
" Gave thee an equal seat on mis'ry's ebon throne.

VI.

" Forgive me, that I try'd *thy* mind,
" Whilst yet disguis'd *my* name ;
" Thy voice was in my heart enshrin'd,
" I trembled for thy fame.
" For *here*, full oft, the harlot's snare,
" In vestal robe's array'd ;
" And many a lamp that's trimm'd for pray'r,
" Lights up lewd riot's bed.

VII.

" So, in our groves and sacred choirs,
" Numbers indulge their base desires ;
" With legacies, *through craft*, bestow'd,
" To pave *the donor's* way to God.
" But not so *all*—there are, who come
" Heart-broke, like me, and wish the tomb :
" Who, so much on futurity depend, and know,
" As not to quit their posts 'till heav'n directs the blow.

VIII.

" Twelve summer suns and winters cold,
" Thy *brother*, *Adeline*, had told,
" Without desire, next morn to see,
" 'Till accident restor'd him thee !
" Restor'd thee—sainted to his arms,
" With sorrow's sympathetic charms.

" *Victrix*

" *Victrix* o'er woe, with hope's angelic mind,
" Companion, mistress, for the monk refin'd.

" Once LAWRENCE BELCIGLIA.

" Now FATHER RAMBELLIUS."

The conclusion put it beyond doubt that
I had done wrong in my former suggestions
of the intimacy and friendship of *Adeline* and
Lawrence. I wept contritely ; and restoring
my papers to their habitation, in melancholy
mood retired to rest.

Morning led me to my second day's labour,
and in pursuit of my ring. I searched dili-
gently, but in vain ; and had just stepped
over a very high hedge to proceed to duty,
when a shrill voice uttered—

" *Norab, norab,* help me, help me, *little
bit* !"

Looking round, I perceived my old ac-
cuser, *Berlengwelfen* ; who, in defiance of
the edict, was in the field before me, and, in
quest of my desired ring, had fallen into a
dilemma frequent with gold-finders. Had
revenge possessed me, it was but to turn me
round, and totally immerse her. Horrid
death,

death, for one who had lived and bafked in
the fmile of princes! *I* hefitated ; *fhe* im-
plored. I was not confidering whether I
fhould fmother her or not, but how I could,
unfoiled myfelf, convey her home. The
fenfes, always kind in extremities, prefented
one of my fhoes as a vehicle : I kicked it off
—by the hair, as if pulling a radifh, drew
her out, and gently laid her in it. She was
fo exhaufted, that I thought it moft prudent
to return immediately, and leave the other
job undone. I therefore directly conveyed
her to her apartment, and waited on *Log-
Ereg,* to explain what had occafioned delay
in my progrefs. At firft, *his* brow loured ;
but *her* majefty taking his hand, faid—

" Come, come, never mind ; *norab* will
make amends—and confider, it was occafioned by his kindnefs to my poor old favourite ; and perhaps fhe has found the ring."

I declare *the queen* was quicker minded,
refpecting my property, than I had been myfelf, for I never thought to afk her, and fo
informed her majefty, who continued—

" *Well,* I'll go fee her."

" *I* go

" *I* too, *I* go too," faid Log-Ereg, " perhaps has been lucky—did right, quite right,
and go laugh at her."

Here the queen frowned. *They* fat off to
pay their vifit of condolence: I, having
nothing to do, the day being rainy, went
home, and amufed myfelf with minuting the
following obfervations in my tablets, which
had occurred during my refidence at *Elfac
Sinwrod.*

" NOTE,

" 1ft. Royal family of Lilliput, all *very*
purblind.

" Q. May not *this* be fictitious, and the
effect of merciful inclination; being
unwilling to fee the faults of their
fubjects?

" 2d. Univerfally triplicate their mono-
fyllables in conversation.

" Q. Is this a royal privilege, or only
from the defire of peculiar elegance in
diction?

" 3d. *Generous* to profufion—promife fomething almoft every day. But never receive
prefents.

" N. B.

" N. B. I think this truly magnificent, and prevents any grofs ideas of royal peculation, or taking gratuity to fcreen the unworthy.

" 4th. Remarkably fond of the arts—painting and poetry : Good authors and artifts fure of reward ; but principal favourite poet, one *Repte Danrip.*

" N. B. Think this rather too partial, as he is *a profeſſed court flatterer.*

" 5th. *Heir apparent* remarkably parſimonious.

" N. B. This would be certainly commendable in a fmall degree ; but not to the extent he carries it—as his royal fire's munificence will leave him little befides honour.

" 6th. Aftronomy in great perfection—very properly fo, being uſeful to navigation.

" N. B. *The king* keeps a planetarian in his houſehold, and has got a ftar of his own—calls it *Log-Ereg.* Told him one day, ' he fhould have named it *little Mars,* in imitation of the *fecond bear,*

he

he being the *earthly god of war.*' Smiled
a good deal at my remark."

I was proceeding in my obfervations, when
a fummons to attend an *immediate council,*
obliged me to difcontinue.

PRESENT.

LOG-EREG,

DRALPONT, VILPI TICO, PEKRUB, ORO-BLUFF,
REC-NEPS, DUNHELDASHIO, VILE—GRIN,
NAVE NPNAEE, SEVRESE, ESOR, GLUL-
PLEW.

VILE-GRIN *Grinvile* was on his legs, reading, when
I entered. He continued *thus*—

" In fhort, fo fatally are we fituated,
hemm'd in, without ordnance, without provifions—our braveft fellows all cut off—the
remnant fo difpirited, that without inftant reinforcement, all is loft."

PEKRUB ftopped him.—

" Conceal the fatal reft ; fend out more
men ! fend money ! fend—would *I* could go
myfelf !"

ESOR *Rose* interrupted him.—

" *Money !* there's none in hand ; and agent
Gonilegs' laft drafts are yet unpaid. Befides,
fome

fome grumbling rafcals fay, when the mare's
dead, too late to give her hay."

Oro-Bluff.—" *How* do they dare fay
that! Sevrefe, inftant hence! double the
number of—*you know* ; away."

Away he went. *I* now rofe to give my
opinion.

" It appears to *me* thefe dangers are mag-
nified ; I would not be vain-glorious, but I
can venture to affert, that with five hundred
of picked men, I would, unmolefted, march
through the whole territory of *Blefefcu.*"

Log-Ereg majeftically rofe, and fhaking
his head, faid—

" No, no, *Glulplew,* that won't do! Told
fo, once before—deceiv'd—believ'd it, and
loft *thirteen of my beft friends* by it."

Bowing duteoufly,

" Sir," faid I, " give me leave to review
your troops, I *may* fuggeft."

" You fhall," he returned ; fat down, and
fighed.

Rec-neps next fpake.—

" The returns of *my department,* I am
forry to fay, are little lefs difaftrous ; what
M   with

with the delays in fitting out, the ſtormy ſeaſon, and the intelligence the enemy have received, our naval hopes are at their loweſt ebb."

Here I felt my conſequence, and (perhaps abruptly) ſaid—

" *The navy of Lilliput* not to be relied on for defence! impoſſible! That your armies have *been laughed at*, I admit—but *your navy*, no! Beſides, matriculated here, give me command, my life ſhall anſwer for your tars' ſucceſs".

VILPI TICO, who had hitherto reſerved himſelf, now took his turn.—

" The taxes propoſed by *Norab Glulplew*, though promiſing, have, in part, failed of their expected produce; and neither fleets or armies can be equipped without great preſent ſums. I have again turned my eyes on all *the neceſſaries of life*, and do not ſee *one article* untaxed: What, therefore, can be done?"

He pauſed; I took advantage, and replied—

" If the neceſſaries of life have been impoliticly and unpopularly aſſeſſed, yet there
remains

remains one great refource, more than amply
fufficient for the prefent vaft occafion. And
I fhould be afhamed, unmeritedly, to continue an eleemofynary receiver, from a diftreffed loyal people."

So faying, I took out my gift of the
penfion, and tore it in pieces. Then went
on—

" If the neceffities or meanneffes of thofe
in fimilar fituations reftrain them from the
like virtuous facrifice to juftice, let them at
leaft bear their proportions of the burden;
and doubly tax the idle, to preferve the meritorious induftrious."

I fear I was too energetic, for at thefe
words *Pekrub fainted!* The little hubbub
occafioned by this accident was, by his removal, done away; and it was refolved,
that I fhould review the army, and give my
fentiments as to farther campaigning. The
command I refufed, and left that to the
continued management of the magnanimous
fo-Kyro.

The fleet was abfolultely forced on me;
which, gratuitoufly, I accepted: But was

compelled,

compelled, againſt inclination, to accept the added title of *quarmſi.*—And the meeting, after reſolving a ſolemn faſt, and that I ſhould on the morrow attend *Vilpi Tico* to *Flubndubnna*, broke up.

CHAP.

CHAP. XIV.

*Political Converfation on the Road, between
Vilpi Tico and Gulliver—The Faft—Vifit
from a Superior of the Church—The Camp
—A Plot difcovered—Sevrefe's Activity dif-
played—Humbug—Congratulatory Addreffes
to Log-Ereg, on the Efcape from what might
have been a Plot—Sets off to view and
equip the Fleet.*

---

*C*INCINNATUS was called from *his* plough
to the conduct *alfo* of armies, and the
prefervation of a mighty ftate! On our way
to *Fluhnduhnna*, *Vilpi Tico* was remarkably
inquifitive—as to " how, without frefh fupplies, I could undertake to fend out the
fleet ?" &c. And laftly, " whether I had
conveyed my own treafures out of the kingdom ?" I affured him to the laft queftion, I
had not : To the firft, I muft view, before I
could determine. We then fettled, that as
the morrow was appointed for *the faft*, I
fhould, on the following, fee the armies en-
camped ;

camped; and the third day, vifit *the fleets.*
Thefe things arranged, we feparated.

THE FAST.

I made a point of fupping well, intending
to obferve the ordinance of abftinence ex-
emplarily. The bells of all the temples
rang betimes, the fhops were all fhut up,
and about two hours after fun-rife I was
vifited by one of the *fuperior religious* : He
was the picture of eafy holinefs—*fat, fleek,*
and *ruddy.* Not like *Rambellius,* a living
fkeleton. His falute was highly dignified.
I thought he was come to prepare me for
confeffion, and kneeled to him ; he fmiled,
as I fuppofe, at my ignorance, for, taking my
hand, he faid—

" Rife, *quarmfi* ; I called to give you
joy of your appointment. I hope you'll trim
the dogs—cut all their throats—exterminate
them."

" Sir! furely I mifapprehend ; are you
not a delegate of heaven?—a minifter of
peace? The very name of war muft grieve
your pious mind, fo oppofite to your bleffed
function ?"

" Oh,

" Oh, oh," faid he, " I muft undeceive you. Come, come, and dine with me to-day; I fhall have a jolly party—and we'll difcufs the moft probable means of fuccefs."

" The *Elbib*," faid I, " which I fuppofe you form the fucceffes of futurity upon, treats not, *father*, as I recollect, on the advantages that can be made or gained in earthly war."

" *Elbib* !" faid he, " what's that? It's a ftatute I never heard of. Is it a treatife on preferment?—Is it the art of getting rich ?"

" Indeed," faid I, " it is, of gathering riches which can never wafte : And I hope the neglect of its principles, which have been the fole caufe of the horrors of Blefefcu, have not been unnoticed in Lilliput !"

" *Elbib*! Oh, oh," faid he again, " I re-collect we ufed to have fuch a book in ufe; but it is now almoft unknown, obfolete, out of print. I fee you was brought up with a falfe notion : We muft rub off this monaftic ruft ; fo come, dine with me."

I peremptorily refufed ; and a flight bow from each to the other feparated us.

Inftead

Inſtead of ſeeing *Vilpi Tico,* as I expeſted, to accompany me, *Eſor* came with an apology, which ſurpriſed me; it was, " That a too copious libation *on the faſt,* had rendered him incapable of the intended honour ; but that *he,* if I would condeſcend to accept his company, would attend me."

Eſor and I, accordingly, ſet forward and arrived at

THE CAMP.

A curſory view diſguſted me. Inſtead of ſeeing, as I expeſted, veteran commanders, both in years and manners equal to, and capable of, joining combat with ſuch as *I had ſeen*—they appeared to me, the followers of *an Anthony* on Cydnus' banks, waiting, fulltrimmed, another voluptuous Cleopatra. And ſo infantine were many of the leaders, if I had not known better, I ſhould have concluded, the ſoldiers, from parental kindneſs, had preferred their children to themſelves. I was well pleaſed I had wiſely refuſed ſuperintendance of ſuch an hazardous taſk ; and returned, fully ſatisfied of my eſcaping the enterpriſe.

A PLOT

A PLOT DISCOVERED.

I was in expectation of finding *Vilpi Tico*
recovered, instead whereof, *Sevrese* was waiting my arrival; he looked very sombrously—
but as I leaped spiritedly from my car, and
handed down my comrade, he exclaimed—

" Welcome, *quarmsi!* how is *dear Esor?*
how did ye both escape the horrors of yes-
terday? *Poison!* fatal poison!—Oh, *Pekrub,
Vilpi Tico, Vile-Grin!*"

I was thunderstruck, and ejaculated—

" Poison! ill-fare, poison'd!"

" Yes," said he, " nor *there* did the
dreadful intention end; 'twas intended to as-
sassinate even sacred precious *Log-Ereg*. A
traitor, with poisoned spittle, was to have
squirted venom in his face the next time he
appears in public; and, if that failed, to have
extracted his brains, by forcing out your
rivet with a powerful magnet. But I've discover'd all—*here, here's* the proscribed list
(holding out a list of names) here they are,
all safe, all caged, all be tried, all bang'd.
Adieu! farewell! I must go—times full of
peril. Take care, take care."

I was

I was afraid this dreadful difcovery would prevent my vifit to the fea-fhore; but in order to know how matters really were, hafted to poor *Vilpi Tico* to condole. I found the *noble trio* all on one fopha, a large wafh-tub before them, which was near full of fhocking red-coloured evacuation—their faces pale, as in the agonies of death. On my entrance, they each lift up their funken eyes, and feebly articulated—

" Ah, quarmfi!"

" Oh, quarmfi!"

" Dear quarmfi!"

And infenfibly funk away. *Dunheldafbio* was ftanding by—a large cloth in his hand, with which he kept alternately wiping the clammy foreheads of his wretched friends.

" Fine efcape," faid he to me, " fine efcape; glad you refufed dining. But the *faft-day*, fee the effeds of treafon—*the fupe-rior's* wine! There, there's the rub; don't though fufped *him*—no! he's right; trufty; drank more than either of thefe unfortu-nates, and *quite well*—fo can't judge *him* guilty."

" God

" God forbid," faid I, which had hardly efcaped my lips, when in came, led by *Sevrefe*, Ahno.

Mahlta. *Latham*

Wifhkan.

They looked very gravely, and the patients as dolefully : However, *Mahlta*, who was a man of true genius, at once difpelled their fears by this developement.—

" As order'd, we have examin'd all the *forty* bottles that were yefterday emptied by *you*, my *noble invalid*, and *the fuperior*. There's no danger : This, this empty bottle (holding up one he had brought away) was the vehicle of the offending matter. *The butler* has confeffed : He fufpected a fellow fervant of addiction to wine, fo infus'd a fmall quantity of emetic tartar in this veffel to difcover him. You, by miftake, were at dinner ferv'd out of it."

Joy fucceeded this news ; and all, but *Sevrefe*, fmiled. Sangrado's beverage was now plentifully beftowed, and a few hours reftored the *tres nobile fratrum*. The worft remained behind !—The intended affaffin was in cuftody, but would not confefs. I begged to fee him.

him. *Sevreſe*, ever ready in theſe matters, ſoon produced the miſerable delinquent. Think my ſurpriſe—it was my own valet!

At ſight of *me* his courage forſook him: " Why, wretch (ſaid I)?"

" Oh, my noble maſter (the poor creature anſwered), forgive, but forgive me! I'll con-feſs all; for you, you only are wrong'd."

I ſigned my perſonal forgiveneſs to him, and *Sevreſe* brought in ten ſcribes to take his exa-mination, which was as follows:

SEVRESE. " Is your confeſſion voluntary, or extorted?"

PRISONER. " Voluntary."

SEVRESE. " Of what was the poiſoned liquid, you held in your mouth when taken, compoſed, and by whom?"

PRISONER. " I don't know."

SEVRESE. " Scribes, obſerve *that*!—There are more yet lurking behind the curtain. Where did you get it? From who receive it?"

PRISONER. " From no one. I—I ſtole it!"

SEVRESE. " Improbable! this is prevari-cation. Who ſteals poiſon!—take him away. I'll try him yet a little further. Where did
                                    you

you procure the fubtle, powerful, death-intend-
ing other inftrument?

PRISONER. " I ftole it."

SEVRESE. "Surely, furely, noble auditors,
here is proof fufficient of my fagacity, my
depth of obfervation, induftry, and loyalty in
hunting out thefe horrible mifcreants, damn'd
complotters—Away with him!

PRISONER. " I have fpoken the truth; I
am innocent of treafon; I have only wrong'd
my mafter."

" By your leaves, my brothers (faid I); I
will propofe him a queftion or two (affent
was bowed)." " Be candid; fpeak out, and
fear not; but you muft anfwer. Where did
you get this dreadful mixture you are faid to
have the defign of ufing? and of what is it
compos'd?"

PRISONER. " I know not its component
parts; nor do I know that it has deleterious
qualities. I only faid to a friend, it was fo hot
that I believed it would blifter the face of a
king, if it fhould touch it.

SEVRESE (impatiently). " Rafcal! rafcal!
How dar'd you fuggeft fuch a thing! How
dare your profane rebellious mouth furmife it

N   poffible

poſſible for danger to approach a royal phiz! Noble compeers, I pronounce this *Conſtructive Treaſon*!"

" Patience! moſt perſpicuous Sevreſe (ſaid I); the manner of his obtaining it, and for what uſes, will, I think, in a great meaſure, elucidate this matter. How did you obtain it ?"

PRISONER. " I had obſerv'd your *Drolſpib* often fill your mouth from a golden cheſt, which one day you left behind you: Curioſity induced me to know the contents; I call'd one of my fellow-ſervants, by whoſe aſſiſtance I open'd the lid. We took out about ten of the rolls, and breaking one in two, I ventured to put it in my mouth. A violent burning enſued, and I ſaid in my haſte as before-mentioned."

I could not help burſting into laughter *at Sevreſe's quid of tobacco plot ;* but he, undaunted, notwithſtanding my explanation of its uſe, and to convince him of the harmleſſneſs of it, by filling my mouth with it, perſevered in his ſecond charge of " *the magnet.*"

SEVRESE. " Where, ſirrah, was this tremendous bar of iron, this diabolically magnetiſed

netifed death-dealing inftrument manufactured ?"

PRISONER. "Indeed I know not; I did
not know its properties; I faw it laying in my
mafter's chamber, and as he never noticed it,
I thought it of no fervice to him; and wanting a bar to my own ftreet door, I one day
took it home. I'm fure I'm a fufferer enough
by it : For the moment I entered my doors,
my houfe fell about my ears, and I faw, to my
terror and aftonifhment, all the iron fpikes,
nails, rivets, trivets, grates, locks, bolts, and
bars of my poor manfion, flying towards, and
fticking clofe to it."

Sevrefe *now did appear* a little creft-
fallen : However, I reprimanded the fellow
for ftealing my pocket-magnet, and with ad-
monition to *be very cautious* of his *political*
converfation in future, he was difmiffed.
Sevrefe, however, recommended, as the force
of the magnet was allowed, and the tobacco
water was acknowledged to have acid qualities, that it was proper *Log-Ereg* fhould have
an additional guard whenever he appeared in
public. That as all the foldiers were nearly
employed, or cut up, in the juft and neceffary

Blefef-

Blefefcudian war, a guard of 500 old women would fufficiently anfwer the purpofe; he fhould therefore move for it. He would, moreover, recommend the command of this honourable *body corps* to *Berlengwelfen*; and if not thought too unworthy, would put himfelf in female attire for a time, and become her adjutant.

This being an affair of moment, the determination was deferred till the next council. Letters of gratulation were, however, immediately difpatched to *Log-Ereg* on his happy efcape from what *might have been a plot*; and the *tres nobile fratrum* having difgorged the offending matter, the day following, as originally fixed, was appointed for our fetting forward to view the fleet.

CHAP.

CHAP. XV.

A new Acquaintance; the Occasion of his Visit —His Character and Business—A little Insight into MONEY MATTERS—*Lenders and Borrowers—Agents—Jackalls and their Advocates.*

WALKING homeward, a thought fortunately struck me of the necessity of taking with me my cork jacket, there being no vessel sufficiently large to convey me to the ships. I therefore directly returned, while the idea was in my head, to pack it up. In my apartments I found a stranger; he had no *mauvaise honte* about him, but at a *coup*, introduced himself thus:

" My name, norab, is *Juknig*; I am *procurator-general* for dissipation in *Lilliput*; understanding you have immense riches at command, I came to offer you my services, in laying out your money to the greatest advantage."

" Sir," said I, " I thank you; but I really think *Vilpi Tico* enables even the most avaricious

N 3   ricious

ricious to gratify their lucrous appetites to repletion."

" Oh dear! dear norab! *I can* double your
fortune in fix years. I can fhew you men,
who, from nothing, as it were, are become
rich, by a traffic unknown when your father
was *here*. If you have an hour to fpare, I'll not
only inftruct you in the myfteries of the inviting merchandize, but delineate to you fome
of the *dealers* and *dealing*, which will convince you I am capable of the undertaking,
many of the characters being well known to
you fince your fojourning with us."

There was fomething fo fingular in the application, that I not only bowed affent, but
told him I fhould thank him for his information, merely to fatisfy curiofity; for I had no
intention of taking *him* for my factor.

" I will firft," faid he, " begin with my
own hiftory :—I am an *ignis fatuus, born* in a
work-houfe, educated in a *charity-fchool*, thence
tranfplanted to the fituation of *footboy* to an
ufurer. I poffeffed perfpicuity, and was foon
noticed ; poffeffed confidence, and became his
clerk. I quickly amaffed fees fufficient to
wing my flight, and honoured myfelf with a
                                    mafter's

mafter's degree ; that is, I held out the fame
lures as *a money lender:* A fmart lodging, well
dreffed footman, and neat advertifement in
the diurnal papers, did my bufinefs. I'll not
trouble you with a recapitulation of the firft
twenty years of my life, the various ups-and-
downs I have experienced, but pafs on to the
prefent ftation I hold (digreffing only thus
far): That about feven years fince I married
an old demirep of quality, whofe titles have
helped me through numberlefs pecuniary ma-
nœuvres. I now live in *Illypaccid,* and keep
equipage, table, fervants ; in fhort, an hotel of
rendezvous for needy, great, expeɛant profli-
gate heirs to titles and eftates : So, norab, if
you have inclination to obtain, with rapidity,
an oriental-like fortune, employ me, and it is
effeɛed."

"Juknig," I replied, "I am fatisfied from
your converfation, external form, and Mofaic
appearance, you have every requifite for the
undertaking offered me—rapid accumulation of
wealth—*that* certainly is inviting ; but before
I embark in the commerce, I fhould wifh to
have the names of, and general opinion the
parties fo trafficking are held in by fociety in
general,

general, that I may afcertain in what clafs I
fhall rank, fhould I be difpofed to engage."—
I fancy he thought he had taken a gudgeon, for
he fmiled acquiefcence to my requeft, took
out his pocket-book, and read as follows :

"*Lift of Lenders and Borrowers in Flubndubnna,
also of their Jackalls, or the Money Adver-
tifers, and their refpective Advocates.*

"LENDERS.

" *Crota-Nojb* deals only in fix years purchafe annuities, by which means, from a fmall
beginning, he has accumulated upwards of
100,000 copars.—N. B. He is always ready
for a frefh chap, and is a certain anchor for
the *firft holding* on the young heir.

" *Bladbis* and *Ceytras.*—Thefe gentlemen
live in the fame ftreet, and frequently hunt bar-
gains in couples, give good prices, and deal
honourably—made their original fortunes in
Aidni, but continue to peculate *here* under the
term—*lend*

" *Nikdrain.*—A *norab,* who, by his marriage
with the daughter of an old ufurer, became
immenfely rich, and fat up general and whole-
fale

ſale dealer in copars—either as agent, truſtee, or ſharer.

" *Cutileg.*—A gentleman equally adroit in the diſſection of a Lilliputian, or in the cutting up his eſtate, docking an *arm*, or a *leg*, or an *entail*; fond of a good reverſion to diſtraction : So that poſſibly, immediately after a kind attendance on an expiring father, he may more kindly attend the ſon to pay him for his purchaſed birthright.

" *Elſig.*—A great merchant, and of high rank in the national repoſitory of wealth—A certain purchaſer of a ſnug ten per cent.

" *Boſkobrank, Dalekrob, Yelterces, Racmas,* and *Ingtonſhul.*—All follow the ſame purſuit."

"To proceed with this liſt is unneceſſary; for I dare ſay, *norab*, you find, even among thoſe few I have mentioned, ſome names from whoſe *rank*, credit, character, and conſequence in life, *you* may be induced to join the train. I will now proceed to the *borrowers*, from among whom you may *ſelect pigeons* to your fancy; then proceed to the *jackalls*, then to their *advocates.*"

I ſtopped him, ſaying,

" *Juknig,*

" *Juknig*, I am much obliged by your wifh
to ferve me; but I cannot conclude that, joining myfelf to a *horde* of *avowed* law-fanction-
ed plunderers, would take from *me* the confcious guilt which I muft feel at the completion of every dirty manœuvre to heap up
wealth: And inftead of coalefcing, I'll be as
candid with you, as you have been to me,
in divulging the contents of your *black lift*;
and, moreover, give you my fentiments of the
difpofition I would make of the varioufly de-
fcribed, if *I* was in power.

" 1*ft*, *The Lenders* I would fine, to the extent of their properties, that they might feel
mifery, fuch as their rapacity muft often inflict
on others.

" 2*dly*, *The Borrowers* I would confine in
private mad-houfes till the age of reafon
dawn'd; for it is obvious, either their fenfes
are loft or unripen'd, otherwife they could not,
would not, fubmit to fuch impofitions.

" 3*dly*, *The Jackalls* I would treat with a
voyage for life to *Yab Ytanob*.—And,

" 4*thly*, *The Advocates* (if any fuch there
are), who debafe an honourable profeffion, by
being inftrumental in forging the fhackles
which

which bind to fuch ruinous, villainous contracts, *they* fhould fwell the fees of the execu-
tioner."

He put up his *black lift*; and, like an arrow from a bow, fhot out of my room. As
he was fhutting to my door, I heard him mut-
ter, " *Great* (alluding to my fize) *virtuous
fool.*"

The infight which he had given me of Lilliputian ufury, put me in mind of one of
Rambellius's manufcripts, which I had never
yet read, it being written in Englifh, of which
language I had but a fmattering. I recollected the title of it was,

" ABUSES OF THE LAW."

Having an hour or two to fpare, I was
minded to fee if there was analogy between
the abufes of the Englifh and the Lilliputian laws ; fo opened my little bundle, tied
with the narrow black ribbon — it was enclofed
in the following letter, directed

" *To* FATHER RAMBELLIUS,

" *Sialac Blefefcu.*

" MY DEAR FRIEND,

" Since my refidence in this country,
chance has thrown me into the fangs of their
lawyers:

lawyers: Thereby I had an opportunity of obferving much mal-practice and deviation from
juftice and rectitude in their proceedings.   I
refolved, in confequence, to put my ideas of
the abufes on paper, which I have done, and am
preparing for the prefs.   As I promifed, on
my departure, to fend you every literary mor-
fel I fhould compofe whilft *here*, I have enclofed you this (to fave the duty a printed copy
would coft you)—a manufcript of my work.

> " I am,
> " My dear Friend, &c. &c.
> " Maurus non Niger.

" *Hatton Garden*,
" *London*, 1794."

I fat down to the perufal, it was *thus titled:*

ABUSES

A B U S E S

OF THE

L A W;

OR

THE TEMPLE,

CITY, AND SUBURBS

EXEMPLIFIED.

A MORAL SATIRIC POEM.

IN THREE PARTS.

" Fie on't—oh fie ! 'tis an unweeded garden
" That runs to seed—*Things* rank and gross in nature
" Possess it merely." HAMLET.

A B U S E S

OF THE

L   A   W.

PART I.

" Quantum mutatus ab illo "—*Temp'c.*

FROM Henry's * days to these, how chang'd the race
   That tenanted this then devoted place;
Where Godfrey's knights from holy war retir'd,
Their spears laid by, yet with religion fir'd,
The world forgot, to pray'r, to fasts return'd,
And with seraphic ardor only burn'd;
True to the cross, and freed from martial strife,
Here pass'd, in cloister'd ease, their rest of life.

How chang'd the scene!—each lance is now *a pen!*
The holders what!—*Truth* dare not call them men,
But knaves and fools, and pert pragmatic sparks,
And what were squires † transform'd to sniv'ling clerks.

* In the reign of Henry II. the Temple was the residence and property of the *Knights Templars,* or *Knights of Jerusalem.*

† Every knight used to have a *squire* or shield bearer.

O 2

The

The muse forbids the honest man to die,
And Kenyon sure will cleanse this filthy sty,
Whence wrongs are hurl'd, th' unwary to enthrall,
This *Temple once, this now* Pandora's hall.

Ye learned few * who grace this latter age,
And turn, for honor's sake, the elab'rate page ;
Who toil, and exercise your minds, to gain
Those heighths ev'n Aristides wou'd attain—
To sit exalted, and decide for right,
Condemn the wrong, and crush oppression's might.
To you the muse with adoration bends,
And hails ye virtue's, freedom's, nature's friends ;
Around your heads eternal laurel's bent,
" *Ye* fall not in the scope of our intent."

Pace we the rounds, and first regard *that pile* †,
Simply magnificent, unmatch'd its style:
The entrance awes, each column stamps effect,
And ev'ry sculptur'd stone commands respect.
Here soldiers, patriots ‡ lie, in firm belief,
To meet (their toils' reward) our hallow'd Chief.
Bless'd be their manes, 'twas for Christ *they* fought !
Light fall the feet, nor wear their mem'ries out.

Yon *shady walk* shall now instruction shew—
Enter *that door*—Heav'n! *fourteen clerks* in row !
Some mighty task employs the master's mind :
How good ! to labor thus to serve mankind!

* The bar and bench.   † Temple church.   ‡ Tombs of the knights.

Tread

Tread, softly tread ! we're sure on sacred ground,
Whence law's pure light throws its broad beam around.
Amazing work!—what depth of science!—see !
Whole reams o'erwritten—Ha! "*fallacious plea!*
Sham judgments, joinders, and *demurrers*"—well—
" *Weil*"—No—'tis bad—This is a task for hell.
Right can be only by the base delay'd,
And English honour shou'd disdain such trade ;
By *this protractive work*, fresh mischief grows,
And *one* is multiplied to *many* woes.

The *wretched debtor*, trembling at a jail,
Asham'd to own, or tell his hapless tale,
When first affliction lays her iron hand,
Flies to *that aid* which nearest seems at hand,
Defence—for *that* he seeks the man of law,
Elate with hope, from *time* relief to draw.
" *A little time*," he says, " is all I want."
The *scriv'ner* * answers, with right scriv'ning cant,
" Bring me to bear th' expences out of purse,
I'll stem the storm, your present evils nurse."
Agreed—*Term* comes, succeeding terms flow on,
False pleas, and *error's process*—all are done.
" *What now?* To Parliament with error?'' " Yes."
" What shall I gain ?" " Let's see—a few day's grace."
" *A few day's grace!* good heav'n ! what then ?" " No
      more ;
Law has not then one other trick in store :
But what of that, *we've* teaz'd them for *their* strife,
They can but send you *now* to jail for life."

* *Scrivener* was the original surname for *attorney.*

O 3   " *To*

" *To jail for life!* Why what you've had of me
Wou'd pay the debt, and I might now be free!"

Unhappy wretch! just in the lion's mouth,
Fly, and conceal thyself, tho' bless'd with youth ;
Rememb'ring this, thou still hadst mix'd with men,
If *quirks* and *special pleading* had not been.
That *this is so*, inspect that *crowded* cell *,
Where thoughtless virtue's doom'd with vice to dwell;
Where, stow'd with those, the very worst e'er born,
The very best in silent anguish mourn.
In the *same* straw-bed frequently are seen,
Debtor and creditor with squallid mien ;
Ask them the cause, thrill at their sad replies ;
" *Me, laws delay :*"   " And me, Sir, false advice.
We're friends, and wou'd *each other* free ; *but then*,
Each other's lawyer lays us fast again!"

Truth, without force of language, thus express'd,
Strikes home, and harrows up each feeling breast.

Oh *thou†!* the learned'st in th' entangling maze,
Pupils were few in thy great pleading days ;
Scoul on th' abettors of *protraction's* scheme,
Exert thy pow'r, and be our gen'ral theme.
Easy the task ; a rule of court does all :
Admit no staying plea within the hall,
Unless 'tis vouch'd beneath some counsel's hands,
That what's adduc'd, *the cause, in fact,* demands.

* King's Bench prison.   † Sir F. Buller.

So

So onwards, till the record meets your eye,
Thus will you knav'ry from desert espy.
Oft thus unmask, where now 'twere sin to doubt,
Unless some master-hand shou'd point it out.

Farewel *false pleading*! Down these steps again,
Not far away, we'll pierce another den :
A worse, a murkier far—lo ! *herein dwells*
The wretched hunter-out * of youngsters' bills.
This is the mart usurious harpies use,
Pawnbrokers' 'change, resort of pilf'ring Jews :
A *scene* where fraudulents may learn to thrive,
Taught by example how a knave can live.
This is the cell from whence such evils rise,
As on the pleader's desk abus'd our eyes.
Trace we the tricks, unknot the blasted spell,
With hope, when seen, the progress you'll repel.
Presto—*a bill* presents itself to sight,
Due, with indorsers' names o'ercover'd quite :
Drawer, a youth of fashion and expence;
Acceptor, such another, void of sense ;
Indorsers, first, a broken broker ; now,
An o'ergrown money-lender's name I vow ;
" Another yet!—I'll see no more." We must,
Or fail to execute the promis'd trust.
These six that follow are the lawyer's friends,
Or *clerks*, whose names assist his roguish ends.
Now mark ! this little bill of twenty pound,
Shall prove a fortune, ere the year roll round.

* So villainously profitable is this traffic, that 2ol. has been given for a bill of 1ol. by one of these jobbers.

We'll

We'll now inquire for what this bill arose :
Was't for their bookseller, or was't for cloaths?
Neither ! a trifling sum they wish'd to raise,
Or for the joy of youth, for wine, or plays.
The papers taught them rapidly t'obtain,
What ev'ry paper offers, golden grain ;
They give their bill, the man * of straw proceeds
To twist, and turn it, somewhere he succeeds.
With *woollen, linnen*, or with *wooden pails,*
Buckles, or *buttons*, or a *bag of nails.*
If those won't do, he makes the matter sure,
His 'polst'rer deals in charming furniture † !
The goods are sold, loss *fifty* full per cent :
" Ten pounds for twenty !" Well, they part content.
The bolder flies to bless his scriv'ner's‡ sight,
With the new lovely morsel of delight ;
Certain default of payment at the first !
But *then*, an ample crop to ripeness nurs'd,
A prize for ingenuity to work,
Where law's broad loom may figure ev'ry quirk,
'Tis grasp'd with thanks, grows due, and as declar'd,
Neglected lies—*direct* the oath's prepar'd.
Ten wills are issu'd, *two* requiring bail,
The rest are sleepers till we close the tale.
Now declaration comes, *defence* grows warm,
But *pleas* and *paper books* conclude *this term.*

    * The advertizer.

    † There are certain pawn brokers, silversmiths, woollen-drapers, mercers, &c. &c. who profess this traffic solely.

    ‡ Scrivener and bill doer often halve the costs.

Inquiries

Inquiries next (vacation's leisure) please,
A sheriff's jury gives with so much case.
Now, term again, with judgment at its heels,
The full completion of extortion seals.
A writ of error here, were slight avail,
Here * 'tis the debt, and not the man to bail.
What's to be done? with money unprepar'd;
The thoughtless youths attend, a little scar'd.
They bow—the well-prepar'd attorney smiles,
And with his oily words their fears beguiles.
" They only want a *little time*"—'tis giv'n;
Warrants † are sign'd, for weeks, some six or sev'n,
Including ev'ry cost, both great and small,
Brokers, indorsers, friendly rogues, and all;
Judgment *now* due, the costs close tax'd are found,
On actions ten—exactly each ten pound:
Now, money present, if they have it, goes,
Else from *post-obit contracts* date new woes.

By arts like these these chambers ‡ are upheld,
These arts, books, music, mirrors, paintings yield,
Dress, tavern, horses, mistress, country seat;
These self-created bus'ness gives complete.

* When bail to a writ of error is given, the undertaking is *for the debt*, not to produce *the party only*, in case he loses the cause; therefore more difficult to be obtained.

† That is, a confession of the damages.

‡ The hero designed by this portrait has left the Temple, but resides within an hundred miles of it.

Two

Two * of law's great abuses thus pourtray'd,
Within the reach of thy all-healing aid;
Observe, good Kenyon! be thy country's friend!
And bring these growing evils to an end.
Let no attorney in such traffic deal,
Which to prevent, mark each cramm'd writ they seal,
And mark the *plaintiff's*; often you'll disclose,
A name that does not wear the plaintiff's nose:
Slaves † who've no int'rest, as *the suit* pretends,
Mere ready engines for the bill-man's ends.

Another stain, to *study, science, law*,
Whence petty scriv'ners their resources draw;
Who, sure to find an advocate of name,
Pliant to torture *truth*, and varnish shame,
In spite of *reason, evidence*, and *sense*,
Their forte the force of mighty impudence,
Protect *chicane* with rhet'ric's glossy shew,
And gain a verdict (oft we wonder) *how?*
Calls, loudly calls *thy* reprobation down,
Whose upright bearing all are free to own.

For, Heav'n! what weight his conscience must uphold,
Who martyrs innocence for sake of gold!

---

* Iniquity of special pleading, and bill jobbing attorney's practice.

† If the C. J. would order an alphabetical list of all writs issued, containing the plaintiffs' and attornies' names, to be delivered him on the first day of every term much light would be thrown on this dark subject.

Who

Who, knowing when th' oppreſſor brings a brief,
Wants the small virtue to return the leaf,
Or tread it underneath his honest feet,
And shew where *learning is,* is *bonor's* seat.

But see our exit—Mitre Court's in view ;
Templar's farewel—we'll travel " eastward ho!"

END OF PART FIRST.

ABUSES

A B U S E S

OF THE

L   A   W.

PART II.

THE CITY.

" While thus *we* play the fool with the times,
" The spirits of the wise sit in the clouds
" And *mock* us."

Durnford * and East to distance we consign,
  Nor envy them their slow wealth-yielding mine;
They can but reap as lagging terms roll round,
While our reports diurnal mischiefs sound.
'Ere we ascend the hill †, abuse of law
Stand full confess'd in whom ‡ we next will draw;
A *now attorney,* t'other day a blade,
Of gen'ral depredations slight-hand trade;
A *broker, sharper, jobber,* ev'ry wile,
Long tried in vain, long lost to fortune's smile;

    * Modern reporters.   † Ludgate-Hill.

  † This worthy is also moved, and lives now almost in the heart
of the city.

                                       But

But one path left for infamy to tread,
This *Son of Israel*, flew *to law* for bread.
Scarce yet sev'n years are gone since huge distress,
Saw him uncoil'd, and shrunk to nothingness:
Somehow (a *Proteus*) to the court he stole,
And swell'd the number of the *monst'rous roll*;
And quite transform'd, e'en Moses faith thrown by,
Started with *Christian name*, and *new nam'd fam'ly.*
It seems success of some sort has ensu'd,
Or whence his equipage, and horse of blood;
Whence each expence, the man of fashion meets,
Supported *now*, by who once swept the streets.
Perhaps a *kindred luck* augur'd his mind,
" Become a lawyer, and (sense cast behind) :
Be only *rogue enough*; act, know not fear.
Shortly the sweets of practice will appear.
Hunt rotten merchants out, their secrets gain,
To whom they owe, by whom are ow'd obtain.
If they've some credit left! your genius here,
Rides in duplicity's meridian sphere.
Advise a while th' accommodating plan,
At private meetings to assist each man;
Paper machin'ry's well suggested use,
The momentary evils may amuse;
Bid creditor and debtor jointly draw,
They'll, jointly failing, yield resource to law.
Awhile supported thus, you'll gain your ends,
They dare not meet as foes, they must be friends.
To you they fly, *your friendship* draws the net,
And *ten commissions* swell the next Gazette :
But ere a docket's struck, *you*, knowing all,
The crazy scantlings that upheld their fall,

P   Cautious

Cautious try round, half words effect your end,
Whoe'er are assignees your zeal commend.
They must, they know, you can a tale unfold,
Will cause the banker's clerk to cry, ' hold, hold,'
When next for discount's aid their bills are brought;
Thus, by *your* scales, *they're* yet of weight, or nought;
To your good guidance *forc'd*, each cause they yield,
To *you* commit the harvest of the field.
Ten men's estates thus grasp'd at once, and none
Who dare inspect, or ask, ' Pray, what is done?'
You, assignees and *bankrupt*, being as one,
Plunder's the word; as good debts come to hand,
Sue for *bad debts** to make *your* balance stand.
Years pass on years, at last suppose the worst,
With which *a nursing docket-hunter's* curs'd;
A dividend demanded, fruitless call!
Your labour, vouchers, sulls, have swallow'd all!"

There are, of truth, who will with grief declare,
Such games are play'd from hence to Finsb'ry's square;
The city thro', each street, each alley yields
Mildews of law, that blight the merchants' fields.

To sweep such from the wholesome face of trade,
And leave the just poor man to just men's aid,
Without chicanry's intermediate theft,
To garble, sift, and wrench the remnant left,

---

* There is an incident of this sort, well attested, in an attorney of
the city, who, becoming bankrupt, had the address to prevail on
his assignees to let *him* recover the debts due to his estate; the consequence was, that he soon produced a balance in his own favour.

Were

Were no Augean task. Of assignees
What is the use ? To swell the lawyer's fees,
That each attendance one may aptly mark,
And keep for t'other matters in the dark.
Oft hand-in-hand trustee, and man of law,
Draw, turn by turn, till nought is left to draw;
And then *walk off †, which long before they'd done,
But that some bankrupt's store their state held on.

Abolish assignees‡, they're frauds on fraud,
Defin'd, exemplified, oft mean *maraud*.

'Tis easy ! and would gain the nation praise;
Wou'd give the *honest failer* halcyon days ;
He'd know the law of right, by which he fell,
Wou'd bear him through ; that his estate wou'd tell
Its full amount : Misfortune's full spring tide
None can avert, yet honour still may ride
Buoyant o'er all. And as, at storm's subside,
The well caulk'd vessel floats in unhurt pride;
So he again clear'd bright, and cleans'd his ways,
Might sail to fortune's isle thro' prosp'rous seas :
Now, without hope, the *Goodwin law* his bane,
Recoverless he sinks, and joins its ooz-sunk train.

* No *scrivener* (attorney) should have his certificate when bankrupt, till the clients he has defrauded are satisfied. At present a gross abuse on the bankrupt laws.

† Assignees should be obliged to find security against breach of trust—the sum according to the magnitude of the dealings of the bankrupt, which should be settled by the commissioners.

‡ This might be well done. The manner is too long for insertion here.

P 2

So

So must it be, till some strong balm is found,
To stay this noisome canker's eating wound :
The fine * impos'd will be of use, but still
There much remains t' eradicate of ill.

'Tis no uncommon thing to see a boy
Leap from the shoe-black's and the groom's employ
Behind the desk.   His merit? He's so keen,
Five years elapse, an imp of law is seen ;
What can the wretch unknown, but hunt his bread,
He may be honest, yet he must be fed :
No patrimonial income to assist,
'Till reputable bus'ness brings its grist.
He must ferment, disreputable strife,
By that maintain a sad nefarious life.
Soon he becomes obnoxious to the court,
And once so mark'd grows callous to retort ;
By dire necessity's strong hand borne down,
And in chicane's full scope a master grown,
Still plunges onward, just within the mark,
That keeps him on the roll a noted shark ;
Dreaded by all, his formidable name
Produces clients of co-equal fame.
Thus, so prepar'd to white-wash dirty work,
His practice gets in this one point—a quirk.

O'er some such single caitiff, mercy's veil,
Pity, perchance, shou'd draw, his faults conceal,

* The fine on admission 100[l].

Extenuate

Extenuate with sighs his fated shame,
And say—" Who such enrol * shou'd take some blame."

Another crew, more formidable still,
Graduates of theft, school'd doctors of each ill,
Tradesmen decay'd (who, pass'd the rubicon,
Certificate, by friendly debts and fraud led on,
Clear'd out by *act of parliament,* survive,
To all law's errors, ev'ry shift alive),
Augment the list—'twere vain to point to one,
And cry, " Behold, lo there's a corner stone!
This was a *mercer* †, that a *draper,* he
Sold *woollen cloth,* and *he* sold *hosiery,*
Till self sold up, he thought ' what next to be;'
Law asks no stock ‡, and I'm but forty-three.
That I have seen, and *that I know* will do;
Oaths, and a fee well plac'd will bear me thro'."—
Attornies now, each spreads his well lim'd snare,
And strides Guildhall as tho' he'd ne'er been there.

Amazing such *abuse* shou'd pass so long,
And not provoke or truth's or satire's tongue!
Oh for the force of language, to narrate
The arts by which such villains hold their state!

---

* That is, who article such paupers, and then turn them loose to
prey on the distressed.

† At least an hundred of the present London attornies have been
bankrupts in other trades, and took to the law, as the *ne plus ultra* to
obtain, or rather enforce a livelihood under.

‡ *No stock* to set up in trade with.

P 3   To

To make those laugh who are above their reach,
Teach those to shun who're falling in their breach ;
Who, deeming aid resultant from their smile,
Are sure at last to pay for us'ry's guile ;
But lacking *wit, more* faults undeck'd we'll bare,
And trust by good intent some fame to share.

Is it not strange that law's perplexities
Shou'd be acquir'd in full with so much ease,
That in *five years* a raw untutor'd youth,
Can pace a lab'rynth of nine cent'ry's growth;
Know ev'ry track, each mazy path unwind,
As tho' the turnpike road were left behind ?
Be *law* or *equity* before him laid,
No case too hard, he's master of his trade!
The meanest mechanist that turns a wheel,
The veriest grub who lives by sawing deal,
The barber, cobler, taylor (ninth of man),
All serve sev'n years, ere competent to plan :
Meanwhile, thro' custom's fault, in five short years*,
The scarcely bearded boy a sage appears ;
Join'd, by admission, to a horde of rooks,
With *chambers, clerk, bag, black coat, ink,* and *books,*
With jargon technical he can't translate,
Nods his advice, his client's adverse fate !
Thus oft *an heir,* an *orphan, widow's* barr'd.
Whose case, tho' just, such ignorance has marr'd.

---

* If the law apprenticeship extended to seven years, they would not only be qualified when admitted, but the great evil, *encrease of practitioners* would be prevented ; then, in seven years, the same number as are now admitted in five, would only be enrolled.

Shou'd

Shou'd we pursue our desultory range,
From Paul's void aisles, e'en to the crowded 'Change,
Small diff'rence shou'd we mark, except in name,
The acting motive nearly is the same—
Bus'ness! it matters not if good or bad,
So long as bleeding clients can be had.
Hence the disgrace that soils a noble shrine,
Which cleans'd of such, as pristine, were divine.

But soft, we'll backward tread, and westward shew,
Who spurning *law*, to lawless Baal bow.

END OF PART SECOND.

ABUSES

A B U S E S

OF THE

L A W.

PART III.

THE SUBURBS.

" *Quæsitor minos* urnam movet, ille silentum
" Consilium vocat, et *vitas*, et *crimins* discit. "

VIRGIL ÆN. B. 6. 432.

TRUTH, our fair herald, thus far have we dar'd,
    And dauntless plung'd amid the pois'nous herd,
Ev'n 'gainst the chiefs, the giants of deceit,
Have kept the field with justice' stedfast feet.
Thus *having* dar'd the leaders to uncasque,
And crucibled perversion's threefold * mask,
Barefac'd their hellish agents we'll display,
And drag to light, altho' they'd shun the day.

Up ——— lane, then bearing to the left,
A nuisance is beheld, a den of theft,

---

* Special pleading, bill jobbing, and impertinence of council.

Head

Head quarters * of oppression, which demands,
Speedy extinction at compassion's hands;
And pity, justice, mercy, honor say,
These cells † of rapine should be swept away.
To prove it, *knock* ; behold ! a brute uncouth ‡,
Like Cerb'rus station'd at Avernus' mouth,
The door unlocks ; enter, the keeper see
|| *Briareus banded*, each stretch'd forth with glee,
Simp'ring he smiles, and hopes for each a fee.
" An *hundred fees!* for what ? what favours, grace ?"
" Patience ! We'll reckon them by scores apace :
Twenty for taking first your word when freed;
Twenty for letters, bidding you take heed;
Twenty for bail-bonds I'll fill up to-day ;
Twenty for poundage I must some time pay ;
The *twenty last* are worth full forty quid §,
You know I wou'd not see you when I did."

These are mere nothingnesses—*these*, the gay,
The dissipated, thoughtless spendthrifts pay,
Who, while they have a *bank-note* ¶ left, may still
Ensure avoidance from this cave of ill;

That

* Spunging houses.

† In one of these receptacles of extortion, the *floor*, scarce 20 feet
square, is divided into four apartments ; each room is six shillings
per day. There are twelve or fourteen of these rooms, which are
almost always all full, about 25L per week !

‡ The porter.

|| This *bandy* gentleman is said to have had an hundred *palms*.

§ The bailiff's cant word for a guinea.

¶ There is one curious method of extortion practised by these
gentry in the case of execution against goods, viz. As soon as the
levy

That wanting, soon the specious brow's o'ercast,
They're snapp'd, they're dogg'd, the word—" *got home
    at last.*"

The cynic here may smile, he'as right, to see,
A bailiff's sideboard, and his library ;
To see his wine free flowing, and his dress,
Equal the gentleman's of former days :
To hear him boast of buying freehold lands,
With rapine squeez'd from mis'ry's clammy hands.

Various the ways by which the plunder's made,
In these barr'd dungeons, diabolic trade :
First, if *th' entrapp'd* requires to see a friend,
Whose presence may the present trouble end,
The house's messenger won't stir a foot,
'Till doubly paid a sum (without) wou'd do't.
If *mis'ry* thirsts, no slacking draft can come,
Unless it bear encreas'd taxation's doom.

Next, search of office two and sixpence takes,
In office hours*, when not, 'tis double stakes ;

levy is made, Mr. Bailiff waits on the defendant, and gives him to
understand, unless *civility money* is copiously given, the broker
must instantly move the effects.   This is practised so often, and so
successfully, when the defendant means to settle the debt, that keeping the execution in is enormously expensive ; for, every instant
Mr. Officer has occasion to squeeze, he attends with, " *I must move,
by God ! the carts are come,*" &c.

  * Surely the sheriff's office might be open from nine till nine, for
the purpose of search ; it would save great impositions to the unhappy.

                          And

And chance deliv'rance prove on holiday,
Then sev'n and sixpence must be paid, or stay.

Th' hotel's expences form the monst'rous mass,
Tho' here each pays as each wretch likes to class:
The first-floor's * grandeur is at nobles' price,
For menials there are rooms not quite so nice.
Each may be squeez'd as each can bear or pay,
From half-a-crown to one pound one per day.
Thus truly coop'd, and waiting destiny,
Each hapless spunge may stay till perfect dry:
When *guineas* fail, *halve;* do, then *crowns, half crowns,*
The threat of Newgate, till return day drowns!

Disgustful as this is to read, or hear,
Pity 'tis true, to wound a British ear!

Now, down the Strand, half down, then halt, near here,
Resides an o'ergrown money-lending seer,
Whose worthiness, if wealth cou'd purchase fame,
Might bid defiance to reproach or shame,
Might tell the trembl'ing thriftless ruin'd heir,
Whene'er he tax'd him with the *six years'* † snare,
" *I've wrong'd you not!* 'twas specie fairly lent,
At int'rest barely *seventeen per cent.*
If in six years your father *wou'd not* die,
And the *sum's doubled,* who's to blame? Not I!
The law allows it ‡; you have had your day,

---

* Why not abolish these arbitrary nuisances, and establish others under limited expences?

† Annuities at six years purchase.

‡ More's the pity! " *The law allows it,*" is Shylock's reply.—Vide *Merchant of Venice.*

And

And I've security enough to pay.
Talk not to me of ' *family once great,*'
Of pictur'd halls and woods—stuff out of date ;
Bring me my bond's amount, or else, with speed,
Your cov'nant's broke, beneath the forfeit deed,
Your oaks I'll fell, to Christie* with your land,
He'll find a nabob buyer out of hand."

Thus of an ancient heritage betray'd,
Ere in the earth his sire is scarcely laid ;
Full many a blooming youth, of promise great,
Laments in exile his purloin'd estate,
And sees *a wretch* (the Indians' curse) preside,
Lord of his soil, an early baron's pride,
Giv'n in the field as glory's just reward,
For patriot worth, or being his monarch's guard.

Six year's † annuities, destructive price !
Wou'd eat up Europe's treasure in a trice;
'Tis blam'd by all, yet 'mong such holder's see ‡
Ladies of rank, and lords of industry,
Stern senators, who this day blame *war's waste*,
To-morrow sign at home such judgment's ‖ rich repast.

* A great auctioneer, and worthy character.

† Often so bought on two and three lives.

‡ For this purpose search the annuity enrollment office.

‖ If, instead of enrollment only, the names of grantor and grantee, sums granted, and consideration, was obliged to be put in the Gazette within one month from the purchase, it would check the evil, and let any false statement of *names* or sums vitiate the contrast.

Enough:

Enough : the jackalls to this tribe we'll view,
And justly lay them down in sombrous hue,
Dub them in colours that can never fade,
Dark brown the ground, and black the pencil'd shade.
Enter this square, let's see if *Tom's* at home :
" A chariot's at the door!—some client's come."
" A client, nonsense! they're his own four wheels,
Got by superfluous skins* and useless seals."
What tho' his father scarcely had a shoe,
Tom's a conveyancer, has much to do,
Or makes it, 'tis the same! His progress mark,
Hall-sweeper, office-sweeper, then a clerk :
A man of bus'ness tried his grov'ling mind,
And found its bias strong to pelf inclin'd ;
Himself grown old, and almost past deceit,
Took him in firm, and renovated *cheat* ;
Thence date his rise, if rise that state you name,
Which hourly fits him for the pill'ry's shame ;
Memorial'd grants proclaim him *man of wealth*,
While robb'd grantees proclaim him *man of stealth*.
Such is *this wretch*, fatt'ning a dross of vice
On *half-pay's pittance*, bought at half its price.

* *This worthy* frequently covers six skins of parchment with various other legal appendants, such as bond, judgment, deed of covenant, &c. and to annuities of 20l. and 30l., the purchase about 120l., expences nearly 30l., so that in one year the annuity of 30l. is half refunded, viz.

Costs	—	—	—	L. 30	0 0
Arrears	—	—	—	30	0 0

And if paid off, generally a quarter of a year is given
for leave — — — 15 0 0

L. 75 0 0

This

This chariot to support, the hardy tar
Endures the dangers of uncertain war ;
And here, escap'd the onset's bloody fray,
The vet'ran of the field yields up his pay.

Comments are useless, words would fail of weight,
To crush this worm that gnaws th' unfortunate ;
The hand of pow'r must root this evil out,
From whose fell trunk new suckers * daily shoot.

Tho last, not least, of the destructive race,
The *advertising spawn* must take *their* place ;
Those who, without a guinea at command,
Proffer " *Immediate coin to heirs of land,*
To jointur'd widows, and *expectant peers,*
Or *merchants of repute* who've disappointment's fears."
Take up *the Herald, Times,* or *Morning Post,*
Each page invites to the pactolian coast ;
" *The bank for money,*" is a specious name,
And " *Craig's Court Office*" boasts peculiar fame ;
" *Great George-street*" some prefer, some few " *Sobo ;*"
Knock where they will, they knock for *certain woe.*

But what of that ? if money *must be bad,*
And, with imagin'd want, a youth's run mad,
Eager he'll dart, and, like the speckled trout,
With artifice's fly, deep barb, his snout
Once hook'd, the more he plunges, less his force,
He's lugg'd on shore to sign *his worth's divorce !*

* The office of this hero has just launched *two solicitors,* who, in the neighbourhood of Grosvenor-square, depredate in their master's manner.

If

If chance he pants, and will not yield his breath,
Swift *execution* stamps his *freedom's death*;
On King's Bench shamble lies, or Fleet's parade,
Sad victim *to the money lending trade!*
Urg'd on *by truth* our proem to support,
One specimen we'll give of such resort.

Suppose the applicant of rank supreme,
Here dabbling first in money's pebbled stream,
His name announc'd, next morning gives a card,
Directing, *to deception's* master-ward.

Hope, pleasure, passion, all are brought in play,
Flatt'ry's perspective is *so rich, so gay,*
Innum'rous liv'ry'd lacqueys at th' approach,
And at the door a gaudy court-like coach ;
To dinner ask'd, the wond'ring boy stares round,
Sees courses change, and hears the silver sound :
Libation follows of the best French wine,
The dames retire, the master springs *the mine.*
Money's the theme—a Pall Mall draft succeeds,
" *Return to-morrow, and we'll sign the deeds.*"
They part, protesting *one* with cash *to-day,*
T' other with schemes that ten-fold will repay.

The lad returns right punctual to the hour,
Signs what's prepar'd, and treads the crouded floor.
Night, dark-brow'd night, brings on the grand attack,
He *now must play,* or *losing players* back.
Wine ply'd, and dazzled with the blaze of light,
He *drinks, laughs, punts,* and empts his pockets quite :

Q 2   Again

Again return'd into its former course,
Again he borrows *that* was late *his purse*;
Again he loses, signs while signing's good,
And grants till payment is past likelihood.
Perchance *then* wakes, *then* finding he's deceiv'd;
What can he do? by what means be reliev'd?
Remonstrance! *foolish*! Shou'd a murmur break,
A villain's honour sets his life at stake.
Thus robb'd, he *must submit*, or else maintain
The hazard of a bullet thro' his brain.

By *ways and means*, like these, each parent's dread,
Here false magnificence uprears its head;
Here us'ry thron'd, presides in high career,
And daily gripes for each to-morrow's fare;
" To-morrow's and to-morrow's" luck the same,
News-paper, puff-trap, yields supply of *game*.

These dreadful facts are known thro' all the town,
From ermin'd peers, e'en to their porters down;
From merchants of the highest rank, to those
Who buy bad shillings, or who vend old cloaths.

'Tis *your's*, and cannot be in abler hands,
Ye present delegates of heav'n's commands,
To crush these dire abusers of the law,
Whom truth has dar'd for virtue's sake to draw;
To scrape the moss from off the noble pile,
And shew it in our great forefather's style,
Grand, simply elegant, earth's purest code,
By freemen form'd, inspir'd and taught by God.

'Bove

'Bove all the world's Britannia's inward boast,
Strong as the cliffs that guard her rocky coast.
Well ye've begun, and well shall be repaid,
Immortaliz'd, your names shall never fade;
Ages to come, feeling the good effect,
Must grateful pay such mem'ry's due respect,
Whose strength of genius stemm'd *for public good,*
Corruption's, rapine's, and *perversion's* flood.

   I could not avoid obferving an exact parallel between the Lilliputian and Britifh money
harpies. As for many other parts of the
poem, they were in a great degree incom-
prehenfible to me, from being ignorant of the
cuftoms of that country; but I hope, for the
honour of that nation, the pictures are mere
caracatures. It was now late; I packed up
the materials neceffary for my journey, and
retired to reft.

Q 3   CHAP.

CHAP. XVI.

Vifits the Fleet—Puts it in good State—Returns to Fluhnduhnna—which he finds in Confufion, owing to Sevrefe's having written a bad Book—Sevrefe tried and hanged—Vifit from Pekrub—Gives him his Sentiments—differs with him—Meffenger arrives from Blefefcu to treat of Peace—Goes to Elfac Sinwrod—Brings Log-Ereg to his Way of thinking—and returns with Commiffion to fee and hear the Ambaffadors.

MY *compagnons de voyage* were with me betimes, and after a very pleafant journey arrived at the port. We were joined by *Norob Ner-pefc*—he was manager of the navy. After the ufual falutations, *it* was agreed we fhould fpend the day together in merriment, and the following morning proceed to bufiness.

Never had I been fo entertained fince my arrival in Lilliput. Every hour encreafed my aftonifhment. And I began to think, that with his tactical affiftance, and my gold, we fhould obtain the defideratum of conqueft. In fhort, he

he was the only minister I had obſerved, fit
for the ſtation he was placed in.

I equipped myſelf á la marine; for, from
the whole ſtock of a ſlop-ſhop, I procured linen
ſufficient for a pair of trowſers. I ſat all the
taylors in the town to work, and time enough
for our embarkation, had them ready to put
on. VANITY once more (and for the laſt time
during this my firſt expedition to Lilliput)
obtruded her ready aſſiſtance—my *cork jacket*
was the immediate offspring of her concep-
tion; it *had* ſaved *me* from drowning, and I
reſolved *it ſhould ſave a nation.*

" A hit! a palpable hit!"

Great minds always endeavour to apply
compariſons from the *great* of antiquity to
ſuit their own ſituations, whether as excuſes
for vice, or parallels of virtue. I exclaimed
with a poet I have ſomewhere read,

" Some are *born great,*
" Some *atcbieve greatness,*
" And some have *greatness thrust upon them.*"

A naval eſcort and band of muſic ſummoned me to the beach; clad in my trowſers, my
cork jacket next my ſkin, my ſhirt only over
it,

it, and flippered, I attended. *Vilpi Tico* and
Ner-pefc were waiting in their state barges. I
walked into the ocean; a falute was fired from
the whole fleet, which lay about a Blefefcudian furlong from us; the boats pufhed off,
and, Neptune like, I majeftically ftalked between them. From topmaft to the hold of
every fhip I examined with attention; much
was wanting to enable them to keep the fea
with effect againft fo formidable an enemy.
I had ftore of ammunition, which I determined patriotically to give; I had alfo gold (fufficient for what could be purchafed) neceffary.
The means of keeping fome of the old hulks
(which were mere parade) above the water,
was the only difficulty that occurred; *that too*
was in my power: But as the enemy's intelligence was by fome means or other always
conveyed fo timely, as to prevent the great defigns formed againft them having effect, I did
not communicate, even to my colleagued minifters, the ready repair in my poffeffion; fo,
only looking very gravely, I fhook my head,
and defired the fleet might return to port.
The anchors were weighed, and the evening
                                        faw

faw us all fafe in harbour. I difpatched trufty meffengers to the capital for my ammunition and gold; and knowing they could not return until the following evening (under pretence of being fatigued), I retired as to repofe, but, in fact, to prepare for the prefervation of my truft.

The gabbling of geefe faved *Rome* ;

The magnanimous *relief* of *Gibraltar* was effected *by a fog*—and,

The *cork jacket* of *Gulliver* was to fave *Lilliput.*

I had in my pocket the hammer and pincers with which I fo happily cured Log-Ereg: *Sacred instruments!* more fit, as being more ufeful, to be depofited for the admiration of futurity, than *the milk, the blood,* or *black members of imaginary prophets.*

I pulled off my jacket, with a penknife ripped it open, took out its inteftines, and piece by piece put them in my pocket. At the expected time, the couriers (in twenty covered waggons) arrived with my money and ftores. With ecftacy, known only to breafts preferring public to private intereft, I faw it unladen.

I now

I now almoſt ſtood alone; for *few*, very *few*, from ten thouſand years before Adam to the preſent hour *(Vilpi Tico, Vile-Grin, Dunheldaſhio* excepted), ever experienced the blifs.

I thought every hour two, till daylight enabled me to go to my taſk. With one coat pocket full of pieces of cork, the other full of gunpowder, my waiſtcoat and breeches pockets crammed with gold, I ſallied to the dockyard : I was determined to do my work effeſtually. I forgot to mention, that being frequently troubled with the ear-ach, I always carried with me a ſyringe for injecting my head : This was of great uſe. I began with the firſt ſhip I came to ; I peeped into all the decks through the port holes, and deſired the commander to ſtate his wants minutely. He ſaid,

" They had ſix foot water in the hold, had no powder, very little biſcuit, and the pay of the men in arrear."

I took out my ſyringe, and at one exhauſtion cleared the water. I then took a piece of cork, with which I ſtuffed the hold. She roſe imme-

immediately to her proper failing depth, and threecheers thanked me for my fervice. I next gave out a fufficiency of ammunition and gold, for *this* my firft recovered patient, and fo proceeded till I had doctored the whole fleet. I was on an average about five minutes employed on each veffel, fo that by noon I faw my work complete; and being defirous that a decifive blow might compel the Blefefcudians to folicit peace, the commander in chief, at my requeft, immediately got under weigh; and by the time I joined my companions, the whole armament was in its ftation again, and only waiting a favourable breeze (fully cleanfed, repaired and ftored) to launch into the main, and hurl defiance at the enemy.

Though unnoticed I proceeded to my work, not fo my return to my comrades; the magiftrates and municipality of the town were drawn out to meet me, and the Governor (as he appeared by the confequential ftep he affumed) advancing, in the name of himfelf and of his brethren, repeated a fort of fpeech of thanks, hundreds of which I remembered to have read in the diurnal prints of Fluhnduhnna,

duhnna, addreſſed to various perſons who had
ridden through towns, or done the honour of
laughing at a good dinner.

Complaiſance, and properly ſubmitting to
the cuſtom of nations, rendered me (ſeeming-
ly) vaſtly pleaſed with *the diſtinguiſhed honour done me:* They, ſubjoining ſome little
common cant of loyalty, &c. went away, and
we departed on our journey back to Fluhnduhnna.

FLUHNDUHNNA.

Although abſent only ſo ſhort a ſpace, we
found the metropolis in confuſion. *Ner-peſc*
and myſelf were not otherways affected by the
diſſentient murmurings which reached our ears,
than as expreſſing our mutual wonder at the
occaſion ; but Vilpi Tico (whether or not conſcious of the cauſe, of which *I however* was
ignorant) trembled exceedingly ; indeed his
fears became ſo great for perſonal ſafety, that
he ſolicited my protection. Where could I
hide him beſt? My piſtols were in my girdle ;
I was convinced they could not be wreſted
from my gripe ; ſo, legs foremoſt, I popped
him

him into one of the barrels. The crowd at the door was far more immenſe than at my departure, but very different the reaſon of its aſſemblage.

" *No Vilpi Tico!*"

" *No Sevreſe!*"

" *No Spies!*"

Were the unpleaſant articulations uttered on our alighting. I was hemmed in, and (without hurting) hardly knew how to clear the populace. A thought ſtruck me—*to fire one* of my piſtols in the air. By miſtake (God pardon me for the unintended accident!) I took out *that* charged with

Vilpi Tico.

Ner-peſc ſaw my error (by his *little leg* hanging out of the mouth), and ſaved him, or I had undoubtedly fired *him* off amongſt them.

Perhaps, in the annals of hiſtory, *no hero* hitherto was ſo fortunately, yet miraculouſly, ſaved from deſtruction.

R   However

However dull the aggregate of thefe travels may prove, yet as the faving of *Vilpi Tico's* life is a fact, known, and *indubitably recorded*, ages to come fhall blefs the chance, and *Nerpefc* with *Gulliver junior*, be remembered, *in perpetuo*, for their care of

LILLIPUT'S Aristides.

A CORPSE

A CORPSE.

A DREADFUL SCENE.

" *One* so spiritless, so pale,
" Drew *Priam's curtain* at the dead of night,
(Tho' in thofe days they had not curtains.)
And wou'd have told him half his Troy was burn'd."

Just fo did *Pekrub,* meeting on my ftair-
cafe, addrefs me; adding, fublimely and pa-
thetically,

" He's gone! he's gone! the prince of fpies is gone!
The *Book*—the *swinish multitude*—*the rope*—
The curs'd determinors!—But, ah! he's hang'd!
Oh! death to pride—For, take him plot for plot,
We ne'er fhall look upon his like again."

I perceived, by this burst of fympathetic
affection, fome accident had happened to the
fo juftly-meriting-praife, cautious *Sevrefe.*
Condoling by action I followed him to my
antichamber, whither, for fafety, to preferve
it from the infults of an enraged mafs, they had
carried it, as I conjectured—'twas *Sevrefe's.*
Around it in melancholy mood were fitting,
Orobluff, Hactham, Dunheldafhio Nave-Npnaee,
and *Efor.*

The awful filence ufual at fuch meetings

was,

was, for its due time, obferved. When I
thought they had fobbed fufficiently, I ventured to afk, " What had occafioned the melancholy fcene before us ?" *Pekrub* ftarting up,
pulled from his bofom, with theatric air, a
little pamphlet, bound in black, and had power
only to utter,

> " *Thefe* bleffed leaves ! ! !
> And tho' they fully picture right *divine*,
> Yet, for this noble work, he's tried, he's hang'd ! ! !"

Down he fat, and gave himfelf up to forrow. *Efor* next rofe :

> " The dead we can't recall ; he did his beft :
> And living was well paid in places, penfions.
> He's gone, 'tis true, 'tis meet we feek his equal.
> Proceed to read his will, then bury him."

This called up *Nave Npnaee*, who produced

THE WILL.

" This is the laft will and teftament of me,
Efpio Sevrefe. As it is uncertain whether I
fhall be hanged in chains or not, I fay nothing
of my burial.

" Not having the luck to be an *acquitted fe-
lon*, my perfonals may be in the power of the
ftate ; but as I poffeffed virtues which confti-
tutional authority cannot diveft my legatees of

till

till they receive *my fate,* I difpofe as follows:

" Imprimis, To my dear friend *Orobluff,*
my conftancy in political friendfhip, which I
hope will bear him fafe through every change
and fhift.

" To my dear friend *Pekrub* all my manufcripts, among which will be found many valuable notes of fufpected perfons, collected at
great expence from confidential relatives and
fervants of thofe intended to be entrapped.
Thefe, difcretionally ufed, may produce him
another penfion.

" To my moft efteemed friend *Vilpi Tico,*
my fcarce collection of 500 curious keys, claf-
fically arranged, which open every door of the
royal apartments from the *ball door* to the
back-ftairs water-clofet. Thefe were the firft
valuable gift to me from his dear protector
alfo, *Quarnfi, Gam-cub-Nibbs,* and I hope he
will efteem them accordingly.

" To my beloved fellow-labourers in the
ftate vineyard in the arduous, painful, gainful,
hateful tafk of eavefdropping and evidence gathering, *Nave-Npnaee* and *Efor,* my perfeve-
rance, apathetic front, and refolution to en-

R 3   dure

dure (when their time comes) my fimilar fate.
The above being all in my power to beftow,
I hereby fubfcribe my name.

"　ESPIO SEVRESE.

Witness—" *Tru-Eb-Notri*,
"　*Crean-Dhuy.*"

This folemnity over, the legatees (perfectly
fatisfied with the liberal donations) feemed
comfortably relieved. The burial was unanimoufly voted to *Pekrub's* management, who
accepted the fame as a mark of high honour.
All except him departed, *we* were left together. After a few deep fighs, jumps, and
ftarts, he broke filence :

" We can't recall the dead ! but *we can kill !*
We will ! and drive to hell this hell-born crew ;
Thefe Blefescudian curs'd king-slaying dogs.
Shall we not, comrade ? say, hah ! shall we not!"

I thought I fhould have burft into laughter;
but biting my tongue, and recollecting for a
moment, I replied,

" Peace, peace will be better far.
What's Hecuba to him, or he to Hecuba ?
Peace ! let us meddle not—or further burn our fingers,
Get snubb'd i' th' nose—or haply singe our beards."

I thought

I thought I had juft hit off his own non-
fenfical verbofe ftyle, and he faw I meant it
ironically. A fallowifh flufh fuffus'd his
cheek—I was almoft forry I had played on his
dotage. However, I had gone too far to re-
tract ; for my fentiments, though farcaftically given, were given according to the dicta-
tion of my heart. He anfwered not, but
wrapped himfelf up in a long black cloak, and
(the very *fac-fimile* of an old monk leaving a
death-bed, where no alms were left to his monaftery) fullenly walked off.

As I wifhed to repofe, and not liking the
memento mori even of a grub in my dor-
mitory, I fpread my handkerchief on the
floor, and in it, tying up *Sevrefe* and his fune-
rœal decorations, carried them (to be out of
my way) to the leaft honoured apartment—
my ——

A ftatefman knows no reft—I had hardly
compofed myfelf, when *Vilpi Tico* knocked
me up.—Ceremony was at an end. " *Glulplew*," faid he, " You muft go with me directly to *Log-Ereg*; your armament has terrified the *Blefefcudians* ; they have fent commiffioners to treat.

" Thank

" Thank God (said I)! peace then shall wave her wings,
And parents cease to wail fresh murder'd sons."

" I fufpect!" faid he coldly : " But come,
hafte, we muft go to *Log-Ereg*."

LAST VISIT TO *ELSAC-SINWROD.*

Log-Ereg met us, embraced me, and exclaimed—

" Done well—done well—frighten'd 'em :
But don't like peace—can't make peace—
won't make peace!"

" Sire," I replied, "*you* have ufed me honourably—I thank you, and hope I have deferved.
I have beftowed *all* I had to give, and thereby
have brought a formidable enemy to fue to you
for peace.—Your fubjects are exhaufted!—If
you, *yourfelf* will, from your amazing private
treafures, furnifh for the exigencies, *humour
your caprice—Still* be the cry, ' *havoc, and let
flip the dogs of war.*' If not, accept my humble
refignation—I'll not uphold certain, haften-
ing, inevitable difgrace."

" Alack! alack!" faid he, "I am poor—
too generous—-no means—-curfed thing
though!—My old hobby horfe—love him as
well as *my white horfe.* But go back; go
        fee

fee what you can do—treat—make terms—
make peace—do any thing but *aſk me for
money.*

Vilpi Tico prepared an inſtrument to which
the ſign manual

" Log-Ereg"

was affixed, and away we again ſet off, like
Jove's precurſors, to act as we could—beſt—
to ſave the Monarch's honour ? No, his purſe !

CHAP.

CHAP. XVII.

Meets the Ambassadors—Result of the Conference—Another Visit from Pekrub—*who, on* Gulliver's *Determination to make Peace or retire, falls in Convulsions, and dies—Extraordinary Manner of his Translation to Eternity—The Catastrophe of his Death related, and recital of his Confessions strike Vilpi Tico, Vile-Grin, and Dunheldashio dumb, blind, and deaf ; from which melancholy Circumstances a Change in the Ministry becomes absolutely necessary.*

NO time was loft. We hasted to meet the commissioners. They were slightly known to me in *Blefescu*, but I was better known by them ; their names were *Gruph-eci* and *Terrenas*. They received me very cordially, but looked very coolly on my friend *Vilpi Tico*. He perceived it, and soon after our authority was notified, under pretence of other very urgent business, made an apology for indispensible absence, resigned the entire conduct of the matter to me, and with a haughty stride left us.

What

What paſſed at this momentous converſation, it would be highly indecorous and un-
ſtateſman-like for me to mention *here*. *Cabinet hiſtory* of the paſſing moment is always reſerved for the admiration and inſtruction of
the following generation; of courſe I ſhall not
deviate from eſtabliſhed rule, and ſuffer the
maſs to ſee, by means of my garrulity, the
weak ſides and mental imbecillities of ſuch
highly-rated names as *Vilpi Tico's*, *Vile-Grin's*,
and *Dunheldaſhio's*.

Our converſation was of conſiderable
length. We agreed that peace was abſolutely neceſſary for *both powers*. My co-inci-
dence pleaſed them; and they ſaid, *their ſtate*
would not heſitate for trifles, their hatred being not againſt the *Lilliputian nation*, but
merely againſt *the few* who had perſevered in
an unneceſſary war, and *who*, they were inſtructed to ſay, muſt be proſcribed from any
congreſs held for pacification : Promiſing to
urge *this* (rather than give up ſo deſirable a
point), I returned home.

Pekrub, in deep mourning, his anger of the
over-night forgotten, was waiting my arrival.
He was ſitting in ſorrowful attitude; before
him

him lay Sevrefe's *black-book* and a manufcript (the contents of which will be feen fhortly); in his right hand a dagger. I thought he was ftudying the part of Cato for theatric reprefentation, and that the book before him was the fubftitute for Plato's Phœdo ; but he was only ftudying a parody. Attentively liftening, I heard him utter,

" If 't must be so !
Thus am I doubly arm'd—*My life* and *death*—
My *bane* and *antidote* are both before me.
This in a moment brings me to *one end*,
By which I certainly shall *'scape the rope*,
While *this* informs me I shall *get a place*
As soon as I behold *another king*,
Or else *that other king can* have no vanity."

My ftep interrupted his foliloquy, and he addreffed me thus :

" Well!—is it well?—What say these caitiff dogs!
Will they yet crouch ?—lick Lilliputian dust?
Ere all compell'd to bite the soil of hell."

" Sublime orator," I replied ; " be compos'd, all fhall be well, and I'll obtain fuch peace—"

" No! no!" said he, " war ! war! no peace! no peace!
Be aristocracy the only joy:
Let commerce perish—Let the world expire;
Or, as at first, let *Adam* whip his brutes."

I was

I was nettled, and faid,

" *Adam*, I think, has flogg'd his brutes enough ;
Their flesh is gone, they are mere skin and bone,
Nor longer shou'd endure the curse of war.
Peace, or my resignation shall take place."

On my faying this he uplifted the dagger,
and, in a ftate of abfolute phrenzy and demo-
niac-like attitude, vociferated,

" And is it come to this ! oh ! then farewel
The paid-for pen ! Farewel the phrafe verbofe !
The spirit-stirring hope of great reward,
Which led me on to varnish monft'rous vice,
The royal rags, and all the tinsel glare,
However base which once *Blefescu* bore !
Printers, and printers' devils too, farewel !
And ye, ye pretty pensions which so long
Have bless'd my fingers for the venal song,
Farewel ! *Old Pekrub's* occupation's gone,
And *the sublime* and *beautiful's no more* !"

He was in the act of ftriking the dagger into his breaft, when a convulfion feizing him,
he fell proftrate on the floor; the manufcript dropped from his hand; I took it up,
and fafely lodged it in my pocket. I thought
at firft it was only a fit, the confequence of
paffion, fuch as I had feen him in before, and
that he foon would recover ; however, he was

S   called

called to eulogize *the court above* or *below*, for
he was ſtone dead. I muſt confeſs I was
ſomewhat ſhocked; though for ſome time I had
conſidered his head a little wrong, and thought
him going. While contemplating his body, a
vapor aroſe from it, and diffuſed a ſcent like the
acrimonious acid ſmell which proceeds from a
neſt of enraged emmets. To get rid of it, I
threw a few grains of gunpowder on the corpſe;
it immediately took fire, and the terreſtrial
part of *Pekrub* evaporated *inſtanter in fumo*,
brains and all, leaving only his empty ſkull:
I was glad it was conſumed, it being ſufficient
to ſhew his ſtrange tranſlation to eternity.
His head being differently formed to that of
others, by producing what had been his *knowledge box*, my word could not be doubted.

Whether his memory may be worth regiſ-
tering, the impartial annals of the next century will ſhew.

As ſoon as I had got the better of my ſurprize, I diſpatched meſſengers to inform *Vilpi
Tico, Vile-Grin,* and *Dunheldaſhio,* of the melancholy event.

" I thought ſome evil planet reign'd,
And ſhed its baneful influence on mankind."

by

By the appearance of my returned fervants, who all trembled as if fhaken with the ague, after fome paufe, one of them, on my repeating the queftion, " *What anfwer ?*" faid, " *None*! *ftruck dumb*!"—" *All dumb?*" faid I, " *fool*!" " *Vilpi Tico, Vile-Grin*, and *Dunbeldafhio dumb*!" " *Slanderous fcoundrel*! impoffible! I'll go and fee."

I found them all fitting on the fame fopha whereon they were placed when the poifoning plot was developed. I began condoling for the lofs of *Pekrub*, but might as well have held my peace. Their auricular faculties were alfo gone. They underftood my actions, and all wept bitterly. There is nothing moves one like *great men* in diftrefs! Their eyes were the only remaining fenfe of mental communication. I was fearful left that fhould go too, fo with all expedition placed pen, ink, and paper before them. *Vilpi Tico*, by their motions, was deputed fcribe. He wrote, and I anfwered as follows:

Vilpi Tico. " Did *Pekrub* make any confeffions before his death ?"

Anfwer. " I did not hear him, but have

poffeffion

poffeffion of this manufcript which fell from his hand in the agonies of death."

I laid it before them ; it contained as follows :

" *Mes Confeſſions a la Rouſſeau.*

" *Rouſſeau* wrote *his confeſſions* from *the the ſpirit,* the *cynical motive,* the *deviliſh deſire,* and *vicious determination* ariſing from *that deſire,* of dragging others forward as objects of difguſt, in the ſame *humanity-degrading, ill-featured, ill-deſigned, baſely-managed, hiſtorical canvaſs with himſelf.* I write mine from no ſuch motive. No! but, *primo loco* (in the firſt place), ' I tranſlate for the benefit of the country gentlemen to clear my memory. *From that hunt of obloquy* which (notwithſtanding my *patriotic virtue, inflexibility, integrity, unſhaken* and *unchangeable)* has purſued me with a full cry through life.'

" *Secundo* (ſecondly), *to inſtruct, to ſhew, to point out, to teach* (I am fearful for want of another ſimile or epithet ſuited to the phraſe, the beauty and ſublimity of this paſſage will fail of my uſual graceful circuity ; however I am at confeſſion) others who may follow *my track,*

track, my walk, my path, my course, or road
through mortality ; how *to enjoy, poffefs,* and
become mafters in old age of *otium,* or eafe,
opes, or wealth."

"The ifland of *Gab-and-face* claims the
honour of my birth ; the Jefuit college of
Remo in *Blefefcu,* my education : There I *un-
tiredly, unremittingly, unceafingly* ftudied many
years, and *wafted, burned, watched*-out many
a midnight lamp, *not* in unprofitable philofo-
phic toil—*not* in the refearches of who were
the moft virtuous of antiquity—*not* how a man
could live and die moft admiredly poor ; *but*
how he might *beft, fooneft,* and *eafieft* arrive
at worldly profit. From obfervation, and
bleffed alfo with a cold, yet commanding, apathetic ftoical vifage and form, I turned to the
pages of modern hiftory, and after, various
revolvings, fixed *on Lilliput* as the ftage whereon to act my part.

"Fraught with polemic fubtlety, and Jefu-
itic complacent confcience and confidence, I
bade adieu to the fathers of *Remo,* and bent
my courfe to the expected *El-Dorado.*

"A few political pamphlets brought me
into notice. I then wrote a treatife on the

S 3   beauties

beauties of Lilliputian ortho and logography.
It was rather impudent in me, being a foreigner; but the fwarm of bookworms infeft-
ing that little infulated atom of land, bite at
any rag, tatter, or fcrap of novelty in literature; the book is now almoft obfolete, but it
anfwered my purpofe.

" I was next noticed by a *ftate party,* formidable to the then adminiftration, and, *from
vanity* and *for bread,* became enrolled in the
Lilliputian fenate as the *firebrand* of freedom.

" *How I rav'd, how I toil'd, how I moil'd,
how I fweated, how I threatened,* the annals of
the times will fhew.

Lilliput, in this my ranting period, became
involved in a war with the inhabitants of fome
patches of land fhe had fettled and eftablifhed.
My party, who were anxious for power, main-
tained the caufe of the revolters, and thus *I*
ftood prominent in the fcene.

Nor *only* in the fenate, I engaged with a
bookfeller to write part of a periodical mifcel-
lany, to which I was the hiftoric Sybil, and
therein dreffed up the heroes of my party *a
la merveil.* From this I got a decent falary,
the beft I could *then* get (my party being *outs);*
                                        I con-

I continued it to the clofe of the war, and the bookfeller, in juftice to me, will confefs it paid him as well as he paid me.

" A fplendid fcene now opened to my view. This war had brought an immenfe debt on Lilliput. The people murmured at the taxes ; and *I*, ever bufy-minded, and anxioufly waiting for the breeze which fhould waft me into power, propofed various phantoms of reform. I attacked the very bread and butter of *Log-Ereg*; faid he ate and drank too much, flept too foft, gave his fervants too much wages, and advifed retrenchments in every article, with curtailment of his income. This obtained me the huzzas of the mob.—But NO PENSION.—Here *I was not blind*; a *penfion* ftill might come. There was a little fund called the FOUR COPARS, from which the monarch had licence to grant indulgencies to his *favourites*. THAT, hoping fome day I might be of the *elect*, *I* prudently, fagacioufly, prophetically left untouched ; yet, it anfwered not—another, and another ftorm came on, ftill—elementally, foaringly inclined, and filled with afpiring gas, fully charged, bloated, fkinful, I rofe in the fenate——' The caufe,'

it

it was 'the caufe my foul'—*auri facra fames*
—defire of

"A PENSION.

" I *now* call God and man to *witnefs*, to
atteft, to *prove* I have been hitherto uniform.
An epifodical (unexpected) opportunity of obtaining the defired *end, metus, goal*, prefented
and gave me hope to exclaim,

" *Mea domo rénidet lacunar.*"
Or,
" I now have filver, brafs, and gold,
" Effect of *changes* manifold.*"

" A *good, faithful, praife-deferving, brave,
politically-fkilled Governor* returned from the
labour of many years' fervice in a diftant
clime, where the only fruit he gathered and
had ftored, was the honour of his country, by
him fully and reverentially preferved. Him
I fingled out as the butt my random arrow
fhould fly at to obtain the high-flavoured
game, *penfion*. Alas! I was deceived. He
heard my oratorical fulmen denouncing him
' the moft abandoned of mankind; charging
him with the crimes of *rapacity, peculation,
cruelty, unneceffary wanton bloodfhed, war*, and
murder.' For all which alledgments I put
him

him to his trial as the *nequiſſimus bipedum.*
Uſeleſsly, alas to me! did I keep him years
on years in the agonizing ſtate of innocence
with an impeached character: For *be* patiently, meekly, prudently, wiſely, bore it out;
and, with the curſed unbluſhing front of integrity, and the conviction of falſe accuſation
againſt him, waited (without ſuing to *me* for
favour) the verdict of

" *Not Guilty.*

" *My bark* was now a little ſhattered by the
many rocks of diſappointment it had daſhed
againſt, and I thought of laying her up in
ſome creek of promiſe for a repair, before I
would venture out again ; but it was ordered
otherways. A prize of the firſt expectation
ſuddenly appeared right before me. I thought
no more of repair, but, with full bent ſails,
gave inſtant chace. She appeared richly
laden, and I made no doubt to find

" A PENSION CHEST on board.

" To drop metaphor, LOG-EREG was ſeized with a malady, the moſt pitiable inflicted
on the human frame—(I am at confeſſion).
If *Log-Ereg* had faults, he had over-balancing
virtues ; the connubial and parental, and
mercy

mercy and compaſſion were undoubtedly his juſt attributes, againſt all which there was only to oppoſe the error of a money-loving appetite ; but I threw down the gauntlet of *invective*. I compared him to the Aſſyrian King puniſhed for his miſdeeds : That heaven had diveſted him of reaſon for his manifold crimes—reduced him to a level with the brutes. I adviſed to hurl him from his throne, and place another in his ſtead. *Juſt* as my ſyſtem began to be approved—*juſt* as my deſired port, *preferment*, was in view, *he*, miraculouſly, ſuddenly recovered; his people followed his footſteps with bleſſings, and I was at ſea again without

"*A Penſion.*

" *Now*, thanks to *Alecto*, *Tiſiphone*, and *Megæra*! Praiſe be to the genius of diſcord, whoſe terror-ſtriking trump ſhrilly and fear-impreſſingly blew the blaſt—

"*Revolution in Blefeſcu!*

" This *revolution*, in a few ſhort months, irremediably, irretrievably overthrew the moſt tyrannous ariſtocracy, though the labour of eleven centuries.

" *Peaſants trod upon the necks of nobles.*

" (I'm

" (I'm at confeſſion) There *it was* right, *it was* to be expected—*it was* even-handed juſtice ; for they had borne them down from generation to generation, even to the groundſil edge. I acknowledge this in ſecret; but I wanted

" *A Penſion.*

" Here begins my fortunate epoch. Hence view me in a new light—no longer a grub—I here caſt my ſlough, and become a fair ſilky moth, fluttering my wings in the genial beams of royalty, and give to the world my

" *Beauties of Ariſtocracy.*

" All my former aſperities againſt *Log-Ereg* were forgotten, and but juſtly ; for I pourtrayed every *earthly majeſty* as *viceroys of the Almighty*, who, to touch with the rod of correction, was ſacrilege, and their every conſort as *earth-treading ſtars, ſiſters of heaven*, immaculate and faultleſs.

" *It did* ; the paſt was ſunk in oblivion, and I got

" A PENSION."

The miſchiefs flowing from my fallacious varniſhing pamphlet were not thought of. I
bolſtered

bolſtered up the cauſe, and made it appear
palatable to the unthinking.

It was fatally anſwered; and had *I* not written, my ſuperior genius could not have replied. But I got my penſion.

I retired ſatisfied, thinking all over, and
that the fortunate Jeſuitic education had at
length given me poſſeſſion of quiet and affluence for my dotage.—I was miſtaken.

Once more I was called to the field of political diſpute.—My tergiverſations, my wan-
derings, my eccentricities were attacked, my
whole life was canvaſſed by two ſcarcely-
bearded boys; yet in ſo maſterly a manner
did they diſſect my conduct, that it appeared to
every diſpaſſionate auditor the life of

A State Harlequin.

It was abſolutely neceſſary to riſe in vindi-
cation, to ſay, or write ſomething, or loſe my
penſion, my darling penſion! It was too
late in the day! *" 1 was now a poor lone man,
and had none to meet my enemies in the
gate."* What could I do? I felt my inſuffi-
ciency, yet I could not, from apparent gratitude, let the ſhuttlecock, I had ſo long kept

up,

up, fall to the ground without one laſt ex-
hauſting effort. I publiſhed a ſtrain of ful-
ſome adulation on my donor, and of ribaldric,
metaphoric, abuſive invective, the refuſe of
my peck of verboſe wheat at the heads of
thoſe I had, when unpenſioned, ſworn almoſt
adoration unto, conſortation, and laſting amity
with.

I ſuppoſe ſome pens will anſwer me. If unpenſioned, let them. While my paid-for
nonſenſe paſſes current, I ſhall defy their attacks ; *and lay, like one of thoſe old oaks,
which the late hurricane has ſcattered round
me*," log-like, unimpreſſibly ſecure. After all,
what have I gained ? After forty years ſtruggle, what am I ?

A penſioned heterogeneous character, and
ſuch as I ſhould deſpiſe, if I was not myſelf
the man. But it is well I am become alone
man, and have no ſon to curſe my memory :
For he could never ſurmount or do away,
though poſſeſſed of all the points in which perſonal merit can be viewed, in *ſcience*, in erudition, in genius, in taſte, in honour, in generoſity, in humanity—(what ſad ſtuff !)—in
every liberal ſentiment, and every liberal ac-
T   compliſhment,

complifhment, thofe undeferved obloquies
which, though retorting on myfelf, I have
fo unneceffarily, copioufly, unfathomably,
groundlefsly lavifhed from my acrimonious
pen on my two young, noble, gallant, free-
dom-defending, affailant detectors; yet I hope
I fhall deferve, and ftill receive

MY PENSION;

for I am refolved ftill on to write, in defiance
of whips, ftraw, chains, and a dark room.

Here the manufcript ended. There were
beginnings of feveral fentences, or notes, but,
from their unconnectednefs, could not be underftood. In all probability had he lived, he
would have continued them.

As foon as they had finifhed reading, they
carefully folded it up; then each, with ftream-
ing eyes, kiffed it.

Vilpi Tico next wrote, " *We muft refign.*"

I anfwered, " *So it is rumoured.*"

Vilpi Tico. " We fuppofe *Nadirefh* and
Calxbosfer will come in with you, and *peace*
be eftablifhed."

I replied,

I replied, " *There* are almoſt *innumerables* who *ſay, wiſh,* and *hope* ſo."

He was proceeding to write another queſtion, when the pen fell from his hand. Stedfaſtly looking at him, I perceived what I had feared was come to paſs ; blindneſs had alſo ſeized him and his companions. I could ſcarcely credit my own eyes, and began to doubt whether all theſe accidents really had happened, or if my own head was ſteady, and my mind ſound. However freſh ſymptoms brought me from my reverie, and proved there was reality in the cataſtrophes ; for they now began to kick and ſtruggle ſhockingly, by which I am afraid their memories remained perfeƈt, and that they were ſtung and tortured by ſome dreadful recolleƈtions. As I could do them no good, I gave them a laſt long look, committed them to the care of their domeſtics, and returned home.

T 2 CHAP.

CHAP. XVIII.

Meſſage by Wholtru *and* Eniſker *from* Log-Ereg *to* Gulliver—*Attends*—Nadireſh *and* Calxhoſfer *taken into favour, and appointed Secretaries of Legation*—*Death of* Orobluff—*More of* Gulliver's *private Hiſtory*—*Prepares for his Embaſſy*—*Affection of a Servant*—*Specimen of* Nadireſh's *Poetical Talents*—*Set off on their Journey to* Bleſeſcu—*Applauded by the People, and named* Prince *of Peace.*

I WAS now *the atlas* that ſupported *Lilliput*, my colleagues being incapacited as before-mentioned. I was conſidering how to proceed, whether to leave the metropolis, and go in perſon to *Log-Ereg* with the doleful tidings, or ſend an official account, when the arrival of my old worthy friend *Wholtru*, accompanied by *Eniſker*, put an end to my deliberations. *Wholtru*, in his uſual, abrupt, mannerleſs, honeſt manner, broke out at me thus:

" By G— what I expected is come to paſs !
You

You muſt come with us immediately, *Log-Ereg* is come poſt to the capital, and there is the devil to pay. We have been cloſeted theſe two hours, and have, at laſt, after much ſolicitation, agreed to come in, in junction with you, for the defirable and defired accompliſhment of peace—ſo! *Pekrub's corpſe* ſtunk d——ly, ha! But come, *d—n that!* make haſte; let's go—we muſt not loiter—*it's to do good.*"

Away we hurried to the *royal refidence—* There were aſſembled an entirely new caſt of feature—*Nadireſh* and *Calxbosfer* were bowing to, and ſimpering at, each other, from the ſeats formerly filled with *Vilpi Tico* and *Vile-Grin.* *Wolthru* popped himſelf into *that* of *Orobluff*; and *Eniſker* with a grace equalized to the confequence of the fituation, placed himſelf in *Y-ko-nens* (the *Scipio* before whom my caufe was heard). To fay truth, I was glad to fee *Eniſker* exalted to the rank his talents deferved, yet I was forry to fee *Y-ko-nen* difplaced, as I believe he was a very honeſt man. But it certainly is right, when feveral fervants in one houſhold are become either indolent, roguiſh, or faucy, to get rid of the

T 3   whole

whole gang at once, fuppofing it might be judged right to do the fame in fuperior fyftems, I fubmitted to fee *Enifker* in his new place, without thinking again of *T-ko-nen.*

The bufinefs we were fummoned on may be eafily conceited, *viz.*

" To adopt the eafieft, moft advantageous, and expeditious means of ending the war."

It was ordered, " That *1* fhould repair to the Blefefcudian Commiffioners, and name fome neutral place for the affemblage of a congrefs to treat. That an armiftice fhould take place, and that *Calxhosfer,* *Nadirefh,* and *I* would meet them, with an additional Commiffioner on their part, at fuch time and place as we fhould refolve on."

Thefe great matters fettled, the council was breaking up, when news was brought that *Orobluff* had been choaked, his fervants having, by miftake, ferved him with a bony fifh, called the *flat* or *refignation*-flounder, inftead of the *plaice-fifh*, of which he was remarkably fond. A circumftance occurred here, which I thought a little cruel : *Log-Ereg* laughed at the relation of his death, and wittily, though furely rather unkindly, faid—

" Thought

"Thought fo—always thought fo!—thought he'd come fhort home—very greedy—always greedy—*always mouthfull of place*—got a bellyfull now—Hah, *Wholtru!*

Wholtru looked gruffly, but foon recovered himfelf. *The principal* withdrew, and after the ufual congratulations between thofe who had been promoted, our affembly broke up.

I repaired inftantly to the Commiffioners, told them the refult, with which, well pleafed, after determining our meeting, we parted, and they gave orders for return.

Every thing now reftored to tranquillity, I intended to indulge myfelf with one day's repofe, and commanded that I fhould be generally denied to all vifitors : And it was well I did, for it was no fooner rumoured that I was departing on the following day diplomatiquement, than there was one continual knocking at my door—perfons of all ranks, ages, and conditions, who, when they found I was not to be feen, retired, and foon again came with their folicitations in writing, every one flattering himfelf fome place in my fuite remained vacant for "*integrity, affiduity,* and *abilities.*"

It was in vain to anfwer them, fo ordered my
fecretary

fecretary to throw the letters, as they were delivered, into a wafte room to abide my return.

After refreshing myself, I recollected it was neceffary to prepare for my departure; fo calling together all my houfhold, I directly put it in hand; the alertnefs of my fervants foon enabled me to finish packing. One little trait of gratitude I am bound to mention: The poor mortal, who I had refcued from *Sevrefe's inquifitorial trial* for the *magnetic* and *tobacco-quid plot*, was refolved (notwithftanding I had protefted againft taking any of the fubjects of the majefty of Lilliput out of his dominions, left they fhould return infected with the *mania Blefefcudiana*) to attend me, and refolutely hid himfelf in *the tobacco-box.* I difcovered him very accidentally, not by his weight, but by taking him out with a bit which I was about to put in my mouth. To fhew I was not angry, I gave him an ingot above his wages, and promifed, if I returned, to take him again into my fervice.

I once more had recourfe to my packet tied with the narrow black ribbon, and the fcrap next prefented

ADELINE'S

ADELINE'S ANSWER

to

LAURENCE.

I.

Has *the grave* open'd to my sight?
Has *ocean* cast her dead?
Or is't the vap'rish gloom of night
Affects my feeble head?
" * Twelve summer months, and winter's cold,"
That time, with *fact* accords!
But *where's thy Julia?* Ah! that's told
Without grief-weak'ning words!
Come! Laurence, come! acknowledgement receive,
And teach me, grace, like thee resign'd to grieve.

II.

'Tis true from morn till night I weep,
And sigh those hours design'd for sleep.
Snow-cold my breast, nerves so unstrung,
Accents scarce murmurs from my tongue;
Care's lines the dimples' place supply,
And orbit-sunk my hollow eye.
So merciless this fiend despair,
His vengeance ev'n has rim'd my hair;
Robb'd me of ev'ry charm and winning grace,
And stamp'd *infirm old age* on woman's *scarce-form'd* face.

---

* Vide page 115, Laurence to Adeline.

Thou

III.

Thou, arm'd with manly reason, hast defi'd
 The tyrant's sapping pow'r,
And mail'd with *sense*, *philosophy* thy guide,
  Could'st stem th' assailing hour:
But what cou'd *I?* my *only comfort* gone!
  Who ne'er the strength'ning aid of science knew,
  Bow'd down by ev'ry blast affliction blew,
Save *hither wend*, wish death, and breathe my *widow'd*
  moan.

IV.

Haste then, my *saint-like brother*, haste!
  Dear comfort of my soul!
Thou only welcome earthly guest,
  With *Adeline* condole.

V.

My cell shall meet thy holy gaze,
  Bedeck'd with nicest care;
An added lamp shall cast its blaze
  Before the fount * of pray'r.

VI.

There shalt thou find me on my knee,
  Arm cross'd o'er either breast,
Grateful for minutes as they flee,
  As each leads on to rest.

VII.

And tho' of ev'ry good bereft,
  When thy dear form I see;
If yet *one* lambent smile is left,
  That one shall beam on thee.

          * The Crucifix.

                                            Our

VIII.

Our parent's *mem'ries then* we'll bless,
   Their *spirits* next invoke,
To view our mutual wretchedness,
   To ease our heavy yoke.

IX.

Trace from our infant happy state,
   To reason's glorious rise;
So on, till rigid, wayward fate
   Stamp'd us, *love's sacrifice.*

X.

When all of Nature was o'erthrown
   From pride 'gainst virtue's worth,
When clos'd *those doors* our birthright's won,
   And all *our wealth?*—wide earth.

XI.

Thou thought'dst because that *orphan mild*
   Engross'd my daily care,
That he was mine, loose folly's child,
   Sad nursling of despair.

XII.

I found him here, his mother dead ;
   I know no more, not ask,
Save *this*, he wept, I gave him bread,
   Fair charity's sweet task.

XIII.

Haste then, my saint-like brother, haste !
   Dear comfort of my soul!
Thou only welcome earthly guest,
   With *Adeline's* condole.

I'll

XIV.

I'll weep thy *Julia lost*, while you,
　　With sympathy divine,
Shall shed *connubial sorrows*, due
　　O'er my lost *Henry's* shrine.

I might *now* be literally confidered *a citizen of the world*, for neither *Adeline* had been my mother, or *Laurence* my father—ftill I might be the *fon of Gulliver*. But my exalted ftation required I fhould find a pedigree of *fome fort* wherewith to ornament the leaves of heraldry, and under my embaffy, one hope of tracing it exifted. *I* was undoubtedly dropped on the coaft of *Ydnamron*, in *Blefefcu*, from whence many others, now titled in Lilliput, are proud to boaft their genealogy, and think it the fummit of fuperiority to be deduced from a baftard *Ramron*. I had ftrong ground for my hope being realized, and, wrapped in that pleafant reverie, funk to flumber.

Early in the morning the fhouts of affembled thoufands awoke me, and I could plainly diftinguifh

" *Nadirefh* and *peace!*
' *Calxhofe r* and *peace!*
　　　　　　　" *Quarmfi*

" *Quarmſi, Glulplew,* and *peace.*

" Succeſs to the friends of humanity, and their embaſſy.

" No more war!—No more war!

" God ſave *Log-Ereg!*

" God bleſs the peace-givers!"

The air rang with the above, and ſimilar expreſſions. My equipage, drawn forth exactly as on my entreé *into* the metropolis, was at my door—and following in high ſtile,

My Secretaries of the Legation.

They alighted, diſmiſſed their carriages, and flew to embrace me. While we were partaking of a collation I had provided for them, *Nadireſh* put a manuſcript in my hand with this preface :

" You remember, *Quarmſi,* the prieſt who aſked you to dine on the faſt day? He has been dabbling ſince in politics, and as I hate churchmen to ſtep out of the bounds of moral propriety, I have compoſed an addreſs to him ; juſt run your eye over it, and I'll ſend it to the preſs before we ſet off."

I did as he deſired me, and at *Calxhosfer's* requeſt, read it aloud. It was as follows :

U   A POETIC

A POETIC EPISTLE

TO THE

PRATING PRELATE OF LILLIPUT,

FROM

HIS ALMA MATER HYPOCRITA.

WITH NOTES.

" Quo, quo scelesti ruitis?
" *Hic est* acerba fata agunt."
HOR.

I.

WHAT have I done, my darling boy,
    That *thus* your mother you affright?
By holy Peter's * keys, I vow
I have not felt such qualms, such fears,
These eighteen † hundred rolling years
    As press my bosom *now*—
No! not when *Julian* ‡ rent my veil.
Ah me! I'm sick from head ‖ to tail.
    Help! or I sink to endless night,
And with *me* dies Fanaticism's joy!

  * St. Peter supposed to keep the keys of heaven:

  † From the year A. D. 1, to 1796.

  ‡ The Emperor Julian, after being a Christian bigot, apostatized, and became the scourge of the church.
  ‖ From the Pope to the sexton.

Then,

II.

Then, then farewel, belov'd tythe goose and pig,
Black gown, and learned-seeming bushy wig ;
    Farewel to coach and couch ;
Farewel to gout, repletion's evil:
But 'stead thereof the starv'd blue devil *
    Beneath your stool will crouch.

III.

Then too, your wife, sweet lady fair,
Nor dress nor cards will make her care,
    Or flaunt the town about ;
From street to street, from square to square,
Boasting the pannel's *mitred glare,*
    At midnight's noisy route.

IV.

If *I* shou'd die, you'd not be able
To keep a hunter in your stable,
    Or game-keeper right brave,
To guard *the hares* for *holy men,*
To mew *the birds* in *priesthood's* den,
    Or shoot † the poaching knave.

V.

You'd not be able *then,* if cash
Runs low, and there's end of *dash,*
    From dissipation's cause,
To visit *Rome,* and leave your *See*
To straining stewards, *absentee*
    From duns and bailiffs' claws.

* Hyp, spleen, or fever of dissappointment.
† There was an accident of this sort once happened in Lilliput, the game-keeper of a priest shooting a poacher. GULLIVER, Jun.

Ere

VI.

Ere then *I go,* as go I quickly must,
And all our trump'ry shall be laid in dust,
   Let us in serious mood survey
     The motley world around,
     From Italy and Spain profound,
   To where the madmen * of the day,
   Spurn at our holy toil, and mystic pay,
And let us try, if yet within our pow'r,
A little to prolong the lazy, stall-fed hour.

VII.

First look for what Blefescu's sons uprose,
And tore to rags the sacerdotal clothes:
Was it that pious meekness they abhorr'd,
Or useless gold in monasteries stor'd ?
Was it fair charity, good will to all,
Or lust and stiff-neck'd pride provok'd your brethren's
    fall ?

VIII.

I fear some haughty, naughty prelate said,
His head uprearing from swoln luxury's bed ;
   " The multitude have nought to do
   But bend, obey, and smile at woe,
   And tho' a murmur breaks for bread,
   Strict law (for slaves) should doom such dead ?"
Why hangs your head ? Why mute thy holy tongue ?
I speak what pass'd abroad, " Your withers are un-
    wrung."

---

* The Blefescudians.

Ah!

IX.

Ah! have I touch'd you, dove-ey'd sacred soul!
What! flowing tears down either ruby jowl.
Just so, I swear, in potteries I've seen
The liquid brimstone glaze the red earth pan ;
But dry them up. 'Tis not so bad I hope.
Some months may scape ere yet you reach the rope.

X.

Oh! 'twou'd be dreadful bad for *you*,
Who *here* have had no work to do,
   But eat, and drink, and w—— ;
Like the Blefes'can priests, poor ragged wretches,
With long lank sides, cropp'd hair, and tatter'd breeches,
   To seek a foreign shore.

XI.

Where cou'd ye go ? I scarce know where ;
To *Rockica*—Oh no, not there !
   For *there* they make no hay.
Perhaps best place, as few require,
Or priesthood's gifts, or pastoral fire,
   Is *Botany's* fair Bay.

XI.

Shou'd you object, and think *that* far,
Perhaps beneath the northern star
   You, who are young, might *rise* ;
In buxom *Cath'rine's* passion'd hour,
Snugly slip in to mitred pow'r,
   The temple's prop, her thighs.

U 3   Sweet

XIII.

Sweet smiles my Shemei's cheeks adorn,
Go, my dear son, for honour born,
    For here, I fear, the game is up;
And if ye strive against the wind,
Justice, perchance, may lift her blind *,
    And you in paradise may shortly sup.

XIV.

Lilliput's mob so wise are grown,
They, croziers, and the scarlet gown,
    Regard with tilted noses,
And thinks *ten thousand cops* † per year,
More than a vap'ring priest need bear,
    Who only gripes and dozes.

XV.

Haste then to Lapland's untaught race,
There's but *one other* vacant place
    On earth's terraqueous zone—
Where yet religion rears her head,
There holy prelates only plead,
    For virtue's sake alone.

XVI.

But *England's* ‡ stall will not suit *you*;
They give, and never grasp a due,
    Men's souls are all their care.

---

* Perhaps the *bandage* she is said to have her eyes covered with.

† *Cops*, abbreviated *copars*, the coin of Lilliput.

‡ England then is the *one place meant*—A just and fine compliment.

You

You stare, and well, right well you may,
I mean'd not you shou'd thither stray,
   Who nothing know of pray'r.

XVII.

No! you'd be lost on England's shore,
Join'd with meek Markham, learned Moore,
   And prudent virtuous North.
Their moral rules, and temp'rate food
Wou'd ill agree with your's, whose blood,
   Boils high for temp'ral worth.

XVIII.

You, too, so us'd to foam and gabble
In *Lilliput's* tax-framing *Babel,*
   On *spies,* and *war,* and *treason,*
Cou'd ne'er contented, silent sit,
And list to *Britain's Saviour, Pitt,*
   Tho' he's arch-prince of reason.

XIX.

You'd be for dipping in your oar,
And 'larm the mob without the door,
   As *here* you lately did;
Therefore, no thoughts of England, there
The *sov'reign mass* have rights, and share,
   And will not be priest-rid.

XX.

My son, but little now remains:
Firstly, we'll reckon up the gains
   You can secure before you hop.

How

How lucky 'twas you turn'd your head,
When weeping mothers knelt for bread,
  And crav'd one stiver from your yellow crop !

XXI.

So now with gold and learning bless'd,
You stand good chance to be carress'd
  Where virtue is not known :
If too you keep your subtle looks,
And lov'd obedient-passive books,
  Withal your Lexicon.

XXII.

None shall dispute your sov'reign claim
To *Metropolitan's* high name,
  In land o'erwhelm'd with vice,
Where despots rule with unyok'd sway,
Where priests receive and never pray,
  Except o'er cards and dice.

XXIII.

There shalt thou rule arch-priest install'd
 (By *you* and *me,* his will enthrall'd) ;
 We'll tax and tythe the *very bear,*
 And frame such acts shall make him stare.
Meanwhile he shall not ope his grumbling throat ;
 For, for the love I owe thy zeal,
 Upon his mouth I'll pop a seal
So close, we will not hear dissention's note.

XXIV.

Thus, yet a little will we last,
And list around *reform's* fell blast,
  There in our wilds safe pent ;

         We'll

We'll lead the monsters such a dance,
Such as was Whilom led —— ——,
'Till *reason's shaft was bent.*

XXV.

But come, my son, too long we stay,
I've mark'd you out a dreary way ;
Yet heed it not : No soil so low,
But for a time church seed will grow—
So haste, I hear reform's curs'd bell
Toll forth oppression's and vile pension's knell.

———————

While I was reading the above, and my colleagues refrefhing themfelves, the mob took the bullocks out of the car, and 10,000 of them harneffed themfelves to it. I remonftrated; but in vain, and was obliged to fubmit.

It was my intention to ufe the fame polite caution with my new comrades as I had obferved in my firft journey to *Elfac-Sinwrod* towards *Vilpi Tico* and his friends ; but there was no occafion—they fcrambled up alertly, and when I expreffed my furprife at their courage, they laughingly replied—

" *We* are not frightened at the elevation— *We* have been all our lives accuftomed to
look

look upwards. We are not afraid of any heigth."

They then began finging a duet. It was fomething about

"Let us take the road."

The populace highly applauded, *I once more unfurled my umbrella*, and away we went on our patriotic journey; and furely fufpicion could not be entertained of our want of integrity; for *my fecretaries* were pennilefs, and I was only enriched with the founding title of

Prince of Peace.

F I N I S.